PRECARIOUS WORK, WOMEN, AND THE NEW ECONOMY

Globalisation, the shift from manufacturing to services as a source of employment, and the spread of information-based systems and technologies have given birth to a new economy, which emphasises flexibility in the labour market and in employment relations. These changes have led to the erosion of the standard (industrial) employment relationship and an increase in precarious work – work which is poorly paid and insecure. Women perform a disproportionate amount of precarious work. This collection of original essays by leading scholars on labour law and women's work explores the relationship between precarious work and gender, and evaluates the extent to which the growth and spread of precarious work challenges traditional norms of labour law and conventional forms of legal regulation. The book provides a comparative perspective by furnishing case studies from Australia, Canada, the Netherlands, Quebec, Sweden, the UK, and the US, as well as the international and supranational context through essays that focus on the IMF, the ILO, and the EU. Common themes and concepts thread throughout the essays, which grapple with the legal and public policy challenges posed by women's precarious work.

Oñati International Series in Law and Society

A SERIES PUBLISHED FOR THE OÑATI INSTITUTE
FOR THE SOCIOLOGY OF LAW

General Editors

William L F Felstiner   Johannes Feest

Board of General Editors

Rosemary Hunter, Griffiths University, Australia
Carlos Lugo, Hostos Law School, Puerto Rico
David Nelken, Macerata University, Italy
Jacek Kurczewski, Warsaw University, Poland
Marie Claire Foblets, Leuven University, Belgium
Roderick Macdonald, McGill University, Canada

Titles in this Series

Social Dynamics of Crime and Control: New Theories for a World in Transition edited by Susannah Karstedt and Kai Bussmann

Criminal Policy in Transition edited by Andrew Rutherford and Penny Green

Making Law for Families edited by Mavis Maclean

Poverty and the Law edited by Peter Robson and Asbjørn Kjønstad

Adapting Legal Cultures edited by Johannes Feest and David Nelken

Rethinking Law Society and Governance: Foucault's Bequest edited by Gary Wickham and George Pavlich

Rules and Networks edited by Richard Appelbaum, Bill Felstiner and Volkmar Gessner

Women in the World's Legal Professions edited by Ulrike Schultz and Gisela Shaw

After National Democracy: Rights, Law and Power in America and the New Europe edited by Lars Trägårdh

Precarious Work, Women, and the New Economy
The Challenge to Legal Norms

Edited by
JUDY FUDGE
and
ROSEMARY OWENS

Oñati International Series in Law and Society

A SERIES PUBLISHED FOR THE OÑATI INSTITUTE
FOR THE SOCIOLOGY OF LAW

·HART·
PUBLISHING

OXFORD AND PORTLAND OREGON
2006

Published in North America (US and Canada)
by Hart Publishing
c/o International Specialized Book Services
920 NE 58th Avenue, Suite 300
Portland, OR 97213-3786
USA
Tel: +1 503 287 3093 or toll-free: (1) 800 944 6190
Fax: +1 503 280 8832
E-mail: orders@isbs.com
Web Site: www.isbs.com

Hart Publishing is a specialist legal publisher based in Oxford, England. To order further
copies of this book or to request a list of other publications please write to:

Hart Publishing, Salter's Boatyard, Folly Bridge, Abingdon Road,
Oxford, OX1 4LB
email: mail@hartpub.co.uk
Telephone: +44 (0)1865 245533 Fax: +44 (0)1865 794882

WEB SITE http//:www.hartpub.co.uk

British Library Cataloguing in Publication Data
Data Available

ISBN-13: 978-1-84113-615-8 (hardback)
ISBN-10: 1-84113-615-8 (hardback)

ISBN-13: 978-1-84113-616-6 (paperback)
ISBN-10: 1-84113-616-5 (paperback)

Typeset by Compuscript,
Printed and bound in Great Britain by
Biddles Ltd, King's Lynn, Norfolk

Acknowledgments

This collection of essays had its genesis in a set of papers which was presented at a Workshop on 'Precarious Work, Women, and the New Economy: The Challenge to Legal Norms' held at the International Institute for the Sociology of Law (IISL), Oñati, Spain, from 30 June to 2 July 2004. The opportunity to present papers at a workshop provided intellectual stimulation, promoted greater understanding of issues, and created an important opportunity for collaborative work on this important topic.

We wish to thank the IISL for the generous support it gave to all the participants at the workshop in providing such congenial surroundings in which to work, for accommodation in the beautiful Residencia de Antia, and for making all transportation arrangements within Spain.

In particular, we wish to thank Professor Dr Volkmar Gessner, the Scientific Director of the IISL, for his gracious hospitality in welcoming us all to the IISL, and for his support and interest in our intellectual endeavours. We would also like to thank all the staff at the IISL whose work ensured the smooth running of the workshop. Ms Malen Gordoa was especially helpful to us. In the months leading up to the workshop she provided us with a high level of professional support, helping to co-ordinate arrangements amongst the participants, who came from three continents, and ensured that everything was in place for our arrival in Oñati.

The contributors to this volume all enthusiastically embraced the opportunity which the IISL provided to work on this project. We thank each of them for that. We also acknowledge with thanks the contribution of Professor Gillian Lester, who participated in the workshop and provided an overview of the issues raised. In the light of the discussions at the IISL, all participants revised their papers in the months immediately following the workshop.

We are also deeply grateful to Professor WLF Felstiner, General Editor of the Oñati International Series in Law and Society, for his interest in this project, and we are indebted to the reviewers organised by him for their careful reading and comments on the manuscript.

Finally, we would also like to acknowledge the skilful editorial work of Ms Naomi Horrox, who helped with the task of preparing this manuscript, and the staff at Hart Publishing for the final publication.

Judy Fudge
and
Rosemary Owens

Contents

Notes on Contributors

Diamond Ashiagbor is currently a lecturer in the Faculty of Laws, University College London. She was previously a Postdoctoral Fellow in the Institute of European and Comparative Law at the University of Oxford, and a lecturer at the University of Hull. She completed a PhD at the European University Institute in Florence, and her research interests include British and European Community labour law and employment policy, European constitutional law, and law and economics.

Stéphanie Bernstein has been a law professor at the Faculty of Political Science and Law of the Université du Québec à Montréal since 2003. Her research and teaching activities presently focus on international and comparative labour, social security, and human rights law, the legal protection of precarious workers, and the role of the state in the regulation of working conditions.

Susanne D Burri is a Lecturer in Gender and Law in the Department of Legal Theory at the University of Utrecht in the Netherlands. She currently teaches the courses 'International Law and European Law and Women' and 'Gender and Law'. She has published widely on the subject of equal treatment of men and women in national, international, and European law, specifically in relation to part-time work. Her doctoral dissertation, in Dutch with an English summary, explores the question of the extent to which the principle of equality and related norms in Dutch labour law may contribute to a new organisation of work, characterised by the redistribution of paid and unpaid activities. She is correspondent for the French review *Liaisons Sociales Europe*, and a member of the editorial boards of a Dutch annual publication on European social law, a loose-leaf publication on flexible labour relations, and an annual publication of the Dutch Equal Treatment Commission.

Joanne Conaghan is a Professor of Law at the University of Kent at Canterbury. Her scholarly interests lie in the areas of labour law, tort law, and feminist legal theory. Professor Conaghan has published widely in all these areas, and she is also the Managing Editor of *Feminist Legal Studies*.

Sandra Fredman is a Professor at Exeter College, University of Oxford. Professor Fredman specialises in discrimination law, labour law, and human rights law, all areas in which she has published. She teaches in constitutional law, administrative law, and labour law to undergraduates; and comparative human rights law and European employment law to graduates. As well as her academic work, Professor Fredman has been active in the field of policy-making.

Judy Fudge is a Professor at Osgoode Hall Law School, York University in Toronto, where she teaches employment and labour law. She has written on a wide range of topics in Canadian labour law, including labour law history, women workers and the law, precarious work and labour standards, and freedom of association and labour rights. She has worked with women's groups, unions, and workers' organisations on topics relating to employment and labour law.

Allison Hoffman, a recent graduate of Yale Law School, is an Associate at Ropes & Gray LLP in Boston. Allison Hoffman specialises in health-care law and has written on the effects of US health-care policy on women and families, focusing on the area of long-term care. Her prior work in management consulting at The Boston Consulting Group and on women's health policy at the National Partnership for Women and Families informs her understanding of women in the workplace and her interest in diverse approaches to social change.

Rosemary Hunter is Dean of the Griffith Law School, Griffith University, Brisbane, Australia. She is a feminist legal scholar specialising in the areas of anti-discrimination law, women's employment, and access to justice. She has undertaken a wide range of consultancies for governments, courts, public and private sector bodies, and the World Bank, and has appeared as an expert witness in several industrial relations matters.

Claire Kilpatrick is a University Lecturer in Law and a Fellow of Emmanuel College at the University of Cambridge. She researches and teaches in the areas of European Union law and labour law. She is Co-Director of the Centre for European Legal Studies at the University of Cambridge and co-editor of the *Cambridge Yearbook of European Legal Studies*. She serves on the editorial board of the *Industrial Law Journal* and edits its 'European Developments' section.

Rosemary Owens is a Reader in Law at the University of Adelaide, where she researches and teaches in the areas of labour and industrial relations law, Australian constitutional law, and feminist legal theory. She has published widely on issues relating to work, law, and women. Her current major research interests are the law of work especially as it impacts upon women in international and national legal systems and social and economic rights. Rosemary Owens is the co-editor of the *Australian Journal of Labour Law*. She is also the Chair of The Working Women's Centre SA.

Kerry Rittich is an Associate Professor of Law and Women's Studies and Gender Studies at the University of Toronto Her scholarly and teaching interests include international law and institutions, human rights, labour law, critical legal theories and feminism. She is the author of *Recharacterizing Restructuring: Law, Distribution and Gender in Market Reform* (The Hague: Kluwer Law International, 2002) and recently completed a report for the Law Commission of Canada, *Vulnerable Workers: Legal and Policy Issues in the New Economy*.

Vicki Schultz is the Ford Foundation Professor at Yale Law School, where she teaches courses on employment discrimination law, feminist theory, and workplace theory and policy. Professor Schultz has written and lectured widely on feminist theory, workplace harassment, sex segregation, work–family issues, and the meaning of work in people's lives. Her *Yale Law Journal* articles, 'The Sanitized Workplace' and 'Reconceptualizing Sexual Harassment' propose a new way of understanding and regulating sexual harassment in the workplace.

Katherine VW Stone is a Professor of Law at the University of California, Los Angeles. She specialises in courses regarding labour law, comparative labour law, employment law, labour and social policy, private justice, and contracts. Professor Stone has published widely in her fields of expertise, and her most recent book is *From Widgets to Digits: Employment Regulation for the Changing Workplace* (2004).

Leah F Vosko is Canada Research Chair in Feminist Political Economy, School of Social Sciences, Atkinson Faculty, York University. Professor Vosko is the author of *Temporary Work: The Gendered Rise of a Precarious Employment Relationship* (University of Toronto Press, 2000), co-author of *Self-Employed Workers Organize: Law, Policy, and Unions* (McGill-Queen's, 2005) and book chapters and articles in a range of scholarly journals. She is also co-editor of *Changing Canada: Political Economy as Transformation* (McGill-Queen's University Press, 2003) and *Challenging the Market: The Struggle to Regulate Work and Income* (McGill-Queen's, 2004). She is currently writing a book on globalisation, gender, and the changing scope of the employment relationship.

Jenny Julén Votinius is a doctoral candidate at the Faculty of Law, Lund University, Sweden. Her research is directed towards the reconciliation of gainful occupation and parenthood, and exploring labour law and social security law in the light of the social context in which parents with young children form their everyday life. Her publications to date have focused on aspects of the protection against discrimination in their working life of employees with parental responsibility, as well as on the actual possibilities for working parents with small children to balance family life and parenthood with the demands of the workplace.

Table of Cases

Canada

European Union

Sweden

United Kingdom

United States

Table of Statutes, Statutory Instruments, Guidelines and International Treaties and Conventions

Australia

Canada

European Union

United States

Table of Abbreviations

AAL	Additional Adoption Leave
ABS	Australian Bureau of Statistics
ACTU	Australian Council of Trade Unions
AIRC	Australian Industrial Relations Commission
AML	Additional Maternity Leave
BEPG	Broad Economic Policy Guidelines
BFOQ	Bona Fide Occupational Qualification
CBI	Confederation of British Industry
CBS	Dutch Central Office for Statistics
CC	Civil Code
CEC	Commission of the European Communities
CML	Compulsory Maternity Leave
Comp time	Compensation Time
EC	European Community
ECJ	European Court of Justice
EEO	Equal Employment Opportunities
EEOC	Equal Employment Opportunities Commission
EMU	Economic and Monetary Union
EOC	Equal Opportunities Commission
ESOPE	European Study of Precarious Employment
ETC	Equal Treatment Commission
EU	European Union
FEMME	ILO Division on Women
FTA	Free Trade Agreements
G-7	Group of Seven
IFI	International Financial Institutions
ILC	International Labour Code
ILO	International Labour Organisation
IMF	International Monetary Fund
LEL	Lower Earnings Limit
MPL	Maternity and Parental Leave

NAALC	North American Accord on Labour Relations
NAFTA	North American Free Trade Agreement
NAP	National Action Plans for Employment
NSWIRC	New South Wales Industrial Relations Commission
OAL	Ordinary Adoption Leave
OECD	Organisation for Economic Co-operation and Development
OMC	Open Method of Coordination
OML	Ordinary Maternity Leave
PPT	Permanent Part Time
SCP	Sociaal Cultureel Planbureau
SER	Sociaal Economische Raad
SZW	Sociale Zaken en Werkgelegenheid
TUC	Trade Union Congress
UN	United Nations
UNDP	United Nations Development Program
UNIFEM	ILO Program on Rural Women
WTO	World Trade Organisation

Part I

Introduction

1

Precarious Work, Women, and the New Economy: The Challenge to Legal Norms

JUDY FUDGE AND ROSEMARY OWENS

THE PROCESS OF globalisation has led to the rapid disintegration of the old industrial model of employment. The manufacturing sector in developed industrialised countries has shrunk as a source of employment, and the share of employment generated by the service sector has massively increased. Women's labour market participation has risen dramatically. Modern information-based systems and technologies have given birth to a new economy, which emphasises flexibility in the labour market and has hastened the change in employment norms. Simultaneously, there has been a profound increase in precarious work—work that departs from the normative model of the standard employment relationship (which is a full-time and year-round employment relationship for an indefinite duration with a single employer) and is poorly paid and incapable of sustaining a household.[1] According to the International Labour Organization (ILO), globally, during the last two decades of the twentieth century there was 'a general increase in the precarious nature of employment and the reduction of workers' protection' (2000a: para 104). The objective of this collection of essays is to explore the extent to which the rise of precarious work is a gendered phenomenon and to evaluate whether the new forms of employment challenge existing legal norms for regulating the labour market.

Our hypothesis is that the rise and spread of precarious work is gendered and that it challenges the existing legal norms of employment and regimes of labour regulation. National regimes of legal regulation are based on norms of employment, assumptions about who workers are and what they need, and ideas about how regulation works. Since the 1940s the industrial model of employment, although it differed in detail between different

---

[1] See the discussion of precarious work below.

countries and regions, was dominant in industrialised liberal democracies. It was premised upon a gendered division of labour in which men had the primary responsibility for paid employment and women were primarily concerned with unpaid care work. National laws and policies not only reflected and reinforced these gendered roles—male breadwinner and female housewife—they were also based upon the assumption that the nation state had an active role to play in regulating the labour market (Supiot *et al*, 2001). During this period, collective bargaining supplemented by 'hard' regulation predominated.[2]

The purpose of this collection is to explore the extent to which the process of globalisation and the growth of the new economy have undermined these understandings, and to determine whether there is any pressure to develop new legal norms for precarious workers and different social understandings of work. Changes in employment norms are situated in a framework that is attentive to the social reproduction of the labour market. Feminist analysis explores the competing demands of social reproduction, which comprises the social processes and labour that go into the daily and generational maintenance of the working population, and production in developed market economies, emphasising how women's unpaid care labour has been used to mediate this tension (Picchio, 1992).

The collection also emphasises the relationship between law and society and the role of the state, placing laws and policies in their social contexts. National case studies from developed countries are supplemented by an examination of how supranational organisations, such as the ILO, and regional governance structures, such as those comprising the European Union (EU), have sought both to develop and disseminate new legal norms. The comparative dimension of the collection is designed to enrich our understanding of how legal norms emerge and develop institutional moorings. The introduction provides a general background for the individual essays in the collection, identifying the broader context, the conceptual framework, and a pluralist approach to law.

GLOBALISATION AND THE NEW ECONOMY

Globalisation refers to the intensification of international economic and political integration:

> Economically, globalisation is marked by increases in international trade and investment, the evolution of global production by transnational corporations,

---

[2] The United Kingdom, with its commitment to collective laissez-faire and eschewal of direct statutory regulation, tended to be an outlier when it came to direct statutory regulation of the employment relationship.

and unregulated flows of capital. Politically, globalisation theorists point to the erosion of nation states as the key unit in which political decisions are made; the leakage of sovereignty to supranational organisations on the one hand and to subnational units on the other; and sometimes, to the emergence of neoliberalism as a global ideology.

(McBride, 2001: 21)

Neoliberalism favours limitations on the exercise of political power for egalitarian purposes and calls for deregulation, privatisation, supply-side rather than demand-side macro-economic measures, and a withering away of the welfare state (Standing, 2000; Rittich, 2002b). It is closely associated with international economic agreements, such as free trade agreements (FTAs), which 'serve as a restructuring tool or, put differently, as a conditioning institutional framework that promotes and consolidates neoliberal restructuring' (Grinspun and Kreklewich, 1994).

These conditioning agreements can be bilateral (such as the FTAs between Canada and the United States and between Australia and the United States), regional (two examples are the EU and the North American Free Trade Agreement (NAFTA)), or international (best exemplified by the group of agreements comprised by the World Trade Organization (WTO)) (McBride, 2001; Clarkson, 2002). At the supranational level, nation states and supranational political organisations such as the World Bank are the key actors and institutions, together with large transnational corporations, which strongly advocate for markets that are open to them. Not only have nation states participated in the construction of a regime of rules and structures governing economic relations between states, they have agreed to abide by the constraints imposed upon national policies contained in these international regimes (Gill, 1995; Schneiderman, 2000). At the heart of such agreements is a concern to preserve the market from political interference.

The market has assumed the central place in the global order, both dominating and driving it, but forged through the interdependency of capital and the state. Since the 1980s, the economy has restructured on a global scale orchestrated primarily by major transnational corporations that have accumulated economic resources far more extensive than those of many nation states. The capacity of these corporate giants to disaggregate and relocate some or all of their activities while simultaneously maintaining a cohesive control over the whole has consolidated their dominance. Often the threat of exit has been enough to ensure that the control of investment capital at a global level has translated directly into a political power at a more local level.

Unsurprisingly, many nation states have been anxious to attract and ally themselves with these transnational corporations. Through policies that deregulate national markets, they have aided and abetted global capital, diminishing the costs of entry to their jurisdiction and freeing from local strictures any trading and financial institutions that might wish to operate from within their borders. Under these policies, the flow of goods and services across national borders has escalated. Paradoxically, as nation states have opened themselves to greater integration in economic markets beyond their borders, their neoliberal policies consolidate further the power of global capital; states are sometimes reduced to mendicant status offering various forms of corporate welfare in the form of subsidy payments, exemptions from local taxes, and other inducements for transnational corporations to stay within their national boundaries. The fear that nation states are forced to compete in a 'race to the bottom' by reducing labour standards is at 'the heart of debates about the need to regulate global labour markets' (Murray, 2001b: 17). Although there is some scepticism about whether there is evidence to support the concern that globalisation results in this race to lower labour standards (Blackett, 2001: 429), 'there *is* evidence of a general deregulation of employment protection since the 1980s by economically advanced states which are members of the OECD' (Murray, 2001b: 17, citing OECD, 1994b).[3]

The discourse of neoliberalism and the language of 'deregulation' serve to erase the significant role of the state in the creation and maintenance of the new economy. Moreover, since the market is considered to be the most efficient mechanism for allocation and distribution, the state itself is required to resile from interfering with the market. The resultant reduction of the state through 'privatisation' has witnessed not only the transfer of functions from the public to the private sphere, but the disappearance of many of the Keynesian state's welfare and redistribution functions (Fudge and Cossman, 2002). Not only have social welfare programmes been contained, they have also been refigured in ways that encourage greater participation by individuals in the market (Collins, 2003a). The diminished state is thus constructed and constructs itself as the very antithesis of the market, imbedding even deeper the public/private dichotomy that has long been a part of western liberal political thought. Citizens are reincarnated as market actors in the new economy.

But the 'new economy' is not merely descriptive of the nature, extent, and scope of change brought about by globalisation. It is for many, as Joanne Conaghan (2003: 12–13) has pointed out, 'aspirational and *normatively* imbued positing the surest route to a progressive future.'[4] The new global

---

[3] There is also a debate about what counts as evidence of the race to the bottom in labour standards. While there may be little direct evidence that states are engaged in an active policy of deregulation of labour standards for the purpose of gaining a competitive edge (Freeman, 1998; Barnard, 1999; Flanagan, 2003), workers may accept lower standards in order to protect their jobs (Langille, 1996, 1997).

[4] For an example where globalisation is claimed to be creating opportunities for sustained economic growth and development of the world economy, see Commission of the European Communities, 2001b: 4.

order promises that the rising economic tide brought by competitive markets and increased productivity will lift all boats, and neoliberals brush aside present inequalities as merely temporary aberrations or natural adjustments in the present evolutionary process. Interference to adjust or eliminate these interim inequalities is said to threaten the long-term success of the project as a whole (Standing, 2000, Rittich, 2002b).

Changing Employment Norms and Work Arrangements

The dominance of the market has impacted dramatically upon the organisation of work. New industries have flourished producing new goods and services marketed on a global level. In that fiercely competitive environment there is a spiralling upward demand for new products, or new improvements, to be made available ever more cheaply and quickly. 'Just-in-time' production methods, through which businesses attempt to respond more immediately to the market pressures, demand increased flexibility from workers as corporations find new ways to structure their operations. With corporations stretching across the globe, production on a single item may involve workers across a number of different continents. At the same time as the global corporate networks have developed, there has also been a proliferation of small businesses, often called micro-enterprises. In many instances, the imperative for efficiency and cost-cutting has spawned arrangements among these smaller operators whereby they are linked through franchising agreements or operate through joint ventures, often in complex webs of interaction (Castells, 1996). There has also been a 'commercialisation' of employment relations, and an increase in self-employment and various forms of subcontracting. Somewhat paradoxically, the competition of businesses in the marketplace has also given rise to their increased co-dependence, as firms seeking to become more specialised loosely integrate with one another in production chains (Collins, 1990).

The changing nature of industry has meant the old 'Fordist' paradigm of the mass of workers performing a standard set of skills in large-scale production enterprises is rapidly becoming a thing of the past. In industrialised countries,

> employment patterns and practices are now primarily determined not in the manufacturing, but in the services sector, which accounts for 63.5% of total Organisation for Economic Co-operation and Development (OECD) employment and close to three-quarters of all employment in a number of major OECD countries.
>
> (OECD, 2000a: 85; Rubery and Grimshaw, 2003: 77)

The dominant image of the archetypical worker of the new informational economy is the knowledge worker. Knowledge workers are characterised as independent risk-takers, who build their own networks that, when linked with their property in knowledge, can invert the relations of power and subordination that have traditionally structured employment (Hyde, 2003). The designation of their skills as 'human capital' signifies the blurring of the traditional boundary between these workers and the businesses for which they work: these knowledge workers are the new capitalists—workers who own the means of production. They are highly mobile and committed to their work above all else, and for this dedication and risk they are richly rewarded, both financially and with interesting and high-status work (Hyde, 2003). Employed primarily in managerial, professional, and technological occupations, these informational workers, according to Yuko Aoyama and Manuel Castells, belie 'the myth of service-sector employment characterised by low skills, low wages and low stability' (2002: 146). But, even though they are not precarious workers, these highly skilled knowledge workers do not fit the traditional norms of employment law (Stone, chapter 11, this volume).

Moreover, simultaneously with the growth of high-skilled occupations in the informational economies of the Group of Seven (G-7) countries, the informal sector has expanded in developing and developed countries, and with it low-skilled, poorly paid, intermittent, and insecure employment (Sankaran, 2002: 854; ILO, 2002; World Commission on the Social Dimension of Globalization, 2004: 14; United Nations, 2005). Initially identified with household labour in small, family enterprises in the developing countries, the informal sector has grown across the world as firms pursue flexible forms of labour, such as casual labour, contract labour, outsourcing, home working, and other forms of subcontracting that offer the prospect of minimising fixed non-wage costs. Guy Standing refers to this process as the 'informalisation' of employment, claiming that:

> although the dichotomy of 'formal' and 'informal' *sectors* has always been misleading, a growing proportion of jobs possess what may be called informal characteristics, ie without regular wages, benefits, employment protection, and so on.
> (Standing, 1999a: 585)

In both developed and developing countries this work is performed primarily by women (Standing, 1999a; Sankaran, 2002; Elder and Schmidt, 2004; United Nations, 2005: 67–88).

The benefits of globalisation and the new economy have not been distributed equally. Even with the rise of the informational economy, Aoyama and Castells note that occupational sex segregation and the gendered nature of work helps to account for the persistence of low-paid and insecure employment in the service sector in G-7 countries (2002: 146, 157). In developed countries such as Australia, Canada, the United Kingdom, and the United States, national labour markets have increasingly become bifurcated into high- and low-skilled jobs as those jobs in the middle have gradually disappeared (Picot and Heisz, 2000; Taylor, 2002; Cully, 2002; Wright and Dwyer, 2003). This dualism is also inscribed in the international division of labour. While knowledge workers from developing countries obtain good jobs in the information sectors of developed countries (Hyde, 2003), their low-skilled counterparts migrate to developed countries to take jobs in the service or agricultural sectors that nationals are unwilling to perform (Bakan and Stasiulis, 1997; Anderson, 2000; Basok, 2002; Caruso 2002; Macklin 2002; World Development on the Social Dimension of Globalization, 2004).

Globalisation has also had an uneven impact upon earnings within countries. At the same time as earnings inequality has grown markedly in some countries (Canada, the United Kingdom, and the United States), it has grown noticeably, although less profoundly, in others (Australia, France, the Netherlands, and Sweden), while diminishing in a few (Belgium, Norway, and Germany) (Bosch, 1999, 137; see also World Dimension on the Social Dimension of Globalization, 2004: 42). Supply shifts alone cannot account for the increased inequality, since, as David Blanchflower and Matthew Slaughter note, 'the quantity of skilled labour and the relative wages paid to skilled workers has been increasing at the same time' (1998: 85). Nor does increased international (freer) trade directly account for increased inequality (Blanchflower and Slaughter, 1998: 85–86). What is clear, however, is that earnings inequality has increased the most dramatically in countries with relatively unregulated labour markets (Blanchflower and Slaughter, 1998).[5] Globalisation has been a factor, albeit one that is indirect, contributing to increased earnings inequality as 'the rise in global competitiveness has caused a change in norms, lowering expectations, especially for the low-skilled workers whose bargaining power has been most eroded' (Rodrik, 1998: 91). According to the ILO, 'the simultaneous inclusion and exclusion of people, regions and economic sectors is a significant characteristic of globalisation and presents some of its greatest challenges' (2002: 9). Moreover, in its recent report the World Commission on the Social Dimension of Globalization (2004: x) asserted that:

> The current process of globalisation is generating unbalanced outcomes, both within and between countries. Wealth is being created, but too many countries and people are not sharing in its benefits. They also have little or no voice in shaping the process. Seen through the eyes of the vast majority of women and men, globalisation has not met their simple and legitimate aspirations for decent jobs and a better future for their children.

[5] In Australia, there is startling evidence demonstrating that the institutions of the law have an overwhelmingly significant role to play with respect to earnings equality. The Australian evidence shows that a centralised regulatory wage system produced more equitable outcomes for both men and women. Women's gains were in part determined by the fact that the centralised system looked after low-paid men better than a more fragmented system. As the Australian system has been 'deregulated', the wage gap, for both men and women, has intensified (Gregory, 1999).

Precarious Work

The demand for flexible labour has resulted in a decline in standard employment (Felstead and Jewson, 1999: 1; Beck, 2000; Zeytinoglu, 2002). Indeed, perhaps the most significant impact of the new economy on employment is the rise in non-standard, contingent, or precarious forms of work experienced by all industrialised countries. But the ascription of an appropriate label to the changes in the nature and composition of employment relations and work arrangements in the new economy is not unproblematic. In part, this difficulty arises because there are regional differences in the usage of the various terms—precarious, non-standard, contingent, atypical, insecure, and flexible—to describe the new work arrangements and, in part, because of a lack of theoretical precision. Moreover, as Kate Purcell has noted, most distinctions, boundaries, or categories in the labour market are conceptual and heuristic rather than descriptive (2000: 2). Thus, whatever terms and definitions are adopted to identify different kinds of work, there is a need to be:

> alert to the instability of all of our concepts about the world of work and ... to the dependence, and indeed the interdependence, between work and workers and the legal, political, social, economic and historical contexts in which they are situated.
>
> (Owens, 2002: 214)

The terms 'atypical' or 'non-standard' are particularly useful in drawing attention to the way in which such work deviates from the 'old' paradigm of the standard employment relationship and the male breadwinner life cycle. The standard employment relationship is best characterised as a continuous, full-time employment relationship where the worker has one employer and normally works on the employer's premises or under the employer's supervision (Muckenberger, 1989: 267; Buechtemann and Quack, 1990: 315; Schellenberg and Clark, 1996: 1; Tilly, 1996: 158–59). Its essential elements include an on-going and indefinite (in terms of duration) employment contract, adequate social benefits that complete the social wage, the existence of a single employer, a standard work day and work week, and employment frequently, but not necessarily, in a unionised sector (Fudge and Vosko, 2001b). The high level of social policies, such as pensions, unemployment insurance, and extended medical coverage, associated with this form of employment are particularly noteworthy since, in combination with the existence of the standard employment contract, they have historically 'incorporated a degree of regularity and durability in employment relationships, protected workers from socially unacceptable practices and working conditions, established rights and obligations, and provided a core of social stability to underpin economic growth' (Rodgers and Rodgers, 1989: 1).

The normative model of the standard employment relationship emerged in a particular context—heavy manufacturing industries after World War II—and reinforced a particular type of work–life arrangement. Men predominated in heavy manufacturing, and their working patterns and histories became the norm. After completing their formal education, they worked full-time (typically with one employer) until retiring at the age of 65. Women, by contrast, worked temporarily until marriage and children, and then withdrew from the labour force to devote their time to care responsibilities

However, defining the work arrangements in the new economy simply in contrast to standard employment can be misleading and risks perpetuating the notion that there is a simple binary divide between the 'old' and the 'new' forms of work. This can mean that important changes in standard employment are ignored (Stone, 2004), that significant differences among the wide range of non-standard work situations are not acknowledged (Bellman and Golden, 2002; Zeytinoglu and Weber, 2002; Watson *et al*, 2003), or that characteristics shared by 'old' work and 'new' work are missed. The increasing heterogeneity in work arrangements suggests that there is no simple dichotomy between work arrangements in the 'old economy' and 'new economy' (Owens, 2002; Vosko, Zukewich, and Cranford, 2003).

An alternative approach to defining the new work arrangements is to focus on some of the distinctive characteristics of work in the new economy. The lack of job and income security is the most striking feature of the new forms of employment (Befort, 2003: 159; Vosko, Cranford, and Zukewich, 2003), and the term 'contingent work' emphasises this dimension. But the problem with an exclusive focus on this factor is that it ignores other important dimensions. While part-time work, for example, might provide employment security, it may not provide enough income to support the worker.

The standard employment relationship promised security along a range of dimensions. What is distinctive about the new employment relationships is the degree to which they are precarious. Precariousness is a complex notion, and involves four dimensions: (1) the degree of certainty of continuing employment; (2) control over the labour process, which is linked to the presence or absence of trade unions and professional associations and relates to control over working conditions, wages, and the pace of work; (3) the degree of regulatory protection; and (4) income level (Rodgers and Rodgers, 1989). There is no shared concept of precarious employment in Europe, although there is an attempt to develop normative regimes governing the contrasting national forms of regulating unstable and low-paid forms of work (European Study of Precarious Employment (ESOPE), 2002). Chapters in this book also indicate that other jurisdictions, such as Australia, Canada, and the United States, do not share a common concept of precarious employment. Moreover, identifying precariousness can be a difficult task because its different dimensions may intersect in numerous ways (Junor, 1998).

Precarious work tends to be associated with the following forms of employment: part-time employment, self-employment, fixed-term work, temporary work, on-call work, home working, and telecommuting, which are united more by their divergence from the standard employment relationship (full-time, indeterminate work with a single employer) than by any common features. While each category of precarious work presents particular challenges for the worker, all tend to be distinguished by low wages, few benefits, the absence of collective representation, and little job security (Fudge, 1997a; Kallenberg *et al*, 1997; Vosko, Zukewich and Cranford, 2003).

Impact of the New Economy upon Women's Work

The Feminisation of Employment

An important dimension of the rise of precarious employment has been its gendered nature. When the standard employment relationship was strong, women predominantly performed precarious work in order to supplement the male wage (Fudge and Vosko, 2003). Since the early 1980s, the standard employment relationship has declined, precarious work has spread, and more men are working in forms of employment previously identified with women. However, women continue to be over-represented in precarious work (Dickens, 1992; Kallenberg *et al*, 1997; Cooke-Reynolds and Zukewich, 2004; Elder and Schmidt, 2004, 10; ILO, 2004b: 11). Thus, the growth of precarious jobs in the paid labour market has been referred to as the 'feminisation of work' (Standing, 1989, 1999a).

'Feminisation' has a double meaning and refers both to the increased labour market participation of women and the proliferation of forms of employment historically associated with women, that is, jobs that are part time, temporary, poorly paid, and lacking benefits and collective forms of representation. Women's participation in the labour market increased throughout the OECD countries, although its form and intensity varies between countries. By the end of the 1990s, there had been a convergence in the labour market experiences of men and women throughout developed industrialised countries (Rubery, Smith, and Fagan, 1999; Cooke-Reynolds and Zukewich, 2004). But this convergence was only equivocally a cause for celebration; in part, it was propelled by deteriorating employment experiences of, and prospects for, men, and increased inequality within the ranks of women. More women were competing on an equal basis with men, although many women continued to be employed in female-dominated sectors that tended to offer low paid work with poor benefits and minimal job security (OECD, 2002b; Cooke-Reynolds and Zukewich, 2004).

However, despite the convergence in men's and women's labour experiences, there are enduring differences. There remains a persistent segregation of men and women into different occupations, and high rates of part-time work for women. Women also continue to earn less than men do, and face a glass ceiling when they climb the occupational hierarchy. Women are more likely than men are to work for very low wages, and they continue to experience a greater risk of poverty than do men (OECD, 2002b: 69, 95, 109–10; Cooke-Reynolds and Zukewich, 2004; ILO, 2004a; United Nations, 2005: 71). However, the increasing polarisation in occupation and income that characterises men's work in the new economy also characterises women's work. More women have made considerable gains in the paid labour market and now occupy good, high-income jobs, such as in high-level management or administration and in professional positions (Cooke-Reynolds and Zukewich, 2004). However, not all women have made gains. Labour markets in Canada and the United States, for example, became increasingly segmented by age, race, immigration status, and educational attainment (Cranford, Vosko and Zukewich, 2003; Wright and Dwyer, 2003).[6]

Social Reproduction

The different nature or character of the participation of men and women in the paid labour market in industrialised economies is conventionally explained by reference to women's responsibility for unpaid care work in the private sphere of the home. Neoclassical economic theory has traditionally viewed the labour market solely in terms of the productive economy, understanding unpaid care work as lacking in value and exogenous to the labour market. While the value of unpaid care work has been persuasively presented (Waring, 1988) and feminist scholarship has demonstrated that the relation of the public and private spheres is most accurately characterised as one of interdependence rather than separation (Thornton, 1995; Boyd, 1997), these insights are resisted by liberal theorists and neoclassical economists.

---

[6] Moreover, it is not accurate to characterise those engaged in precarious work as an homogenous group. Available evidence in Canada suggests that precarious work is not only a gendered phenomenon but is also racialised (Vosko, Zukewich and Cranford, 2003: 16–17). In Australia, indigenous workers and people of colour face systematic discrimination in obtaining decent paid employment (Behrendt, 2003 Australian Bureau of Statistics, 2004). Erik Wright and Rachel Dwyer (2003) note that in the United States gender differences in job expansion were less noticeable in the 1990s compared with the 1960s, but that the racial polarisation increased, along with a marked clustering of immigrants, especially Hispanics at the bottom of the employment structure.

The separation of the home from the market is one of the key characteristics of advanced industrialised economies, and therefore understanding the ways in which the functioning of the marketplace depends upon social reproduction as a crucial source of labour is critical to understanding the operation of the new economy and especially its impact on women (Fudge and Cossman, 2002). Although separate, these two spheres—the household and the market—are inextricably linked (Rittich, 2002a, 2002b). But while the household is linked to the process of production through the wage, both in influencing the cost of labour power and by providing access to the means of subsistence, it is not subject to the same logic as the production process (Acker, 1988). This separation of production from reproduction gives rise to an essential tension in industrialised market economies, and the state plays a crucial role in mediating this tension by helping to organise social reproduction—through immigration, providing public education, health services, and assistance for the elderly, for example (Picchio, 1992).

A central component of the state's role also involves stabilising a specific gender order (Connell, 1987).[7] Every gender order encompasses a sexual division of labour and gender discourses that either support or contest that division (McDowell, 1991). Social reproduction has predominantly been organised in households through normative families and kin relations, characterised by a gendered division of labour (Acker, 1988; Seccombe, 1992). Gendering is a process in which social significance is attached to sexual difference, which, in turn, 'structures organisations, affects social and political relationships, and becomes intrinsic to the construction of significant social categories and political identities' (Frader and Rose, 1996: 22). Labour markets, because they 'operate at the intersection of ways in which people make a living and care for themselves', are bearers and reinforcers of gender (Elson, 1999: 612-13). The gender order is stable to the extent that it has been institutionalised in certain key sites such as the family, labour market, and state policies (Connell, 1987; Acker, 1988; Laslett and Brenner, 1989; Walby, 1990). For this to occur, there must be some fit, however temporary, fragile, and incomplete, between the processes of reproduction and production.

The male breadwinner worker and female housewife household model was at the centre of the post-war gender order in advanced industrialised countries. However, with the feminisation of labour, which began in the 1960s, this model is no longer dominant. The shift from unpaid domestic labour to paid wage labour for providing services—whether delivered publicly or through the private market—had a profound impact on women's labour (Rubery and Grimshaw, 2003: 77). So too did welfare and tax

---

[7] This section draws upon Fudge and Cossman, 2002.

regimes, which shape the opportunity of the population to participate in paid work (L White, 2001; Philipps, 2002). Changes in the labour market, which involve a fundamental shift away from the male breadwinner employment norm, are part of the broader reconfiguration of the gender order. Increasingly, there has been a move to a new multi-earner family mode (Bruegel, 1998; Bosch, 1999: 141). However, institutionalising a new gender order is a difficult task, especially as there has been a simultaneous intensification and erosion of gender in the labour market (Fudge and Cossman, 2002). In spite of the increased participation of women in the paid labour market, women's share of unpaid work has scarcely diminished at all. Care for children and other family members, housework, and emotional labour have all remained the primary responsibility of women (ILO, 2004b, 10). This is true for all women, even for those women who also work full time in paid employment, although in developed countries the time women spend on household labour is slowly declining (Gershuny and Robinson, 1998).

For some women who work full time in well-paid, high-status jobs, the solution has been to outsource to the paid labour market some of their responsibility for unpaid care work (Bernstein, chapter 10 in this volume). Not only does this solution tax the economic resources of women and require them to confront and reject in their own life powerful societal conceptions of 'the good wife/mother/daughter', it creates a demand for women, many of whom are migrants, who are paid to perform domestic labour (Anderson, 2000). Many women work part time and in other forms of non-standard employment because it allows them the flexibility to accommodate their responsibilities within the family. In this new gender order, women are no longer entirely financially dependent on a male breadwinner, but nor have they become totally financially independent. The precarious nature of their employment means that women continue *partially* to rely on a partner's income (Bruegel, 1998). And when this income is removed at separation or divorce, women continue to be at high risk of falling into poverty, notwithstanding their labour market participation. Single-parent families, especially those headed by women, have risen in number dramatically in recent decades, although there are variations by country (Kamerman *et al*, 2003: 17; Pocock, 2003: 26–31). Where precarious work cannot produce a living wage for a single worker, the social consequences are even more severe for those who support children, and the tensions more pronounced as they try desperately to reconcile social ideals of what it is to be a good mother/parent. Women workers, regardless of their occupation and social status, have an increasingly difficult time balancing their need for paid work and their obligations to care. Thus, it is not surprising that the work–family or work–life conflict has been elevated to the top of the labour law and policy agenda (Conaghan, 2002; OECD, 2002a, 2003a, 2004a; Pocock, 2003; Fudge, 2005).

LEGAL NORMS AND INSTITUTIONS

Convergence or Divergence in Legal Norms

Globalisation, the new economy, the growth of precarious work, and the feminisation of labour create great pressure for changes in the legal norms, discourses, and institutions that regulate labour markets and employment relationships (Ashiagbor, in chapter 4, and Rittich in chapter 2 of this volume). Deeper economic and political integration across national boundaries places constraints upon the ability of elected governments to develop and implement policies that are at odds with the central tenets of neoliberalism. Thus, globalisation challenges both the centrality of the nation state (Arthurs, 1996), which traditionally has been the main author of labour legislation, and labour protection and enhancing workers' agency through democratic participation as the major goals of labour legislation (Blackett, 2001: 418). Simultaneously, economic restructuring across advanced industrialised countries has led to an increase in precarious work and a feminisation of labour, which, in turn, tends to undermine employment and labour legislation that traditionally has been based upon standard employment relationships and male breadwinner workers.

However, in the face of global pressures towards greater convergence in deregulating labour markets, and labour legislation that emphasises competitiveness and flexibility, national regimes of labour regulation and legislation have been remarkably resilient. Employment and labour laws and institutions are path dependent; they are historically determined and tend to follow specific institutional patterns (Boyer and Drache, 1996; Deakin 2002; Kilpatrick 2003). However, the general influence of globalisation and neoliberalism has resulted in an increase in precarious employment and women's labour market participation across OECD countries. But the legislative and regulatory response to precarious employment differs from country to country (ESOPE, 2002: 3). Regulation of precarious or atypical employment arrangements may serve either to reinforce or to reduce differences in access and employment protection between those in standard and those in precarious work. As Christine Cousins has noted, the broader 'forces for change are mediated through social, political, and institutional structures within each country' (1999: 116). Thus, it is useful to compare labour legislation and regulatory regimes among different nation states 'where the institutional arrangements, social conditions, the forms of economic organisation, and the roles and attitudes of social actors all vary' (Rubery and Grimshaw, 2003: xvii). Such a comparison provides a basis for evaluating the extent to which globalisation is transforming national regimes of labour legislation and the extent to which the regimes are converging.

Legal Pluralism

The essays in this volume focus on only one aspect of the institutional and social arrangements that shape labour markets and regulate employment relations and work arrangements—the legal regime—and only one element of that regime—labour and employment law. This focus tends to downplay the contribution of welfare arrangements, tax regimes, education systems, trade unions and collective bargaining, and custom. However, although narrow, this focus provides an opportunity to deepen our understanding of legal norms and institutions by attending to what Karl Klare has described as 'complex, multivalent legal regimes' comprised of 'multiple, overlapping layers of sovereignty and norm-creation' (2002: 27).

Globalisation has contributed to legal pluralism with the growth in 'supranational institutions, the expanded reach of international law, and the proliferation of bilateral and multilateral treaty organisations' (Klare, 2002: 27). Multi-level governance, especially in the European Community, has had a profound impact on domestic labour legislation (Kilpatrick, 2003), although the 'boundaries between various sovereignties and sources of law—for example whether a particular matter falls within European Community or member State competence—are distinct, porous, and constantly shifting' (Klare, 2002: 21). Federal systems, such as those of Australia, Canada, and the United States, have long grappled with the problem of the hierarchy between layers of sovereignty, although on a subnational basis.

But multi-level governance not only creates jurisdictional issues and conflicts, it can also result in the dissemination of norms across jurisdictions. These norms can be expressed in 'hard' or 'soft' laws; the former are the traditional binding norms emanating from central authorities, while the latter take the form of non-binding recommendations, codes of practice, and guidelines (Hepple, 2002: 238). Hard law takes a variety of forms and has a variety of functions. The ILO Conventions, which have the status of international treaties for the countries that ratify them, exemplify 'the universal framework of mid-twentieth century public international labor law' (Hepple, 1999: 360). However, there is no effective means of enforcing the ILO Conventions against countries that have ratified them (Gould, 2003), let alone any sanctions to apply against countries that have not ratified key Conventions. Although a form of 'hard law' addressed to nation states, ILO Conventions are not legally binding (Murray, 2001b).

By contrast, the EU provides transnational binding labour regulation via pre-emptive legislation, which includes treaty provisions and EU regulations, and harmonisation, directly through EU Directives and indirectly by virtue of collateral regulation (Stone, 1998). The use of Directives had been the preferred approach to transnational labour regulation in the EU. Directives give member states a degree of flexibility in achieving their goals, while the European Court of Justice provides a means of enforcing these standards against member states by individual workers. However, with the adoption of the open method of coordination—which is an administrative mechanism and not a judicial method of enforcement—as the means of achieving the European Employment Strategy expressed in Lisbon in 2000, the EU has moved more towards 'soft' law when it comes to employment policy (Ashiagbor, chapter 4 in this volume). It is also possible that this form of soft regulatory technique within a system of core constitutional rights 'may become the emblem of modern supranational labour law' (Sciarra *et al*, 2004: 15).

The North American Accord on Labour Cooperation (NAALC), which is the side agreement regarding labour rights that was negotiated as a counterpart to NAFTA, was the first multilateral agreement that linked a regional FTA to a commitment of governments to respect labour rights in their territories. But, unlike in the EU, where (in a restricted way) the rights of sovereignty in the area of employment policy were relinquished, the NAALC preserves national sovereignty (Dombois, Hornberger, and Winter, 2003). This is because the NAALC seeks neither to equalise labour standards nor to establish a minimum floor of labour standards as rights; it is confined to requiring parties to enforce existing labour laws (Stone, 1998).

Soft laws also take a variety of forms. An example of soft law is the ILO's Declaration on Fundamental Principles and Rights at Work, which was adopted in June 1998 and is strictly promotional (ILO, 1999; Alston, 2004). Increasingly, the European Community uses soft law measures that are purely persuasive to achieve social policy (Barnard, 2000: 82–83). Moreover, in the NAALC, 'fundamental rights' of freedom of association and collective bargaining, unlike the 'technical rights' regarding occupational health and safety, have no enforcement mechanisms, and thus function as 'soft law' (Gould, 2003: 103).

Soft law measures are often promoted because they are regarded as more flexible than hard law. But, as Bob Hepple (2002: 243) notes, flexibility can be achieved in other ways, such as giving member states optional methods of implementing a Directive, allowing derogations from certain standards, or giving lengthy periods for implementation. The EU's atypical work directives on part-time and fixed-term work are an example of flexible or reflexive regulation, since they establish a framework setting out shared goals, leaving a space for diversity and national self-regulation (Kilpatrick, 2003). According to Hepple, the 'difference between flexible directives, which leave a measure of discretion to member states, and codes of practice or guidelines, is that the objectives of directives are legally binding on members states, while codes and guidelines are not' (2002: 243).

The EU's atypical work directives also provide an illustration of the pluralism in the normative discourse about the role and function of labour law. To the traditional goal of labour law of providing protection for workers has been added the goal of increasing flexibility 'in a way which both fulfills the wishes of employees and the requirements of competition' (Kilpatrick, 2003: 138; see also Ashiagbor, chapter 4 in this volume).[8] The new governance discourse appears to be an attempt to avoid the efficiency–equity trade-off, which is a core assumption of neoliberalism, by defining a third way in which flexibility is aligned with security and competitiveness and designed to promote social inclusion (Collins, 2002; Kilpatrick, 2003; Fredman, chapter 8 in this volume).

Accompanying the shift in norms of governance has been a move in the technique of regulation away from command and control to enabling and coordinating a range of public and private actors to define and pursue objectives (Kilpatrick, 2003; Sciarra *et al*, 2004). The emphasis is on smarter regulation, which leaves it to the parties to negotiate mutually suitable arrangements in light of legal instructions rather than imposing standards. Once again the goal is upon reflexiveness or responsiveness in regulation— the freedom to adapt regulatory standards to local conditions or individual situations by way of agreement (Ayers and Braithwaite 1992; Collins, 2002: 466). Whatever its merits and shortcomings, this 'market model' of regulation (Pal and Maxwell, 2004: 13) has increased the range of regulatory techniques available to labour law.

There has also been a shift from law to the market as the mechanism for achieving labour standards and rights. Voluntary codes that incorporate labour standards have been adopted by many transnational corporations, either at the behest of governments and non-governmental agencies or under pressure from consumers (Blackett, 2001; Fudge, 2001; Arthurs, 2002; Hepple, 2002; Picciotto, 2003). Increasingly, corporations are urged to follow 'best practices' rather than just the minimal standards set out in labour legislation or international labour standards (Cooney, 1999; Godard, 2003).

Legal pluralism challenges state-centered understandings of legal norms and legal institutions, and its multi-faceted approach captures the multiple and overlapping layers of sovereignty and norm creation that is a feature of globalisation. Legal regimes comprise different levels of governance, forms of law and authority, norms and discourses, and regulatory techniques.

The Challenge to Legal Norms

Just as globalisation compromises the conventional state-centred approach to law, the changes to the labour market wrought by the new economy

---

[8] Preamble 5 of both the Part-time Work Directive (Directive 97/81/EC, [1998] OJ L 14/9) and the Fixed-term Work Directive (Directive 99/70/EC, [1999] OJ L 175/43) states:

whereas the conclusions of the Essen European Council stressed the need to take measures to promote employment, and called for measures to increase the employment-intensiveness of growth, in particular by a more flexible organisation of work in a way which fulfils both the wishes of employees and the requirements of competition.

challenge the standard employment norm that is the foundation of 'Fordist' labour law. Standard employment relationships, which derive from the male model of employment in the manufacturing sector, became the basis both of social protection and labour law, under which workers are guaranteed passive individual security, uniform working hours, and relatively independent collective bargaining (Conaghan, 1986; Owens, 1995b; Fredman, 1997b; Fudge and Vosko, 2001a; Supiot *et al*, 2001: 216; Dickens, 2004). From an institutional perspective, the Fordist or 'classical' labour law model 'may be seen as a triangle whose three sides are companies, trade unions, and the state' (Supiot *et al*, 2001: 215).

The standard employment relationship and Fordist labour law predominated not only at a national level in advanced industrialised countries, but also internationally through the ILO (Prugl, 1999; Vosko, chapter 3 in this volume). Since its members consist of employers, trade unions, and nation states, it is little wonder that the ILO concentrated on the core constituency of Fordist labour law—male workers in standard employment relationships in formal enterprises. Feminised forms of employment were treated as marginal or peripheral forms of work that fell outside the purview of the ILO's standard-setting and technical cooperation activities (Prugl, 1999; Sankaran, 2002; Vosko, 2002).

But the changes in the nature and form of employment relationships that have occurred in both developed and developing countries as a result of economic globalisation have prompted the ILO both to focus on the informal sector and to develop standards for atypical and precarious forms of employment (ILO, 2002; Sankaran, 2002: 856; Vosko, chapter 3 in this volume). Non-governmental organisations, especially women's groups, have pressed the ILO, with some success, to broaden its activities to include non-standard and marginal forms of labour (Prugl, 1999). Beginning in 1994 with the Convention Concerning Part-time Work (No 175), which was followed in 1996 with the Convention Concerning Home Work (No 177), the ILO began to craft standards specifically designed for feminised and precarious work (Prugl, 1999; Sankaran, 2002). Although neither part-time employment nor home working are new, the spread of these feminised forms of employment has meant that many of the ILO's standards simply do not apply to ever-increasing numbers of workers.

The ILO's new programme of action, which is known as 'Decent Work', shifts the ILO's attention to 'workers beyond the formal labour market— ... unregulated wage workers, the self-employed, and home workers' (ILO, 1999: 3–4; Vosko, 2002: 26). The ILO's conception of decent work is far wider that the domain covered by the standard employment relationship and Fordist labour law (Sen, 2000; Hepple, 2002). Decent Work's 'focus on marginalised workers is ... a display of the ILO's new commitment to bring workers once deemed to be outside of its constituency into its standard- and norm-setting activities', and is, in part, 'the product of longstanding efforts of officials in the International Labour Office aiming to "mainstream gender", take seriously the conditions of workers in the informal economy, and address the proliferation of non-standard employment' (Vosko, 2002: 32). Moreover, the ILO's shift in focus is indicative of a growing recognition of the need to revise the basis of labour law (Owens, 2002: 218). In 1999, a group of experts appointed by the European Commission released a report that recommended moving 'beyond employment' in formulating policy responses that will guarantee decent work for all workers (Supiot *et al*, 2001).

Increased attention to non-standard and precarious forms of work combined with the dramatic increase in women's labour market participation is also forcing policy makers and legislators to address the relationship between paid and unpaid work in labour law. The standard employment relationship is based upon 'an anachronistic notion of the division of labour in the household' (Deakin, 2002: 196) in which women did not work outside the home for pay and 'a linear and homogeneous concept of working life that begins upon leaving school and continues without interruption until retirement age' (Supiot, 2002: 152). The notion of standard working time 'was established around a wholly male reference point, defined in opposition to female reproductive time' (Supiot *et al*, 2001: 184–85). Standard working-time arrangements were generalised in most OECD countries after World War II, and they consisted of a norm of standard working time—continuing full-time employment of approximately 40 hours a week, distributed in equal daily segments over daytime, and joined with paid annual leave and public holidays—combined with carefully designed provisions for formal variation (Campbell, 1997). The increased labour market participation of women has resulted in the demand for the flexible adaptation of working time. Simultaneously, employers are demanding increased flexibility in working-time arrangements. Under these pressures, the norms of working time are breaking down.

The growth of precarious employment and the feminisation of labour present a number of challenges to labour law on a range of different levels. The traditional work–family divide that has been at the heart of labour law is troubled by attempts to expand the activities that count as work to unpaid care labour (Waring, 1988) and by the location of paid work in the home (Prugl, 1999; Gurstein, 2002). Conventional understandings of the standard life course, on the one hand, and standard working hours, on the other, do not fit with women's employment histories or patterns (Conaghan, chapter 5 in this volume; Kilpatrick, chapter 7 in this volume). Even the concept of employment, which has long determined the personal scope of labour protection, is no longer sacrosanct (ILO, 2000b). Moreover, changes in how work is organised challenge the adequacy of traditional forms of anti-discrimination and equality legislation for protecting women workers' rights (Fredman, chapter 8 in this volume; Vosko, chapter 3 in this volume).

STRUCTURE OF THE BOOK

The chapters in this volume explore the hypothesis that the spread and rise of precarious work is gendered and that it challenges the existing legal norms of employment and regimes of labour regulation. They are designed to provide a comparative approach, which has a strong tradition in labour law (Sciarra, 2004), to understanding the relationship between legal norms and institutions and precarious work and women. One benefit of a comparative approach is that it brings the distinctiveness of each nation's norms and institutions into relief. Different European states, for example, have very different understandings of precarious work (Ashiagbor, chapter 4 in this volume). Working-time norms differ from country to country, as do arrangements for providing care for young children, and these social norms and institutions shape the specific legal response to precarious work.

The majority of the chapters are national case studies that focus on the legal regulation of either specific forms of precarious work or on how legal norms and institutions generate precariousness for women workers. Each of the national case studies are of advanced industrialised liberal democracies, and the majority of the countries selected share a common law foundation—Australia (Hunter, chapter 13; Owens, chapter 15), Canada (Fudge, chapter 9), the United Kingdom (Fredman, chapter 8; Kilpatrick, chapter 7), and the United States (Hoffman and Schultz, chapter 6; Stone, chapter 11). Chapters that examine facets of the legal regulation and production of work in Quebec (which, although a province of Canada has a civil law), the Netherlands, and Sweden broaden the scope of the comparison beyond jurisdictions that share a common-law heritage. The national case studies from Europe also provide a basis for evaluating the impact of European integration on national legal norms and institutions.

Another benefit of a comparative approach is that it provides evidence that can be used to assess the impact of supranational institutions, norms, and discourses at the national level. Three chapters in the book focus on national supranational institutions, norms, and discourses, and they function as a frame for the national case studies. The chapter by Kerry Rittich (chapter 2) places precarious work within a larger set of governance debates over labour market reform in the international financial and economic institutions. She argues that the governance agenda of the World Bank and the International Monetary Fund (IMF), which promotes 'flexible' labour markets regulated only by contract and property law, influences the ILO at the level of tone and substance, and strategy, and 'normalises' precarious work. Using two recent reports, *A Fair Globalisation* (ILO, 2004a) and *Time For Equality at Work* (ILO, 2003c), Rittich illustrates the extent to which the World Commission on Globalisation and the ILO share the 'good governance' agenda of the international financial institutions and the limits of a traditional concept of equality that does not address head on the problem of unpaid care. Flexibility and equality are themes that recur in the chapters that follow.

Leah Vosko, in chapter 3, examines the new constellation of international labour standards developed by the ILO that are aimed at limiting or mitigating precarious work. She shows how the ILO's embrace of an equal treatment approach, in which the male norm continues to function as a benchmark for women's and men's labour-force activity and the issue of caregiving remains marginal, limits its response to the regulation of precarious work. Vosko contrasts the ILO's approach to legal regulation, precarious work, and gender with approaches proposed by two groups of experts, one appointed by the European Commission and the other by the US federal government.

Diamond Ashiagbor, in chapter 4, places the EU's response to the phenomenon of precarious work in the context of the European Employment Strategy, which promotes the use of non-standard forms of work as a means of boosting labour supply. Within the EU, Ashiagbor shows that there exists a preference for procedural norms over substantive standards with the move to the soft regulation of the open method of coordination. The question she poses is whether this open method of coordination is a new form of responsive governance that can ensure security for workers in an era of labour market flexibility or whether it simply sacrifices worker protection to job creation. She also points out that, whilst hard law measures do exist, for example, in the atypical work directives, their effectiveness in bringing workers in non-standard employment within the scope of employment protection legislation or social protection systems is questionable because gender equality is a secondary, and not primary, goal of these policies.

The next group of chapters explores various dimensions of the legal treatment of working time. Working-time regimes include the set of legal, voluntary, and customary regulations that influence working-time practices, which include daily and weekly working hours, shifts, overtime premia, vacation leaves, and public paid holidays. In their study of the relationship between time allocation and women's paid employment, Jill Rubery, Mark Smith, and Colette Fagan (1999: 72) found that, although women performed the bulk of the domestic labour across Europe, the extent and degree of the inequality in women's paid work varied between countries, and depended upon the national working-time regime.

Joanne Conaghan, in chapter 5, describes the law's role in the construction of working-time norms in the United Kingdom that have been central to normalising men's employment and marginalising women's work. She argues that one effect of the new economy is to disrupt conventional norms of working time captured in the notion of a standard employment relationship. Focusing on recent developments that both give workers greater input into determining working time and enable them better to balance work and care responsibilities, Conaghan attempts to determine whether this breakdown in conventional working-time norms is a 'feminisation' of these norms in favour of more precarious arrangements or presents an opportunity to realign the division of time between paid and unpaid work and life.

Vicki Schultz and Allison Hoffman in chapter 6 also focus on the legal rules that establish norms of working time and how they marginalise women workers who bear a disproportionate share of the burden of unpaid care responsibilities. They show how labour law in the United States functions to create incentives for employers to employ workers either for very long hours or for very short hours, and how this polarisation of working time has negative consequences for society at large, and women in particular. They consider a range of policy options that would promote a more equitable distribution of paid and unpaid work.

Claire Kilpatrick (chapter 7) explores another dimension of the legal treatment of working time—how employment breaks have been conceptualised by contract and statute in the United Kingdom, and the gender implications of those conceptualisations. She shows how regulatory choices concerning how to treat employment breaks make women's employment more or less precarious. Kilpatrick focuses on the legal treatment of formal and extensive periods of leave for family reasons, and she demonstrates how casual workers and workers on various forms of family leave, who are disproportionately women, are detrimentally affected by a twentieth-century male-worker paradigm of employment patterns.

The next three chapters are concerned with the question of employment status, since workers who are not legally recognised as being employees are not entitled to employment rights and protections. They show that the failure to develop legal norms that are responsive to women's care work, whether unpaid or paid, makes many women's employment more precarious.

Sandra Fredman, in chapter 8, illustrates how, in the United Kingdom, women's need to navigate the obligations of paid and unpaid care leads them to take non-standard forms of employment, which results in their exclusion from the protection of labour law. This is because non-standard employment does not conform to the traditional bipartite notion of contract that continues to dominate the area of employment law in the United Kingdom. Fredman shows how non-standard workers pose particular challenges for contract-based labour law, because their services are not wholly at the disposal of their employer. This arrangement gives them a semblance of autonomy and independence, which appear to be the hallmarks of the independent entrepreneur, and thus the courts exclude them from employment protection. There has been some attempt to change this at a legislative level, where legislation providing minimum wages, limits on working time, and rights for part-time workers was extended beyond the contract of service to the contract to provide personal services. However, the courts have given a narrow interpretation to this concept, too. Fredman demonstrates how a fault-based model of employer limits the potential of equality laws to improve the terms and conditions of non-standard workers. By contrast, she argues that duties should 'fall on employers not because of their immediate power to command the time and commitment of an individual worker, but because of their labour market power and civil responsibility that attaches to those with power' (Fredman, chapter 8).

Judy Fudge also argues that expanding the scope of employment protection legislation is necessary to improve the situation of women in precarious work. She explores what the growth in women's self-employment reveals about the legal norms of employment and independent contracting, and the fit between contemporary work arrangements and the scope of labour protection. She maps the scope of employment in labour-related law, and legislation in Canada against a statistical portrait of women's self-employment and assesses the extent to which the law contributes to the precarious nature of self-employment for women. Fudge also describes the ILO's recent activities on the scope of employment and considers the impact the ILO's work is likely to have in Canada. She concludes that women's self-employment demonstrates the need to go beyond employment to consider self-employment and unpaid caring labour in order to develop policies that promote women's equality.

In chapter 10, Stéphanie Bernstein shifts the focus from unpaid care work to paid work caring for children, the elderly, and people with disabilities, and the related work of managing households that takes place at (either the worker's or employer's) home. She reveals how the law in Quebec has classified paid care work along dimensions such as the identity of the employer, the type of work, and the place of work in order to exclude many forms of paid care work from the scope of labour legislation. Moreover, she shows how conflicts over the terms and conditions of care workers have a potential to divide women, and how women who provide child care in their home are divided over employment status. The status, rewards, and distribution of paid care work are highly contentious, and increasingly so with the trend toward the international commodification of paid labour, and Bernstein questions whether this trend may have a positive effect on the visibility and legal recognition of paid care work.

The next chapters explore the lack of fit between the employment norms of the Fordist economy and the employment relationships in the new economy. Kathy Stone, in chapter 11, shifts focus from non-standard to standard workers and explores how facets of the boundary-less workplace make standard workers more precarious. She shows how new employment practices that diffuse authority make women and minority workers vulnerable to forms of discrimination for which there is little legal redress. Stone argues that, although the new workplace, with its rejection of implicit long-term employment guarantees and its repudiation of job ladders, offers the possibility of creating new opportunities for women and minorities, discrimination takes new forms in the new boundary-less workplace. Because US anti-discrimination law was developed for the hierarchal job structures of internal labour markets, it does not fit the new employment practices, making workers in standard employment relationships more precarious. Stone offers a number of proposals that would alleviate the discrimination faced by the workers in the boundary-less workplace.

Jenny Julén Votinius provides a critical analysis of the problems in Sweden associated with the working-life norms of the 'typical employee' focusing on questions relating to working time and the form of employment (chapter 12). In labour law, it is the norm of the typical employee that both governs the assessment of which needs of the employee should be accorded the status of rights and provides the foundation upon which legal protection is constructed. Votinius emphasises the extent to which legal norms contribute to the formation of perceptions about employees and their fundamental needs.

Rosemary Hunter, in chapter 13, argues that Australian labour law has been a large part of the problem in relation to precarious work for at least the last 15 years, and that there are few signs that it has much to contribute by way of solutions. She examines the relationship between labour regulation, the entrenched gender divisions of labour in the private and public spheres, and the production of different kinds of precarious work. Hunter also looks at the opposite side of the ledger: how law has attempted to ameliorate precarious work. She finds that, although some state governments, industrial tribunals, courts, and unions have sought to improve the status of non-standard workers, these efforts have been piecemeal and largely unsuccessful. Hunter concludes that attempting to change legal norms while the state of the labour market and the gendered practices in paid employment and the home remain constant can only have a limited effect on improving the conditions of women in precarious work.

The final section of the volume focuses on the theme of flexibility that has threaded throughout the chapters. Susanne Burri, in chapter 14, describes and assesses the attempt in the Netherlands to reconcile the diverging demands of flexibility of employees and employers. The challenge was to realise the flexibility of working time, employment contracts, and working conditions without giving up employment security and employees' rights, and the Dutch legislator has enacted several statutes with a view to improving the working conditions of employees with flexible employment contracts, while at the same time not disregarding the needs of employers. Burri concludes that the Working Time Adjustment Act has the most potential to weaken the dominance of the full-time norm and provide for a greater pluralism in working time. However, she notes that little attention has yet been paid by policy makers to the structural risks relating to career interruption and part-time work, and that the long-term consequences of this may continue to be very hard for women.

Rosemary Owens, in the final chapter, examines three strategies that have the potential to transform flexibility from a negative process for women workers in Australia to one that is potentially transformative in that it allows them to navigate better the boundary between unpaid care and employment. Through an analysis of anti-discrimination cases, she shows that anti-discrimination law in Australia has not been a very successful strategy for producing workplaces that enable women to accommodate better the competing demands of unpaid care and employment. The second strategy discussed involves converting casual employment into standard employment. But the problem with that strategy, according to Owens, is that it simply requires the line between precarious and standard employment to be redrawn; it does not eliminate precarious employment. Like the anti-discrimination strategy, conversion offers an individual solution to a structural problem. The third strategy entails developing flexible standards via facilitative provisions that aim to allow individuals to tailor a wider range of workplace rights to suit their own needs. Although Owens also identifies problems with this strategy, in that it does not challenge in a fundamental way the norms that underpin the law of work, the standard worker, she suggests that the 'public' supervision of otherwise 'private' arrangements may be a more productive route to attaining 'decent' flexible work.

Part II

Supranational Norms and Discourses about Precarious Work

2

Rights, Risk, and Reward: Governance Norms in the International Order and the Problem of Precarious Work

KERRY RITTICH*

INTRODUCTION

THE DECLINE OF the standard employment relationship and the increase in precarious work—work that is insecure, badly remunerated, unprotected, and largely beyond the control of employees—is widely recognised as one of the most fundamental and worrying problems of the new economy. While precarious forms of work are neither new nor unusual in the history of work (Deakin, 2001), they have become a focal point in contemporary discussions of work because of their apparent structural links to globalisation and the new economy. Moreover, precarious work remains deeply associated with constituencies which have always lacked significant leverage and power in the labour market; notwithstanding the extent to which it has spread within labour markets as a whole, those engaged in precarious work remain disproportionately women, racial and ethnic minorities, young people, and disabled workers (Fudge and Owens, chapter 1 in this volume). In short, precarious work both constitutes a general problem in the new economy and marks a persisting zone of secondary status in the labour market.

While the rise of precarious work is closely related to the proliferation of atypical, flexible, or 'contingent' work arrangements, it is fundamentally a governance problem. The persistence and proliferation of precarious work and the marginal status of those engaged in such work are not phenomena that can be attributed to the nature of investment, production, and

* Thanks to Judy Fudge and an anonymous reviewer for very helpful questions and comments; all errors remain mine.

exchange in the new economy alone. Rather, they are intimately linked to the institutional structure in which work takes place and the choices states make about the structure of legal entitlements; the distribution of resources through taxation and income transfers and expenditures on public goods; and the sharing of risk through legal and social institutions. Those choices, in turn, have much to do with perceptions of the available institutions and their appropriate roles, as well as the assessments that are made about their capacity to deliver particular social and economic outcomes. For these reasons, both the problem of precarious work and the range of possible responses to it are tightly tied to a larger set of governance debates in which we are now immersed.

This chapter aims to suggest how and why the international financial institutions (IFI), the World Bank and the International Monetary Fund (IMF), have become important to the international debates on labour market reform and, by extension, to the issue of precarious work. The point of entry is the connection between these issues and questions of governance and institutional design. Although the IFI have no direct mandate over the global labour agenda, they have become centrally involved in the general question of governance within market societies, which they define in broad terms as both the exercise of political powers and the management of human, natural, and economic resources (Shihata, 2000). Since their conclusion that 'good governance' and institutional reform are the key to economic growth (World Bank, 1989; Wolfensohn, 1999; Rittich, 2002b), the IFIs have developed a set of governance norms and progressively elaborated an institutional or structural reform agenda which, in their view, provides a framework or matrix, if not a blueprint, for economic success in the global economy. This agenda both sets the general justifications for the regulation of markets and frames the analysis and the range of possible responses to specific labour market problems and concerns such as precarious work.

The IFI exercise direct influence over the governance and policy choices of developing and transitional states through mechanisms such as the attachment of conditions to loan agreements and the provision of 'technical' legal assistance (Shihata, 1997). However, they also exercise influence in a variety of other soft or indirect ways, primarily because of their surveillance and comparisons of different market economies and role as arbiters of 'good governance' and best practice in respect of institutional or structural reforms (IMF, *World Economic Outlook*, various years; World Bank, 2004). Here, their reach is not limited to developing and transitional states but extends to industrialised states as well. This soft power is enhanced by the fact that they are the largest, most well-funded sources of development research in the world. Both the IMF and the World Bank now generate an avalanche of research and policy reports on the legal and institutional bases of economic growth; however, many are designed to confirm a set of propositions about the connections between economic growth and the structural and institutional reforms that they have already been promoting as best practice for some time (see, for example, World Bank, 2004).

The IMF recently encapsulated and justified these reforms in the following way:

> Structural reforms entail measures that, broadly speaking, change the institutional framework and constraints governing market behavior and outcomes. In general, structural reforms have been associated with the notion of increasing the role of market forces – including competition and price flexibility, and the term is often used interchangeably with deregulation – reducing the extent to which government regulations or ownership of productive capacity affect the decision making of private firms and households ... [Structural reforms rest on] a variety of factors, inducing growing evidence that not only markets but also governments can fail – that is, governments' regulations can in practice fail to deliver what they are supposed to do in theory, namely to resolve problems related to market failure or inefficiency. ... Fundamentally, structural reforms aim at adapting institutional frameworks and regulations for markets to work properly.
>
> (IMF, 2004, 104–5)

As this passage indicates, the reform strategy is deeply functionalist in orientation, and the functionality of institutions is defined in a very particular way: their contribution to the efficient allocation of resources and the facilitation of market transactions. Resistance to these reforms is typically presented as the carping of specal interest groups at the expense of the general interest in economic growth; while concessions to losers may sometimes be required, it is only to the extent necessary to sustain the political support for reforms (IMF, 2004; World Bank, 2004).

This agenda might be of limited interest on its own but for the fact that it appears to be gaining weight and credence through an iterative process within the international system, and visibly influencing other institutions such as the United Nations (UN), United Nations Development Programme (UNDP), and the International Labour Organization (ILO) at the level of tone, substance, and strategy. Recent reports across a range of international institutions are either marked by or explicitly framed in the language of good governance and their recommendations increasingly operate within the basic institutional and policy parameters that have been established by the IFI. Indeed, other international institutions, or specific projects within them, now simply invoke IFI research findings, incorporating them without more into their own analyses and policy reports (see UNDP, 2004, referencing World Bank, 2004). There is no easy or certain way to account for their influence. However, as few, if any, of the other international institutions have comparable resources at their disposal, the sheer quantity of analyses generated by the IFI and the categorical terms in which their conclusions are articulated often go a great distance to establish the terms of contemporary debates around institutional reform within the international order. One result is that where previously the different concerns of the international institutions were clearly visible and distinguishable, as were the constituencies for whom they spoke, now they are becoming more difficult to tease out. Goals are increasingly merged as policy analysis is organised around exhortations for better governance.

Establishing a causal relation between economic growth and specific structural reforms is notoriously difficult; moreover, the track record of reforms promoted by the IFI is marred by the fact that they have often failed to generate their predicted consequences and sometimes made things worse even by their own standards (Stiglitz, 2002). Despite this, within the IFI little research has been directed at testing their foundational assumptions, or even at investigating why it is that states that have varying institutional structures and governance norms and that have taken different reform routes also seem to have been able to generate economic growth. Yet however limited or problematic the research might be and however questionable or spurious some of the resulting claims, they gain legitimacy as they are adopted and recirculated within other institutions. The result is a rapidly consolidating foundation of maxims and principles about the nature of the new economy and the institutional bases of efficient markets that are increasingly pervasive and difficult to contest at the political and institutional levels, even if they are far from unassailable at the analytic level. Among them is a set of basic propositions about labour markets, including: the foundational role of continuous growth through private sector investment; the inefficiency and distorting effects of labour market institutions; the primacy of labour market policies that enhance workers' skills; and the limits of the regulatory and redistributive state in the global economy. While there might be disagreements over the desirability of particular rules and policies, more and more of the discussion now takes place within a broader zone of convergence over the institutional foundations of growth.

Although one conclusion might be that we really have reached the 'end of history', that all this convergence merely marks the dawn of market enlightenment in respect of the regulation of market societies, it is belied by the ongoing disputes over the institutional bases of growth and the efficiency of different legal rules (Deakin and Wilkinson, 2000; Rodrik, Subramanian, and Trebbi, 2002; Stiglitz, 2002); it also ignores the well-established critiques of functionalist analyses of legal regulation in market societies (Gordon, 1984). Whatever the outcome of these debates, the entrenchment of this particular governance frame is a particularly fateful turn of events for workers because of the way that the aims and justifications of regulation and policy in general and labour market regulation and social protection policy in particular are represented within it. One effect is substantially to normalise the emergence of precarious work. Refracted through the lens of best practices and good labour market governance, precarious work emerges re-branded as flexibility and opportunity. As a problem, precarious work is not so much engaged as displaced, overwhelmed by a counter-narrative of progress for workers through the opening of markets, the accumulation of skill, and the use of entrepreneurial savvy.

The rest of this chapter will attempt to outline how this occurs, by describing the vision of labour market reform that predominates within the IFI and outlining the features that make it an uncongenial, even perilous, frame within which to resolve the problem of precarious work. It will then describe the ways in which that agenda is increasingly reflected in the analyses of the ILO, notwithstanding its efforts to advance the position of workers through initiatives such as the Decent Work Agenda.

GOOD GOVERNANCE AND THE NORMALISATION OF PRECARIOUS WORK

Describing the New Labour Market

Both the World Bank and the IMF have weighed in heavily on the debate around the future of work, devoting major policy reports and substantial portions of their analysis of institutional or structural reforms to the question of labour market reform. Labour market flexibility is a linchpin of this agenda. Developing countries repeatedly have been advised to maintain flexible labour markets and eschew the introduction of burdensome regulations (World Bank, 1995). Industrialised countries have been exhorted to reduce existing levels of job security and the costs of their provision to employers, to move from passive income support to 'active' labour market policies, and to 'make work pay', largely by eliminating rules, policies, and programmes that have the effect of reducing the incentives to work (OECD, 1994b, 1999).

The most unvarnished arguments for such structural reforms to labour markets along these lines can be found in the analyses of the IMF. In a series of reports over the last six years, the IMF has hewed to a consistent line on reforms, couching its analysis first in terms of causes of and cures for unemployment (IMF, 1999a: chapter IV) and, more recently, restating the benefits of such reforms (IMF, 2003: chapter IV) and proposing ways to manage the political obstacles toward what, in its view, is a self-evidently more desirable state of affairs (IMF, 2004: chapter III).

In these reports, the Fund has been explicit about the need to exert downward pressure on wage levels, benefits, and security for workers in industrialised countries in order to combat the excessive labour market rigidity that, in its view, is a source of both inefficiency and distributive injustice. It argues relentlessly that what is needed in the new economy is not protection for workers against the risks of the new economy, but rather a greater emphasis on skills and greater worker adaptability to the demands of the market. While many of the arguments relate to efficiency concerns, the arguments for reform are not grounded only in the demands of growth and competitive labour markets; rather, labour market institutions are undesirable because they cost jobs and produce protected classes of labour market 'insiders' at the expense of outsiders. To inject greater flexibility into labour markets, the Fund proposes a set of institutional reforms, the overall aim of which is to reduce the constraints on labour market contracting on the theory that those constraints prevent prospective workers and employers from reaching bargains that they otherwise would. To this end, the Fund proposes that bargaining be decentralised as much as possible, job security reduced, and access to unemployment and other benefits significantly curtailed. But the constraints that in its view contribute to labour market rigidity traverse the entire field of labour and employment regulations; they include not only the rules listed above but working time regulations, those governing part-time work and minimum wages, and health and safety regulations as well (IMF, 1999a: 99–100).

The governance norms espoused by the World Bank and the IMF have shifted somewhat in recent years in response to a range of factors and forces including: internal and external critiques of their evident shortcomings in particular contexts (Stiglitz, 2002); a reconceptualisation of development as freedom (Sen, 1999); the recognition of human rights as both a constitutive part of development and an aid to growth (Wolfensohn, 1999; World Bank, 2000); and a new recognition of the problems of market distortions and the possibilities of regulating for efficiency (World Bank, 2004). The inclusion of human rights within the development framework may have induced the World Bank and the IMF to move some distance towards the recognition of 'core' workers' rights, although the OECD had already argued persuasively that freedom of association posed no barrier to trade (OECD, 1996), while freedom from discrimination has independent economic appeal because of its role in ensuring general access to labour markets. However, both the World Bank and the IMF have been careful to qualify their support for freedom of association, largely because of their concerns about the negative impact of unions and collective action by workers on efficiency, investment, and economic growth (World Bank, 1998; IMF, 1999a; Rittich, 2003a). Moreover, labour market institutions beyond the core continue to attract critical scrutiny notwithstanding the many arguments that have been made in respect of their efficiency-enhancing properties (Deakin and Wilkinson, 2000).

Thus, the logic animating labour market reform has not (yet) significantly changed. The World Bank and the IMF continue to promote a greatly decentralised structure of bargaining and workplace norm-setting within a 'deregulated' market governed largely by the property and contract rights of employers. The assumption is that the end result will be a dispersion of economic reward commensurate with the level of human capital of the worker, its value to the enterprise, and the degree of risk and individual work undertaken.

Recoding Precarious Work

Animating the regulatory agenda of the IFI is not only the standard neoclassical account about the efficiency- and growth-impeding effects of labour market rules: there is an image of the ideal worker and a set of assumptions about the nature of contemporary work as well.

At the heart of the new labour agenda is a new regulative ideal, the entrepreneurial worker. The archetypal worker emerging from this agenda is the skilled, knowledge worker of the post-industrial world (see Fudge and Owens, chapter 1 in this volume). This is a worker who both cooperates with his employer in the pursuit and successful execution of commercial ventures but maintains an entrepreneurial approach to work, seeking not the security of a long-term employment relationship but rather continuously improving opportunities in which to deploy his skills and maximise his returns in the market. This worker is also largely unencumbered by outside constraints and is both willing and able to devote his primary energies to positioning and advancing himself in the market.

If the archetypal worker is the highly skilled knowledge worker, then the archetypal workplace is a site of continual innovation embedded in a high-velocity market (Barenberg, 1994; Hyde, 2003). Whether the task is the production of goods or the provision of services, the operating assumption is that the demands for greater efficiency now place a premium on continual innovation at work. Both at the level of the organisational structure and at the level of work processes, the assumption is that this will translate into networked production and more transitory contractual and employment relationships counterbalanced by flattened workplace hierarchy and a higher degree of input and control on the part of workers. Wages and income are supposed to rise with investment in human capital and increased skill, so that there is a direct relationship between conformity to the regulative ideal and income and employment security in the new economy.

Various scholars and analyses have suggested why such labour market reform strategies might radically underplay the complexity of work relations in the new economy. In addition to new problems such as the generation of trust and commitment in transitory relationships (Stone, 2001) and the organisation and financing of skill acquisition in a knowledge-based economy (OECD, 2003b), there are on-going problems centred around the role of employer power and control at work (Klare, 2000), the provision of collective goods and other issues requiring collective action, as well as the persistence of other labour market imperfections and social norms that systematically prevent both workers and employers from behaving according to script. While many of these problems are associated with the old economy, it is not obvious that they have disappeared in the new (Deakin and Wilkinson, 2000).

Although the assumptions that make the entrepreneurial ideal seem attractive are descriptively accurate for only a segment of the labour market (Standing, 1999a), this ideal still has a powerful hold on contemporary debates about work. Like the ideal or normative worker so critical to the fate of women workers of the post-war world, the intersecting images of the entrepreneurial worker and the innovative workplace dominate the regulatory and policy agenda and play a constitutive role in precarious work.

Much of the work is done through a shift in the frame in which we view the world of work. It is not difficult to see how on the basis of a changed set of assumptions and norms precarious work might take on a different cast. Once the optic is adjusted, for example, short job tenure and instability in employment appear as inherent parts of the process of 'creative destruction' at work analogous to the on-going cycle of start-up, competitive selection, adaptation, and consequent success or failure that characterises life in the commercial world as a whole. Insecure employment becomes simply the natural fate of those who have inadequate skills for the new economy. Lack of control over work is something that can be remedied by the contribution of more valued skills, not the exercise of collective worker power. Wages are not 'low', indeed, they cannot be low in any absolute sense; they are set by the market, and set correctly once regulatory 'distortions' are removed. While there is no promise of a secure employment, there is the promise of wages commensurate with productivity, merit, performance, and marginal product or value to the enterprise. In this world, as in the wider commercial world, the mantra might be, 'worker prove (and be prepared to continually reprove) your worth'.

In other words, according to the logic animating this idea of good labour market governance, it is not clear that precarious work emerges as a problem, at least one that merits any specific legal response beyond the general reforms that are thought to be beneficial to workers and labour markets as a whole. To the extent that it does, because, for example, precarious work is also associated with labour market inefficiencies, any response would differ fundamentally from the classical post-war approaches to labour market regulation and social protection. As the standard 'deregulatory' prescriptions suggest, greater worker rights and protections, labour market regulation, and union-inspired collective action are themselves figured as the problem, the central reason that labour markets fail to produce the good jobs that would otherwise emerge from well-functioning labour markets.

Notwithstanding the strength of this narrative and the power of the new regulatory ideal, there is another story to be told about contemporary labour markets. Part of it concerns the organisation of work. Whatever the decentralising pull of networked production and the enhanced possibilities for cooperation in innovation-driven markets, workplace hierarchy stubbornly persists: employers continue to control the operation of enterprises and the organisation of work. This is not merely a matter of employer preference, although the desire to maintain rather than share control surely plays a part; the wider structure of legal rules is also implicated. For example, corporate law in the Anglo-American jurisdictions induces, even compels, employers to give primary attention to the interests of shareholders, not the wider 'stakeholder' community of which workers are a part (Barnard and Deakin, 2002). In the drive to increase shareholder returns, workers are still often treated as costs to be managed and reduced rather than as assets to be cultivated.

Another part of the story concerns the nature of work. Whatever the importance of human capital, much work still is, and may be organised to remain, relatively unskilled. It has long been observed that the global cities which are the engines of economic growth in the global economy and the natural repositories of high-skilled work simultaneously produce a set of low-road counterparts, a sort of third world within the first (Sassen, 1991). It is also clear that modernisation and growth are no longer the route out of labour market informality; rather they generate informality as well (Castells, 2000). Moreover, there is accumulating evidence that wage gaps, especially those that track gender or racial lines, persist even when the human capital of those on the wrong side of the line exceeds that of those on the right (McColgan, 2000c). These complications put significant dents in the contentions that precarious work is a supply-side problem and that attention to human capital largely solves the poor prospects in the labour market.

Sceptics could obviously raise a host of additional problems. While concerns about the disparity of bargaining power may be allayed by the specific skill set some workers bring to the table, or even the advantages some labour forces as a whole bring to particular industries, is the typical worker now on a level footing with her employer? Has conflict at work really been supplanted by cooperation? How do we square this with the constant reminders that replacement workers stand by ready to claim jobs in the next jurisdiction if workers' demands are too high? What place is there in this narrative for the specific risks faced by women, many of which contribute to their vulnerability at work?

In this labour market governance agenda, these issues are not so much confronted as avoided, subsumed within the dream of market solutions. The power of this agenda seems to lie in the fact that it marries propositions that are attractive, persuasive, and at least partly true to others that are speculative, disingenuous, or simply objectionable. But the failure to address concerns that, whether from the standpoint of efficiency or distributive justice, are painfully easy to point out suggests that, notwithstanding the description of workers as a whole making progress, poor jobs and precarious work may be integral to the labour market reform agenda in a more fundamental way. The labour market governance narrative is a bold attempt to persuade everyone to buy into a new set of propositions about the global road to progress in the world of work. However, it may also function to distract attention from labour market problems both old and new. For these reasons, we should be alert to the manner and extent to which it becomes entrenched and accepted.

DIFFUSING GOOD GOVERNANCE NORMS

The ILO has an explicit mandate to advance the conditions of labour and further the cause of social justice, and in these capacities has launched a number of initiatives to respond to the social deficit of globalisation. By contrast with the IFI, whose engagement with the issue is collateral to their main concerns, the ILO is intimately, and directly, involved in the problem of precarious work. Indeed, it is possible to understand the ILO's 'Decent Work Agenda' (ILO, 1999) as fundamentally a response to the centrality of precarious work in the global economy. The Decent Work Agenda seeks to reverse the slide toward precarious work by holding up its mirror image as the goal. Stressing the four 'pillars' of decent work, the ILO now promotes the protection of workers' 'basic' or core rights and seeks a reinvigorated commitment to employment, social protection, and dialogue at work.

Rather than assess these efforts on their own terms (see Vosko, chapter 3 in this volume), the following analysis considers the extent to which the ILO appears to accept, qualify, or reject the governance agenda promoted by the IFI. Recent reports suggest that, despite the effort to promote decent work through core rights, employment, social protection and social dialogue, and to do so at least partly by relying upon the policy and regulatory tools of the old world so disparaged by the IFI, the ILO also increasingly operates within the parameters defined by the IFI as good governance. The intuition pursued here is that the acceptance of the overall framework and the failure to scrutinise the ways in which the institutional infrastructure associated with it might itself be implicated in current labour market problems both diverts attention from issues that are critical to the interests of workers and weakens the overall analysis of the issues that are considered. In particular, it undercuts the capacity to deal comprehensively with precarious work because it fails to give serious attention to its institutional substructure but rather leaves much of it intact.

Two recent examples, both of which are pertinent to the issue of gender and precarious work, give some indication of the reach of the governance norms now promoted by the IFI within the ILO and, indeed, the wider policy-making community. The first is the Final Report of the World Commission on the Social Dimension of Globalization, *A Fair Globalization* (ILO, 2004a); the second is the fourth global report following the Declaration on Fundamental Principles and Rights at Work, *Time for Equality at Work* (ILO, 2003c). The first aims at a comprehensive response to the social deficit of globalisation; the second addresses the question of discrimination and equality in labour markets.

A Fair Globalization: A Summary

The World Commission on the Social Dimension of Globalization was specially constituted by the ILO as a group of diverse and broadly representative actors and experts charged with the task of making a systematic attempt to find common ground on the question of the social dimension of globalization. As the title of its final report suggests, the animating impulse was the sense that there was an urgent need to generate proposals for 'righting the imbalances' of globalisation. (ILO, 2004c). The 'common ground' from which the analysis proceeds is, for this reason, critical to understanding the report itself; in many ways, it is the very object of the exercise.

At first glance *A Fair Globalization* seems like a welcome response to the emergence of precarious work; it is certainly possible to find references to problems such as growing insecurity and pressures on the quality of employment (ILO, 2004a: para 283). Yet, read as a whole, and in the context of the governance agenda in particular, it begins to look less promising. What follows are some observations about the continuities and discontinuities of *A Fair Globalization* with both the governance agenda and the traditional concerns and optics of labour.

The language of governance is all over the report. But *A Fair Globalization* does not simply endorse the centrality of rules and institutions, it adopts a general vision of good governance that sounds remarkably like the one promoted by the IFI. References to the need for 'sound institutions' and a 'well-functioning market economy' appear right off the bat. Here, as in the analysis of the IFI, they end up functioning as codes for specific institutional reforms. The general policy focus is on 'enabling' strategies for labour market participation, a strategy that is consistent with the role figured for the state by the IFI of 'enabling' market processes and creating a market- and investment-friendly environment.

The most basic message of the report is that 'globalisation is good'; it just needs to be made to work better. The report does not question the basic proposition that greater economic integration is beneficial for workers. This is a position that should be at least somewhat controversial: whatever the aggregate efficiency gains and ultimate economic benefits of trade and integration-driven growth, the distribution of those gains and benefits remains highly uneven, both between and within states and regions. As the report notes, the imbalance of power between countries is a central governance problem in the global economy. However, it is striking that the report says almost nothing about the imbalance of power between workers and unions on the one hand and employers on the other, as there is general agreement that, so far, the process of integration has very much favoured capital holders over labour. While in theory these defects (and other distributional concerns too) could be at least partly remedied by institutional reforms, the barriers to such reforms remain formidable. Whether in their absence the ILO should remain so sanguine about the benefits of greater economic integration for workers should be the question, not the presumption.

There are repeated pleas for greater policy coherence among the international institutions and 'enhanced coordination of macroeconomic policies to attain a more balanced strategy for sustainable global growth and full employment' (ILO, 2004e). This is hardly undesirable, especially given that pro-worker reforms in one arena might be completely undone by reforms with cross-cutting effects elsewhere. However, 'failure of coordination' seems to understate the problems with, and the gravity of, an institutional agenda that has had labour market deregulation at its heart. The report places great stress on the benefits of social dialogue, which the ILO defines as 'all types of negotiation, consultation or exchange of information between or among representatives of governments, employers and workers on issues of common interest relating to economic and social policy' (ILO, 2004d). Such dialogue may range from completely informal discussions among any of the social partners to arrangements that are entrenched and supported by institutions and legal entitlements both substantive and procedural. In practice, the framework in which such dialogue occurs is crucial, not peripheral, as freedom of association and rights to collective bargaining may ring hollow depending on their particular institutional form, the manner in which they are adjudicated, and the extent to which they are enforced (Human Rights Watch, 2000). For this reason, the call for greater 'social dialogue' seems a totally ineffectual response to the actors and institutions on the other side who reject any automatic role for unions and are explicitly seeking to break corporatist arrangements, decentralise bargaining, and weaken the collective power of workers by dismantling many of its institutional supports.

There is great stress on the imperative of growth and many references to growth as the best route to full employment. However, *A Fair Globalization* contains relatively little analysis of the specific demands of pro-employment growth (ILO, 2004a: paras 281, 282). This issue should be much more central to a global labour or social justice analysis; whether growth without employment is desirable in itself raises some of the issues discussed above.

Throughout the report, the language of cooperation between workers and employers dominates this analysis, totally eclipsing the spectre of conflict. Equity and efficiency are generally presented as complementary objectives. Rather than devices for worker empowerment and protection, labour market rules and institutions are typically characterised as a response to some market failure and repeatedly justified in terms of their contribution to efficiency. To state what may be obvious, the decision to characterise them in this way ignores their role in redressing the inequality of bargaining power between workers and employers. Apart from displaying a startling amnesia about the history of labour market institutions and controversies out of which they emerged, this account stands in tension with the longstanding view within the ILO that 'labour is not a commodity' and has the effect of instrumentalising worker protections in the service of growth. While this frame provides a justification for labour market institutions that is consistent with the overall logic animating the governance agenda, it ignores their role in redistributing power and authority among workers and between workers and employers and mediating conflicts of interest at work, many of which still exist. As well as obscuring the trade-offs and choices among different objectives, it may also have the collateral effect of delegitimating rule, institutional, and policy responses that cannot be easily or uncontroversially subsumed under the rubric of efficiency.

In common with the labour market strategies of the IFI, *A Fair Globalization* stresses the importance of investments in human capital, making this the major orientation of labour policy and regulation in the new economy. What might be expected in this analysis, and what is largely missing, is more attention to the demand side of the equation too: without it, we are invited to conclude that a skilled, educated labour force creates its own market (Amsden, 2001). Although the report suggests that there is global responsibility for ensuring demand, we learn nothing about what this might mean in policy or regulatory terms. Notably absent is a serious consideration of issues such as jobless growth; structural and cyclical unemployment; and the emergence of low-skill work. Most troubling is the lack of attention to making low-skill work 'good' work, that is, to contesting the assumption that, basic rights aside, skill is an adequate index of terms and conditions of work. These are all problems that either will not or cannot be solved by improving the value of workers to their employers.

In general, the regulatory and policy focus of the report is on compliance with core labour rights and the creation of a basic socio-economic floor. The discussion of labour market rules and institutions, by contrast, is surprisingly thin, given that even the IMF understands that the real conflict is over the institutional implications of those core rights or standards (IMF, 1999b) and appreciates that structural reforms that improve productivity may also increase earnings inequality and poverty (IMF, 2004: chapter III). While the references to a socio-economic floor add something to the institutional vision promoted by the IFI, viewed in historical perspective and in light of the total corpus of ILO activities, these are very modest, chastened objectives.

Beyond this, the most prominent regulatory concerns are the promotion of agreements on the cross-border movement of workers and the formalisation of labour markets. Although they are important, they do not begin to touch, let alone exhaust, the wide range of institutional concerns that are relevant to workers in the new economy. Whether these are the most important regulatory issues for workers, rather than those that are least contentious and most compatible with other regulatory objectives, is unclear. What is clear is that hard distributive justice goals such as improving wages or strengthening workers' bargaining power receive little attention; at best, they are addressed indirectly through social dialogue.

If, on the one hand, *A Fair Globalization* contains some surprising omissions and concessions, on the other, it contains concerns that seem primarily explicable in terms of their centrality to the larger market reform agenda. The protection of property rights, for example, receive a degree of prominence that is puzzling in a discussion about social justice; it is less puzzling once we realise that property rights have been discovered by the World Bank as a major poverty-reduction tool (De Soto, 2000; World Bank, 2003). One of its more bizarre effects is to cast workers in the developing world as future entrepreneurs. Yet even if property rights work their magic and markets in land develop as predicted, many people are likely to remain in marginal self-employment. In addition, the ownership changes that accompany greater commodification of land will almost certainly result in greater inequality and produce numbers of workers with limited or no capital who face a quite predictable set of labour market issues. In other words, whatever their benefits, property rights do not solve the dilemma of precarious work: they will almost certainly produce more of it as well.

Assessing *A Fair Globalization*

Notwithstanding that it was the perceived defects of the current global order that provoked the creation of the Commission and the report in the first place, *A Fair Globalization* reads less as a sober analysis of the requirements of distributive justice for workers than as a consensus document reminiscent of the negotiated outcomes of international conferences. Indeed, compared to at least one such document, the Copenhagen Declaration of the World Social Summit in 1995 (UN, 1995), it is less forthright about the challenges for workers in the current economy, advocates less on their behalf, and is more accommodating to the economic and regulatory norms that now prevail in the international economic order. Rather than confront the limits of the current paradigm, *A Fair Globalization* fiddles at the margins, hoping to stake out more promising territory for workers within it. At best, it raises cautions without going on to consider the extent to which problems are created by or can be resolved within the basic governance framework. This makes the analysis seem in the alternative vague and unhelpful or internally incoherent and unpersuasive.

A Fair Globalization begins in a promising vein by centring the problem of the social dimension in the distribution of costs and benefits in the global economy; moreover, it attributes the problem to deficiencies in governance (ILO, 2004a: xi). However, it does not then go on seriously to consider or contest the basic thesis, advanced by the IFI and increasingly found elsewhere too, about the efficiency or non-efficiency of various labour market institutions, nor does it seek to implicate the other institutions that facilitate global markets in the current position of workers. Instead, it merely reproduces the idea that 'sound market institutions' are key. In so doing, it leaves untouched the deeply problematic proposition that labour market rules 'distort' otherwise neutral markets, as well as the assumption that other rules associated with 'well-functioning markets' necessarily operate to the benefit of both workers and societies in general.

These are concessions with very, very long legs. They arguably take the analysis away from where it most needs to look: the role of a wide range of rule and institutional choices in either aggravating or ameliorating the maldistribution of resources, authority, and power in the global economy. They have particularly profound implications for analysing and responding to the precarious work of women, for they work to normalise a contingent allocation of powers, risks, benefits, and burdens among market actors; this in turn helps to naturalise the very division between market and non-market spheres and concerns that must be challenged in order to address some of the basic sources of labour market disadvantage for women (Rittich, 2002b). But they also render a wide range of other proposals, many of which are still part of the ILO's Decent Work Agenda and other projects, 'second best' solutions that constitute deviations from optimal policies, if they even make sense at all.

A Fair Globalization situates the plight of workers within the larger context of developments in the global economy; this is both its strength and its weakness. It seems clearly right that the fate of workers is tied to the larger economic and institutional climate rather than to a narrow set of workplace issues alone. However, the sense conveyed by *A Fair Globalization* is that the ILO is desperately trying to navigate a better path for workers within the global economy without challenging conventional institutional wisdom held in other quarters. The real question may be why the ILO chose to adopt this approach to analysing such a central problem for workers and societies in the current economy. Whatever the reason, the 'common ground' approach reflected in the Report of the World Commission may be perilous, if it induces the ILO to hold its fire and adopt a compromised set of reform objectives that are designed to merely soften the adjustment process for workers. Whether governance norms that challenge this 'common ground' are feasible right now is a live question; however, by subsuming the agenda for social justice within them, not only does *A Fair Globalization* accommodate those norms, it subscribes to, rather than questions, the theory that workers, too, stand to benefit from them. The failure to come to grips with the extent to which precarious work may be structurally related to current governance norms and emerging labour market practices eliminates some of the key analytic and policy tools to address one of the most pressing labour problems of the new economy. When the ILO, too, simply recirculates the promise of the high-skill labour markets without scrutinising the other face of the new economy, the effect is to suggest that the problem of precarious work lies with workers. To the extent that the ILO adopts this approach, it risks abandoning its most vulnerable constituency.

Time for Equality at Work

Time for Equality at Work is the fourth global report on the ILO Declaration on Fundamental Principles and Rights at Work. Its purpose is to explicate the context and implications of one of the 'core' rights—freedom from discrimination—and to generate a consensus about the general direction of policy and regulatory reform to support it. As part of the 'soft' regulatory machinery of the Declaration, it bears a family resemblance to a range of other strategies to negotiate convergence in labour standards among states with diverse histories and institutional structures (Trubek and Mosher, 2003; Ashiagbor, chapter 4 in this volume.).

While this once lay beyond its interest and purview, the World Bank too has recently developed an interest in equality—gender equality in particular (World Bank, 2001, 2002, 2005). The World Bank now asserts that gender equality is good for growth; it simultaneously (and more controversially) claims that growth is good for gender equality, too, by advocating more and higher value labour market participation for women as the route to equality for women. For the purposes of this discussion, it is important to note the following things: in the name of protecting 'choice' for women, the World Bank explicitly endorses an 'opportunity' model over a 'substantive' model of equality; it focuses policy interventions on enhancements to women's human capital; and while it recognises that some rights are essential for gender equality, basic anti-discrimination rights aside, it categorises labour and employment regulations as matters of economic policy that are subject to a cost–benefit analysis. In short, the Bank has a vision and model of gender equality that operates quite comfortably within the general regulatory framework it promotes in the name of economic growth.

Here my aim is to identify some of the similarities and differences between *Time for Equality* and the World Bank's market-based approach to equality. While some aspects of the analysis would be weighted differently and some of the remedial strategies might be contested outright—for example, *Time for Equality* rejects equality strategies that stop with education and explicitly endorses remedies such as affirmative action (ILO, 2003c: part II), whereas the World Bank is much more cautious about such labour market regulations, fearing their efficiency-impairing properties—what is noteworthy is how much of *Time for Equality* could have been generated by the staff of the World Bank.

Like *A Fair Globalization*, *Time for Equality* is pervaded with arguments about the importance of equality for other ends. On the one hand, it endorses a 'rights-based' approach to development (ILO, 2003c: paras 44, 357). Precisely because the animating idea is to subordinate market reforms to a set of normative commitments that prevail notwithstanding their consequential effects, rights-based approaches to market design and structural reforms are something that the IFI have been clear to resist (Shihata, 1991; IMF, 1999b). However, *Time for Equality* actually advances countless instrumental arguments for attention to equality; indeed, references to the links between equality and growth, efficiency, political stability, and social inclusion arguably outstrip arguments for equality as an end in itself. The discourse of efficiency is salient throughout—for example, the merits of equality are often couched in terms of greater efficiency to society (ILO, 2003c: xi)—as is the 'business case' for equality. Whether it is for strategic reasons—for example, an effort to speak a language that policy makers and other international institutions are presumed to both hear and endorse—the burden of justification on those advocating on behalf of equality is unmistakable.

Second, the report proffers a very confined, formalistic definition of equality. Equality is defined as 'free choice in the selection of occupations, an absence of bias in the way merit is defined and valued and equal opportunities in the acquisition and maintenance of market-relevant skills' (ILO, 2003c: para 83). While the World Bank would probably be comfortable with this definition, it leaves intact a raft of equality concerns that arise from the structure and organisation of work and it fails to raise a host of questions that have been central to feminist inquiries into labour market equality, including the effects on women of otherwise neutral norms, and the market and non-market constraints on labour market choice for women.

Discrimination in the labour market is identified not as a function of the relationship of particular workers to emerging labour market or workplace norms (Brodsky and Day, 1996) or as a problem in the organisation of productive and reproductive work (Conaghan and Rittich, 2005), but as a problem of treating people differently (ILO, 2003c: paras 1, 7, 20). Framed in this way, discrimination becomes a wrong because it is an affront to the right of the individual worker to choose her destiny and pursue her options in the market, the result of perceptions, rather than objective 'facts', that are falsely ascribed to particular groups. This definition maps on to one of the enduring fantasies of those promoting market-centered approaches to equality, which is that the only thing barring workers from full participation in markets is either inadequate skill and effort or invidious discrimination on the basis of personal characteristics that can be remedied with a right to non-discrimination.

Apart from the inherent limitations of conceptualising equality in this way (Minow, 1990; Brodsky and Day, 1996) and the consequent inability to resolve the equality dilemmas, especially for women, that tend to arise at work, this analytic framework has the effect of making the report seem uncertain of its central thesis; it also introduces discontinuities between the concept of equality and the way in which it is addressed. For *Time for Equality* does in fact make references to wider conceptions of equality (ILO, 2003c: para 8) and it advocates labour market strategies, such as minimum wages and pay equity, that go well beyond the requirement that people be treated as 'the same'. At the level of institutions and implementation, if not at the level of concept, *Time for Equality* registers significant divergences with governance norms. For this reason, it raises a number of questions: is the definition of equality strategic, designed to establish common ground with other institutions, while the real battle is fought over the operational details? Or does the definition of equality do significant work in itself, shifting the terrain and the burden of justification in ways that make it harder to respond to complex problems of equality?

At the same time, *Time for Equality* differs from the labour market strategies of the IFI, and even from *A Fair Globalization*, in key ways. There is no presumption that either markets or economic growth necessarily eliminate discrimination on their own. Solutions to discrimination are not limited to the supply side; consequently, there is less stress on human capital. There is explicit acknowledgement that regulatory choices such as 'deregulation' and decreased social protection as well as the fragmentation of labour markets place constraints on the elimination of discrimination at work. This puts it at odds with the IMF, whose concerns run towards restraining public expenditures and curbing 'disincentives' to work. *Time for Equality* also gives a prominent role to unions and collective bargaining in addressing workplace discrimination (ILO, 2003c: paras 304–6). While the IMF and the World Bank remain preoccupied with the negative effects of unions and collective bargaining on labour market efficiency, *Time for Equality* stresses the benefits of centralised over decentralised bargaining (ILO, 2003c: para 330) and the positive relationship between union membership and increases in women's wages (ILO, 2003c: para 309).

The most significant difference between *Time for Equality* and *A Fair Globalization*, however, appears to lie here. While *Time for Equality* uses the discourse of the new economy and frames the task as sustainable development and poverty-reduction too, it retains a fundamentally interventionist role for the state, stressing the importance of regulation, administrative structures, and enforcement, including traditional labour market institutions, for equality objectives. *A Fair Globalization*, by contrast, simply cautions that, however desirable, liberalisation and deregulation can go too far, and offers only the most parenthetical reminder that there may still be a role for the state in limiting the impact of globalisation on inequality (ILO, 2004a: 246–51).

Perhaps for related reasons, *Time for Equality* fails seriously to engage with many of the features and characteristics of the new economy; these are central to the entire *raison d'être* of *A Fair Globalization*. For example, the whole question of the reorganisation of work receives relatively scant attention. However, work organisation is directly related to the rise of precarious work, which, in turn, is not randomly distributed among the workforce, but is disproportionately associated with women, racial and ethnic minorities, disabled workers, and other groups with marginal social power, in short the very groups that are invariably the subject of equality initiatives. Nor, despite the references to the salutary role of unions in remedying workplace discrimination and the continuing need for affirmative action, is the rise of labour market flexibility norms and the declining role and power of unions confronted directly. This risks leaving the misleading impression that flexibility norms are not relevant to the problem of discrimination; it also stops the analysis short of its target. While noting a trend towards the implementation of laws that impose a positive duty to promote equality (ILO, 2003c: xii), *Time for Equality* fails to probe the fate of other rules that may be inseparable from the practical realisation of equality such as pay and employment equity laws and affirmative action programmes; because of emerging governance norms, the regulatory picture looks much less rosy from here.

Despite its defence of traditional labour market institutions, *Time for Equality* fails to engage the relationship between equality and the drive for efficiency and competitiveness in any systematic way. This is significant, given that the relationship between equity and efficiency is one of the most deeply contested, and important, regulatory questions in the new economy. On the other hand, *A Fair Globalization* fails seriously to engage with the problem of labour market discrimination; this too is puzzling, if only because a major dimension of the social deficit of globalisation is growing labour market inequality along a variety of axes.

Finally, although *Time for Equality* might look responsive to the problem of discrimination if compared to the policy reports of the World Bank and the IMF, when juxtaposed with other research, the analysis seems thin. The matter of care does not receive much attention in *Time for Equality*. Despite the fact that the relationship between 'productive' and 'reproductive' tasks and spheres has been identified as central to the matter of gender equality in a range of analysis, scholarly and institutional, for at least a decade (Waring, 1988; UNDP, 1995, 1999; Beneria, 1999; Elson, 1999) and is now central to the transformation of work (Supiot *et al*, 2001) and the general crisis afflicting welfare state regimes as well (Esping-Andersen, 1999), the issue comes up quite late in the discussion of equality and is relatively marginal to the report as a whole (ILO, 2003c). This is highly suggestive: it indicates that the equality analysis in *Time for Equality* is still securely anchored within, rather than across, the boundaries that divide the market from other social institutions. While this comports with the approach in the current governance agenda, for the reasons discussed below it severely limits the possibilities of tackling the gendered dimensions of precarious work.

Precarious Work and Gender Equality

Although the normalisation of precarious work suggests that we may now be moving toward a state in which women's labour market position converges with men's through the perverse route of downward harmonisation (Standing, 1999b), there are reasons, some of which are intimately related to current governance norms and assumptions, that precarious work can be expected to retain some of its gendered character in the new economy.

Among the sources of enduring labour market inequality for women is the idea that only market work is 'real' work. Feminist scholars have repeatedly demonstrated that women's disproportionate representation in secondary and precarious work is a structural, rather than contingent, feature of labour markets, one that is intimately related, moreover, to the very assumption that real work is paid work. It is well documented that women perform, by a very large margin, most of the unpaid, 'reproductive' work that is crucial for both the reproduction of societies and the operation of markets (Beneria, 1999; UNDP, 1999). This unpaid work operates as a constraint upon women's labour market participation and disadvantages women relative to men in economic terms. Rather than of purely private benefit, it confers at the same time a benefit upon those who labour in markets and those who profit from that labour. The reason is that all market activity is dependent, if in often unrecognised ways, upon the on-going processes of social reproduction (Waring, 1988; Picchio, 1992; Elson, 1999).

The extensive empirical literature documenting the extent and value of unpaid work has begun to register in the literature of the World Bank (2001). However, women's non-market work still remains entirely excluded from the calculus of economic growth. This work is, not surprisingly, often still absent from the considerations that are relevant to market design and structural reforms (but see OECD, 2001). Indeed, the disadvantage to women is increased by policies that are driven by a pervasive fear of fostering 'dependency' or are designed to decrease the fiscal burden on states.

The failure to recognise the extent to which unpaid work underwrites economic activity allows those costs to be externalised; this, in effect, means that women's contribution to economic activity is destined to remain undercompensated. It is not only that anyone with non-market obligations does not, in fact, have equal 'opportunity' to participate in the market, thus undermining both emerging labour market ideals and equality norms at the most basic level. Nor is it that the market needs to 'accommodate' those with family obligations because of moral or social imperatives (ILO, 2004a: 4). It is that the assumption that the only real work is market work obscures the basic distribution of costs, risks, and benefits within the economy itself. The promise for workers within the narrative of the new economy is reward commensurate with skill, effort, and adaptability to the demands of the market. However, the presence of unacknowledged goods and services in the context of production, the costs and burdens they impose, and their association with particular groups skews the outcomes of labour market participation against those with obligations of care in predictable and well-documented ways. Analysts familiar with the gendered effects of economic restructuring and recent development policy (Rittich, 2002b), and neoliberal reforms in industrialised economies (Fudge and Cossman, 2002) could complete the story at this point. Residual support for critical but non-market 'reproductive' activities will be provided privately, much of it on an unpaid basis. Very often it will be women who do it; this in turn will impair women's labour market prospects in predictable if varied ways.

CONCLUSION

To return to the beginning, there is a close nexus between precarious work and the issue of governance. On the one hand, it seems possible to imagine many different ways of responding to the current (mal)distribution of costs and opportunities associated with precarious work, at least some of which might be justified within the larger governance objectives and the logic now informing market design. For example, they may be necessary to induce higher levels of market participation among women; in so doing, they may both generate growth and actually reduce, rather than increase, the fiscal pressure on states. On the other hand, we could also use the problem of precarious work as a way to reread, and reconstruct many of the prevailing norms about good governance themselves; it is clear that a serious investigation of the gendered nature of precarious work is a productive way to uncover, and critically interrogate, many of the assumptions organising the current approach to labour market reform.

The two ILO reports represent two modes of engagement with the debates around the new economy. *A Fair Globalization* represents the possibilities for workers of the new institutional path at their most optimistic with a few cautions at the margins; *Time for Equality* represents a less sanguine view, but locates the solutions in regulatory institutions and strategies that are under siege. Both reports arguably fail to come to grips with the extent to which governance norms might themselves function as a mechanism by which workers are legally, materially, and ideologically disempowered. More than anything, *A Fair Globalization* and *Time for Equality* document the current struggle and uncertainty, part of which is being played out within the ILO, to come to terms with the new economic and institutional terrain and its implications for workers. Whatever the outcome, the stakes for workers, particularly those in precarious work, seem high.

3

Gender, Precarious Work, and the International Labour Code: The Ghost in the ILO Closet

LEAH F VOSKO*

P RECARIOUS WORK HAS been a central object of international labour regulation since the inception of the International Labour Organization (ILO) in 1919. So, too, has the regulation of paid work performed by women. However, in its decades-long history, the ILO has scarcely recognised or addressed the relationship between gender and precarious work. Major international labour standards are only beginning to acknowledge the gendered character of precarious work. Over the last three decades, the ILO's recognition of the erosion of the standard employment relationship and the gendered character of precarious work has been sporadic, receiving focused attention only recently with the publication of reports such as *Transformation of Labour and Future of Labour Law in Europe* (European Commission, 1998), country studies commissioned by the ILO, and a growing corpus of government and independently commissioned studies.

Changes in the International Labour Code (ILC), the ILO's compendium of international labour standards, signify an effort to resuscitate the standard employment relationship by stretching several of its central elements. And they entail an implicit embrace of a dual-earner/female caregiver gender contract. Efforts to address the rise of precarious work are mounting in the ILC. Yet the ILO's capacity to advance a viable model for re-regulation

* I thank the Law Commission of Canada and the Social Sciences and Humanities Research Council of Canada (Grant No 510186) for providing the financial support necessary to conduct the research for this chapter. I am also grateful to Judy Fudge and Rosemary Owens, as well as Gerald Kernerman, for reading and commenting on earlier drafts of this chapter, and to Kim McIntyre and Sandra Ignagni for their able research assistance.

This chapter develops an argument first advanced in a report titled *Confronting the Norm: Gender and the International Regulation of Precarious Work* (Vosko, 2004a), see especially Part Two).

is limited by its orientation to an equal treatment approach, where the male norm continues to function as a benchmark for women's and men's labour force activity and the issue of caregiving remains marginal.

To make this case, this chapter examines the new constellation of international labour standards aimed at limiting precarious work. The first section sets out core concepts and describes the equal treatment approach in the ILC with reference to the central problem in this collection—the relationship between gender and precarious work. With this backdrop, the second section surveys new conventions and recommendations on part-time work (1994), home work (1996), and private employment agencies (1998), as well as discussions on the scope of the employment relationship. Using the triad of time, place, and status as a heuristic device, its objective is to reveal the stretched employment norm fostered by these instruments and the modified gender contract implied by this vision. Section three builds on this analysis by locating ILO instruments and initiatives in relation to proposals to move 'beyond employment' in the European Union (EU), attentive to the need for changes in the gender contract, and the direction of change in the United States, where there are attempts to revive an employment norm based on wage earning that is, however, silent on gender.

THE OLD MALE NORM IN THE NEW INTERNATIONAL LABOUR CODE

Several linked concepts are central to understanding the international regulation of precarious work: the normative model of employment, the gender contract, and equal treatment.

The normative model of employment is a relational concept capturing the interplay between social norms and governance mechanisms linking work organisation and the labour supply (Deakin, 2002: 179; see also Vosko, 2000; Supiot, 2002). The standard employment relationship—the normative model throughout the twentieth century—is a full-time continuous employment relationship where the worker has one employer, works on the employer's premises under his or her direct supervision, normally in a unionised sector, and has access to social benefits and entitlements that complete the social wage (Muckenberger, 1989: 267; Buechtemann and Quack, 1990: 315; Tilly, 1996: 158–59; Fudge, 1997a; Vosko, 1997: 43; 2000: 15). In the post-World War II period, most nation states, especially liberal industrial democracies, came to organise labour and social policies around this ideal type (Fudge and Vosko, 2001a).

Manifestations of the standard employment relationship vary by country, but the broad features of this employment norm are partly a product of international labour regulation. International labour regulation, broadly conceived, encompasses both the package of conventions, recommendations, and other instruments devised by international institutions and advanced through supranational agreements (Cooney, 1999)—the principal focus of this chapter—and the process of interaction between national and supranational schemes. The ILC does not represent a stand-alone system of regulation that could ever replace any individual set of national labour laws. Rather, national, supranational, and international systems of regulation are mutually constituting, and the ILC is thereby important as a transnational space.

The ILC is composed of conventions and recommendations that do not fall easily into the conventional categories of 'hard' and 'soft' law. Once ratified by a nation state, ILO conventions have the status of treaties; however, the sanctions imposed for violations of the conventions are weak. Recommendations are a pure form of 'soft' law, and increasingly guidelines, protocols, and codes of conduct are the favoured instruments for labour standards in the ILO. The ILC has influence through its construction of normative principles and frameworks that can be used by individual nations to translate principles into substantive labour standards.

At the inception of the ILC, the Hours of Work (Industry) Convention (No 1) (1919) and the Utilisation of Spare Time Recommendation (No 21) (1924) advanced the notion of regular weekly hours. Shortly thereafter, the Unemployment Provision Convention (No 44) (1934) and Minimum Wage-Fixing Machinery Convention (No 26) (1928) institutionalised the bilateral employment relationship. Two decades later, the Freedom of Association and Protection of the Right to Organise Convention (No 87) (1948) and the Right to Organise and Collective Bargaining Convention (No 98) (1949) helped to establish the right to associate freely among both self-employed workers and wage earners and normalised collective bargaining among the latter. Finally, the Convention on Social Security (Minimum Standards) (No 102) (1952) helped organise the provision of social benefits and entitlements around employee status, the presence of a bilateral employment relationship, and, to a lesser extent, continuity of service. In these ways, over its first four decades, the ILC moulded the standard employment relationship, influencing its emergence elsewhere, especially in countries such as Canada (Vosko, 2000), Australia (Owens, 2002; Paterson, 2003), and the United States (Piore, 2002). From the outset, the standard employment relationship was a male employment norm linked to a particular gender contract. The gender contract is the normative and material basis around which sex/gender divisions of paid and unpaid labour operate in a given society (Rubery, 1998: 23). As the standard employment relationship gained ascendancy, the male breadwinner/female caregiver gender contract grew up to accompany it (Fraser, 1997). The term 'gender contract' is used to capture social and legal norms surrounding the exchange between breadwinning and caregiving, protection and freedom, and public and private responsibilities. This 'contract' assumed a male breadwinner pursuing his occupation and employment freely in the public sphere, with access to a standard employment relationship and in receipt of a family wage, and a female care-giver performing unpaid work, and possibly earning a 'secondary wage', and receiving social insurance via her spouse. It fostered policies and prac-tices encouraging women to assume responsibilities attached to biological and social reproduction.

Given their mutually reinforcing relationship, it should not be surprising that many of the same international labour standards normalising the stan-dard employment relationship were also central to cementing the male breadwinner/female caregiver gender contract. The Convention on Hours of Work (1919) set maximum hours for wage earners, excluding casual labour, as well as workers in family enterprises (to preserve the sanctity of the private sphere). As Jill Murray (2001a) demonstrates, the Recom-mendation on the Utilisation of Spare Time (1924) was designed to encour-age nation states to permit men to participate in leisure and to allow them the rest and relaxation necessary to support their familial role. Around the same time, the prime objective of the early Night Work (Women) Convention (No 4) (1919) and Maternity Protection Convention (No 3) (1919) (and even the mid-century revision to the Convention on Maternity Protection in 1952) was to protect women (and their infants) through encouraging women's confinement to the private sphere. The Convention on Social Security (Minimum Standards) (No 102) (1952), in turn, cast the standard beneficiary of social insurance as a man with a wife and two children. Together, these instruments defined female caregivers as dependent. They worked in tandem with international labour standards positioning the stan-dard employment relationship as a male employment norm, each shaping women's and men's familial obligations and labour force patterns, as well as dominant household forms.

Protective measures around maternity as well as measures assuming a female caregiver norm persisted in the ILC throughout the twentieth centu-ry. Yet as early as the mid-1950s, economic pressure to increase women's labour force participation coinciding with women's collective struggle for political, economic, and social equality prompted adjustments in the male breadwinner/female caregiver contract at both the national and internation-al levels. In the ILC, the adoption of an equal treatment approach reflected and facilitated these adjustments (Hunter, 1995; Fredman, 1997a; Conaghan, 2002; Fudge, 2002). An equal-treatment approach entails 'the removal of formal legal impediments because of the effective harnessing of liberal concepts to the cause of women's emancipation' (Fredman, 1997a, 15–16). It seeks to eliminate policies and practices excluding women from the rights to full civil, social, and political citizenship (Hirshmann, 1999).

The Convention on Discrimination (Employment and Occupation) (No 111) (1958) exemplifies this approach. Its stated aim is to contribute to the elimination of discrimination in the field of employment and occupation so that 'all human beings, irrespective of race, creed or sex, have the right to pursue both their material well-being and their spiritual development in conditions of freedom and dignity, of economic security and equal opportunity' (Preamble; see also Article 2). It defines discrimination as including any distinction, exclusion, or preference made on these and other bases that 'has the effect of nullifying or impairing equal opportunity or treatment in employment or occupation' (Article 1.1). Among other measures, the Convention on Discrimination calls on nation states to promote educational programmes fostering the elimination of discrimination and to repeal legislation permitting discrimination. Its orientation towards formal equality is evident in the exceptions it allows, such as where it permits '*special measures of protection* or assistance provided for in other ILO instruments' (Article 5, emphasis added) and deems 'any distinction, exclusion or preference in respect of a particular job based on *inherent requirements*' not to be discrimination (Article 1.2, emphasis added). In this familiar way, policies promoting both equal treatment and protective measures towards women may coexist.

Understanding the dynamics of the liberal equal treatment approach operating in the ILC is central to the present analysis since it orients new and emerging instruments on precarious work. The liberal equal treatment approach was renewed under the Declaration on Fundamental Principles and Rights at Work and Its Follow-up (the Social Declaration) (ILO, 1998c), successor to the Declaration Concerning the Aims and Purposes of the International Labour Organization (the Philadelphia Declaration) (1944), which committed the ILO to expand its mandate to emphasise the 'role of economic and social policies, as opposed to only labour legislation for attaining social objectives' (p i). The Philadelphia Declaration was a key constitutional moment (Langille, 2002) in ILO history as it simultaneously renewed the organisation's founding mandate and enlarged it to include social security issues pivotal to the post-war welfare state (Vosko, 2000, 105–6). So, too, was the enactment of the Social Declaration, which was designed to break the impasse in standard setting, precipitated by unresolved debates over the appropriate relationship between international trade and labour standards, by reviving a rights-based approach to international labour regulation. The Social Declaration articulates a narrow set of fundamental international labour rights, casts the promotion of these rights as a constitutional obligation, and establishes a mechanism for monitoring adherence among member states. It aims to promote freedom of association and the effective recognition of the right to collective bargaining, the elimination of all forms of forced or compulsory labour, the effective abolition of child labour, and the elimination of discrimination in respect of employment and occupation. In its renewed emphasis on 'equality at work', the Social Declaration names the Convention on Discrimination as one of a select group of core Conventions, Conventions to which nations are bound under the ILO Constitution regardless of whether they have been ratified.

The Social Declaration, however, is only one of two recent initiatives framing the new constellation of instruments on precarious work. The other is 'Decent Work', a platform emerging from a major organisational review where the ILO examined its role and determined how it could best respond to its chief constituencies in the face of globalisation. Initiated in 1999 by ILO Director-General Juan Somovia, the first Director-General from the global south, 'Decent Work' epitomises the new strategic emphasis of the ILC in the face of the unravelling social pact around which international labour regulation operated in the latter half of the twentieth century. Through 'Decent Work', the ILO is attempting to reassert its influence by rehabilitating old standards, while also adopting new ones. The purpose of 'Decent Work' is to improve the conditions of all people, waged and unwaged, working in the formal and informal economy, through the expansion of labour and social protections (Vosko, 2002: 26). 'Decent Work' identifies people on the periphery of formal systems of labour and social protection as requiring greater attention. It also recognises that, while 'the ILO has paid most attention to the needs of waged workers—the majority of them men ... not everyone is employed' (ILO, 1999: 3–4). This assertion represents, for the ILO, an unprecedented acknowledgement of unpaid work, performed by women, and its link to precarious work, and provides a vital opening for improvements in standard setting.

The Social Declaration and 'Decent Work' are very different types of initiatives. While the Social Declaration aims to reassert age-old principles through constitutional means, 'Decent Work' seeks to rearticulate, and, in some instances, expand, and reinterpret procedural and substantive components of the ILC through other, broader means. Where gender and the international regulation of precarious work are concerned, the almost simultaneous appearance of the Social Declaration and 'Decent Work' is paradoxical. On the one hand, 'Decent Work' attempts to dislodge the standard employment relationship as the normative model of employment in the ILC, partly by acknowledging the significance of unwaged work. On the other hand, the mandate of the Social Declaration is to establish meta-rights (Sen, 2000), a move that, in its narrow rights-based focus, bows to mounting pressure to limit the creation and expansion of substantive international labour standards. Furthermore, while equality at work is cast as a fundamental right in the Social Declaration, it maintains a male norm, addressing inequalities only between individuals who are 'similarly situated' (Scott, 1988), promoting 'consistent' treatment rather than minimum standards (Fudge and Vosko, 2001b; Fredman, chapter 8 in this volume), and neglecting the question of who should bear the cost of caregiving (Fredman, 1997a; Picchio, 1998; Fudge and Vosko, 2003; Fredman, chapter 8 in this volume). In these ways, the Social Declaration fails to employ the broader conception of work embraced in 'Decent Work'. It reproduces a familiar equality/difference-type opposition, where women must either seek formal equality by conforming to a male norm or seek equality through problematic forms of difference, where 'women' are understood as a homogeneous category characterised by stereotypical biologistic and/or culturalist assumptions that reinforce women's subordination (Scott, 1988; Fraser, 1997; Fredman, 1997a).

NEW INSTRUMENTS OF THE INTERNATIONAL LABOUR CODE: REGULATING PRECARIOUS WORK

In 2000, a Committee of Experts convened by the ILO to investigate workers in situations needing protection observed that 'a tendency which appears to be a *common denominator* in recent changes in employment relationships, irrespective of the specific factors at their origin, is a general increase in the precarious nature of employment and the decline of workers' protection' (ILO, 2000a: para 104, emphasis added). This observation focused attention on disguised, ambiguous, and triangular employment relationships, bringing the growing misfit between the normative model of employment and the realities of the labour market into full view. And it accelerated efforts to regulate part-time work, home work, and private employment agencies already underway. The new constellation of international labour standards aimed at limiting precarious work thus seeks to resuscitate the standard employment relationship by addressing deviations from it based on time, place, and status.

Time

> Until a few decades ago, it used to be assumed that the vast majority, if not all workers, would automatically conform to the standard full-time working pattern, particularly in terms of their hours worked.
>
> (ILO, 1993a: 1)

> When examining the rights, protections and terms and conditions of employment of part-time workers, the yardstick generally used, in the same way as for defining part-time work, is the treatment enjoyed by comparable full-time workers. In effect, this amounts to asking whether part-time workers are discriminated against in terms of their shorter hours of work.
>
> (ILO, 1993a: 31)

The product of intense debate, the Convention on Part-Time Work (No 175) evolved over several decades. Adopted in 1994, its roots date to the

Declaration on Equality of Opportunity and Treatment of Women Workers (1975), which called for measures 'to ensure equality of treatment for workers employed regularly on a part-time basis' (Article 7.4). The Convention seeks to extend protections to two groups: those who cannot find full-time work, including the unemployed, people with disabilities, and older workers, and those who 'prefer' part-time work due to family responsibilities (Part-Time Work Convention, Article 9). According to the report that led to the Convention:

> although part-time work responds to the aspirations of many workers, there are those for whom it spells low wages, little protection and few prospects for improving their employment situation ...This is partly because labour legislation and welfare systems... were designed largely for the full-time workforce.
>
> (ILO, 1993a: 3)

The Convention on Part-Time Work is built on the acknowledgement that a growing segment of workers engage in part-time work because of a shortage of full-time work, even as it characterises specific groups, such as workers with family responsibilities, as freely choosing part-time work. Of course, as Murray has argued, 'for many workers, the fundamental issue of part-time work is not their willingness to be flexible, but the price they have to pay for flexible work' (1999b: 14). This common assumption around 'choice', advanced in the justificatory parts of the Convention (eg Article 9), is the ideological backdrop of the instrument as a whole.

The Convention on Part-Time Work includes within its purview 'employed person[s] whose normal hours of work are less than those of comparable full-time workers' (Article 1a). In its first Article, the Convention limits its coverage to those part-time workers for whom a comparable full-time worker may be found. The term 'comparable full-time worker' is then defined as a full-time worker with the same type of employment relationship who is engaged in the same or similar type of work or occupation and employed in the same establishment or, 'where there is no comparable full-time worker in that establishment, in the same enterprise' or, 'when there is no comparable full-time worker in that enterprise, in the same branch of activity' (Article 1c). These definitions circumscribe the scope of the Convention, limiting it to those part-time workers working normal hours for whom comparable full-time workers exist.

In addition to these definitional limitations, the Convention allows ratifying states to 'exclude wholly or partly from its scope particular categories of workers or of establishments' (Article 3.1). States may limit the group of workers covered to permanent part-time wage earners employed in establishments, enterprises, or branches of economic activity where permanent full-time wage earners exist. In this way, the Convention extends equal treatment to workers whose employment situation deviates only marginally from the standard employment relationship—on the basis of 'normal' hours alone—and who lack access to certain labour and social protections as a consequence. In other words, it permits the exclusion of many, if not most, part-time workers, such as those engaged on temporary, seasonal, and casual bases as well as those in certain establishments, enterprises, or branches of activity.

Before the Convention on Part-Time Work was adopted, a Resolution on Equal Opportunities for Men and Women in Employment (1985) recognised 'the need for national legislation to ensure that part-time, temporary, seasonal, and casual workers, as well as home-based workers, contractual workers and domestic workers suffer no discrimination as regards to their terms and conditions of employment' (p LXXX). This resolution characterised the growth of part-time work as part of a larger set of trends. Early in the negotiations, employers and some member states, including Australia and the United Kingdom, objected to creating a convention covering all part-time workers. Referring to part-time workers with irregular hours, the government representative from the United Kingdom stated:

> what may be considered reasonable in the case of part-time workers employed for a large number of hours in relation to normal working time, may be unnecessary in cases where hours worked are minimal.
>
> (ILO, 1993b: 24)[1]

In the end, these opponents were so successful that the written proceedings note that:

> part-time workers should not be grouped with other 'non-standard' or 'atypical' workers ... the Governing Body did not intend the conference to include, under the item on part-time work, such questions as temporary, casual, or seasonal work.
>
> (ILO, 1993a: 9)

The consequence of this limitation is that part-time workers who are also employed on casual, seasonal, and/or temporary bases may be compelled to have their rights enforced through other (largely procedural) international labour standards (eg conventions on freedom of association and discrimination) that lie outside the Convention on Part-Time Work. This result is paradoxical, given the Convention's focal emphasis on promoting part-time work, in part, through extending social and labour protections to part-time workers. The Convention on Part-Time Work asserts that its provisions do not 'affect more favourable provisions applicable to part-time workers under other international labour Conventions' (Article 2). This clause, which is known as a 'savings clause', is designed to set limits on the exclusions

---

[1] The employer representative also called for excluding the self-employed, family members, persons working a very small number of hours over a given period, and seasonal workers (ILO, 1993b: 24).

permitted under the Convention. However, in practice, the combined effect of the exclusions and the savings clause is to extend second-class rights to part-time workers who are temporary, casual, and seasonal. As Jill Murray notes, 'those who rely on the savings clause to enforce their fundamental rights are at a disadvantage compared with those granted ... positive right[s] ... in light of their part-time status' (1999b: 10).[2]

The part-time workers that the Convention on Part-Time Work *does* cover are to be treated in terms equivalent to comparable full-time workers. This means the same level of protection with respect to the right to organise, collective bargaining, basic wages,[3] occupational health and safety, and discrimination in employment and occupation (Articles 4 and 5). However, in other areas, part-time workers are to 'enjoy conditions equivalent to those of comparable full-time workers.' Equivalency, here, is defined proportionally: protections related to social security, certain types of paid leave, and maternity are determined in relation to hours of work, contributions, earnings, or by other means (Article 6). There is no provision for minimum standards. Instead, benefits are extended on an equitable basis; prorated entitlements are perceived to amount to equivalent conditions (Articles 6 and 7). Ratifying states may also disqualify part-time workers falling below a certain hours threshold from prorated social security schemes altogether; maternity and employment injury are the only exceptions to this permissible exclusion (Article 8). This approach adopts a common baseline for all categories of workers. As a consequence, only those workers in employment relationships closely resembling the standard employment relationship are assured of benefits.[4] The protections extended under the Convention on Part-Time Work are accessible only to those part-time workers capable of squeezing into a narrow norm. The Convention simply *stretches* the employment norm marginally—since the employer has a duty to redress only those inequalities for which it can be found to be directly responsible. In these ways, the Convention on Part-Time Work could contribute to improving the situation of some part-time workers while condoning the continued marginalisation of many others.

---

[2] The Recommendation on Part-Time Work (No 182) qualifies the exclusion of particular categories of workers or establishments permitted under the Convention (para 21). It aims to limit exclusions that relate to establishment size and the resort to part-time workers solely as a means of escaping employment-related obligations. However, it cannot undo the practical effects of the savings clause.

[3] Notably, the Convention on Part-Time Work sets a far lower standard in the area of wages than the Convention on Discrimination, which includes 'any additional emoluments whatsoever payable directly or indirectly whether in case or in kind' (Article 2.1). It prohibits the payment of differential wages, but it allows differential non-pecuniary benefits.

The Recommendation calls for equitable formal compensation beyond the basic wage, although, once again, it is non-binding (Recommendation on Part-Time Work, para 10).

[4] The non-binding Recommendation on Part-Time Work attempts to limit the exclusions permitted in this Article by calling for a reduction of hours thresholds generally, and especially in the areas of old age, sickness, invalidity, and maternity (paras 6 and 8).

Place

> home work implies an employment relationship between the home worker and
> the employer, subcontractor, agent or middleman . . .
>
> (ILO, 1990a: 3)

> the sometimes invisible link between employer and employee is a source of vul-
> nerability ... repugnant work conditions, low pay . . .
>
> (ILO, 1990a: 15)

The Convention Concerning Home Work (No 177) and the Recommendation Concerning Home Work (No 184) address the persistence
of work arrangements in liberal industrialised countries, and their proliferation in industrialising countries, where the worker performs a service or
produces a product outside the employer's premises.[5] These instruments
preceded the 'Decent Work' platform, although their promotion is central
to it. They are the product of the collective struggles on the part of insiders
in the ILO Division on Women (FEMME) and the ILO Programme on
Rural Women (UNIFEM), and trade unions and emerging labour organisations, to expand the ILC to cover home workers in a meaningful way
(Vosko, 2002: 33). Together, they alter what constitutes a worksite and thus
the work arrangements and places or locations of work that are subject to
international labour regulation.

The main modification to the employment norm in the Convention
Concerning Home Work is achieved by its characterisation of home workers as wage earners. This Convention casts the relationship between a home
worker and an employer and/or an intermediary as an employment relationship so long as the home worker does not have 'the degree of autonomy
and of economic independence necessary to be considered an independent
worker' (Article 1). The Convention therefore moves beyond the assumption dominant in the ILC, as elsewhere, that wage earners work on their
employers' premises, under their direct supervision. Instead, it adopts a
broader notion of the worksite that extends into the home and ascribes a

---

[5] In analysing the approach to regulating home work in the ILC, this chapter takes labour
laws, legislation, and policies on this topic (or their absence) in liberal industrialised countries
as its point of departure.

The approach to regulating home work varies dramatically between countries, especially
between industrialised and industrialising countries. Factors shaping the increase or revival of
home work are also often distinct in industrialised and industrialising countries. To this end,
in considering the persistence of home work in industrialising countries, a Meeting of Experts
on the Social Protection of Home Workers convened preceding the adoption of these standards
emphasised the 'growing pressure to maintain trade competitiveness and reduce labour costs
is prompting enterprises to make structural changes that may involve reallocating work to
regions of the world with limited social and physical infrastructure' (ILO, 1990a: 7).

These pressures clearly have implications for the reallocation of production in liberal industrialised countries but it is important to stress their global dimension.

wage relationship to what has historically been characterised as piecework. A home or other premises of the worker's own choosing is equivalent to an employer's premises and piecework is cast as 'work carried out by a person ... for remuneration ... irrespective of who provides the equipment, materials or other inputs used' (Article 1a).

These modifications have significant implications for the gender contract. By labelling the home as a potential site of work, the Convention encourages registration and labour inspection in this location of paid work. The Recommendation goes further, asserting that home workers should receive compensation for costs related to the use of 'energy and water, communications and maintenance of machinery and equipment as well as time spent maintaining equipment and packing and unpacking goods' (paras 8, 16). However, little attention is given to hours of paid work, even though overwork was noted as a common problem associated with piecework in discussions leading up to the instruments and one with gendered effects (ILO, 1990a; Recommendation Concerning Home Work, para 23). As delegates to a regional meeting in Asia concluded, the tendency towards overwork blurs

> the line between working life and family life. Because work is remunerated on a piece rate basis, the pressure to earn adequate income and the need to meet quantity and quality targets tend to require the allocation of a significant amount of time to work. Interwoven with other family tasks, the workday may therefore stretch to excessively long hours ...
>
> (ILO, 1988: 42)[6]

In an innovative move, the Convention on Home Work also characterises as an employer a person who 'either directly or through an intermediary gives out home work in pursuance of his or her business activity' (Article 1c). It encourages the allocation of employment-related responsibilities by labelling those who purchase products or services as employers and by drawing a linkage between employers and intermediaries, as well as recognising two or more employer-like entities (Article 8).[7] These interventions effectively characterise home work as 'an employment relationship between the home worker and the employer, subcontractor, agent, or middleman' based on an 'agreement that may be implicit or explicit, verbal or written' (ILO, 1990a: 3). The Convention thus retains the bilateral employment

---

[6] They went further to note that 'the intrusion of work into the domain of family life is not confined to the "plane of time", it also involves the intrusion of work-related equipment into family space, which might mean a situation where children have to play close to dangerous machinery and chemical products' (ILO, 1988: 42).

[7] The Recommendation also asserts that where an intermediary is involved, it 'should be made jointly and severally liable for payment of remuneration due to home workers' (para 18).

relationship at the core of the employment norm while promoting account-ability up the subcontracting chain.

No exclusions are permitted under the Convention Concerning Home Work (Article 2). Furthermore, the approach to equal treatment advanced in it takes 'into account the special characteristics of home work', and it does not assume a rigid comparator. It simply indicates that national poli-cies on home work promote, 'where appropriate, conditions applicable to the same or similar types of work carried out in an enterprise' (Article 4.1).[8] The absence of a comparator at the enterprise level is by design: it aims to encourage improvements for home workers' right to establish or join organisations of their own choosing,[9] protections against discrimination in employment and occupation, occupational health and safety protection, remuneration, social security protection, access to training, minimum age requirements, and maternity protection.

The Convention Concerning Home Work has considerable promise in advancing more inclusive employment norms. It achieves a delicate balance, meaningfully addressing the question posed by trade unionists at the outset of the negotiations: namely, 'what is it that can be done to preserve the social protection and gains achieved by organized labour and extend these gains and protection to home workers while at the same time providing for the economic needs of enterprises and workers that resort to home work?' (ILO, 1988: 44). However, the risk is that legitimising the home as a site of wage earning could contribute to the maintenance of a caregiving norm that encourages women's confinement to the home. Extending labour protection to home workers and moving towards legitimisation without prescribing minimum standards and without addressing unpaid caregiving could fore-stall changes fostering shared caregiving. In assessing new instruments on home work, it is important to recall that 'women are involved in home work not only because of their family responsibilities but also because of their generally weaker position in the labour market' (ILO, 1990a: 10).

Status

> The conditions governing the method, time and place of the performance of serv-ices may not bear any similarity to the elements considered by the courts of a rela-tionship of this kind [ie an employment relationship].
>
> (ILO, 2000a: para 14)

Efforts to address the vexed question of status are longstanding in the ILC, not surprisingly since questions of status rest at the foundation of the

---

[8] Prior to the adoption of the Convention, there were numerous attempts to take wording from the Convention on Part-Time Work, yet these attempts failed (ILO, 1995).

[9] The Recommendation also calls on states to encourage collective bargaining (paras 8, 16).

labour law platform itself (European Commission, 1998; Davies and Freedland, 2001; Engblom, 2001; Langille, 2002; Fudge, Tucker, and Vosko, 2002, 2003b). There is a growing movement to redraw the boundaries of the employment relationship throughout the ILC, to extend labour protections to workers 'who are in fact employees but find themselves without the protection of the employment relationship' (ILO, 2004c: para 56). This movement dates to 1990, when the promotion of self-employment was a central item of discussion at the annual international labour conference. While the emphasis of this discussion was promotion, a report prepared for the conference both recognised the diverse nature of self-employment and drew attention to the growing problem of what it labelled 'nominal self-employment', especially among OECD countries. In response, negotiations centring on the report concluded that:

> Employment relationships are complex and do not fit into neat conceptual categories. While the polar cases of pure wage and self-employment are simple to categorize, there are *hybrid and intermediate cases* which need to be recognised. Among these an important category is the *nominal self-employed—those who are sometimes classified as self-employed in national statistics and who may consider themselves to be such, but who are in reality engaged in dependent employment relationships more akin to wage employment than to genuine autonomous self-employment.*
>
> (ILO, 1990b: para 4, emphasis added)

These conclusions are highly significant. Reflecting greater concern with questions of status, they introduced notions of dependent and nominal self-employment in the ILO lexicon while simultaneously promoting independent and genuine self-employment. The result was a resolution calling for 'freely chosen and productive forms of self-employment' and, at the same time, guarding against 'the growth of precarious and dependent forms of nominal self-employment stemming from attempts to bypass protective social legislation and to erode the employment security and earnings of affected workers' (ILO, 1990b: paras 6e, 12). Importantly, the resolution noted further that the self-employed should ultimately enjoy similar social protection, including labour rights, to other protected groups. It also called on countries to institute measures to raise the levels of social protection of the self-employed to 'levels comparable to those enjoyed by wage employees' (ILO, 1990b: para 17c; see also para 6d). However, discussion on self-employment after 1990 ended with this resolution, since there was strong resistance, on the part of employers, to setting limits on commercial activities.

Although it was not focused as narrowly on employment status, the Convention Concerning Private Employment Agencies (No 181) was the next standard to touch on this issue. Adopted in 1997, it is also the weakest convention relevant to status since it legitimises triangular employment relationships without putting proper safeguards in place (Vosko, 1997). Its passage represents a defeat for workers since, unlike the Convention Concerning Home Work, it fails to address squarely the importance of regulating employment relationships where responsibility does not rest solely with one entity. It focuses too narrowly on a single labour market institution, and it mandates only 'adequate' protections to workers employed by private employment agencies. This instrument is relevant here since it defines workers in triangular employment relationships as employees of agencies whose services consist of 'employing workers with a view to making them available to a third party ... which assigns their tasks and supervises the execution of these tasks' (Article 1.1b). It constructs an employment relationship between a worker and an intermediary, a strategy with merits and shortcomings,[10] and calls on member states to allocate responsibility between the agency and the user in various areas (Article 12).

Shortly after the adoption of the Convention Concerning Private Employment Agencies, attention shifted to contract labour. The draft version of the Convention on Contract Labour, which failed in 1998, provides clues as to the direction of change. This draft Convention defined contract labour as 'all situations in which work is performed for a person who is not the worker's employer under labour law but in conditions of subordination and dependency that are close to an employment relationship under that law' (ILO, 1998a: 2). It sought to cover workers engaged directly by the user enterprise as well as workers who are employees of enterprises making them available to the user enterprise but 'whose subordination or dependency is in relation to the user enterprise', excluding workers employed by private employment agencies (ILO, 1998a: 2; see also draft Convention, Article 2). One of its main aims was to eliminate disguised employment relationships by ensuring 'that rights or obligations under labour or social security laws or regulations are not denied or avoided when contract labour is used' (draft Convention, Article 3).

This draft Convention sought to bring the protection offered by labour standards to contract labour by promoting 'adequate' protection in areas similar to those covered under the Conventions on Part-Time Work and Home Work.[11] Here, the term 'adequate' was defined as affording protection to contract workers 'to correspond to the degree of the worker's subordination to and/or dependency on the user enterprise' (ILO, 1998b: 65).

---

[10] In some instances, temporary agency workers benefit from having the agency treated as the employer, specifically, for the purpose of rights based on length of employment with a single employer. In others, these workers may have better access to rights if the user is treated as the employer; this can be the case with collective bargaining, where the ability to participate in a bargaining unit with permanent employees of the client of the agency yields important gains (Trudeau, 1998; Vosko, 2000; Commission on Labor Cooperation, 2003).

[11] Namely, the right to organise, the right to bargain collectively, freedom from discrimination, minimum age, payment of wages, occupational safety and health, compensation in case of injury or disease, and payment of social insurance contributions (draft Convention, Article 5).

The draft Convention on Contract Labour situated the standard employment relationship as a reference point in advancing a model of graduated protection (Vosko, 1997). The draft Convention also called for allocating 'the respective responsibilities of the user enterprise and the other enterprises in relation to employees' in triangular relationships (Article 9). Rather than making workers in triangular employment relationships employees of the user enterprise, it attempted to improve protections accorded to them regardless of the nature of the contract labour arrangement.[12]

In the wake of failed deliberations over contract labour, a committee of experts was mandated to inquire into and report on 'workers in situations needing protection.' Between 1998 and 2003, the committee commissioned 39 country studies focused on four types of situations: subordinate work; 'triangular employment relationships'; self-employment; and self-employment under conditions of dependence. Notably, authors were asked to pay particular attention to truck drivers in transport enterprises, construction workers and salespeople, and to explore the grey area between formal and informal sectors as well as the situation of women workers. The commission thus interpreted its mandate broadly to encompass a research agenda probing not only changing employment relationships across the labour market but looking within occupation and industry, a unique approach opening space for the renegotiation of the labour policy 'platform' (Langille, 2002) at the international level (see Fudge, chapter 9 in this volume; see also Vosko, 2004, 2005). The 2003 report growing out of its work, *The scope of the employment relationship*, focused on 'dependent workers' in disguised, ambiguous, and triangular relationships (ILO, 2003a: 37). To fill out this threefold typology of dependent work, it surveyed criteria for defining the employment relationship, explored the consequences of the absence of labour and social protections for workers in the situations concerned, and canvassed several models for re-regulation. The report maintained that the employment relationship is a universal concept and an appropriate basis for extending labour protection. However, it acknowledged the need to adapt the scope of the regulation of the employment relationship (ILO, 2003a: 53). It called for the creation and adoption of promotional conventions and recommendations 'designed to encourage the formulation and implementation of a policy to protect dependent workers, taking account of recent developments in employment relationships' (ILO, 2003a: 77). It also proposed internationally sanctioned mechanisms and procedures to determine who is an employee to serve as guidelines at the national level (ILO, 2003a: 77).

---

[12] To this end, the draft Recommendation also offered a hybrid test for establishing subordination and dependency covering the various forms of contract labour (ILO, 1998a, 1998b).

In negotiations following up on this report at the International Labour Conference in 2003,[13] workers and employers were polarised over the question of expanding the scope of the employment relationship. Nation states, too, and even communities of nation states, such as the industrialised market economies, lacked a common overarching position. Nevertheless, the various parties reached a consensus that 'the concept of the employment relationship' is 'common to all legal systems and traditions' and that 'in many countries common notions such as dependency and subordination are found' (ILO, 2003b: para 2). They also concurred on the need for clear rules in cases where laws are 'too narrow in scope', where the employment relationship is disguised or ambiguous, and 'where the worker is in fact an employee but it is not clear who the employer is' (eg triangular employment relationships). Ultimately, they called on the ILO to pursue the issue of disguised employment relationships in its standard-setting activities (ILO, 2003b: para 25) and to develop guidelines for dealing with objectively ambiguous situations, although the issue of triangular employment relationships was unresolved in the negotiations. Internationally sanctioned mechanisms and procedures to determine who is an employee to serve as guidelines at the national level, in the form of a recommendation, are the likely outcome of this call (ILO, 2003a: 77; see also ILO, 2003a: 7; 2003b: part 25; 2004c, para 5; Fudge, chapter 9 in this volume).

Discussions on the scope of the employment relationship aim to bring more workers under the umbrella of the employment relationship, although the gender dimension largely lay below the surface until the end of negotiations in 2003. Gender scarcely surfaced as an issue of concern in the 2003 talks themselves due primarily to employers' attempts to avoid the topic through repeated claims (which workers' representatives vehemently rejected) that 'the gender aspect of the issues under discussion ... was not fully understood' and that there had been 'insufficient analysis of the scope of gender issues' by the ILO (ILO, 2003c: para 53). Indeed, at the conclusion of negotiations, the employer representative went so far as to suggest that 'there was no evidence or data available demonstrating that lack of labour protection exacerbated gender inequalities' (ILO, 2003c: para 123), despite the evidence marshalled by delegates of women's high representation in various forms of dependent work. One outcome of the discussion was the affirmation that 'the lack of labour protection to dependent workers exacerbates gender inequalities in the labour market' (ILO, 2003b: para 15). Another was a directive for clearer policies on gender equality and better enforcement of relevant laws and agreements based on the notion that the

---

[13] The author was an observer in these discussions, which took place in June 2003, as well as initial discussions on the subject of contract labour in 1997, conducted follow-up field work in 1998 and 2000, and observed discussions on the related subject of the informal economy in 2002.

Convention on Discrimination applies to all workers. Still another was the assertion (which challenged the male norm and the limits of an equal-treatment analysis) that the Convention on Maternity Protection 'specifies that it "applies to all employed women, including those in atypical forms of dependent work"' (ILO, 2003b: para 16). Against the backdrop of a broad recognition that a lack of protection reinforces inequalities between the sexes, the juxtaposition of a call for adhering to the now core Convention on Discrimination and a solemn reminder that maternity protection is applicable to *all* employed women is paradoxical. Silences still remain over the female caregiving norm assumed and its links to the gender of dependent work—a profound consequence of the continuing endorsement of a narrow vision of equal treatment in the ILC.

RECONFIGURING TIME, PLACE, AND STATUS: PITFALLS OF AN EQUAL-TREATMENT APPROACH

New international labour standards aimed at curbing precarious work and discussions on the scope of the employment relationship seek to revive a standard employment relationship, albeit with important modifications. Collectively, they aim to stretch this norm to incorporate more part-time workers, home workers, and dependent workers whose employment relationships are either obscured by the presence of multiple parties, blurred by a greater margin of autonomy than that typically associated with wage earning, or wilfully disguised. Yet they espouse relatively low levels of labour protection because their approach to regulating precarious work is preoccupied with minimising deviations from the employment norm, specifically those based on time, place, and status. For part-time work, accommodation within the employment norm translates into identifying a comparable full-time worker to set a baseline for prorated social and labour protection schemes rather than the adoption of minimum standards. For home work, it entails viewing the home as a worksite subject to inspection and other forms of regulation, establishing as the employer the person that parcels out work directly or through an intermediary, and reconfiguring piecework to fit the mould of wage earning. And, for dependent work, it entails bringing a variety of workers exhibiting qualities of subordination and economic dependency under the scope of labour protection by adapting mechanisms and procedures for establishing an employment relationship where it has previously gone unrecognised.

In each instance, deviation from the norm is gendered. Women's family responsibilities are a central justification for both new conventions and recommendations on part-time work and on home work, while men's role in wage earning is tacitly affirmed. 'Reconciling work and family' also forms the rationale for promoting these types of work (ILO, 1990a; Murray,

1999b). In turn, women's predominance in certain occupations and sectors, such as domestic work, nursing and care professions, and home work, is linked to their high prevalence in ambiguous and disguised employment relationships (ILO, 2003b: para 15). Approaches to expanding the employment norm uphold male norms surrounding wage earning and they fail to advance strategies for equalising caregiving responsibilities among men and women. In this way, they follow the path of equal treatment advanced in the Social Declaration, but they also place the goals of 'Decent Work' out of reach because they fail to acknowledge how gender structures divisions of labour in *both* labour markets and households.

Gender, Precarious Work, and the International Labour Code in Context

> Today there is less justification than ever before for differences in protection between stable workers and those who are employed in precarious conditions, when there are so many forms of instability in contracts of employment. The same may be said of men and women ... the very marked difference separating protected workers and those who lack protection in the end only helps swell the ranks of the latter, entering into competition with the former.
>
> (ILO, 2000a, para 125)

The approach to gender and precarious work in the ILC is by no means fixed. Nor is the ILC alone in its attempts to re-regulate the employment relationship. Rather, a range of approaches is surfacing. Some use a historical lens to tackle the question of the 'many futures of the employment contract' (Deakin, 2002). Others focus on a single aspect of regulation, corresponding to time (Bosch, 2000; Golden, 2000; Mutari and Figart, 2000), place (Boris and Prügl, 1996), or status (Deakin, 1998; Freedland, 1999; Fudge, Tucker and Vosko, 2002). Few approaches consider these elements together, although two prototypes may be seen as marking the terrain of constructing new employment norms, each offering different responses to the challenge of limiting precarious work and each with distinct implications for the gender contract.

One prototype, exemplified by developments and proposals in the United States (Dunlop *et al*, 1994; Hyde, 2000), focuses on reviving an employment norm based on wage earning and characterised by an inferior set of labour and social protections than that associated with the standard employment relationship. This prototype is largely silent on gender issues. The other prototype arises from proposals to move 'beyond employment' in the EU, and it is acutely sensitive to the need for fundamental changes in the gender contract.

The first prototype embraces the idea that all adults should be engaged in paid employment, preferably full-time, and supports maintaining a system of delivering labour and social protections by tying eligibility to a single job,

such as with continuous service requirements. It entails a continuing emphasis on private decision making in the workplace as a means to furnish benefits ranging from health insurance to vacation pay (Dunlop *et al*, 1994: 16;
see also Hyde, 2000; Applebaum, 2001; Piore, 2002). While recognising the
growth of time-based deviations from the standard employment relationship, not only does it fail to prorate social wage benefits for part-time workers, it permits employers to treat 'part-time employees/workers differently
from those with permanent or indefinite relationships with the employer'
(Commission on Labor Cooperation, 2003: 5). Place-based exclusions are
also permissible under this model.[14] Where establishing employee status is
concerned, the only area where subtle changes are evident relates to the
tests used to determine the scope of coverage. The United States is an exem-
plar here, once again, as most US laws still use a 'common law agency test',
which places greatest emphasis on the right of control. Yet some laws
employ an economic realities test (eg the federal Fair Labor Standards Act
of 1938 and the Occupational Health and Safety Act of 1970), which
allows for fuller examination of other factors suggestive of what is often
labelled 'economic dependence', an approach growing in popularity in
international discussions concerned with disguised employment.[15]

Furthermore, even the Dunlop Commission on the Future of Worker-
Management Relations (Dunlop *et al*, 1994), a major Commission exploring goals for the twenty-first century US workplace, took an ambivalent

[14] For example, in the US, domestic workers are generally excluded from collective bargaining rights and many minimum standards as well as access to workers' compensation and
unemployment insurance benefits (for extensive discussions of these exclusions, see Fudge,
1997b; Commission on Labor Cooperation, 2003).

[15] Historically, US courts have used three tests in distinguishing between employees and independent contractors: the common law agency test and the economic realities test—both noted
here—and the hybrid test. However, the common law agency test operates as the default position. Unless a statute specifies otherwise, this is the test to be used. The Commission on Labor
Cooperation (2003: 31) offers a concise summary of the list of factors normally, although not
exclusively, considered under this test (also called 'the thirteen factor test') which include: (1)
the hiring party's right to control the manner and means by which the work is accomplished;
(2) the skill required; (3) the source of the instrumentalities or tools; (4) the location of work;
(5) the duration of the relationship between the parties; (6) whether the hiring party has the
right to assign additional projects to the hired party; (7) the extent of the hired party's discretion over when and how long to work; (8) the method of payment; (9) the hired party's role
in hiring and paying assistants; (10) whether the work is part of the regular business of the hiring party; (11) whether the hiring party is in business; (12) the provision of employee benefits;
and (13) the tax treatment of the hired party (as an employee or a self-employed worker).
One of the foremost recommendations of the Dunlop Commission on the Future of Worker-
Management Relations, an important Commission whose mandate is discussed briefly below,
was to adopt a single definition of employer and a single definition of employee 'for *all* workplace laws based on the *economic realities* of the employment relationship' (Dunlop *et al*,
1994: 12, emphasis added). Quite controversially, it endorsed shifting away from the common
law agency test towards an economic reality test where chances for profit and risks of loss and
capital investment have greater weight. However, this recommendation has not been taken up
in the United States. See also Fredman and Fudge, who discuss the history and evolution of
parallel tests with particular attention to the British and Canadian cases, in chapters 8 and 9
of this volume, respectively.

approach to the growth of 'contingent work': on the one hand, it opposed the introduction of 'contingent arrangements ... simply to reduce the amount of compensation paid by the firm for the same amount and value of work' (Dunlop *et al*, 1994: 61). Yet, on the other hand, it 'affirmed the valuable role contingent work arrangements can play in diversifying the forms of employment relationship available to meet the needs of American workers and companies' (Dunlop *et al*, 1994: 62). Attesting to the gender contract implied by this conception of new employment norms, it claimed further that the 'flexibility' that 'contingent arrangements' provide 'helps some workers, more of whom must balance the demands of family and work as the number of dual-earner and single parent households rise' (Dunlop *et al*, 1994: 61). There is growing acknowledgement in the United States that most women are wage earners, 'who do not receive pay and benefits commensurate with the work they do' (Dunlop *et al*, 1994: 37). Still, under this prototype, the worker whose situation approximates most closely to the norm is still assumed to be male:

> Anyone—male or female–can work. The only requirement is that, as employees, they should conform to the norm of the ideal worker. An ideal worker is a worker who behaves in the workplace as if he or she has a wife at home full-time, performing all of the unpaid care work that families require. Personal problems do not belong in the workplace. Conflicting demands are expected to be resolved in favour of requirements of the job.
>
> (Applebaum, 2001: 29)

The 'personal' problems to which Applebaum refers include care for children and other dependants as well as training work, voluntary work, and work in the public interest. In practice, this philosophy encourages women to be 'flexible', to bear the costs associated with accepting part-time work to accommodate caregiving. However, leave entitlements in the United States, while they rest on a version of equal treatment, are meagre. The outcome is a gender contract that embraces wage earning to the exclusion of caregiving.

Efforts to move 'beyond employment' differ sharply from the first prototype and its associated gender contract. Originating from *Transformation of labour and future of labour law in Europe* (European Commission, 1998), this prototype embraces a broad concept of work that covers 'people from the cradle to grave ... in both periods of inactivity proper and periods of training, employment, self-employment and work outside the labour market,' where 'work outside the labour market' includes training at one's own initiative, voluntary work, and care for other people (Supiot *et al*, 2001: 55). It calls for replacing the paradigm of employment with a paradigm of labour market membership based on the notion of '*statut professional*' or the notion that 'an individual is a member of the labour force even if her or she does not currently have a job' (Supiot *et al*, 2001: x). The idea is to allow for breaks between jobs as well as lifecycle changes, to reject a linear and homogeneous conception of working life tied to the employment contract and, specifically, the relationship of subordination it establishes between the worker and the party to whom services are rendered (Supiot *et al*, 2001, chapter 1). Rather than treating 'regular' part-time work as a valid variation on the norm and calling for an extension of benefits, the 'beyond employment' prototype calls for reducing working time for all and for developing models of production oriented to the entire lifecycle, a suggestion posed at the outset of ILO discussions on part-time work but rejected quickly (ILO, 1993a). It embraces 'worker-time' to reconcile occupational and personal life, to encourage genuinely work-centered flexibility, and to share employment (Supiot *et al*, 2001: 84; see also Fudge and Vosko, 2001b). The Working Time Adjustment Act[16] adopted in the Netherlands, and discussed by Suzanne Burri in chapter 14 in this book, uses this type of life-course approach. It grants employees a statutory right not only to reduce but to extend working time unless an employer can demonstrate that serious business reasons preclude the granting of such a request.

Social drawing rights are this prototype's response to the problem of minimum standards that the equal treatment model is ill equipped to address. These rights are essentially a new type of social right related to work in general (work in the family sphere, training work, voluntary work, self-employment, working the public interest, etc) based on a prior contribution to work, but 'brought into effect by the free decision of the individual and *not as a result of risk*' (Supiot *et al*, 2001: 56, emphasis added). On the question of status, the 'beyond employment' prototype also casts as central the need for freedom to work under different statuses, without forfeiting social rights and entitlements (Supiot *et al*, 2001: 10). It is concerned less with quantitative changes, such as those documented in discussions on the scope of the employment relationship, than with qualitative changes across the employment relationship.

The vision for the gender contract is underdeveloped in 'beyond employment'. Still, this prototype is attentive to the danger that the emerging social and legal system of production 'will be built along strongly biased gender lines, discriminating against women from the standpoint of economic independence and professional careers; and against men with respect to the developments of bonds of affection and family relations' (Supiot *et al*, 2001: 180).

It rejects a policy direction compelling workers to trade off precarious conditions for the flexibility necessary to engage in unpaid caregiving, volunteer work, training, or working in the public interest. Its explicit call for

---

[16] The Dutch Act on Working Time Adjustment (*Wet aanpassing arbeidsduur*, Stb 2000, 114 en 115).

high-quality opportunities for training and paid work for both men and women, and its implied support for universal caregiving, suggest an endorsement of a gender contract characterised by universal and integrated earning, learning, and caregiving.

CONCLUSION

The ILO approach to new employment norms lies at a midpoint between proposals to move 'beyond employment' and efforts to revive an employment norm based on wage earning, characterised by an inferior level of labour and social protection. Its approach to the gender contract, in turn, may be placed along a continuum defined by a male breadwinner/female caregiver model at one end and a universal learner, earner, and caregiver model at the other end. On this axis, the ILO approach more closely approximates to the latter model. However, its orientation towards equal treatment limits the ILO's capacity to address the rise of precarious work.

The equal treatment model is forcing the stretching of the standard employment relationship in the ILC to cover more employment situations, but without altering fundamentally the male norm itself. In doing so, it is fostering a shift to a 'new' *dual*-earner/female caregiver contract, where there is greater equality between men and women in terms of occupational choice as well as terms and conditions of work, at least among those who are similarly situated. But, because this contract neglects fundamental 'social structures of power' (Fredman, 1997a: 15), it is unconcerned with minimum standards and it leaves women the responsibility of caregiving. The neglect of caregiving extends far beyond these instruments to international labour regulation writ large, both in its organisation and its substance. In the ILC, as elsewhere, caregiving remains marginalised—a factor decisive in shaping the gender of precarious work.

4

Promoting Precariousness? The Response of EU Employment Policies to Precarious Work

DIAMOND ASHIAGBOR

INTRODUCTION

THIS CHAPTER CONSIDERS the response of the European Union (EU) to the phenomenon of precarious work against the backdrop of, first, the various attempts to regulate or regularise *atypical* work in its various forms; and second, the European Employment Strategy, which promotes the use of *non-standard* forms of work as a means of boosting labour supply.

There appear to be a number of differing, possibly conflicting, objectives underlying the regulation in the EU of those forms of work that diverge from the standard employment relationship. First, there is the desire to increase the employment rate in the economy: the use of non-standard work is promoted as a means of improving the human capital of those formerly excluded from the labour market—in particular women—and encouraging entry to the paid labour force. A second, related, objective is to enhance the competitive efficiency of enterprises: the use of flexible work patterns and flexible work organisation will, it is hoped, help to match the supply of labour to the demands of employers for workers. A third objective has been to improve or protect workers' quality of working life, or their 'work–life balance'. Such regulatory objectives are being pursued within the overarching framework of the European Employment Strategy, through which the EU is seeking to promote a 'skilled, trained and adaptable workforce and labour markets responsive to economic change'. Much of the employment policy emerging from this strategy is dominated by a supply-side rhetoric, and indeed a great deal of the policy discourse at EU level sees the spread of what might be seen as precarious work (certainly, forms of employment previously considered atypical or peripheral to mainstream patterns of employment) as instrumental to the modernisation of European labour markets so that they can better match the changing demands of goods and services markets. Although the European Employment Strategy calls on member states to create not just 'more' but also 'better' jobs, it remains to be seen whether the EU's discourse on full employment can avoid the pursuit of higher labour market participation rates leading to low quality jobs, and the encouragement of precarious jobs as a route to job creation. Such promotion of non-standard forms of employment is of particular concern in light of the 'disincentive discourse' prevalent within European economic policy, which presents extensive work protection and social benefits as disincentives to taking up work and thus as obstacles to job creation.

The original attempts, dating back to the 1980s, to regulate the whole range of atypical work patterns foundered due to lack of political consensus, and gave way to the disaggregation of forms of atypical/precarious work and to discrete measures to regulate them, such as the directives on part-time work, fixed-term work, and the proposed directive on temporary agency work. These 'framework' directives do not aim at harmonisation, but set out some of the goals of European social policy, leaving a space for diversity and national self-regulation. However, by eschewing binding norms and decentralising decision making, such regulatory techniques risk privileging economic policy imperatives and job creation over social protection. In the absence of a sufficiently strong normative framework at EU level to balance the 'hard coordination' mechanisms of economic policy (for example, the Economic and Monetary Union (EMU)[1] and the Stability and Growth Pact[2]), there is the danger that the requirements of competitiveness and labour market flexibility will hamper efforts to incorporate a discourse on 'quality' into the discourse on 'quantity', and impede the development of worker-friendly responses to precarious work and the regulation of precarious work in ways which could sustain that other key EU goal of 'mainstreaming' respect for equal opportunities.

---

[1] The EMU has been a (contested) goal of European integration since the early 1970s, taking the European Community (EC) or EU from a mere common market to an economic union, in the complete unification of monetary and fiscal policies. EMU involves: (a) closer coordination of member states' economic and monetary policies; (b) the establishment of a European Central Bank; and (c) the replacement of national currencies by a single European currency— the 'Euro'. To date, all but three of the old member states have joined the Euro; the 10 new member states that joined the EU on 1 May 2004 do not have a fixed timetable to join. Fiscal restraint, stability-oriented macroeconomic policy, and structural reforms are Treaty obligations imposed on *all* member states.

[2] The Stability and Growth Pact refers to a cluster of policies designed to ensure budgetary discipline within EMU, by setting targets in order to constrain excessive levels of national debt and excessive budget deficits, and imposing sanctions if a member state runs a budget deficit of more than 3% of gross domestic product (GDP): see Resolution of the European Council on the Stability and Growth Pact [1997] OJ C 236/1.

DEFINING AND MEASURING PRECARIOUS EMPLOYMENT IN THE EU

The absence of adequate international indicators of precariousness and the prevalence of subjective *social* representations of employment precariousness have led some scholars to spurn the search for 'objective' statistical measures of precarious employment. Examples of the divergent social understandings of precariousness are provided by a recent comparative study of precarious work across five EU member states, the European Study of Precarious Employment (ESOPE).[3] ESOPE researchers identified heterogeneous definitions and understandings of employment precariousness, with differences between countries premised on different understandings of what constitutes a 'normal' job. Public discourse in France, Spain, and Italy, for example, can be seen to share a similar conception of the standard employment relationship, at the core of which is a stable, open-ended contract, with protection from unfair dismissal. This much is made explicit through legislation, which regularises and entrenches such public understandings; for example, the Spanish *Estatuto de los Trabajadores*,[4] the French *Code du travail*,[5] and the Italian *Statuto dei lavoratori*.[6] Moreover, social protests, such as the general strike in Italy in May 2002 over the proposed labour market reforms of the Berlusconi government,[7] further illustrate the strong consensus *within* certain European countries over the content of a 'normal' job, with all other types of employment being seen as 'more or less exposed to "employment precariousness" of some sort' (ESOPE, 2003: 13).

The lack of consensus *between* European countries is highlighted by the case of the United Kingdom. Within the United Kingdom, in contrast to the above-mentioned Latin European countries, there exists little public discourse around the notion of precariousness; the closest alternative is the reference in public discourse to 'low-quality' or 'dead-end' jobs. This contrast with other European countries is partly explained by the fact that there has

---

[3] ESOPE is a research project conducted by academics based in the five most populous EU countries: France, Germany, Spain, Italy, and the UK. It is funded by the European Commission.

[4] *Estatuto de los Trabajadores, Ley 8/1980, Boletín Official del Estado* (Spanish Workers' Statute, Law 8/1980 of 10 March 1980, Official Bulletin of the Spanish State).

[5] *Code du travail* (French Labour Code), *Journal Officiel*, 1989. The first Labour Code was promulgated between 1920 and 1927; the current one dates from 1973 but is continuously updated by decree.

[6] *Statuto dei lavoratori, Legge 300/1970, 20 maggio 1970, Gazzetta Ufficiale della Repubblica Italiana, n 131 del 27 maggio 1970;* (Italian Workers' Statute, Law 300/1970 of 20 May 1970, published in the Official Journal of the Italian Republic on 27 May 1970).

[7] The most heavily contested part of the reforms was the proposed amendment to Article 18 of Law 300/1970 (the *Statuto dei lavoratori* or Workers' Statute), which provides for reinstatement of workers dismissed without 'just cause' or 'justifiable reason' to replace reinstatement with financial compensation for certain groups of workers.

been such a dominant discourse of labour market flexibility within the United Kingdom, a vision of labour market regulation that privileged the employer's freedom of contract over the terms on which labour was engaged, as well as by the operation of the background rules of the common law framework (see Fredman, chapter 8 in this volume). With the regulation of the employment relationship rooted in the common law contract of employment, wherein almost all types of employment contract are lawful, 'atypical' contracts have thus not required any particular permissive legislation, resulting in a very broad public perception of 'regular' or 'normal' employment, which excludes only those 'dead-end jobs' of the lowest quality.

Further, to date, there has been little explicit mention of 'precariousness of employment' at EU level, in spite of the fact that EU social, employment, and economic policy has been for some years concerned with precisely the phenomenon of the social exclusion of unemployed, under-employed, and marginalised workers, a social exclusion which is at the heart of the debate on precarious work. Within the policy documentation of the European Employment Strategy, a strategy which is intended to coordinate the national employment policies of the individual member states, one is hard-pressed to find reference to 'precarious' work or employment, and, arguably, it is very unlikely that this term could feature in the European Employment Strategy in the near future (ESOPE, 2003: 18). However, this does not mean that debates on precarious work and the gendered nature of such work have no resonance within EU employment law and employment policy. Rather, this concern is expressed as a desire to promote 'high value' jobs based on 'high skill, high trust and high quality' (Commission of the European Communities (CEC), 1997a).

As an alternative to the search for 'objective' statistical measures of employment precariousness, which could have meaningful resonance across all EU countries, as well as within EU policy making, the ESOPE research project suggests replacing the notion of employment precariousness with more precise features or characteristics of employment relationships, such as instability, insecurity, risk of unemployment, risk of working poverty, low pay, bad health risks, and working conditions (ESOPE, 2002: 36). This classification is similar to that other useful starting point for measurement and comparison of precariousness across EU member states, the set of guidelines provided by the International Labour Organization (ILO) study in 1989, which suggested four dimensions along which to evaluate precarious employment: job stability and security; working conditions; nature and stability of income; and access to social protection (Rodgers and Rodgers, 1989; ESOPE, 2003).

This more functional approach to the understanding of precariousness has gained ground within the European Commission, in particular (see ESOPE, 2003: 18). Certainly, what one notices in policy discussions within the EU institutions and with the member states is the use of terms such as 'low quality', in a broad sense, or 'social exclusion' as *proxies* for precariousness, partly because there is so much diversity in social conceptions of precarious employment across EU countries (ESOPE, 2002).

However, in light of the broad employment objectives of the EU (see below), there is a need for some consensus about how to categorise the phenomenon of precarious employment, in order to develop policies to combat it in the course of job creation. In the absence of a uniform definition of precarious employment, studies of the European labour market by employment type have adopted various methodologies, including cluster analysis, to measure the prevalence of low-skilled, low-quality, unstable employment (CEC, 2003a: 138–42). What such analyses reveal is that women are typically clustered in jobs of poorer quality than those of men. In their report for the European Commission on social precariousness and social integration, Duncan Gallie and Serge Paugam (2003: 65) found that this gender difference remained constant between 1996 and 2001. A further finding was that '[l]ow task quality, higher levels of work pressure and job insecurity undermined commitment to employment, reduced job satisfaction and increased work-related stress' (Gallie and Paugam, 2003: 110).

The Commission's own research has identified three broad clusters into which women's employment falls: first, a cluster of highly skilled women in supervisory or intermediate positions and high-paid permanent employment with access to training, working in non-manual, skilled occupations in the private sector; second, a cluster of relatively younger, highly skilled, highly paid women in non-manual, skilled occupations in the public sector with relatively high access to training—the common feature of this cluster across all member states is work in the public sector, with women somewhat more often in part-time employment, in temporary employment, and in non-supervisory positions; third, a large cluster of low-skilled women in low-paid, short-term or casual employment without access to training, in manual, low-skilled or unskilled occupations, mainly in small private sector firms in industry (CEC, 2003a: 140).

Adopting the more functional approach to the definition and measurement of precariousness highlights the strongly gendered aspect of precarious work within the EU. Viewed along the dimensions of job stability and security, risk of unemployment, working conditions, stability of income and the risk of working poverty, and access to social protection, it is worth noting that whilst differences in employment and unemployment rates between men and women across the EU have decreased in recent years, important gaps remain (CEC, 2003b: 11). With the exception of Finland, Germany, Ireland, Sweden, and the United Kingdom, women have higher rates of unemployment in all member states, and higher rates of long-term unemployment (CEC, 2003a: 24–25). In all member states of the EU prior to enlargement, the proportion of employees on temporary contracts was higher for women than for men (Eurostat, 2002b; Franco and Winquist, 2002). Employees on temporary contracts are not only at considerably higher risk of job loss and labour market exclusion, they also receive lower wages than permanent employees with the same qualifications engaged in the same work (CEC, 2003a: 129). Women are also over-represented in low-income groups, accounting for almost 60 per cent of all those employed in the lowest quintile (CEC, 2003b: 11).

In general, women are more likely than men to be engaged in non-standard employment, such as fixed-term and part-time work. Women predominate in the numbers of those engaged in part-time work within the EU, accounting for about 83 per cent of all part-time workers. Compared to 6.2 per cent of all employed men, for instance, 33.4 per cent of all employed women work part time. Women's employment shares in fixed-term employment also exceed female employment shares in total employment in all member states except Germany (CEC, 2002b: 36). Although it is true that part-time and fixed-term work *can* operate as bridges into the labour market and facilitate labour market participation, the evidence is that employees under these forms of contracts 'risk discrimination in pay and pensions and have less [sic] opportunities to participate in continuous training and to improve their career prospects' (CEC, 2003b: 14).

However, to adopt the terminology used in British public policy-making, there is a lack of 'joined-up government' within the EU. Whilst there is awareness within the European institutions of the feminisation of poverty—arising in part from the gendered nature of precarious work, or work without the protective embrace of employment protection legislation or social protection systems—nevertheless, such awareness does not always filter through to influence policy- and law-making in the area of employment and labour market policy. The Commission proposal for a framework strategy on gender equality, for example, recognised that many women do not have equal access to social rights either because some of these rights are based on 'an outdated male breadwinner model' or because they do not take into account that women predominantly carry the burden of having to reconcile family and professional life (CEC, 2000: 9). This recognition is not, however, apparent in the policy recommendations emanating from those different sections of, or constituencies within, the Commission whose responsibilities include initiating and coordinating policy on active labour market policies and employment creation.[8]

---

[8] It is worth remembering, however, that the European Commission is not a straightforwardly monolithic organisation which can speak with a single voice on any one policy issue. It is an internally complex institution, comprised of a college (the Commissioners) and administrative units (the Directorates-General), which have considerable internal autonomy.

THE EUROPEAN EMPLOYMENT STRATEGY AND WOMEN'S PRECARIOUS WORK

From the perspective of an EU committed not only to reducing unemployment, but also to increasing employment, especially the labour market participation of previously under-represented groups such as women, the gendered nature of precarious employment represents a challenge. The difficulty lies in increasing women's labour market participation whilst remaining true to the goal of 'high skill, high trust and high quality' employment in light of the evidence that much of women's employment has been clustered into precarious jobs—those forms of non-standard or atypical work which have historically been outside the scope of employment protection legislation and outside most (national) schemes of social protection.

The guiding principles of EU employment policy, to promote a 'skilled, trained and adaptable workforce and labour markets responsive to economic change', contained in Article 125 of the European Community Treaty, were forged in response to the economic and employment context in the 1990s, in particular the sense of crisis pervading the Union. At the time of the introduction of the Employment Title into the European Community Treaty in 1997, unemployment remained 'stubbornly high', at a rate of 10.8 per cent (CEC, 1997a: 1), more than double the US rate of 5.0 per cent.[9]

In response, the coordinated strategy for employment launched at the Luxembourg European Council was structured around four main strategic priorities, or 'pillars': improving employability; developing entrepreneurship; encouraging adaptability in businesses and their employees; and strengthening the policies for equal opportunities. Since the aim is to achieve a 'coordinated strategy' for employment, rather than to impose a common EU policy on the member states, what policy instruments were adopted to achieve such goals? The core of the Employment Strategy, set out in Articles 125 to 130 EC, is a power vested in the Union, supplementary to that of the member states, to promulgate common guidelines. The elaboration and implementation of employment policy revolves around the setting of guidelines, benchmarks, and indicators at European level, their translation into national policies, and the periodic monitoring of such implementation, mostly by means of peer review. The second strand of the Employment Strategy (translation into national policies) involves action by member states, which are obliged to report annually, in National Action Plans for Employment (NAPs), on the principal measures taken to implement employment policy in light of the Union's broad economic policy guidelines (BEPG) and the Employment Guidelines.

---

[9] Eurostat, 1999. However, by June 2004, the EU unemployment rate had fallen to 8.1% for the EU15 (but 9.1% for the EU25), compared with 5.6% for the United States (Eurostat, 2004b).

Flexibility or adaptability of labour markets is central to this project, but at least two notions of flexibility often exist in parallel. The Commission describes the equal opportunities pillar as recognising 'both the social need to counter discrimination and inequalities between women and men, and the economic loss resulting from not making full and effective use of the productive capacities of all sections of the population',[10] suggesting the use of non-standard work as a means of encouraging those formerly excluded or discouraged from the labour market to (re)enter paid employment. This was seen as particularly important in view of women's low participation rates historically: in 1997, the proportion of women employed in the EU was around 51 per cent of women of working age, some 20 percentage points below the rate for men (CEC, 1997b: 74), a gap which narrowed to only 17.2 percentage points by 2003.[11] However, the Commission also advocated the use of non-standard patterns of work and employment contracts primarily because such flexibility of labour is seen as a logical response to flexibility in goods and services markets.[12]

Two examples should suffice to illustrate the centrality of 'flexible' or 'atypical' work to the European Employment Strategy. First, the Employment Guidelines for 2002, which make reference to part-time work as one of several types of flexible working arrangement that are essential to encourage 'active aging' (Guideline 3), to help reconcile work and family life (Guideline 17), and to promote modernisation of work organisation more generally (Guideline 13). Further, the 2002 BEPG, with which the Employment Guidelines must comply (Article 128(2) EC), stress the role of part-time work in enhancing labour market efficiency and promoting employment: '[l]abour markets have also tended to become more flexible, as indicated by the large contribution of the development of part-time and temporary employment to overall job creation.'[13]

The Lisbon European Council in 2000 further sharpened the Employment Strategy by setting the Union a new strategic goal for the next decade: 'to become the most competitive and dynamic knowledge-based

---

[10] The Commission's summaries of the four pillars are taken from DG-V on the European Employment Strategy, online: http://europa.eu.int/comm/employment_social/empl&esf/pilar_en.htm (date accessed: 19 September 2004).

[11] CEC, 2004: 31. As the Joint Employment Report for 2001 argues, 'A re-balancing of policies is essential to actively encourage women's participation in the labour market, not only at the point of entry, also especially at mid-career, to help women stay in the labour market longer. Fundamental in this respect are the issues of equal pay, adequate care facilities combined with reconciliation of work and family life, and lifelong learning' (CEC, 2002a: 36).

[12] CEC, 1997b. See also CEC, 1997a: 17: 'Flexibility in product markets means flexibility at the level of the firm. Such flexibility will require an increasing focus on new types of work organisation, which may lead to more flexible patterns of working time. The "flexible firm" should become the norm, not the exception.'

[13] EC Council Recommendation 2002/549 of 21 June 2002 on the broad guidelines of the economic policies of the Member States and the Community [2002] OJ L 182/1, at 6.

economy in the world capable of sustainable economic growth with more and better jobs and greater social cohesion.'[14] Over time, this goal has been distilled into the three objectives of full employment, quality and productivity at work, and social cohesion and inclusion (CEC, 2003c: 9–10). Whilst there is no explicit definition of full employment, an indication is given in the targets set for member states: raising the overall employment rate to as close as possible to 70 per cent by 2010, and the female employment rate to more than 60 per cent.[15] Lisbon is important in marking a shift in thinking, with the EU institutions drawing a clear link between economic, employment, and social policy, indicating a political willingness to prioritise the 'European social model', by means of 'activating' the welfare state and modernising social protection.[16]

The modernisation of social protection envisaged by Lisbon and the version of full employment here being promoted essentially mean a shift from comprehensive employment protection and social benefits, towards an emphasis on investment in human capital, thus improving 'employability' and equipping individuals to be self-sufficient. The conclusions of subsequent European summits devoted to employment issues serve to reinforce this assessment of the Employment Strategy as a heavily supply-side oriented policy that strongly echoes a workfare-inspired 'Third Way' approach. For example, in order to 'make work pay' and encourage the search for jobs, member states are urged to review aspects of tax and benefit systems such as the conditionality of benefits, eligibility, duration, the replacement rate, the availability of in-work benefits, the use of tax credits, administrative systems, and management rigour.[17] The work ethic—the obligation, even, to accept work—is accordingly to be fortified by making prolonged reliance on benefits either impossible or less desirable.

---

[14] Presidency Conclusions, Lisbon European Council, 23 and 24 March 2000, Bull EU-3/2000, 7–17, at para 5 (Lisbon European Council).

[15] Lisbon European Council, above n 14, at para 30. The Stockholm European Council set intermediate targets, aiming for employment rates of 67% overall and 57% for women, by January 2005, as well as a new target of 50% employment for older workers (aged 55 to 64) by 2010: Presidency Conclusions, Stockholm European Council, 23 and 24 March 2001, Bull EU-3/2001, 1–40, at para 9.

[16] The phrase 'European Social Model' is used so often in discussions of European social/ employment policy as if it does not require definition. However, the Commission's Communication on 'quality' in employment and social protection does state that '[q]uality is at the heart of the European social model', a model linked with continually rising productivity and living standards, and benefits that are widely shared. The model is 'distinguished from others by its framework and design, and by the nature, focus and distribution of the policies. ... funding is mainly public in Europe, and much more private in the US' (CEC, 2001a: 3 and 5).

[17] Presidency Conclusions, Barcelona European Council, 15 and 16 March 2002, Bull EU 3/2002, 1–56, at para 32. The employability discourse within EU employment policy bears an uncanny resemblance to the policy prescriptions urged on the EU by the international financial institutions (IFI), most strongly advocated by the OECD (1994b), but also by the IMF (1999a). For an analysis of the IFI's labour market flexibility discourse, see Rittich, in chapter 2 of this volume.

WHAT DOES THE EUROPEAN UNION'S EMPLOYMENT POLICY AGENDA MEAN FOR POLICIES ON PRECARIOUS WORK?

Precarious Work and 'Quality' in Employment

As mentioned above, the EU employment and social policy discourse does not make explicit use of the language of 'precariousness' in order to address the social phenomenon of marginal employment; the main proxies for precarious employment and its social consequences are 'quality' in employment and 'social inclusion'. Adopting terminology that resonates with the ILO's call for 'decent work' (ILO, 1999), the Presidency Conclusions of the Lisbon European Council prioritised not just 'more' but 'better' jobs and 'greater social cohesion'.

The Lisbon, Stockholm, and Nice European Councils all affirmed the importance of 'better' jobs or 'quality' in employment. With regard to 'quality', the Commission views this as a 'relative and a multi-dimensional concept', which involves taking into account factors such as the wider work environment and the specific characteristics of the job; the characteristics the employee brings to the job; and the subjective evaluation (job satisfaction) of these characteristics by the individual worker. Accordingly, a broad approach to quality in work implies not only pay and minimum standards but attention to the character of individual jobs and the character of the wider work environment including how the labour market works as a whole, particularly with respect to movement between jobs, and in and out of the labour market (CEC, 2001a: 7).

Whilst generally dismissing fears that increasing employment in the service sector would lead to a proliferation of dead-end jobs of low quality (CEC, 2001a: 9), the Commission's upbeat assessment of the harmonious interaction between social and economic policy does acknowledge that new and flexible employment patterns may conflict with some of the main dimensions of job quality, especially in jobs that combine low or no skills with temporary or precarious status and a lack of career development opportunities. The challenge becomes to 'combine flexibility with security in ways that benefit workers and companies alike' (CEC, 2001a: 9).[18]

The language used assumes a harmonious interaction, or 'synergy' between quality and new patterns of atypical, flexible, or non-standard work. For example, in order to meet the challenge of combining flexibility with

---

[18] Modernising the labour market so as to achieve a balance between flexibility and security—'flexicurity'—has long been a key theme of Dutch labour market policy, which has influenced EU policy discourse. One of the main legislative measures to achieve this balance in the Netherlands has been the Flexibility and Security Act (*Wet flexibiliteit en zekerheid*), which came into force in January 1999. See Burri in chapter 14 of this volume; see also Wilthagen, 1998.

security, the Employment Guidelines for 2002 urged member states to 'examine the possibility of incorporating in national law more flexible types of contract, and ensure that those working under new flexible contracts enjoy adequate security and higher occupational status, compatible with the needs of business and the aspirations of workers.'[19] The reference to 'adequate security' for those workers in atypical or non-standard forms of employment is recognition of the historical exclusion of atypical workers from employment protection; often, the very *purpose* of atypical work was to provide a way of circumventing legislative and collective regulations, and their associated costs (Jeffrey, 1998: 210). This dilemma, highlighting a distinction between 'good' and 'bad' types of atypical work, was evident in the Joint Employment Report for 1999, which praised the attempts made to reconcile flexibility with security referred to in member states' implementation reports, whilst also noting that 'this trend towards increased flexibility has reached an *excessive* proportion in Spain, where more than 90% of new contracts are temporary with a high rate of turnover' (CEC, 1999: para 4.3, emphasis added). Repeated annual Employment in Europe reports have analysed quality in work in European labour markets, finding wages—as well as job security, access to training, and career development—to be 'crucial determinants of both subjective job satisfaction and objective job quality.' The conclusion of the report for 2003 is that:

> [w]hile according to these criteria, the majority of jobs in the EU are of relatively high quality, *up to a quarter of Europeans remain in jobs of relatively low quality*, having either low pay, and/or a lack of job security, access to training or career development.
>
> (European Commission, 2003b: 126; emphasis added)

The European Employment Strategy thus has to steer a difficult path between two opposing perspectives on the utility of what is variously described as 'atypical', 'non-standard', 'marginal', or 'precarious' work. On the one hand, there is the view that atypical work serves a bridging function, providing an entry route to the standard employment contract for labour market 'outsiders'. On the other hand, there is the view that atypical work is a trap, leading to the marginalisation of atypical workers, with temporary and part-time workers being kept within a segmented and peripheral labour market (see Buechtemann and Quack, 1989; Gash, 2003). This is an area where, in the discourse of the European Commission at least, one can point to a virtuous circle. The policy documents speak of the synergies between quality in work, productivity, and employment, with the EU's most recent annual employment report asserting that quality in

---

[19] EC Council Decision 2002/177 of 18 February 2002 on guidelines for Member States' employment policies for the year 2002 [2002] OJ L 60/60, at 67.

work and subjective job satisfaction are positively correlated with employment performance and labour market participation. In particular, for women, 'greater shares of jobs of higher quality are associated with higher female labour force participation and employment' (European Commission, 2003a: 10). Improvements in the quality of work are viewed instrumentally in the European employment policy discourse, as having a key role to play in increasing labour force participation.

To use the terminology adopted within the EU institutions, the protection of women in various forms of precarious employment and the task of ensuring that their work contributes to the wider goal of employment creation would require the reconciliation of the 'adaptability' goal, with the 'equal opportunities' goal. In particular, the following dimensions must be recognised and safeguarded:

> intrinsic quality at work, skills, lifelong learning and career development, gender equality, health and safety at work, flexibility and security, inclusion and access to the labour market, work organisation and work-life balance, social dialogue and worker involvement, diversity and non-discrimination, and overall work performance.[20]

Post-Lisbon, in an effort to promote 'better' not just 'more' jobs, there has been a shift to measuring 'qualitative' aspects of employment, where hitherto the emphasis had been on observing quantitative indicators. As a way to balance the quantitative indicators which had previously dominated the coordination of national employment policies, the European Commission identified ten 'dimensions' of job quality in its Communication in 2001 (CEC, 2001a). For each of these, one or more indicators have been proposed, and were adopted at the Laeken summit in December 2001,[21] as a means of assessing the quality of work in Europe and of monitoring its evolution over time.

A review of progress in 2003 concluded that, whilst there had been some improvements, for example, in rising levels of educational attainment and skills, nevertheless, there was 'scope for considerable improvement under each of the ten dimensions of quality' (European Commission, 2003b: 3). Using the classification of jobs suggested in *Employment in Europe 2001* (CEC, 2001b), the share of 'low-quality jobs' in the EU remained virtually constant in the second half of the 1990s. According to this classification, three main job types were distinguished: 'high-quality jobs', which, in addition to reasonable pay, offer either job security or access to training and career development; low-pay/low-productivity jobs, namely jobs with gross

---

[20] EC Council Decision (2003/578/EC) of 22 July 2003 on guidelines for the employment policies of the Member States, [2003] OJ L 197/13.

[21] Presidency Conclusions, Laeken European Council, 14 and 15 December 2001, Bull EU-12/2001, 1–26 (Laeken European Council).

hourly wages of less than 75 per cent of the country-specific median; and 'dead-end jobs', ie jobs which, independently of their pay level, offer neither job security nor access to training or career development (European Commission, 2003a: 127).

To return to the 'virtuous circle', the post-Lisbon aim of reconciling economic, employment, and social policy is reinforced by the assertion that there is a 'positive link' between overall employment performance and job quality: for example, that those who move from unemployment to jobs of low quality, in particular jobs without training opportunities, often remain at high risk of becoming unemployed again, with almost a third of these workers out of work again a year later, in comparison to around 10 per cent of those taking up jobs of high quality (European Commission, 2003b: 6). However, it is not clear how quality in employment, along the dimensions mentioned above, is to be reconciled with the requirements of full employment, since this is understood in the EU discourse to require a repositioning of welfare state provision and employment protection away from 'protecting' those in jobs towards 'facilitating' workers' employability and mobility between jobs. The Lisbon version of full employment would appear to necessitate greater wage flexibility in the form of increased labour cost dispersion, and relaxation of the 'overly restrictive elements of employment protection legislation';[22] in all, a risk of privileging quantity over quality, as evidenced, for example, by the declaration by the Laeken European Council that '[w]e must accelerate our efforts to achieve by 2010 the 70% employment rate agreed in Lisbon. That must be the first objective of the European Employment Strategy.'[23]

Precarious Work and 'Social Inclusion'

Within EU policy discourse, another proxy term for precarious employment and its social consequences is the phenomenon of 'social exclusion'. The development of policies to combat poverty and to promote social inclusion has been on the European policy agenda since the Lisbon Summit, as part of the Union's goal of 'modernising the European social model by investing in people and building an active welfare state.'[24]

As with 'precariousness', there is an absence of commonly defined and agreed indicators on poverty at EU level, with member states using different definitions for measuring and characterising current levels of poverty

---

[22] EC Council Recommendation of 25 June 2003 on the Broad Guidelines of the Economic Policies of the Member States and the Community for the period 2003–2005 (Luxembourg: EC, 2003), at para 2.2.

[23] Laeken European Council, above n 21, at para 23.

[24] Although the need to tackle poverty more generally has been on the agenda of the EC and EU since the first Social Action Plan of 1974: see Armstrong, 2003: 174–75.

and social exclusion. Most member states, however, refer to the key indicator of the 'risk of poverty' rate, central factors of which are unemployment (especially when long term), low income, low-quality employment, homelessness, weak health, immigration, few qualifications and early school leaving, gender inequality, discrimination and racism, disability, old age, family break-ups, drug abuse and alcoholism, and living in an area of multiple disadvantage (CEC, 2001c: 7).

The *modus operandi* of the Employment Strategy—a Joint Report, the establishment of common indicators, and then the submission of NAPs— was crystallised at the Lisbon European Council and identified as a form of governance (the open method of coordination, or OMC) that could have greater application beyond employment policy. This iterative, soft law process, employing the use of guidelines, benchmarks, and indicators, has accordingly been applied to combating poverty and social exclusion. It was agreed that member states should coordinate their policies for fighting poverty and social exclusion on the basis of an OMC combining common objectives, national action plans, and common indicators, with the aim of promoting more ambitious and effective policy strategies for social inclusion (CEC and Council, 2004: 3).[25]

Although the term 'precarious work' is not often employed within EU discourse, EU policies to combat social exclusion nevertheless place a great deal of emphasis on improving participation in economic activity and on strengthening fragile attachments to the labour market, as the following definitions illustrate:

> Social exclusion is a process whereby certain individuals are pushed to the edge of society and prevented from participating fully by virtue of their poverty, or lack of basic competencies and lifelong learning opportunities, or as a result of discrimination. This distances them from job, income and education opportunities as well as social and community networks and activities ...
>
> Social inclusion is a process which ensures that those at risk of poverty and social exclusion gain the opportunities and resources necessary to participate fully in economic, social and cultural life and to enjoy a standard of living and well-being that is considered normal in the society in which they live.
>
> (CEC and Council, 2004: 8)

Whilst the EU's *employment policy* provides the overarching framework for the formulation of specific policies for the integration of disadvantaged groups in the labour market, its *social inclusion policy* focuses on action

---

[25] In due course, the Laeken European Council in December 2001 reported how the first Joint Report on Social Inclusion and the establishment of a set of common indicators had furthered the policy defined at Lisbon for eradicating poverty and promoting social inclusion: Laeken European Council, above n 21, at para 28.

that facilitates participation in employment for those individuals, groups and communities who are most distant from the labour market (CEC and Council, 2004: 43).

At the risk of oversimplification, a central part of the policy to combat social exclusion replicates the initiatives to ensure full employment, starting from the premise that work is the best way out of poverty. So, whilst the key priorities of social inclusion policy include decent housing, quality health, preventing early school-leaving, and so on, nevertheless, many of the social cohesion and social inclusion objectives touch on social and labour market integration. Accordingly, the NAPs for social inclusion must be closely coordinated with the NAPs for employment, and both plans should be read together to get a fuller picture of the measures being taken to combat social exclusion through participation in the labour market (CEC and Council, 2004: 43). In turn, the Employment Strategy itself is increasingly concerned with the objective of an inclusive labour market, with many of the employment guidelines touching on social and labour market integration, for instance: active and preventative measures for the unemployed and inactive; promoting integration of and combating discrimination against people at a disadvantage in the labour market; promoting the development of human capital and lifelong learning; making work pay through incentives to enhance work attractiveness; and gender equality.[26]

This shift from passive management of mass and long-term unemployment towards the greater encouragement of job acquisition and labour market attachment has major implications for women engaged either in precarious work or outside the paid employment force. Just as the search for 'quality' in employment risks being undermined in the attainment of a particular form of full employment, similarly there is the danger that precarious workers, underemployed or unemployed workers, namely the 'socially excluded', are to be 'included' by being required (through the removal of 'disincentives' in tax and benefits systems) to undertake paid employment, even if that is employment of low quality.

REGULATING OR REGULARISING PRECARIOUS WORK

What does it mean for the regulation of women's precarious work that the regulatory frameworks within the EU adopt the language of 'quality of jobs' and 'social inclusion'? Can such means of framing the phenomenon of precarious employment be effective to regularise these forms of employment and protect women engaged in precarious work?

---

[26] EC Council Decision 2003/578 of 22 July 2003 on guidelines for the employment policies of the Member States [2003] OJ L 197/13.

The EU's response to precarious work has been located within the context of its employment policy, which is committed to the achievement of full employment. However, as Eddy Lee points out, any definition of full employment must also include notions of what constitutes an acceptable job (Lee, 1997: 47). In the EU context, the emphasis on quality in work and social inclusiveness are therefore crucial to balance the weight given to full employment, but it is questionable whether the appeal to quality and inclusion are sufficient to redress the economic imperative of increasing labour market participation. I would argue that there are insufficiently strong substantive employment protection norms to guarantee high-quality employment. Indeed, one of the reasons why the political commitment to full employment had waned in recent decades was that it was tied to the existence of labour markets contained within national boundaries, to a belief in Keynesian macroeconomics, and, most importantly, to conventions of social responsibility—in particular, that the state would underwrite job security or provide income security—which are all now fragmenting (Stråth, 2001).

The Lisbon version of full employment shies away from a full-blooded commitment to extending labour standards and social protection to previously unprotected (non-standard) workers. Instead, these workers are to achieve employment security by virtue of making themselves more employable. Further, in the modern welfare state, member states are urged to withdraw from a commitment to providing income guarantees in the form of generous unemployment insurance or social benefits. In terms of employment protection law, the lack of substantive 'bite' to measures that might otherwise provide security to workers in precarious jobs can be seen in the new generation of directives, which aim to protect atypical workers.

The 'Atypical' Work Directives

Forms of work previously regarded as marginal or atypical—such as part-time work, fixed-term work, agency work, and home working—are moving to the centre of EU discourse on employment regulation. Whilst the use of non-standard patterns of work and employment contracts has been advocated by some within the EU because such labour flexibility is seen as a logical response to flexibility in goods and services markets, this economic justification for liberalising labour markets contrasts with the rationales given in the debates leading up to the adoption of the Part-time Work Directive and the Fixed-term Work Directive, which stressed the equality of treatment of atypical workers.[27]

[27] EC Council Directive 97/81 of 15 December 1997 concerning the framework agreement on part-time working [1997] OJ L 14/9; EC Council Directive 99/70 of 28 June 1999 concerning the framework agreement on fixed-term work [1999] OJ L 175/43.

The stated aims of the Part-time Work Directive are, first and foremost, to provide for the removal of discrimination against part-time workers and to improve the quality of part-time work; second, to facilitate the development of part-time work on a voluntary basis; and only third to contribute to the flexible organisation of working time in a manner which takes into account the needs of employers and workers. The aims of the Fixed-term Work Directive are to improve the quality of fixed-term work by ensuring the principle of non-discrimination and to establish a framework to prevent abuse arising from the use of successive fixed-term employment contracts or relationships. It is noteworthy that, in contrast to the Part-time Work Directive, the Fixed-term Work Directive is not steeped in the discourse of promoting this form of atypical work. This is a reminder of the position adopted by the European Trade Union Confederation during the social partners' negotiations over the proposed directive, and also by the Commission, that fixed-term work is a low quality form of employment, the use of which should be limited (see Murray, 1999a).[28]

Has something been lost in the separate treatment of the different forms of atypical work, and in the form that such regulation has taken? In the 1997 Green Paper on Partnership for a New Organisation of Work, the Commission envisaged the need to move 'from rigid and compulsory systems of statutory regulations to more open and flexible legal frameworks' (CEC, 1997b: 44). The preference seems to be to leave regulation of the social field to agreements between the social partners, which are seen as being somehow less interventionist.[29] As a result of the desire for a 'light touch' to regulation, the regulatory techniques adopted within the atypical work directives thus far enacted would appear to fall halfway between soft law and hard law, as traditionally understood. Both directives, products of the social dialogue procedure, are departures from the 'classic' Community method of law-making—a style of law-making established in founding Treaties, wherein the Commission has sole right of initiative; the European Parliament has an increasingly important voice, the Council of Ministers takes the final decision, and the resulting Community hard law is enforced by the Court of Justice.

Not only does the *process* by which the atypical work directives are drafted differ from the 'classic' Community method, the actual *content* of the

---

[28] Similarly, the aims of the draft Temporary Work Directive are to ensure the protection of temporary workers and to improve quality of temporary work by ensuring non-discrimination, as well as to establish a framework for the use of temporary work to contribute to creating jobs: Amended proposal for a directive on working conditions for temporary workers, Brussels, COM (2002) 701 final.

[29] Such agreements are the product of the social dialogue procedure (Articles 136–39 EC) under which the Commission is obliged to consult with the social partners (representatives of management and labour) prior to the submission of legislative proposals. The social partners, if they so wish, can then negotiate 'collective agreements' which are subsequently transformed into binding directives by virtue of Council decisions.

framework directives so far produced has eschewed the prescriptive approach traditionally favoured in directives. The atypical work directives simply give legal effect to the unamended social partners' agreements; they were not subject to the usual drafting process for EC legislation, leading to vaguely worded principles, and details to be filled in by member states (Jeffery, 1998). An example of this in the Fixed-term Work Directive is the decision to leave it to each member state to determine 'the conditions under which fixed-term contracts shall be regarded as successive'; further, clause 5(3) of the social partners' agreement leading to the Part-time Work Directive urges that employers should '*give consideration to requests*' by workers to transfer between part-time and full-time work. Would greater use of hard law, such as the granting of a positive right to transfer between part-time and full-time work, better meet the objective of improving or protecting workers' quality of working life and reducing the precariousness of such non-standard work? A more positive perspective on the two directives is that by setting minimum standards, they represent a form of framework regulation which is suited to the social policy area since it leaves so much room for diversity in member states to take account of national social and economic differences.

With regard to improving the quality of such atypical work, the Joint Employment Report for 2001 noted a general trend towards new and flexible forms of work, facilitating the introduction and use of fixed-term contracts, temporary work, and part-time work through collective agreements. These measures, however, tended to adopt a narrow approach to work organisation—typically, with member states restricting their activities to the minimum required to implement the atypical work directives and the Working Time Directive[30]—with 'little focus on the quality of work' (CEC, 2002a, 32–33).

The inability of member states to reconcile quality of part-time and fixed-term work with the objective of creating employment raises the question of the extent to which such non-standard work is truly *voluntary*. Indeed, in the EU as a whole, more than half of all employees on temporary contracts—equivalent to 7 per cent of all employees—would have preferred a permanent job but could not find one (European Commission, 2003a: 127). In this context, temporary work (employment on fixed- or short-term contracts) is particularly important, not least because job security and employment stability are key determinants of both job satisfaction and job quality, and are central to reducing the precariousness of work. The Commission's own report on trends in employment found little evidence that quality in work and employment stability had improved over the second half of the 1990s: 'Despite the strong employment performance

[30] EC Working Time Directive 93/104 [1993] OJ L 307/18.

observed in European labour markets ... recent data on the evolution of both subjective job satisfaction and objective job quality over this period do in many cases not indicate significant changes in quality in work' (CEC, 2003a: 151).[31] Thus, an increase in the employment rate brought about by an increase in the use of temporary contracts or involuntary part-time work can be problematic, given the aim of ensuring quality in employment, since both these forms of atypical work are generally related to strong degrees of workers' dissatisfaction with their jobs.

CONCLUSIONS: SOFT REGULATION AND PRECARIOUS WORK

Alongside the functional approach adopted within the EU to the definition and measurement of precarious work, there also exists a preference for procedural norms over substantive standards. As discussed above, numerous indicators of *quality* in work are now embedded within the Employment Strategy, such that member states are judged by how successfully they meet targets in relation to factors such as the percentage of undeclared work, the numbers of working poor, job satisfaction rates, the gender pay gap, and rates of gender segregation.[32] Similarly, with regard to those aspects of precarious work that fall within the rubric of *social inclusion*, member states are subject not to hard law requirements to meet certain substantive standards, but to the soft law expectations of the benchmarking and peer review process at the heart of the OMC.

Are the policy instruments adopted, namely the 'soft regulation' of the OMC, sufficient to tackle the social exclusion of those women who are unemployed, underemployed, or engaged in non-standard work? The OMC holds out great promise as a new form of governance that has the potential to overturn the assumption that labour standards in the form of (judicially) enforceable hard law are the *only* means to ensure security for workers in an era of labour market flexibility. However, after more than six years of OMC in the employment policy field, the policy experimentation permitted by this new governance method, whilst ostensibly conferring greater legitimacy on the EU to act due to the *responsive* nature of this regulation, nevertheless runs the risk of relegating worker protection to a poor second place behind employment creation.

Whilst hard law measures do exist, for example, in the atypical work directives, their effectiveness in bringing workers in non-standard employment

---

[31] This reinforces the earlier finding that 'changing forms of employment and ever-tighter rhythms of work have prevented working conditions from improving' (CEC, 2001b: 65–66).

[32] Employment indicators have grown in number, type, and complexity from the relatively straightforward first generation of indicators in 1997, numbering eight in total, to over 60 indicators in 2004: CEC, 2004: 97–116.

within the scope of employment protection legislation or social protection systems is questionable. Even with the development of indicators to evaluate quality in work and social inclusion, there remain difficulties in reconciling the promotion of flexibility and wage dispersion, on the one hand, with the labour standards necessary to achieve work of 'high skill, high trust and high quality', on the other. This is likely to continue to be the case as long as labour standards such as gender equality are seen as means to a particular goal (full employment and competitiveness) rather than as goals in themselves.

What does appear to offer some hope for the protection of women engaged in non-standard work is the development of a gender mainstreaming approach, which requires gender equality issues to be built into all policy programmes, at all stages by the actors normally involved in policy-making (CEC, 2000; Rubery, 2002; Rubery *et al*, 2004). This would mean, for example, that a gender perspective would have to be incorporated into EU measures to prevent and combat social exclusion, particularly in view of the increasing feminisation of poverty. As the employment guidelines for 2003–05 suggest, gender mainstreaming in employment policy would require particular attention to be given to reconciling work and family life, notably through the provision of care services for children and other dependants, encouraging the sharing of family and professional responsibilities, and facilitating return to work after a period of absence. Further, there is the need not just to remove financial 'disincentives' from women entering the labour market (such as taxation systems and the gender pay gap), but also to improve working arrangements, with measures to boost the attractiveness of part-time work and facilitate career breaks and flexible working (European Commission, 2004: 47).

However, as the latest Joint Employment Report (CEC, 2004a) points out, with the exception of Sweden, gender mainstreaming continues to be weak and non-systematic, lacking gender impact assessment of existing systems and new policy proposals. Whilst the gender mainstreaming approach has served to consolidate the position of equal opportunities as a mainstay of the EU Employment Strategy, nevertheless, national level policy makers have yet to internalise the full implications of a mainstreaming approach: for example, few NAPs articulate the tensions between competitive flexibility and worker-protective flexibility from the perspective of the gender impact, or consider the specific circumstances and requirements of women workers when developing strategies for organisational change (see Webster, 2001: 37).

As with the OMC, gender mainstreaming provides a new governance mechanism that offers an alternative to the traditional 'command and control' techniques of the EU, which seem increasingly ill suited to the regulation of complex fields and of diverse jurisdictions. Such new regulatory techniques can lead to the creation of norms which are *responsive*—due in part to the process of partnership, deliberation, and participation—but they also highlight the conundrum of enforceability in the absence of hard law: namely, how to ensure member states comply with their soft law obligations to mainstream gender equality into employment and social inclusion policies, and to minimise the precariousness of non-standard employment for women.

Part III

Working Time and Precarious Work

5

Time to Dream? Flexibility, Families, and the Regulation of Working Time

JOANNE CONAGHAN

... when we Home are come,
Alas! we find our work but just begun;
So many Things for our Attendance call,
Has we ten Hands we could employ them all.

... Our toil and labour daily so extreme,
That we have hardly ever *Time to dream**

INTRODUCTION

IT IS REMARKABLE how the words of an eighteenth-century washer-woman still resonate with her twenty-first century counterparts. Women have no more time to dream now than they had then. The promise of a world in which sweeping technological advances would shorten working hours and create greater leisure time has not materialised. The 'new economy' remains one in which time to dream is a commodity which only the most affluent—women and men—can afford to buy.

This chapter reflects upon the relationship between work and time in the wake of the continued absence of a time to dream. The object is to probe the conceptual and discursive boundaries of our understanding of working time, in particular, by assessing the impact of recent developments in working time regulation in Britain through the broader lens of law's role in the construction of working time norms. These norms are arguably crucial to our understanding of 'work' and 'workers', and a primary reference point in the classification of some workers and/or forms of work as 'atypical', 'contingent' or 'precarious'. Time norms therefore have concrete privileging and exclusionary effects with, inter alia, gendered consequences (Smith,

---

* Mary Collier, Washer-woman from Petersfield, Hampshire in *The Woman's Labour*; an epistle to Mr Stephen Duck in answer to his late poem *The Thresher's Labour* (1739, 10–11), reproduced in Thompson (1991, 381)

2002). Moreover, although appearing to emerge spontaneously from the discourses and practices of management, working time norms are, to a significant extent, the product of legal regulation.[1] One impact of the new economy has been to disrupt conventional norms of working time, captured in the idea of the full-time, long-term job. While this is widely perceived to have led to the 'feminisation' of working time norms in favour of more precarious arrangements (Fudge and Owens, chapter 1 in this volume), it has also opened up a space where the question of how working time is delineated and by whom has come to the fore. In this space issues relating to the organisation of work and family life are seen to collide. An obvious question is how far the fallout from such a collision can produce benefits for workers, and the potential role for law in this process. More broadly, the challenge to and disruption of working time norms raise fundamental questions about how we understand and construe work.

This chapter proceeds as follows. It begins with the story of two women whose brief encounter with law over changes in their working hours signals the onset of an apparent convergence between gender, work, and time now a hallmark of the new economy. It then draws upon EP Thompson's analysis of work and time in the context of the transition from feudalism to capitalism in Britain. Here, the focus is on the gendered aspects of Thompson's analysis—which, while present, are fairly undeveloped—with a view to providing a theoretical framework through which to critique current understandings of work and time, as expressed in British working time laws. The chapter then tracks the development of working time norms over key periods of regulation (and deregulation), locating contemporary developments within a broader historical context. Throughout the exploration, a central concern is to consider closely the relationship between working time and the construction and maintenance of gendered social norms. The chapter concludes by considering law's role in the construction of new working time norms, in particular, the extent to which law contributes to the production of precarious forms of work with gendered distributive consequences.

LORD DENNING ON (GENDER), WORK AND TIME

In 1974, two women police clerks, who lost their jobs for refusing to accept changes in their working hours, failed in their claims for redundancy pay.[2]

---

[1] Legal regulation of working time may take a number of forms, including: (1) standardised limits on the working day/week/year; (2) restrictions on the scheduling of work (limits on shift work, provision for rests, breaks, etc); (3) regulation aimed at the protection of particular groups of workers, eg women and/or children; (4) the regulation of 'new' working time arrangements, eg part-time work, temporary work, and/or leave provisions (Bosch, 1999). Legally prescribed norms operate alongside voluntary and customary norms (including those derived from collective bargaining) to establish particular working time regimes.

[2] *Johnson v Nottinghamshire Combined Police Authority*, [1974] ICR 170 (*Johnson*).

The women had worked together for over 20 years on a standard five-day week, commencing at 9.30 am and ending at 5.00 pm. The police authority, in pursuit of efficiency gains, sought to introduce a shift system, requiring them to work separate shifts, from 8.00 am to 1.00 pm and from 1.00 pm to 8.00 pm, alternating weekly. The women refused to accept the new working hours because they clashed with their domestic responsibilities. They were dismissed and replaced, embarking subsequently on claims for redundancy pay.

At issue was the question of whether the women's dismissals arose from a redundancy situation. A redundancy occurred, inter alia, where a dismissal could be attributed to the fact that 'the requirements of [a] business for employees to carry out *work of a particular kind* have ceased or diminished.'[3] Thus, what had to be determined was whether the changes in the women's hours of work effected a change in the *kind* of work they did. Could it properly be said that 'work of a particular kind' had ceased? The Court of Appeal thought not, holding that where the tasks carried out remained the same the fact that they were performed at different hours did not generally suffice to change the character or kind of work.[4] Moreover, Lord Denning cautioned against a wide interpretation of redundancy in this context, suggesting it could encroach unduly on the freedom of management to take sound business decisions: '... an employer is entitled to reorganise his business so as to improve its efficiency and, in so doing, to propose to his staff a change in their terms and conditions of employment; and to dispense with their services if they do not agree.'[5] Lord Denning viewed the determination of working hours as falling squarely within an employer's 'entitlements' in this respect.

One can reflect almost sentimentally upon the efforts of Mrs Johnson and Mrs Dutton to preserve their working hours. Their story is a symbolic representation of a moment of collision between the old world of work and the new, a moment when standardisation gave way to flexibility, when core working practices were displaced by more contingent arrangements, when working time began to assume a vital significance in the on-going process of economic restructuring. Against this background, it is interesting to revisit the Court of Appeal's stance on the relationship between work and time. What is striking is how little weight their Lordships place on time as a characterising feature of work. For them,

---

[3] Redundancy Payments Act 1965, s 1(2)(b) (emphasis added). The same definition can now be found in the Employment Rights Act 1996 (ERA 1996), s 139.

[4] Above n 2 at 178B–D (per Cairns LJ). His Lordship acknowledged that in some cases work and time might be so integrally related as to affect the character of the work, citing the example of a night nurse whose work might be 'different from that of a day nurse' (178D).

[5] *Ibid* at 176F–G (per Denning LJ).

time is not intrinsic to work but tangential; hence their decision not to recognise a redundancy situation when the hours of work are radically altered. In fact, when *Johnson* was decided, this point was arguable in law. The existing case-law was scant and inconsistent and at least one prior decision clearly held that a change in working hours could give rise to a redundancy situation.[6] Moreover, as the applicants' counsel argued, there was some indication that Parliament viewed time as a fundamental aspect of work, evidenced in the legal requirement that working hours be included in the written statement of particulars which employers were obliged to distribute to their employees.[7] Thus, when the matter was considered, what attributes were deemed relevant to a determination of the 'kind of work' and whether time was properly among them was at least an open question.[8]

What was not open was the issue of who determines hours of work. The idea that the interests of employers should give way to the personal needs of employees, that employer 'entitlements' should be compromised by employee concerns was quite alien to this Court. Thus, the time regime which underpinned the Court of Appeal's decision was unequivocally one set by employers and driven solely by their interests. And it is within this normative framework of the primacy of employer interest that flexible working arrangements have subsequently developed, arrangements in which (ironically) time has become a key indicator of the type or *kind* of work. Indeed, it is now common to categorise work expressly in terms of time as, for example, when we speak of full-time, part-time, fixed-term, or temporary work, all of which are time-referential. Even where time is not the sole or express classifying feature of work, it is generally an important dimension of work's characterisation: the number of working hours and the time the work is performed undoubtedly go to the question of whether particular types of work may be characterised as 'atypical', 'non-standard', 'contingent', or 'precarious'.[9]

Thus, in the new flexible workplace, it seems more difficult to discount time as a relevant feature of the 'kind of work' or to say that time is not generally

---

[6] See *Pollock v Victor Value (Holdings) Ltd* (1967), 2 ITR 338 (*Pollock*), considered by Lord Denning in *Johnson*, above n 2 at 167D–E, and also involving a dismissal in the context of a clash between working hours and an employee's domestic responsibilities.

[7] At that time, the obligation to issue employees with written statements of particulars was governed by the Contracts of Employment Act 1972; see now ERA 1996, s 1.

[8] Subsequent case-law has for the most part confirmed the judicial stance taken in *Johnson*. See in particular *Lesney Products & Co Ltd v Nolan*, [1977] ICR 235 (*Lesney*), in which Lord Denning adopted similar, managerially oriented reasoning. A number of cases have, however, found that night work can be different in kind to day work, eg *MacFisheries Ltd v Findley*, [1985] ICR 160 (*MacFisheries*).

[9] For a discussion of these terms, see Fudge and Owens in chapter 1 of this volume. Obviously, features other than time may also inform such characterisations of work, including where the work is performed (offsite/in the home) and how the worker–employer relationship is conceived (contracting out/agency/self-employment arrangements).

a defining feature of what a job *is*. On the contrary, time and work now appear closely interrelated. Of course, one can continue to distinguish them at an abstract conceptual level (as their Lordships do) but, contextually and culturally, our understandings of time and work are quite difficult to disentangle. Moreover, this is arguably not such a recent phenomenon. Writing in 1967, social historian EP Thompson[10] charted the relationship between changing apprehensions of time and the organisation of work during the transition to industrial capitalism. Thompson's essay demonstrates that our understanding of time is not universal but contingent and culturally embedded. Perceptions of time are strongly shaped by the environment in which we live and labour and, simultaneously, by the social relations which shape that environment. Moreover, changes in the way in which we work may effect or necessitate changes in how we perceive time: the two concepts are to an extent interconstitutive of one another. And, because our understandings of time and work are so deeply enmeshed, control over time is often crucial in struggles for self-determination in work. This was apparent in nineteenth-century campaigns for a shorter working day and remains so in current efforts to make flexibility serve worker interests. It is also at the crux of the dispute between Mrs Johnson and Mrs Dutton and their employers.

There is a further dimension to *Johnson* inviting reassessment, and that is the gender dimension, the fact that the court's deliberations about the relationship between work and time take place against the backdrop of two women's struggle to secure some redress for concrete disadvantages sustained as a consequence of gendered social arrangements which limit their availability for and access to paid work. In retrospect, one is struck by the casual way in which the women's need to reconcile work and family responsibilities is discounted as a relevant feature of their legal position. For example, while Lord Denning acknowledges that the women have 'good reason' for refusing to accept the new working hours, endorsing their willingness to place family duties above work-based considerations,[11] he does not view the women's dilemma as any concern of their employers. Likewise, the argument of John Bowyer, counsel for the applicants, that 'as a matter of policy, if redundancy payment is not payable in a situation like the present it will reduce the value of the scheme for many women workers',[12] falls entirely on deaf ears.

Were this issue to arise now, Nottinghamshire police authority might well be met by a claim of indirect sex discrimination under the Sex Discrimination

---

[10] In an essay first published in (1967) *Past and Present* 38 and reproduced in a collection of the author's essays in 1991.

[11] Above n 2 at 175D.

[12] *Ibid*, at 173E.

Act 1975[13] and, possibly, an unfair dismissal claim.[14] More generally, the assumption that pervades *Johnson*—that conflicts between work and family obligations fall outside the scope of legitimate managerial consideration—is now seriously open to question. This is particularly so in the United Kingdom, where the past few years have witnessed the vigorous state pursuit of 'family-friendly' policies designed to effect a fundamental 'change [in] the culture of relations in and at work ...to reflect a new relationship between work and family life.' (Blair, 1998)

In the light of these developments, *Johnson* represents a portentous convergence of gender, work, and time, presaging new challenges by workers to the organisation of working time during a period of intense labour market restructuring. And it is no coincidence that gender, work, and time come together here; historically, as we shall see, they have always been closely aligned. For this reason, gender offers a particular lens through which we can not only better understand the relationship, historical and contemporary, between work and time, but also more fully appreciate, in a legal context at least, the possibilities for disrupting and reshaping that relationship in ways that deliver not precariousness, but rather arrangements which genuinely enhance the opportunities for workers to engage in decent work.[15]

EP THOMPSON ON (GENDER) WORK AND TIME

In 'Time, work-discipline and industrial capitalism', Thompson explores the relationship between changing apprehensions of time and rhythms of work in early industrial capitalism (1991). He argues that the period saw a shift from notations of time around 'task-orientation', where time is measured according to the tasks to be done, to 'timed work', where tasks become subject to the discipline of time, which is in turn broken up into smaller and smaller units of measurement. This effects significant changes in patterns of work, from pre-industrial labour, where the rhythm of work varies according to natural cycles (day, season, life) and the immediacy of needs (producing

---

[13] See *Edwards v London Underground (No 2)*, [1998] IRLR 364 (CA) (*Edwards*), in which a London underground train driver successfully claimed that a proposed shift system with which she could not comply for family reasons constituted indirect sex discrimination (discussed in Conaghan, 2000).

[14] Although unfair dismissal protection had been introduced in 1971, Mrs Dutton and Mrs Johnson did not plead it, probably because the law was then so underdeveloped. Were they to do so now, the decision to dismiss would be subject to the requirement that the employer acted reasonably, which, in the context of economic dismissals, has been interpreted to require the adoption of fair procedures, including consultation and consideration of suitable alternative employment: *Williams v Compare Maxam*, [1982] ICR 156 (*Williams*). However, where proposals to reorganise the workplace are shown to be based on sound business reasons, the determination of the fairness of any dismissals that result does not tend to give much weight to the disadvantages which reorganisation imposes on employees: *Richmond Precision Engineering Ltd. v Pearce*, [1985] IRLR 179 (*Richmond Precision Engineering*).

[15] On 'decent work' as a normative ideal, see Owens, 2002.

less regular, more diffuse work patterns), to industrial labour which demands much greater predictability as well as exclusivity in work patterns. Thompson argues that this shift from task orientation to timed work cannot be understood solely in terms of technological advances in techniques of time measurement but must also be understood within the broader context of the transition from feudalism to capitalism:

> What we are examining here are not only changes in manufacturing technique which demand greater synchronisation of labour and a greater exactitude of time-routines in *any* society; but also those changes as they were lived through in nascent industrial capitalism. We are concerned simultaneously with time-sense in its technological conditioning, and with time-measurement as a means of labour exploitation.
>
> (Thompson, 1991: 383)

Thompson highlights a number of distinct features of this new timed work regime. First, time becomes currency: as Thompson observes, 'it is not passed but spent' (1991, 359). Moreover, time-thrift norms emerge as a dominant feature of working life, indeed of life in general: 'in mature capitalist society, all time must be consumed, marketed, put to use' (1991: 395). In a sense, Thompson is saying, we have lost the ability merely to pass time. Second, the transition to timed work signals a relinquishing of control by the worker over the conduct and fruits of his labour, for it is precisely in the context of dependent labour—when a distinction is drawn between the worker's time and the employer's—that time becomes money: 'the employer must use the time of his labour and see it is not wasted: not the task but the value of time when reduced to money is dominant' (1991: 359). A timed work regime thus creates the conditions for struggle between capitalists and workers over the allocation of time, specifically about how time is divided between work and other activities.[16] This leads to the third distinct feature of a timed work regime, the emergence of a greater demarcation between 'work' and 'life'. Under task orientation, labour, family and social activities are easily intermingled but timed work generally requires their separation in order to maximise the use of the time the employer has bought. Under timed work, life is presumed to carry on elsewhere. Thus, Thompson's analysis directly links the transition from task orientation to timed work to

---

[16] Marx, in his analysis in *Capital* (vol 1, 1983) of the working day, compares the compulsion of the capitalist to consume the worker's time with the bloodsucking of a vampire (224) or the 'hunger of a werewolf' (233). He continues:

> capital ... usurps the time for growth, development and healthy maintenance of the body. It steals the time required for the consumption of fresh air and sunlight. It niggles over mealtime ... it reduces the sound sleep (252);

> Hence it is that in the history of capitalist production, the determination of what is a working day, presents itself as the result of a struggle, a struggle between collective capital ... and collective labour (225).

the emergence of a separation, physical and conceptual, between work and family life.

What are the gender implications of this transition? In particular, how does Thompson's analysis improve our understanding of the gendering effects of working time norms? Thompson himself has very little to say about gender but, to his credit, he does say something. In particular, he acknowledges the difficulties working women faced adjusting to a timed work regime given their continued care responsibilities (1991: 381). Thompson notes that, while paid work gradually succumbed to the discipline of time, unpaid labour in the home remained task-oriented, further adding to the weight of the burden carried by women. He goes on to observe:

> This remains true to this day ... the rhythms of women's work in the home are not wholly attuned to the measurement of the clock. The mother of young children has an imperfect sense of time and attends to other human tides. She has not yet altogether moved out of the conventions of 'pre-industrial' society.
>
> (1991: 381–82)

Thompson's observation of the task orientation of care work may go some way to explaining why such work, particularly in an unpaid context, is not regarded as productive of value. It also sheds some interesting light on the difficulties paid care workers have in conforming to models of employment and in accessing legal entitlements that accompany employment status. For example, live-in carers are often exempt from working time regulation, in part because their residential status makes the demarcation of a clear boundary between work and life difficult, if not impossible, to draw[17]; but the task orientation of care work is problematic even in a non-residential context. There is almost always a sense in which, in the provision of care, completing the task and putting in the time do not quite coalesce. Thompson's analysis pinpoints a recognisable tension between the quality of care and its subjection to disciplines of time and cost: put simply, our expectations of care are task- not time-governed.

What remains missing from Thompson's analysis of the transition from task orientation to timed work is acknowledgement of the reliance of such a transition upon a particular gender division of labour. For workers to be free to engage in timed work, arrangements must be in place to ensure that other essential activities—particularly tasks associated with reproduction and the rearing of children—continue to be carried out.[18] There are many

---

[17] See Mundlak, 2005 for a comparative study of time norms governing live-in workers.

[18] Obviously, caring work extends beyond the care of children to include, for example, looking after the sick, disabled, and elderly. However, from a purely functional perspective, eg from a perspective that considers the value of care to capitalists seeking to exploit labour, it is the reproduction of the workforce which is most essential.

ways in which this might be done—there is nothing 'natural' about the arrangement that emerged in which men were free to labour on a timed work basis while women assumed primary responsibility for reproductive tasks—but the arrangement did serve the purpose of providing a supply of workers who, by virtue of being unencumbered by care responsibilities,[19] could commit their time exclusively, predictably and over the long term, to the benefit of their employers. In other words, it is not just that a timed work paradigm operates to exclude or restrict the ability of (mainly) women with care responsibilities to participate in paid work. It is also that such a paradigm is only possible because women assume those responsibilities. Women's unpaid labour is a crucial enabling feature of the transition from task orientation to timed work. In particular, it effects the necessary demarcation between 'work' and 'life' which a timed work regime requires.

Looking forward (from 1967), Thompson identifies the erosion of the work–life boundary as a potential indicator of a positive shift in our apprehension of time, away from the dominant notion of how best to 'use' time towards a perception of time which allows us to experience its unpurposive passing: 'People might have to relearn some of the arts of living lost in the industrial revolution, how to fill the interstices of their day with enriched, more leisurely, personal and social relations, how to break down once more the barriers between work and life' (1991: 401). Yet, while the ever-increasing participation of women with care responsibilities in the twenty-first century labour market, and the impact of this participation on the gendered allocation of working time might be said to have precipitated precisely the kind of breakdown in the work–life dichotomy that Thompson favourably anticipates, it has *not* brought with it anything resembling a return to lost arts of living, if by that we understand a retreat from the dominance of a timed work regime and a growth in the understanding of and capacity to experience time as anything other than in woefully short supply. While a preoccupation with the need to reconcile work and family obligations, to yield a better balance between work and life, is clearly a key feature of current labour policy and discourse across a range of states and within a variety of political and institutional contexts, it cannot really be said that work and life are coming together in the sense understood by Thompson. Indeed, what arguably is happening is that time norms are being deployed to ensure the continued *separation* of work and life, to effect clear demarcations between work time and life time, through, for example, the emergence of a range of working time packages as well as enhanced, more diverse leave arrangements. It is in part for this reason that time has become more significant as a feature of work's classification: the conflict between work and

[19] An arrangement sometimes characterised as a 'gender contract' (see eg Fudge, 2005, and Vosko, chapter 3 in this volume).

family, which women's increased workplace participation has occasioned, has not so much displaced a timed work regime as forced the adaptation of working time norms to ensure its continuance. This process of adaptation and its consequences—for women workers in particular—will now be considered against the background of a broader historical account of the legal regulation of working time.

THE LEGAL REGULATION OF WORKING TIME IN BRITAIN

The legal regulation of working time can be subdivided into three historical stages: (1) the introduction in the nineteenth century of protective legislation governing the hours of work of women and children in factories; (2) the deregulation of working time following the abolition of protective legislation in the 1980s; and (3) the development of new legal norms of working time in the 1990s primarily in the context of work–life policies. Under each working time regime, gender is a central feature. Moreover, at each stage, the need to ensure a functional balance between work and life limits the freedom of employers unilaterally to determine working time.

The Origins of Modern Working Time Regulation: Gender-specific Protective Legislation

A central concern of Thompson's analysis was to tease out the various ways in which the demands of early industrial capitalism forced the labouring classes to assume new time-compliant working habits. 'In the first stage,' he observes, 'we find simple resistance. But in the next stage, as the new time-discipline is imposed so the workers begin to fight not *against* time but *about* it' (Thompson, 1991: 388, emphasis added). Thus, the mid-nineteenth-century struggle for shorter working hours marks the beginning of the end of the process of transition to a timed work regime. It also witnesses the emergence of a role for law in mediating the competing demands of workers and capitalists over time.[20] It is therefore unsurprising to discover

---

[20] This is not to suggest that the role of law was neutral—clearly workers had little purchase on the political process at this time and lawmakers very much reflected broader power relations in society. However, in the context of working time, law was arguably a necessary brake on the time-devouring and potentially self-destructive tendencies of capitalism. As Marx argued,

> the working day has a maximum limit. It cannot be prolonged beyond a certain point. This maximum limit is conditioned by two things. First by the physical bounds of labour power ... a man can only expend a definite quantity of his vital force ... besides these purely physical limitations, the extension of the working day encounters moral ones. The labourer needs time for satisfying his intellectual and social wants ...
>
> (Marx, 1983: 233).

that for much of the nineteenth century working time was a central focus of political and legal struggle, with working hours a frequent subject of parliamentary debate. What is more remarkable is the form which legislation on working time eventually took, in particular, the gender-specificity of the regulation of adult factory workers in nineteenth- and twentieth-century Britain.

To understand why gender featured so prominently in the legal regulation of factory working time requires, *inter alia*, an awareness of the origins of working time regulation and the social, cultural and economic circumstances in which it emerged. From the outset, the campaign for shorter working hours, manifest in particular by the Ten Hours Movement of the 1830s and 1840s, took place against the backdrop of a growing allegiance among the educated and commercial classes to the tenets of political economy, characterised by adherence to principles of contractualism, free trade and the laissez-faire state. In this context, demands for general limits on the working day met with deep political opposition. By contrast, arguments for limiting the working hours of 'vulnerable' groups of workers—for example, women and children—were better received, as it was not considered inconsistent with the predominantly liberal outlook to protect those who did not possess the (contractual) capacity to protect themselves.[21] Allied with arguments about the immorality of depriving children of the benefits of family life and subjecting them to the full harshness of the factory regime,[22] the Ten Hours Movement secured its first victory in the Factories Act 1833, limiting the working hours of young people and providing for the appointment of a factory inspectorate (Wedderburn, 1965: 157).

The first example of gender-specific legislation was the Mines Regulation Act 1842, which prohibited the employment of women and children underground. Again, moral concerns, particularly about the corrupting influences of women and men working in close proximity, combined with the appeasement of liberal scruples through the designation of women as less than 'free agents', to push the legislation through with fairly limited opposition. This was quickly followed by the Ten Hours Act 1844, restricting the working hours of women in the textile industry for the first time. Over the course of the century, the scope of protection gradually spread to other industries, until eventually, in the Factory Act Extension Act 1867 it was applied to women and children in factories and workshops generally, thereafter establishing the basic model for twentieth-century regulation. Thus, before its repeal in 1986, Part VI of the Factories Act 1961, together with the Hours

---

[21] However, Walby notes the 'principled' objection of many manufacturers to restrictions on the freedom even of women to contract (1986: 122ff).

[22] The chief proponent here was Lord Ashley, later Earl of Shaftsbury.

of Employment (Conventions) Act 1936, placed restrictions on the hours women worked, the frequency and length of intervals and breaks, overtime, night work, weekend work, and work during annual holidays.[23]

There has been much debate about the significance of gender-specific protective legislation within the broader context of the on-going conflict between capital and labour over time. It is widely acknowledged, for example, that many in the early Labour movement viewed women's legislative protection as a means of securing the practical extension of similar protection to men as, where the two sexes worked together, it was often uneconomical to keep factories open for male workers alone. This is clearly the view of Marx, who hailed the Factories Acts as a victory for the British working class: 'It was the first time that ... the political economy of the middle class succumbed to the political economy of the working class' (reproduced in Kamenka, 1983: 362). Likewise, the Webbs are thought to have endorsed a strategy of fighting for a shorter working day by campaigning for women's legal protection, famously citing the remarks of one trade unionist that the men's battle for shorter working hours was fought 'from behind the women's petticoats' (Wedderburn, 1965: 162).

On the other hand, it has also been speculated that the restrictions on women's working hours were an attempt on the part of working men to exclude women from areas of competition for paid work, suggesting that the Factories Acts privileged the interests of working men over working women (Walby, 1986). There is certainly evidence that this was an issue among men and women trade unionists, particularly at the time of debate over further extension of protective legislation in the 1870s.[24] There are also signs that the development of the legislation was influenced by views about the proper scope of women's social role. For example, in the early factory movement, a view is clearly detectable, expressed by Lord Ashley, Marx, and Engels, that men not women should be the breadwinners of the family. Engels observed that a man's demotion from this particular role 'unsexes' him (Engels, 1977: 163),[25] while a Deputation to Sir Robert Peel in 1842 described it as '... a reversion of the order of nature and of

---

[23] Under s 7 of the Sex Discrimination Act 1986, these provisions 'ceased to have effect except in relation to young persons'. Section 7 also repealed certain provisions in the Mines and Quarries Act 1954 relating to the employment of women above ground. The section took effect in 1987, although night work restrictions continued to apply until 1988. Some regulation of the working time of children and young persons remained; see further below n 35.

[24] For example, Emma Paterson, founder of the Women's Protective and Provident League in 1874 and the first woman to attend the TUC in 1875, was a vociferous opponent of the legislation, insisting that the proper way to improve women's working conditions was through collective organisation. She also maintained that protective legislation perpetuated the idea that women, like children, could not protect themselves (Paterson, 1874).

[25] Although elsewhere Engels recognised paid work as crucial to women's economic emancipation (Engels, 1962: 233).

providence—a return to a state of barbarism in which the woman does the work while the man looks idly on' (reproduced in Hollis, 1979: 76).

This focus on the effect of women's employment on family life relies in part on patriarchal endorsements of women's 'natural' role as carers, but is also expressive of a concern—of Marx and Engels in particular—with the assault which early capitalism inflicted on the quality of working-class life. Both writers, for example, comment on the high rate of infant mortality, which Marx directly attributes to the employment of mothers away from the home '... and to the neglect and maltreatment consequent upon her absence' (Marx, 1983: 375). Marx appears to be identifying childcare as a social problem arising from the separation of home and work in early industrial capitalism. This suggests that protective legislation may at least in part be understood as an early 'family-friendly' policy, that is, as an attempt by the state and/or the working class to preserve the proper functioning of the reproductive sphere in the wake of a capitalist onslaught on its form and operation. Whether we conceive of this in Marx's terms, as an attempt to preserve a better quality of life fast being eroded by social and economic organisation, or, as has been posited by some feminists, for example, Walby, as an effort by working-class men to re-establish the patriarchal family form threatened by women's employment in factories,[26] in any case, the presence of a particular gendered conception of family life within early debates around protective legislation is undeniable.

By the end of the century, the focus had shifted to a broader emphasis on the *welfare* of women and children. This welfarist concern is one important reason why many women, for example, defended protective legislation in the early twentieth century (see eg, Hutchins and Harrison, 1926). However, like earlier emphases on family life, the basic underlying assumption of a welfarist approach was to justify restrictions on women's employment on the grounds of their biological and social functions as reproducers and rearers of children.

Thus, conceptions of gender, gender difference, and the relationship between work and family life were at the heart of debate and struggle over the regulation of factory working time. Moreover, this struggle created a space in which particular gendered norms of working time eventually emerged and crystallised in the form of the full-time male breadwinner earning a family wage. Moreover, within this time regime, while much of women's employment became subject to formal legal restrictions, men were able to craft for themselves, through collective bargaining arrangements, more beneficial working time norms, including the financial privileges

---

[26] Cf Humphries (1981), who argues against such an interpretation in the context of a detailed study of the Mines Regulation Act 1842.

attached to overtime and night work.[27] It was only in the second half of the twentieth century, when this (by then traditional) model of work came under threat in the wake of an increased industrial demand for labour market flexibility, that gendered legal norms of working time which had governed British workplaces for over a century became subject to serious critical reassessment.

The Deregulation of Working Time

Gender-specific protective legislation was abolished by the Sex Discrimination Act 1986. At that time, the legislation affected the hours of work of about 1.3 million women workers, approximately 45 per cent of the (then) female manual labour force.[28] Although presented as a gender equality measure, thus lending it an element of progressiveness, the removal of restrictions on women's hours of work corresponded with the active pursuit by the (then) Conservative Government of a programme of deregulation aimed at freeing the labour market from the 'rigidities' imposed by employment legislation and the 'restrictive practices' of trade unions.[29] Unsurprisingly, therefore, the strategy met with a mixed response. While the main employers' organisation, the Confederation of British Industry (CBI), welcomed the abolition of the legislation, the Trades Union Congress (TUC) advocated its retention. The Equal Opportunities Commission (EOC) had recommended abolition of the provisions in 1979 on the ground that they limited women's employment opportunities. Consequently, it welcomed repeal, although its approval was qualified because of reservations about the government's failure to ensure that affected workers were not unduly disadvantaged (EOC, 1979: chapters 3, 4, and 96). Meanwhile, the National

---

[27] Nor did these arrangements necessarily result in shorter working days for women. As Simon Deakin and Gillian Morris observe, 'women workers covered by the Acts frequently worked longer hours than men who had the protection of shop-floor or trade-level agreements setting a nine or nine and a half hour day' (1998: 308).

For an account of the collective regulation of working time in twentieth-century Britain, see Barnard *et al*, 2003: 227–28.

[28] And about 17% of the entire female workforce (Equal Opportunities Commission, 1979: 23).

[29] For a useful account of Conservative neoliberal policies during this period, see Deakin and Morris, 2001: 32–46. The stated aim in abolishing the Factories legislation was to get rid of 'unnecessary restrictions on women's hours of work' (Cmnd 9571, *Lifting the Burden* (July 1985, para 5.10)), a strategy which simultaneously purported to promote equal opportunities and minimise the burden of regulation on employers. However, Lord Wedderburn's comments at the time may be a better reflection of how the measure was perceived, eg as 'more concerned to relieve business of burdens than [to] proffer real social equality to women' (Wedderburn, 1986: 408).

Council of Civil Liberties, which had opposed the EOC Report when it was first published (Coussins, 1979), described the prospect of repeal as 'catastrophic', while, in the House of Commons, it was decried by the Opposition as a 'licence to exploit'.[30]

At the heart of debate over the abolition of the Factories legislation lurked a series of familiar tensions—between sameness and difference of treatment of men and women, between deregulation and social protection, and between middle-class and working-class concerns.[31] However, overriding all other considerations was a government determination to foster the economic, political and legal conditions in which flexible working practices could thrive. This entailed, inter alia, a movement away from a preoccupation with the standardisation of working time, characterised in nineteenth-century struggles over the length of the working day, towards the cultivation of more diverse working time norms within a broader climate of decollectivisation and casualisation of labour.

The pursuit of labour market flexibility may be viewed as a response to wider economic changes occurring at that time. These included greater market fluctuation, accelerated technological development, closer integration of domestic and world economies, and a change in the focus of production away from high-volume mass production to smaller, more differentiated products, prompting a process of labour market restructuring in most developed economies during the late twentieth century. In the United Kingdom, studies carried out in the 1980s already revealed the increasing utilisation by managers of 'non-standard' working practices, including part-time, temporary, agency, and self-employed arrangements (Atkinson, 1987; Hakim, 1987). This trend received particular attention in Atkinson's influential articulation of the 'flexible firm' as an emerging managerial strategy, with its division between 'core' and 'periphery' workers and its emphasis upon internal labour market flexibility (Atkinson, 1984).[32] Within this discursive context, working time emerged as central. The need for managerial strategies to raise levels of productivity in a more competitive, increasingly global economic environment characterised by fluctuating and insecure markets required, inter alia, numerical flexibility, that is, the enhanced ability of employers to adjust the number of workers and the times they worked as market conditions varied, and in particular to dispense with workers during slack periods and call upon them when demand intensified (Atkinson,

---

[30] See Legislative Assembly, *Hansard* (22 October 1986) at 1260.

[31] The feminist movement has often been divided along social class lines on the issue of protective factory legislation—see Banks, 1981: chapters 7 and 9.

[32] The extent to which Atkinson's flexible firm actually constituted a concrete strategy adopted by managers at the time has been contested (see eg Hunter *et al*, 1993). However, it is not disputed that the period in question witnessed a significant growth in flexible forms of employment.

1984). The legal removal of working time restrictions fell squarely within a policy agenda aimed at strengthening managerial freedom in this regard and was part of a broader Conservative attack on the level of social protection. Thus, during the same period, access to unfair dismissal protection was substantially restricted (with particularly dire consequences for the job security of workers who failed to correspond to the standard norm of full-time, long-term employment),[33] maternity rights were curtailed (Conaghan and Chudleigh, 1987), and wage protection mechanisms (in the form of Wages Councils governing the level of pay in particular low-paid sectors) were weakened, and eventually removed altogether.[34] In addition, as *Johnson* illustrates, the judiciary had already embarked on a path with regard to redundancy protection which limited the scope for workers legally to challenge unilaterally imposed changes in their working time. Allied with a substantial drop in unionisation and collective bargaining coverage, to which Conservative policies undoubtedly contributed (Brown *et al*, 1997), the end result was the almost total absence of any form of working time regulation in Britain from 1987 until the introduction of new Working Time Regulations in 1998[35] within a legal climate of declining social protection for workers engaged in non-standard working time arrangements.

How may we characterise the timed work regime that emerged in the wake of Conservative deregulation? First, this was a working time regime affirming unequivocally the prerogative power of management to determine working time, reflecting and reinforcing the stance taken by Lord Denning in *Johnson*. The primary policy emphasis was on the need for greater *employer* flexibility, not on flexibility for employees. Although the ideological backdrop to the Conservative political stance acknowledged the validity of employee choice, captured in an allegiance to freedom of contract as the preferred model of the employment relation, the practical effect of such deference to contract in the context of an (almost always) unequal bargaining

---

[33] The unfair dismissal provisions already included restrictions on the ability of part-time, fixed-term, and/or casual workers to access protection. By extending the qualifying period from six months to two years, the government successfully excluded a number of additional workers from the scope of protection. Needless to say, the distributive effects of such legal limitations were profoundly gendered, producing challenges to their legal validity in the 1990s (discussed below).

[34] See respectively the Wages Act 1986 and the Trade Union Reform and Employment Rights Act 1993.

[35] On the Working Time Regulations 1998, SI 1998/1833, and their legal progenitor, the EC Council Directive of 23 November 1993 concerning certain aspects of the organisation of working time, [1993] OJ L 307/18 (see below). Some vestiges of working time regulation remained after 1986. Controls on the working hours of young people were not removed until the Employment Act 1989. Legislation prohibiting the employment of children continued, as did controls on the employment of young people under school-leaving age. These are now governed by the EC Directive 94/33 of 22 June 1994 on the protection of young people at work and implementing Regulations (see below). In addition, the opening hours of shops, including substantial limits on Sunday opening, continued until the Sunday Trading Act 1994.

relationship was the unilateral power of employers to determine working time arrangements. In circumstances in which a substantial number of workers were legally beyond the scope of employment protection while simultaneously deprived of collective representation—whether by virtue of their lack of employment status[36] or because of the inhospitable legal and political climate for unions then prevailing—the net effect was the legal production of favourable conditions for the promotion of precarious work, that is, work characterised by non-standard working time arrangements accompanied by low levels of pay, increased job insecurity, and limited worker control.

It is tempting to view deregulation as a kind of return to the working time arrangements against which the Factory Acts were directed. However, while no doubt including shades of its nineteenth-century counterpart, the emergence in Britain of a flexible regime of working time is better understood in its own terms. According to Thompson's analysis, the primary task of early industrialists was to *discipline* workers by standardising working time, thus displacing the task-oriented and often highly irregular approach to labour which had characterised the pre-industrial period.[37] By contrast, the object of Conservative policy in the 1980s was not to standardise time norms but to weaken them, and to facilitate the adoption by managers of diverse arrangements according to their particular economic needs. This prompted a retreat from a standardised approach to the length and scheduling of the working day—during this period, the number of actual working hours substantially increased, especially among male workers, as did the number of unsocial hours worked (Rubery *et al*, 1998; see also Marsh, 1991)—but what characterises the period more particularly is greater dispersion of working hours, indicative of the erosion of 'standard' working time in favour of divergent working time arrangements (Rubery *et al*, 1998: 75–78).[38]

According to Jill Rubery *et al* (1998), this tendency towards dispersal in British working time norms is not necessarily identifiable in other European countries during the same period, and certainly not to the same extent. Highlighting significant differences in patterns of working time across countries, they suggest a correlation between particular working time norms and national regulatory regimes, with varying distributive effects.[39]

---

[36] See, in particular, here the notorious case of *O'Kelly v Trusthouse Forte plc*, [1983] IRLR 369, in which 'casual' workers, dismissed for trade union organising, failed to qualify for legal protection because they were held not to constitute employees.

[37] 'The work pattern was one of alternate bouts of intense labour and idleness wherever men were in control of their own working lives' (Thompson, 1991: 373).

[38] Rubery *et al* report that no standard or 'modal' category of working time can be detected for women in the United Kingdom, while for men, in so far as a modal category emerges, it is 50-plus hours per week (1998: 75).

[39] 'Regulation' here includes both norms derived from legislation and those that are the product of collective agreement.

Gerhard Bosch (1999) similarly associates divergent patterns of working time with the institutional and regulatory environment in which they operate, expressly linking working time trends in the United Kingdom with the pursuit of deregulatory policies. Bosch also asserts a relationship between increased income inequality and working time patterns manifest in particular in the prevalence of polarised working time arrangements (in which working hours tend either to be too short or too long).[40] This leads Bosch to conclude that 'policies of labour market deregulation ... lead[ing] to a widening of income inequalities are not compatible with strategies for work redistribution'. In other words, deregulation encouraged inequitable distributive outcomes including inequalities in the allocation of time.

Inevitably, such inequalities were strongly gendered.[41] In particular, women's continued prevalence in part-time work increasingly characterised by conditions of precariousness ensured their prominence within the ranks of the least well-off.[42] At the same time, the Conservative attack on maternity benefits—on entitlements to pay, leave, and dismissal protection for pregnant workers (Conaghan and Chudleigh, 1987)—not only placed substantial practical obstacles in the way of women workers seeking to combine work and family responsibilities, but was also illustrative of an ideological stance which viewed women's workforce participation as essentially subordinate to their primary role as homemakers. This added a further gendered element to the pursuit of policies actively producing precarious work. Because such work was regarded, to a significant extent, as women's work,[43] and because women's work in the labour market was widely understood as a mere supplement to their central role in the home, it was thought less necessary to endow that work with any of the features which might make it meaningful and rewarding. Simply put, women needed no rewards from

[40] A TUC study (2002) also highlights this as a distinct feature of British working time patterns.

[41] Although, interestingly, Bruegel and Perrons (1998) contend that the overall net effect of deregulation on gender inequality was neutral. They account for this in terms of a rise in the numbers of women entering higher paid occupations aligned with a decline in men's pay at the lower income levels. What most characterised women's employment during the period, Brueghel and Perrons conclude, was the increased diversity in women's experiences, although they confirm that the period saw a deterioration in the conditions in which non-standard forms of work (in which women predominate) were performed (1998: 113).

[42] In 1994, the proportion of women working part time in Britain was among the highest in Europe (59.9%). Moreover, a much larger number of part-time jobs in Britain were characterised by short (eg less than 20) working hours, and thus were much more likely to be characterised by poor working conditions and limited opportunities for advancement (Rubery *et al*, 1998: 81).

[43] Studies of the time suggest that the gendered character of non-standard work was to a considerable extent a product of employer perceptions of the labour supply. In particular, employers actively recruited women for part-time and temporary work, because they assumed men would find such arrangements less acceptable or thought they might get away with paying women less (Hunter *et al*, 1993: 394–403).

paid work. More specifically, as the bulk of women's time was properly consumed by their domestic duties, their *working* time required little in the way of close consideration.

This enabled the government to argue that deregulation was good for women. Thus, in proposing further restrictions on the right of part-time workers to access unfair dismissal protection, they claimed such measures would make part-time jobs more attractive to employers, thereby benefiting women workers.[44] This rationale for deregulation echoed a similar argument made by the EOC, when proposing the abolition of the Factories legislation in 1979, that the demise of gender-specific protective legislation would 'free' women to make more flexible working time arrangements and thus facilitate the accommodation of their work and family responsibilities (EOC, 1979: para 367). In both contexts, the deregulation of working time was presented as a positive strategy for promoting a better balance between productive and reproductive activities.

What is most striking here is the change in the configuration of gender, work, and time that the deregulatory agenda yielded. During the course of nineteenth-century struggles over working time, the need to carve out time for necessary reproductive activities became a crucial feature of the case for legal regulation. Yet, in the context of the Conservative pursuit of deregulation, the absence of working time regulation was said to effect a better reconciliation of work and family needs. In both contexts, however, there is a common thread, that is, the continued attribution of primary reproductive responsibility to women, along with a corresponding assumption that their labour market participation must necessarily be limited in ways that men's is not.

Viewed within the analytical framework articulated by Thompson, the picture of gender, work, and time emerging from a consideration of deregulation looks roughly as follows. While 'work' and 'life' remained conceptually separate, the working time norms supporting that separation began to dissolve, leading to a practical blurring of the boundaries between work and life particularly where women's work and family responsibilities came into conflict. In this context, a continued ideological deference to managerial authority with regard to working time determinations, accompanied by the crafting of a normative legal framework reinforcing that authority, contributed to a social and economic climate in which 'work' began to encroach upon 'life' in unforeseen ways, as both men and women scrambled to respond to the economic uncertainties and hardships that deregulation brought in it wake. This upset the delicate balance between reproductive

---

[44] Cmnd 9794, 1995, 'Building Business not Barriers', paras 7.6–7.11, proposing an increase in the hours threshold for part-time workers' access to unfair dismissal protection to 20 hours. Fortunately, the proposals were later shelved, in part because their gendered distributive effects threatened to bring them into conflict with EU sex equality law.

and productive activities which a standardised working time regime entrenched in a strongly gendered division of labour had effected. Within a context of limited female labour market activity, the retreat from standardisation might have been less problematic because reproductive work could have continued to be performed by women while men remained at the disposal of their employers' time needs. However, in circumstances where women's labour market activity had substantially increased and men's earnings were no longer sufficient to sustain a family, the changes in working time practices which the pursuit of flexibility produced did not serve the purpose of facilitating a functional balance between production and reproduction. Rather, they appeared to be set directly on course for collision.

The Reconstruction of Working Time Norms in the Context of Work–Life Policies

Deregulation flexibility, as it has been observed, was largely understood in the narrow terms of employers' efficiency needs. However, at the same time, a counter-discourse was emerging, one that highlighted the potential benefits of flexibility to workers—particularly those with family responsibilities—in terms of the possibilities it posed for enhancing worker choice of, and control over, working time arrangements. Early expressions of such a counter-discourse can be detected in reports published by the EOC (EOC, 1979; Marsh, 1991). The theme is also evident in Labour policy documents of the period, with its strongest articulation in the Labour Party Report of the Commission of Social Justice in 1994 (see also Hewitt, 1993). Meanwhile, in Europe, a growing focus on the need for measures to 'promote the reconciliation of work and family life' (Caracciolo di Torella, 2001; McGlynn, 2001), as well as health and safety concerns, evident in particular in debates about the regulation of working time,[45] worked to preclude the development of a narrow employer-based flexibility agenda at the European policy-making level, forcing some consideration of the wider benefits of flexibility to employers and workers alike.[46] With the election of a new Labour Government in Britain in 1997, the stage was set for a more expanded debate about what flexibility entailed and how best it might be achieved.

---

[45] See EC Council Directive 93/104 of 23 November 1993 concerning certain aspects of the organisation of working time, [1993] OJ L 307/18 (below), which was expressly adopted as a health and safety measure.

[46] Such a wider conception is evident in the European Employment Strategy first introduced in the Amsterdam Treaty 1997, which has as its goal the development of 'a co-ordinated strategy of employment and particularly for promoting a skilled, trained adaptable workforce and labour markets responsive to social change ...' (Treaty of Rome (as amended), Title VIII, Art 125). See further Ashiagbor, chapter 4 in this volume.

This shift in focus to the wider benefits of flexibility may be attributed to number of intersecting factors. Chief among them is the growth in women's workforce participation and, most strikingly, the increased employment of women with responsibilities for young children.[47] This, allied with a gender equality agenda highlighting the limits that traditional workplace arrangements place on workers with care responsibilities (Rittich, 2002a; Conaghan, 2002), has worked to create a strong case for more 'family-friendly' working arrangements in the form of flexible deviations from the standard full-time norm. Social policy and welfare concerns have also been a factor, in particular, the need to tackle unemployment. In this context, flexibility is viewed as a key route to job creation.[48] Flexibility is also attractive to policy-makers seeking to induce people off welfare benefits and into work, as 'diverse working arrangements' are believed to offer better opportunities for traditionally excluded groups, for example, lone parents, to engage in paid work activities.[49] In this way, flexibility can be linked to social justice and distributive goals through the pursuit of policies of social inclusion (Collins, 2003a).

Even in an economic context, the discursive emphasis has begun to shift away from a preoccupation with employer flexibility towards a wider conception of business flexibility which embraces the need to develop workers and to encourage them to take on new responsibilities and acquire new skills in order to raise productivity in a more competitive market environment (Commission of Social Justice, 1994: 160). This has led the Labour Government to ally flexibility with fairness:

> The keys to securing efficiency and fairness are employability and flexibility. Employability means ensuring that people are well prepared, trained and supported, both initially as they enter the labour market, and throughout their working lives. Flexibility means businesses being able to adapt quickly to changing demand, technology and competition. By enabling business success, flexibility promotes employment and prosperity.
>
> (Blair, 1998: para 2.13)

Thus, some accommodation of workers needs is now posited as necessary to enhance their adaptability and, ultimately, usefulness to employers (Collins, 2001).

All these factors have conspired to produce a new legislative and policy agenda aimed at reconstructing working time norms to embrace the wider benefits of flexibility and promote a better work–life balance for all (Collins, 2005). Much of the legislative impetus has been European-led,

---

[47] For details see DTI Green Paper 2000, *Work and Parents: Competitiveness and Choice*, Cm 5005 (London: Stationery Office), chapter 2.

[48] See Department of Work and Pensions, *UK Employment Action Plan 2003*, especially Guideline 3, paras 49–55.

[49] *Ibid*, paras 55 and 112.

although not all. In particular, the introduction of a National Minimum Wage in the United Kingdom in 1998 was a home-grown initiative which, in raising levels of pay at the lowest end, held out at least the promise of tackling the growing problem of long working hours which a low pay climate inevitably fostered.[50] At the same time, because of the strong European influence on policy development, the turn away from deregulation does not coincide neatly with the advent of a Labour Government in 1997. Throughout the Conservative period, European law inhibited the wholesale pursuit of deregulation, with sex equality principles in particular placing necessary brakes on the legislative erosion of employment rights. Matters came to a head in 1994 when the House of Lords concluded[51] that the existing limitations on part-time employees' access to unfair dismissal protection violated the government's obligations under Article 119 of the Treaty of Rome and the Equal Treatment Directive.[52] The decision forced the government reluctantly to remove limits on part-time workers' access to employment protection generally.[53] It also highlighted the potential of European law to enhance the rights of at least some non-standard workers. Shortly thereafter, a second legal challenge, also sex-based, was launched against the two-year qualifying period inhibiting access to unfair dismissal protection.[54] Although the case was eventually lost, it was not until after a new Labour Government had come in and reduced the qualifying period to one year as one of its earliest legislative initiatives.

Thus, even before Labour came to power, a process of reconstruction of working time regulation was already underway in the form of enhanced social protection for part-time employees. Similarly, the adoption of a new Pregnant Workers' Directive in 1992 forced the framework of meagre maternity provision to give way to a much more comprehensive set of entitlements, including expanded rights to maternity leave, pay and dismissal protection.[55]

---

[50] In fact, its impact in this respect has been minimal; for a general assessment of Labour's minimum wage legislation, see Simpson (2004).

[51] In *R v Secretary of State ex parte Equal Opportunities Commission* [1995] 1 AC 1 (*Equal Opportunities Commission*).

[52] EC Council Directive 76/207of 9 February 1996 on the implementation of the principle of equal treatment of men and women in employment [1976] OJ L 039/40.

[53] Employment Protection (Part-time Employees) Regulations 1995, SI 1995/31; although note that, as with most employment protection measures, the scope of protection remained confined to employees, as opposed to the broader category of 'workers' (see further Fredman, chapter 8 in this volume).

[54] The litigation was prolonged, involving, inter alia, a reference to the ECJ, after which it was eventually resolved in the government's favour: *R v Secretary of State ex parte Seymour-Smith and Perez (No 2)* [2000] IRLR 263.

[55] EC Council Directive 92/85 of 19 October 1992 on the introduction of measures to encourage improvements in the safety and health at work of pregnant workers and workers who have recently given birth or are breastfeeding [1992] OJ L 348/01 (implemented in the Trade Union and Employment Rights Act 1993). The Directive substantially enhanced the scope of maternity protection in the United Kingdom, although the position of British pregnant workers remained unfavourable in comparison to their European counterparts.

With the arrival of Labour, the pace of progress increased with a series of working time-related initiatives being enacted since 1997. Chief among these are provisions prescribing general limits on the working day and the working week, along with requirements for regular breaks and rest periods, including a four-week period of paid annual leave.[56] This new framework also regulates the employment of children and young people, essentially prohibiting the employment of children (defined as below school-leaving age or below the age of 15) and subjecting the employment of young persons (aged between 15 and 18) to more stringent limits with regard to the duration and organisation of their working time.[57] In addition, pregnancy-related leave provision has been substantially increased, as has the level and duration of maternity pay. More strikingly, entitlement to leave has expanded to include new rights to paternity and adoption leave, parental leave,[58] and limited short-term emergency leave for family reasons (for details, see Conaghan, 2002). In this way, the legislature has formally incorporated some consideration of reproductive needs into its current design of working time. Finally, the adoption of two additional European directives on part-time and fixed-term work[59] has required the introduction of a new legal framework placing limits on the ability of employers to subject part-time and fixed-term workers to less favourable terms and conditions of work.[60]

At first blush, this new raft of legislation looks like a pronounced move towards the (re)standardisation of working time, in particular in the laying down of legal limits on the duration and organisation of working time, as well as restrictions on the ability of employers to avoid the costs of social protection through the creation of non-standard working time arrangements. This return to some degree of working time standardisation might be viewed as a reasonable compromise between flexibility and security, between employer needs and worker interests. However, there are grounds

---

[56] Working Time Regulations 1998, SI 1998/1833, implementing EC Council Directive 93/104 of 23 November 1993 on aspects of the organisation of working time [1993] OJ L 307/18. The adoption of the Directive was staunchly resisted by the Conservatives, even to the point of (unsuccessfully) challenging its legal validity—*UK v Council of the European Union* [1997] IRLR 30—and was not finally implemented until after the Labour Government came to office.

[57] EC Council Directive 94/33 of 22 June 1994 on the protection of young people at work [1994] OJ L 216/12. For details of implementing regulations, see Deakin and Morris (2001: 316).

[58] See EC Council Directive 96/34 of 3 June 1996 on the framework agreement on parental leave [1996] OJ L 145/04, from which the UK regulations are derived.

[59] See EC Council Directive 97/81 of 15 December 1997 concerning the framework agreement on part-time work [1997] OJ L 014/09, and EC Council Directive 99/70 of 28 June 1999 concerning the framework agreement on fixed-term work [1999] OJ L 175/43. For an overview of family-friendly legislation at an EC level, see Caracciolo di Torella (2001).

[60] In fact, the provisions on fixed-term work apply only to 'employees' and are therefore very narrow in their coverage. Similar efforts to limit the scope of part-time protection were shelved during the consultation process. See further McColgan (2000b), and below.

for thinking that the balance struck is not as 'fair' as it seems and that, the articulation of legal standards notwithstanding, the continued trend is towards greater diversity of working time and continued inequalities in the scope and reach of legal protection.

In part this is a product of problems inherent in the structure and content of the relevant provisions. For example, the Working Time Regulations 1998 are hedged by limitations, exemptions, weak enforcement procedures, and an individual opt-out from the prescribed maximum of a 48-hour week. The consequence is a regulatory framework that is simply insufficiently robust to make any serious impact upon existing working time practices.[61] This legislative lack of teeth is in turn attributable to a concern to ensure that any efforts to prescribe standards do not unduly inhibit labour market flexibility, encouraging the eschewal of fixed rights in favour of 'softer' regulatory techniques which allow for some degree of alienability and modification through agreement (Collins, 2002).

A further problem lies in the construction of legal protection of part-time and fixed-term work. Here, the relevant provisions,[62] both at a European and national level, adopt an equal treatment model, purporting to prohibit less favourable treatment of non-standard workers than of their 'comparable' (full-time or permanent) counterparts.[63] As much of the work carried out on a part-time or fixed-term basis does not readily compare with full-time or long-term work, the principle of equal treatment effectively limits the scope of protection to job packages that conform most closely to the 'standard', full-time, permanent model of employment. In this way, a male norm of working time, albeit dissolving on the ground, continues to be the benchmark against which women's work is measured (see Vosko, chapter 3 in this volume).

A final problem with the working time regime now emerging in Britain is the absence of a sufficient collective presence in the crafting of working time norms. Although most of the relevant legislation makes provision for collectively agreed arrangements to take precedence over norms which are statutorily prescribed,[64] the absence of a sound infrastructure for collective

---

[61] The TUC reports that working time regulation has only reduced the number of workers working long hours by 3%, leaving the United Kingdom with 'an entrenched long hours culture with an incidence of long hours working that is twice the EU average' (TUC, 2003: 2). This has led them to campaign for the removal of the individual opt-out currently under review.

[62] Above n 59.

[63] Note that the prohibition of less favourable treatment is subject to an employer claim of business justification.

[64] For example, the Maternity and Parental Leave etc Regulations 1999, SI 1999/3312, leave much of the application of the law to workplace- or enterprise-level agreements between employers and employees with the provision of a default position in the absence of agreement. This is in line with the genesis of the parent directive as a product of European social dialogue.

bargaining in post-Thatcher Britain means that in practice only a minority of workplaces are governed by collectively agreed working time arrangements (Barnard *et al*, 2003: 243–45). As it is clear from cross-country studies (eg Rubery *et al*, 1998; Berg *et al*, 2004) that a strong collective framework tends to produce more equitable working time regimes, the lack of a significant collective dimension to the current process of working time reconstruction is a telling indicator of the likely limits of that process in terms of the possibilities it presents to challenge working time arrangements that are productive of precarious work.

It is within this general context of a lack of correspondence between the rhetoric of reconstruction and the reality of a deregulated system of working time whose 'familiar features ... remain largely intact' (Barnard *et al*, 2003: 228) that we come to consider the Labour Government's most recent legislative initiative. New regulations on flexible working purport to address directly the vexed problem of how workers can turn flexibility to their own ends, by conferring a right on employees to request contractual variations—including, most centrally, variations in working hours—for reasons related to childcare.[65] In fact, through the creative application of sex equality law, a refusal to accommodate a request to access flexible work could already constitute a colourable legal claim of indirect sex discrimination.[66] However, the scope of protection here was haphazard and depended on statistical showings of gendered disparate impact and the absence of a judicial finding of employer justification. This produced complexity and inconsistent outcomes. Moreover, it confined coverage in practical terms to applications made by women. A call from equal rights campaigners for more robust and gender-neutral provision of access to flexible work for parents combined with exhortations at a European level that employers be encouraged to give full consideration to requests by workers to transfer from full-time to part-time work[67] to place increasing pressure on the Labour Government to act, and, after fairly extensive consultation over a limited range of options (Anderson, 2003: 37–38), a new, essentially procedural, right to request flexible working has been introduced.

---

[65] Employment Act 2002, s 47, amending the ERA 1996 by the insertion of Part 8A. See also the Flexible Working (Procedural Requirements) Regulations 2002, SI 2002/3207, and the Flexible Working (Eligibility, Complaints and Remedies) Regulations 2002, SI 2002/3236. The scope of the regulations is very closely delineated. In particular, they apply only to employees with six months' continuous employment and in relation to the care of children under six for whom they have responsibility. Most crucially, they confer only the right to request a contractual variation, with a corresponding duty on employers to consider the request and refuse it only on the basis of one or more listed grounds. The reasonableness of an employer's decision to base the refusal on a particular listed ground is not tested. See further Anderson (2003).

[66] See *Home Office v Holmes* [1984] IRLR 299, and *Edwards*, above n 13.

[67] See, in particular, the Part-Time Workers Directive, reg 5(3).

It is difficult at this early stage to gauge the likely impact of this new enactment on working time norms. Many commentators are rightly sceptical as to whether any positive benefits for workers have been conferred, given the narrowness of the provision's scope and coverage and its largely procedural content. Lucy Anderson characterises it as 'soundbite' legislation which 'will not provide harassed parents with any real additional rights to challenge unsympathetic managers' (2003: 41–42). By contrast, Hugh Collins characterises the new 'right to flexibility' as introducing 'a seismic shift' in key elements of the contract of employment, the beginning of a transformation in the legal construction of the employment relation (Collins, 2005). For Collins, the radical character of the new provisions lie not in their detail but in the challenge they pose, at least potentially, to the underlying assumption pervading the legal construction of the employment relation that employers should unilaterally determine the content of job packages according to their assessments of the imperatives of productive efficiency. In this sense, he is claiming that the relationship between work and life is changing; in particular, that our understandings of and aspirations for work are increasingly being informed by the need to preserve adequate time for 'life' activities.

But is this really so novel? Surely a functional balance between work and life has always been necessary. What is changing is the way in which it is being achieved. In the past, the operation of a male breadwinner/female caregiver model of work allocation relied upon and reinforced a regime of working time in which 'life' was presumed to carry on elsewhere. The collapse of that model has required a reconfiguration of the relationship between work and time in which gender considerations have come to the fore. In this context it is pertinent to ask questions about the gendered distributive outcomes that may result. As things stand, there is little evidence to suggest that more equitable gendered arrangements are emerging. Many women continue to adopt patterns of work that diverge from the traditional full-time norm, enabling them to combine paid work with unpaid care work at home and in the community.[68] Much of this work remains characterised by poor pay and conditions and job insecurity and may properly be described as precarious[69] thus ensuring that women remain at least in part

---

[68] For example, women continue to comprise the bulk of part-time workers in Britain. Moreover, of women workers, the proportion in part-time employment remains high at 44% (cf 10% of male workers). There is too strong a correlation between motherhood and part-time work, with 67% of employed women with children under school age working part time as opposed to 50% of women with children of secondary school age; the figure drops to 33% where there are no dependent children (EOC, 2004). There is no discernible statistical relationship between fatherhood and part-time work.

[69] The wide pay gap (40%) between the average hourly rate of part-time women workers and the average hourly rate of full-time male workers remains a key factor in the overall gender pay gap (EOC, 2004: 8). For a summary of the various ways in which women's work in Britain exhibits features of precariousness, see Fredman, chapter 8 in this volume.

dependent on men's income (Fudge and Owens, chapter 1 in this volume). At the same time, many men are working long hours and are having to adapt to a new time regime in which 'full-time work' (with its implicit promise of additional compensation for overtime and/or anti-social hours) is giving way to an expectation of infinite compliance with an employer's time demands.[70] This suggests that the broad picture is not one in which any greater gender equity in the allocation of work or time is detectable. It seems, rather, that gender roles are becoming further entrenched in productive needs. In particular, to facilitate the continuance of a timed work regime, women are having to carry a double burden of paid and unpaid work[71] in circumstances where men, by virtue of substantial increases in their working time, are less able to assume a more equal share of domestic work.

The question is: is such reliance on gender inequality necessary to the preservation of a timed work regime or can we still carve out models of working time which are more equitable?

CONCLUSION

Deborah Figart and Ellen Mutari (2000) propose a typology of working time regimes and rate them according to whether they effect 'high' or 'low' gender equity outcomes. They identify four models of working time: the male breadwinner model, liberal flexibilisation, high-road flexibilisation, and what they describe as a 'solidaristic gender equity model'. The first model corresponds to the timed work regime which emerged in Britain under the application of the Factory Acts. Figart and Mutari unsurprisingly rate this as low in terms of its gendered equitable outcomes. The second, liberal flexibilisation, corresponds with the deregulatory approach characterised by 1980s and 1990s Conservatism. It is also classified as low. The third model, high-road flexibilisation, is one 'which provides workers as well as employers with control over work schedule and input into the production process' (Figart and Mutari, 2000: 854) and is one which holds the promise of delivering high gender equity outcomes. The model of timed work emerging under new Labour might be said to correspond to the high road in some aspects, but weaknesses in the regulatory regime appear to be

---

[70] For a detailed report on long working hours in Britain, see TUC (2002). Although four times as many men as women work long hours (48 plus hours per week), the number of women, especially professional women (eg teachers) working long hours, is steadily increasing.

[71] The increase in single-parent families (currently around 25% of UK families), nine out of 10 of which are headed by women, further adds to the double burden carried by many working women.

resulting in working time arrangements which are not dissimilar from those of liberal flexibilisation. The final model, solidaristic gender equity, is one in which men and women are equally distributed among the possible schedule of working hours. Correspondingly, their share of unpaid work is likely to be evenly spread, resulting in a high gender equity outcome.

Figart and Mutari argue that the best route to solidaristic gender equity is an overall reduction in working hours in the form of a shorter working week for all.[72] The argument that a shorter working week will enhance gender equity has been made by others, including, for example, Schulz and Hoffman in chapter 6 of this volume, and it is a highly persuasive one. As things stand, this is not the direction Britain is currently taking, although a concern to shorten working hours is clearly on the agenda of the British trade union movement (TUC, 2003). However, it may be that in current circumstances the model of high-road flexibilisation offers more possibilities for improving gender equity in a British working time context, particularly because, in form at least, it does attempt to marry the economic benefits of flexibility with workers' interests. And it is unclear that flexibility as a labour market strategy can realistically be eschewed in the current economic and political context.

What is clear is that, in the pursuit of flexibility, law must serve a dual purpose of facilitating more flexible forms of work while accommodating the needs of flexible workers, many of whom have care responsibilities. These two purposes are in tension because the encroachment of unpaid care responsibilities upon the domain of work threatens the timed work paradigm. Thus, law must mediate carefully between the need for flexibility on the one hand and considerations of family life on the other. Within the framework of these competing demands, there is room for variations in outcome. While the overall structure of work and family may remain broadly the same, differences in the detail of working time regulation may have substantial gendered distributive consequences. Moreover, and perhaps more radically, the tension between flexibility and family which law is called upon to mediate does at least throw open to question the assumption—articulated so confidently by Lord Denning in *Johnson*—that employers are entitled to reorganise working time without taking account of workers' personal needs. It is arguable that this assumption does not fit a flexible timed work regime in which employers and workers must to some extent *plan together* to ensure that the boundaries of work and life remain clearly and

[72] Figart and Mutari suggest that four European work time regimes exhibit characteristics of solidaristic gender equity, namely Denmark, France, Belgium, and Switzerland. They identify the United Kingdom as 'the clearest personification of liberal flexibilisation'. The Netherlands they identify as a 'transitional work time regime' which cannot be neatly characterised, concluding 'no country has as yet blazed as path which could be called high road flexibilisation'.

unambiguously delineated. It is in this sense that Collins is right when he recognises the radical character of recent developments. However, my fear is that, as a model for which to strive, high-road flexibilisation, is at best elusive and at worst illusory. And it is surely not the safest or most straightforward path to greater gender equity in the allocation of work and time. It may be that we remain some distance away from a world in which work and life easily intermingle and we can once again experience time's unpurposive passing. We are still without a time to dream.

6

The Need for a Reduced Workweek in the United States

VICKI SCHULTZ AND ALLISON HOFFMAN

INTRODUCTION

FIFTY YEARS FROM now, what kind of lives will women and men in the United States and other advanced industrial societies lead? Will women still do more of the work of raising the children and running the household, unable to pursue paid work on equal terms, while men devote themselves to their jobs, unable to participate fully in family life? Will people continue to face problems of overwork and underwork, with the highest earners putting in Herculean hours at their jobs, while the lowest earners work at less-than-full-time, even temporary, jobs that do not pay enough to make ends meet? Or, will we find ways to ensure that all workers, particularly women, can change this pattern and have the time and resources needed to combine working at decent jobs, caring for themselves and their loved ones, and participating meaningfully in civic life?

In the United States, as elsewhere, increased globalisation has ushered in a new paradigm of production and work—one in which many employers demand 'flexible' workers whose jobs and hours can be altered easily in order to match rapidly changing production demands. This shift has created new vulnerabilities that our eroding system of worker and welfare state protections is not equipped to address. Our regulatory system presumes that most families have a full-time (typically male) breadwinner and a supportive, near full-time (typically female) caregiver (Kessler-Harris, 2001). This image no longer fits reality. In today's economy, most men are not sole breadwinners; few jobs provide a family wage or promise the long-term security or generous benefits needed to fulfil such a role. Nor do most women now specialise in family care alone; the great majority of families with children now include a mother who works for pay, either as a dual earner or as a single head of household (Kalleberg *et al*, 1997; Jacobs and Gerson, 2004). Just as women have come to depend more on paid work, the protections traditionally accorded employment have eroded. A growing number of men and women now occupy what is sometimes called 'contingent' or 'precarious' employment—meaning jobs that are characterised by less security (Stone, 2003), shorter hours, less regular schedules, lower wages, less union support, weaker pension or health care benefits, and fewer opportunities for voice and community than previous breadwinner jobs (Kalleberg *et al*, 1997; Lester, 1998; Fudge and Owens, chapter 1 in this volume). In the United States, as elsewhere, women are disproportionately employed in such precarious work, especially in the least remunerative, least secure forms (Kalleberg *et al*, 1997; Lester, 1998). But many men have also lost security and real wages, as men's employment patterns have come to resemble women's (Schultz, 2000). Unfortunately, the social supports that might alleviate these new insecurities have not materialised, but have actually diminished as traditional welfare state protections have weakened. As the family wage has all but disappeared and the government has withdrawn support for raising families, the burden of providing sustenance and care has fallen more than ever on individual Americans—all too often, on women, who continue to provide the lion's share of unpaid family labour. In a real sense, women are bearing disproportionate costs of the new economy.

Some of the same factors that have led to a rise in precarious employment are causing new stresses around working time. Over the past few decades, as employers have sought greater flexibility in the deployment of workers, many Americans have moved away from the 40-hour workweek (Schor, 1991; Jacobs and Gerson, 2004). At one extreme, with the rise of precarious employment, many employees now face a problem of underwork, with growing numbers working fewer than 30 hours per week at paid jobs (Bell, 1998; Jacobs and Gerson, 2004), even though almost half of them want or need to work more hours (Tilly, 1996, citing Shank, 1986). At the other extreme, growing numbers of employees now experience overwork, often working more than 50 hours a week. These patterns create gender- and race-based inequalities, as well as broader class-based vulnerabilities. The long hours associated with the higher-paying, white-collar jobs disproportionately held by college-educated men often conflict with family caretaking and other important commitments, while the lower wages and opportunity sets associated with the low-hours, contingent jobs disproportionately held by women, racial minorities, and the unskilled create short- and long-term economic insecurities that also threaten family life and individual well-being.

The policy interventions made at this juncture will shape people's lives, and their available choices, for years to come. In contrast to dominant US legal feminist approaches, which define the problem as one of work–family conflict and seek reforms that will take account of women's caretaking responsibilities, we argue that, in order to alleviate time stresses and address the related problems of overwork and underwork in ways that make genuine equality for women possible, feminists must call for broader measures to reduce and reorganise working time for everyone. Perhaps paradoxically, our analysis reveals, equality for women can best be achieved through universal measures that benefit all workers.

FEMINIST APPROACHES TO WORKING TIME IN THE UNITED STATES

Dominant Legal Feminist Approaches

American feminists have long been concerned with working time. In the past, feminists attributed economic disparities between men and women primarily to women's inferior position in the labour force. Feminists sought to promote equality by eliminating various forms of employment discrimination that denied women equal access to paid work, including higher-paying, full-time breadwinner positions that had historically been reserved for men (Hartmann, 1976; Bergmann, 1986). Over the past decade, many feminists have shifted away from the earlier focus on sex segregation and have begun to attribute remaining gender-based economic disparities to women's disproportionate responsibilities for family caretaking.

In the US legal feminist literature, two basic approaches have emerged: a 'compensation' approach that seeks to fund and increase the time available for women's family caretaking *outside* the workplace and an 'accommodation' approach that advocates workplace reforms that will accommodate family caretaking roles *inside* it. Both approaches assume that women will continue to do most of the unpaid family caretaking and urge mechanisms to eliminate the costs and burdens associated with it.

The first approach aims to provide economic security for women by increasing the economic value of their unpaid family labour. Some scholars promote private family law-based 'joint property' solutions (see Siegel, 1994), which require husbands to share more of the income and assets made possible by their wives' family labour. Joint property advocates have proposed a number of solutions, including giving married mothers a greater portion of their husbands' ongoing income, for a longer period, after divorce (Williams, 2000b), and treating a homemaker's non-monetary contributions on a par with a spouse's monetary contributions in premarital contract cases (Silbaugh, 1998). Moving away from such private law solutions, other feminists have called for greater public subsidies to support care work. Law professor Martha Fineman, one of the earliest and most powerful advocates for this position, emphasises the 'inevitable dependency' experienced by mothers and calls for broad-ranging subsidies to support those who have primary care of children (1995). Anne Alstott proposes that primary caretakers receive an annual grant to spend on child care, self-education, or retirement savings—all enabling greater lifetime security (2004).

Writers in this tradition reject an emphasis on paid work and stress that women should have the choice to perform childcare on a full-time or near full-time basis if they so desire (Zatz, 2004).

The accommodation approach, by contrast, assumes that, even though women will continue to be the primary family caretakers, most will also spend time working for pay. As a result, advocates call for reforms to make the workplace more 'family friendly' by accommodating women's caretaking responsibilities. For example, some writers urge the use of employment discrimination law to attack practices, such as requiring long hours or providing inadequate leaves, that are said to have a disparate impact on women as primary caregivers (see Kelly, 2003; Travis, 2003; Williams, 2003). Proposed reforms include creating more and better part-time options, more flexible work schedules, and more generous family leave, all of which restructure caregivers' working time in an attempt to alleviate their 'time crunch' at work (Williams, 2000b; Kelly, 2003; Glass, 2004). Some feminists even speculate that the rise of part-time and other non-standard forms of employment could ultimately prove beneficial to caregivers by undermining traditional breadwinner norms (Pateman, 1988).

Problems with the Dominant Approaches

Many of these proposals could, in the short-term, alleviate problems people face in obtaining resources for caretaking or balancing it with paid work. Yet, ultimately, by focusing so narrowly on caretaking issues, the dominant feminist strategies fail to address the broader socioeconomic and quality of life problems that the current crises around working hours poses. Most proposals risk reproducing existing gender, class, and racial hierarchies rather than seizing the opportunity to address and deal with structural inequalities in a more comprehensive, and equality-enhancing, way.

By tying compensation for caretaking to a spouse's income, for example, joint property proposals presume and perpetuate a middle-class, married family structure in which one spouse (typically, the husband) earns enough to support the other's caretaking activities. But, given that in most couples women earn lower wages than men, increasing intra-couple compensation for caretaking only increases the incentive for women to invest in caretaking and their spouses' careers at the expense of their own—a trade-off that can lower their labour force attachment, earnings capacity, and economic security in the long run. Not only do these trade-offs potentially harm the women who make them; they harm all working women, by lending credence to employers' stereotypes about women's lack of career commitment that foster statistical discrimination (Mahoney, 1995). In fact, as feminists of colour have noted, focusing on the situation of middle-class wives and mothers who care for their own families neglects the plight of the many low-wage workers who care for other people's families, while struggling to provide for their own (Romero, 1999; Smith, 1999). Furthermore, joint property proposals would do nothing to help those who care for their own loved ones outside marriage, including a larger share of men and women of colour (who are less likely to marry), gays and lesbians (the legality of whose marriages remains uncertain), and single parents (Schultz, 2000).

Although public subsidies for caretaking alleviate some of the biases in joint property proposals, most schemes still encourage women to invest more heavily in caretaking at the expense of developing their own job skills, while still failing to deliver adequate funding for intensive caretaking. Scholars have shown that, as important as it is to spread the cost of family caretaking more equally throughout society, proposals to pay people to invest primarily in care work for long periods can reinforce the gendered division of labour, hurting both women and men in the long run (Bergmann, 1996; Fraser, 1997; Lester, 2005). Caretakers are left to rely on a second wage earner, or on part-time or other precarious forms of paid work that they can combine easily with caretaking, which in turn increases pressure on their partners to work longer hours. Thus, the compensation approach seems likely to reproduce existing inequities.

The accommodation approach at first seems more promising because, at least theoretically, it could lead to reforms that would enable men and women alike to combine paid work with caretaking. Yet, in practice, such proposals can reproduce traditional arrangements. For example, using disparate impact lawsuits to obtain accommodation reforms requires claiming that women are less likely to be able to comply with standard work requirements. Furthermore, the proposed reforms, such as more and better part-time work options, would segregate women into separate 'career-primary tracks' and 'family-and-career tracks' (Schwartz, 1989), rather than incorporate them as full equals into workplaces that provide all employees more time for outside commitments. Without reforms to address the larger structural problems underlying the 'time crunch', work–life balance remains an individual problem, requiring difficult trade-offs between meaningful participation in market work and sufficient time for family, community, and leisure.

Ultimately, many legal feminists in the United States have missed the opportunity to address the broader problems posed by the new economy, including rising insecurity, unpredictable work schedules, decreased benefits, and serious problems of both overwork and underwork. Resolving work–family conflict and providing adequate resources for caretaking must be addressed in this larger context. Feminist solutions that encourage part-time or flexible work for women, in isolation, risk exacerbating current disparities in which well-educated, white men hold higher-paying, more mobility-enhancing positions, and women and minorities occupy more precarious jobs. Such solutions also neglect the gender-based burdens placed on higher earners (typically, men) who feel pressure to support intensive caretaking by their spouses or partners. To enable their partners to stay at home or to work part time, many men must work overly long hours in ways that may compromise their health or their relationships with their children. There is a need for newer approaches that treat work–family conflict as part of a larger set of issues confronting workers and citizens, both men and women, in the twenty-first century.

The Need for a More Transformative Approach

By combining redistributive policies with more imaginative gender politics, newer feminist initiatives seek to chart a future in which both men and women have more freedom to lead lives that combine paid work, intimate care, and civic involvement in more empowering ways (Bergmann and Hartmann, 1995; Fraser, 1997; White, 2001; Young, 2003; Lester, 2005). Barbara Bergmann, for example, has criticised traditional welfare programmes in the United States for penalising poor women's involvement in paid work. She advocates creating a publicly funded system of high-quality, universal child care such as that provided in France, supplemented by other benefits such as health care and rent vouchers (Bergmann and Hartmann, 1995) to assist poor working parents. Along similar lines, Lucie White argues that funding diverse forms of child care will facilitate poor people's employment without forcing them into low-wage jobs on employers' terms (2001). Gillian Lester offers a carefully crafted proposal for paid family leave that will allow both mothers and fathers to make lasting commitments to their careers, while minimising the potential for women to harm their long-term career-building prospects (2005). Other feminists have advocated broader workplace reforms, including stronger disability protections and personal sabbaticals for workers to minimise backlash against women and parents and to facilitate better work–life balance for everyone (Schultz, 2000; Young, 2000). Many feminists have also agreed on the need for earnings subsidies or other basic income supports to ensure that people have sufficient economic resources to avoid both poverty and overwork (Bergmann and Hartmann, 1995; White, 2001; Young, 2003).

More recently, feminists have begun to recognise that current problems cannot be resolved without addressing the issue of working time itself (Schor, 1991, 1994; Jacobs and Gerson, 2004). A society in which large numbers of people feel pressured to work overly long hours at the expense of their families and communities, while other people are limited to low-hours, sub-standard jobs that offer no prospect of mobility, is an inherently divided and unequal society.

THE NEED FOR A REDUCED WORKWEEK

Workweek Trends and Preferences in the United States

Over the past 30 years, as stated above, Americans have moved away from a 40-hour workweek. Some older literature portrayed this trend as an increase in working time for most Americans (Schor, 1991; Hochschild, 1997). But newer work by Jerry Jacobs and Kathleen Gerson disaggregates averages of hours worked to reveal that the real story of working time in the United States is its increasing dispersion, moving away from the 40-hour norm to higher incidence of both longer *and* shorter weeks (Jacobs and Gerson, 2004).

In the United States, in particular, the rise in women's employment and in the hours worked by women, with no countervailing decrease in hours worked by men, has created a 'time crunch' (Jacobs and Gerson, 2004). Compared to nine other countries with a similar level of economic and social development, the United States has the highest average working week for women (37.4 hours), and also the highest percentage of women (11.3 per cent) and men (26.8 per cent) who work over 50 hours per week. Because both men and women work slightly more hours in the United States than in most other countries, American couples put in the most combined time at work as well. The typical American couple with at least one employed spouse works 72.3 hours per week, compared to 57.4 in the United Kingdom and even less in the Netherlands. Dual earner couples, the fastest growing household type, in the United States work a combined average of 81.2 hours per week, longer than their dual earner counterparts in other countries; the United States also has the highest proportion of couples working over 80 and over 100 hours per week (Jacobs and Gerson, 2004).

Contrary to popular explanations, these increases are not attributable to Americans' penchant for overwork. Most Americans, men as well as women, regardless of marital and parental status, say they would like to work less and devote more time to personal and family care (Jacobs and Gerson, 2004). Some people even report being willing to trade wages for reduced working time (Jacobs and Gerson, 2004). At the other end of the spectrum, around 20 per cent of Americans would like to work more, reflecting a coordinate problem of underwork (Jacobs and Gerson, 2004). Evidence suggests that this phenomenon may be magnified for African-American workers, who experience higher unemployment and underemployment, and more often express the need for additional hours of work (Bell, 1998).

While the majority of Americans would like to work less, most feel they cannot afford to do so or that their employers would not allow it. In general, survey data show that workers perceive a trade-off between their use of family-friendly policies and their own advancement, and recent empirical work suggests this perceived trade-off may be grounded in reality

(Drago *et al*, 2001; Glass, 2004; Jacobs and Gerson, 2004). Women in the United States may be particularly reluctant to risk sacrificing hard-won career advances by using gender-stigmatising forms of family-friendly policies. For example, a study at Pennsylvania State University revealed that faculty members utilised family-friendly policies at very low rates, probably out of a fear that they would be marginalised or discriminated against for doing so (Drago *et al*, 2001: 40, 46). Such fears may be realistic. For example, studies show that US companies with the most family-friendly policies are not those with the best records for promoting women (Dobrzynski, 1996). Moreover, a recent study suggests that actually using such policies results in negative wage growth for women over time (Glass, 2004). In particular, months worked at home and months of part-time work hours show significant negative effects on wage growth for women who remained working for the same employer, suggesting that employers may stereotype workers who use family-friendly policies (Glass, 2004).

Survey evidence shows most Americans do not want part-time work because they perceive that such work would harm both their short-term economic well-being and their long-term career-building prospects (Jacobs and Gerson, 2004). In some countries, including the Netherlands and Sweden, family-friendly policies have been purchased at the expense of US versions of equality; women in these countries are more likely to work in part-time jobs as a way of accommodating family responsibilities. Despite shorter average workweeks, the workforce in these countries is more highly gender-segregated than in the United States (Jacobs and Gerson, 2004). Thus, feminist strategies to promote part-time work as a way to alleviate work–family conflict may risk compromising more comprehensive versions of equality by limiting women's opportunities in the workplace.

American workers state a preference, not for part-time work, but rather for the ability to set their own hours, to work from home, and to have the benefit of employer-sponsored or funded child care (Jacobs and Gerson, 2004). Such preferences correspond to social support policies that have enabled greater gender equality in other countries. In the countries studied by Jacobs and Gerson (2004), for example, a greater public investment in child care was associated with a more gender-egalitarian distribution of working time between mothers and fathers. Thus, evidence suggests that policies such as subsidised child care and greater employee control over scheduling may both be preferred by American workers, and more conducive to gender equity in workforce participation.

The Advantages of a Reduced Workweek (and Related Reforms)

Reforms to US overtime and benefits law are required to eliminate the current incentives for employers to utilise employees for overly long, and overly short, hours. At one extreme, managerial and professional salaried workers are exempt from receiving overtime wage premiums (time and a half) mandated for most other employees under the Fair Labor Standards Act (FLSA),[1] the law setting a 40-hour workweek standard. This exemption, plus the fixed costs of benefits for managerial and professional employees, sets up incentives for employers to utilise them for longer hours, rather than incur the costs of additional wages and benefits that would be entailed by hiring more employees to do the work. Indeed, while comprising one-third of the workforce, such workers constitute nearly 50 per cent of the workers who work 50 or more hours a week (Jacobs and Gerson, 2004). At the other extreme, the Employee Retirement Income Security Act (ERISA)[2] regulates private employer benefit plans but does not mandate them. As a matter of custom, most employers in the United States voluntarily offer benefits such as health care and pension coverage only to regular full-time employees, and not to part-time, temporary, or contract workers (Langbein and Wolk, 2000)—a pattern that creates strong incentives for employers to create these more precarious forms of work in order to avoid paying benefits. Particularly in light of the rising costs of benefits, the ERISA and the FLSA create incentives for employers to achieve flexibility in their workforces by resorting to overtime and contingent work, even in the absence of genuine market efficiencies for such patterns.

In order to avoid the extremes of overwork and underwork, some scholars have called for eliminating the FLSA exemption for managerial and professional employees and requiring employers to pay pro-rata benefits to all who work for them, regardless of their employment status, proportional to the number of hours they work (Jacobs and Gerson, 2004). Under such an approach, someone who worked 20 hours a week would receive one-half the usual benefits, despite not being a regular 'full-time' employee. At the other extreme, someone who worked 80 hours a week would receive double the employer's usual contribution to benefits—just as if the employer had actually hired a second full-time employee. These measures would remove the current incentives to overutilise existing employees and contingent workers as a way to avoid paying for additional benefits.

Even apart from the extremes, however, the traditional 40-hour workweek is overly burdensome for many people, including the dual-earner and single-parent households that have become the new American norm. Reducing the standard workweek would decrease the stress on all workers, provide a foundation for greater equality in working time between spouses or partners, and create a more level playing-field for single parents who are balancing wage-earning and family responsibilities.

---

[1] Fair Labor Standards Act of 1938, 29 USC § 201 *et seq* (2004). The executive exemption can be found at 29 USC § 213 (2004).

[2] Employee Retirement Income Security Act of 1974, 29 USC § 1001 *et seq* (2004).

More moderate workweeks are associated with greater gender equality in a number of countries. In seven out of 10 countries studied by Jacobs and Gerson, more moderate household workweeks—those in which married couples' combined work hours averaged in the 60–79 and 80–99 ranges— were associated with greater equality in working time between husbands and wives (Jacobs and Gerson, 2004). Greater equality in time spent at work creates the potential for a more equitable division of time spent on family caretaking, as well. Wives who have more equal work hours and earnings to their husbands enjoy more economic and social independence, which in turn can give them greater bargaining power to demand more equitable division of household responsibilities (see Mahoney, 1995; Deutsch, 1999; sources cited in Schultz, 2000). Simultaneously, men with more moderate working hours, and less demand on their time by employers, have a greater capacity to spend more time on childcare and household work (Mahoney, 1995). Thus, it is not surprising that studies show that families with more egalitarian distribution of household labour are those in which both spouses have more similar working hours (Coltrane, 1996; Deutsch, 1999). A shorter workweek would also allow single parents to create communal child care or other options, by arranging care with friends, neighbours, and relatives.

Adopting a universal approach that aims to bring the workweek towards 35 hours for *everyone* would also free women and parents from the stigma and disproportionate costs associated with more targeted policies. Employer mandates, when narrowly designed, can result in the employer passing off costs onto the group that is intended to benefit from the mandate, either in the form of reduced employment or wages (Summers, 1989; Jolls, 2000; Lester, 2005). Creating a new universal reduced workweek norm would allow all employees to share in the costs and benefits, and would simplify the process of finding ways for government to redistribute some costs among taxpayers in general (discussed further below).

For all of these reasons, we believe feminists in the United States should join with other concerned groups to advocate a coordinated series of steps designed to achieve a more moderate, more controllable workweek norm as the foundation for a restructured regime of working time. Our programmatic vision of the changes necessary to achieve a more equitable organisation of working time would include:

- reducing the standard workweek from 40 to 35 hours for *all* employees;
- mandating pro-rata benefits for all who work for an employer, tied to the number of hours they work, to reduce artificial incentives for employers to use workers for overly long or overly short hours (alternatively, detaching important benefits, such as basic health care and adequate pensions, from employment and providing them to all citizens as a matter of right);

- eliminating the executive exemption for overtime, to reduce artificial incentives for employers to require long working hours for managerial and professional employees;
- providing reasonable, but not overly long, paid family leave and personal sabbaticals to protect jobs for employees who must care for loved ones or meet other important personal commitments;
- adopting strong anti-discrimination measures to ensure that those who take advantage of reduced hours are not discriminated against for doing so; and
- providing earnings subsidies or other basic income supports to allow low-earners to work a shorter workweek, while still having the economic means to support themselves and their families

(Schultz, 2000; White, 2001; Jacobs and Gerson, 2004; Lester, 2005).

Introducing these elements into American society could occur through a number of approaches, ranging from top-down legislation to voluntary efforts by employers, as explored below.

PROBLEMS ACTUALISING A REDUCED WORKWEEK IN THE FACE OF GLOBALISATION AND NEW LIBERALISM

While a new working time regime would produce immeasurable benefits for workers and provide a foundation for greater gender equality within and beyond the workplace, the current political and economic environment is not conducive to such large-scale reforms. New initiatives around working time have encountered serious problems, even in western and northern European countries and Canada, where there is more political and institutional support for worker protections than in the United States. The new paradigm of labour regulation and widespread employer control over the workplace makes any egalitarian vision difficult to achieve, and serious challenges face any approach.

Legislative Mandates

Traditional 'top-down' mandates to regulate hours currently exist in the United States, including most notably in the FLSA, which established a 40-hour workweek for most workers at the federal level, and state or local extensions, such as legislation in California that established an eight-hour workday. The primary goal of the FLSA was work spreading. By requiring employers to pay premium wages for overtime work, Congress believed it would discourage companies from overworking existing employees, as opposed to hiring new ones (Malamud, 1998). In the current version of the

FLSA, compensatory time ('comp time') is permitted in lieu of overtime pay in limited circumstances—only for public employers, and at a rate of at least 1.5 hours for each hour over 40 hours worked in any one week.[3]

New Overtime Legislation to Reduce Standard Workweek to 35 Hours

One possible approach to restructuring the workweek is to amend the FLSA to require overtime pay or comp time for hours worked beyond 35 in a week, instead of 40. Federal legislation could also incorporate the other elements of a new working time regime. The FLSA could be amended to eliminate the executive exemption, and the ERISA, likewise, to mandate pro-rata benefits. Anti-discrimination laws could be amended to protect people from discrimination based on their hours. Anti-retaliation provisions under the FLSA[4] could be strengthened to include punitive damages when employers retaliate or discriminate against employees who enforce their rights under the law. The federal Family and Medical Leave Act,[5] which requires employers to provide up to a total of 12 workweeks of unpaid leave during any 12-month period, could be amended to require paid leave instead. The Earned Income Tax Credit could be expanded, or other basic income supports adopted, to ensure that everyone is brought up to an income level that will protect them from the need for overwork.

Even if the ideal legislative package were enacted, its success in actually reducing the workweek would not be guaranteed, depending on the response to the regulation (Trejo, 1991; Hunt, 1999; Costa, 2000; Hamermesh and Trejo, 2000; Trejo, 2001). Economic models estimate differing responses from employers, depending on the economic and political conditions in place when legislation was enacted, and the quality of the data set and the methodology used by the researchers (Trejo, 1991; Hunt, 1999; Costa, 2000; Hamermesh and Trejo, 2000; Trejo, 2001). A traditional demand-side model predicts that employers will decrease working hours as marginal hours become more expensive, discouraging employers from using overtime or comp time. By contrast, a compensating differential model predicts that employers will simply lower straight-time wages to achieve the same total hours and salary as before the legislation was enacted, resulting in no change in hours worked (Trejo, 2001). There is some evidence that employers adjust base wages downward in non-minimum wage jobs, reducing the effect of the statutory premiums but not neutralising it completely (Trejo, 1991). Some writers believe that overtime wages create incentives for employees to work overly long hours, so that both employers and employees become locked into overtime as a way of meeting production demands (Schor, 1994).

---

[3] 29 USC § 207(o) (2004).
[4] 29 USC § 215.
[5] Family and Medical Leave Act of 1993, 29 USC § 2601 (2004).

Comp Time Instead of Overtime

One option for dealing with these problems is to replace overtime with comp time, essentially mandating a limit on the total numbers hours worked until they reach desired levels. This type of proposal might require that for any hour worked beyond 35 hours in a week, or seven in a day, an employee would receive 1.5 hours (or one hour) of comp time to use as additional time off work. This type of programme currently exists for many US government employees and has been implemented in some industries in France, Germany, and elsewhere, where workers must average no more than 35 hours per week over a predetermined number of weeks.

Where employers enjoy sole control over the structure of the workplace, workers may suffer in a comp time system. In US government positions currently offering comp time, the risk of abuse is relatively low (Eisenbrey, 2003). Record keeping is reliable and transparent, so employees can ensure they receive the right amount of comp time. Turnover is low, so employees are unlikely to lose time off when leaving a job. Labour unions, which are more prevalent in the public sector, can protect employees' rights to use comp time or to resist compelled overtime work. Problems still arise, however. For example, some employers require or pressure employees to use up their comp time quickly in order to avoid accumulating large quantities of 'banked' time.[6]

Concerns about employer power over decisions about comp time use may be magnified in the private sector. Comp time makes overtime hours less expensive to employers, who do not have to pay for them when they are worked. Employers can increase hours to match levels of maximum production, while at the same time saving money if employees fail to use up their accrued comp time hours or use them during less busy times (Golden, 1998). Because most employees in the United States are 'hours takers' instead of 'hours makers', employers are likely to control when employees work longer hours and weeks and when they can take time off, as has occurred in both the German and French cases (Golden, 1998).

By confronting such problems, however, comp time could be shaped in a way that renders it beneficial for employees. Potential policies would include penalising employers for unreasonable denial of employees' requests to use comp time; allowing 'borrowing' of comp time in advance by workers instead of just 'lending' comp time to employers; prohibiting employer substitution of comp time for vacation, holiday, sick-leave, and personal days; insuring comp time in case of employer bankruptcy or relocation; and banning or limiting mandatory or coerced overtime hours (Golden, 1998: 537).

---

[6] See, eg, *Christensen v Harris County*, 529 US 576 (2000).

Government Incentives and Negotiated Solutions

In face of the decline of the New Deal regulatory regime, US policy-makers are seeking new models of regulation, replacing legislative mandates with more flexible regulatory approaches to achieve policy goals in a way that can still support democratic principles and encourage innovation (Ayres and Braithwaite, 1992; Estlund, 2004; Lobel, 2004). The proposals attempt to find a middle ground between older 'command and control' models, which involve top-down government mandates, and deregulation, which has the potential to unleash free industry reign. Under various names including 'workplace governance' and 'responsive regulation,' these negotiated solutions seek a balance by using 'carrots', 'sticks', or some combination of both to encourage industry to comply voluntarily with government policy goals. A reduced workweek could be achieved through a negotiated solution, under which the government would set guidelines or policy goals and then provide industry some level of autonomy in determining the means with which to reach those goals.

Legislative Incentives

Legislative incentives could stand alone or could form the backbone of a more complex negotiated solution aimed at creating a 35-hour workweek by providing financial support for employers who agree to implement it for their employees. Incentives must be accepted widely to avoid stigmatising employees with shortened workweeks; programmes that call on employees to volunteer for lower hours may ultimately backfire. For example, in a reduced workweek trial in mid-1990, Finnish municipal governments attempted to implement six-hour days in order to decrease hours and increase jobs in the face of high unemployment (Mutari and Figart, 2001). Some studies suggest that, in practice, 94 per cent of the employees who opted for the shorter days were women in what tended, in Finland's sex-segregated workforce, to be female-dominated fields of social services and health services. These women expressed shame over their short shifts, relative to men (Antilla, 2004). As soon as the subsidies were lifted, the shorter days disappeared, as unions and some employees were unwilling to accept the salary cuts that accompanied the reduced hours (Mutari and Figart, 2001). Thus, Finland illustrates how subsidies for 'voluntary' programmes can fail.

France offered subsidies to all employers as one part of a legislative attempt to ameliorate high unemployment levels by reducing the workweek from 39 to 35 hours. Through a two-stage legislative process, France moved toward a 35-hour standard workweek beginning in 1998. Initially, the law passed in 1998, known as Aubry I,[7] offered an incentive grant for

---

[7] Loi No 98-461 du 13 juin 1998, Journal officiel, 14 juin 1998, 9029.

companies who would create new jobs equivalent to 6 per cent of their company's workforce, maintain staffing levels for at least two years, and reduce working time by 10 per cent before year 2000 deadlines (Bilous, 2000; Bloch-London, 2004). Employers who sought the subsidy had to follow a set method of calculating working time: in order to achieve an *effective* working time decrease of 10 per cent, employers could not exclude break time or holidays when calculating the total number of hours worked (Bloch-London, 2004). Many employers declined the subsidies under Aubry I, because they anticipated being able to avoid the government's terms if they waited to implement a reduced workweek under the second phase of the law (Bloch-London, 2004). Aubry II,[8] enacted in 2000, replaced the earlier incentives with a broader structural aid scheme, which subsidised low pay (up to 1.8 times the minimum wage) on a sliding scale to cushion wages until 2005 when the minimum wage would be increased. In contrast to Aubry I, receipt of aid under the second law was not contingent on job creation or on the old method of calculating working time. Employers could comply, in part, by changing the way they calculate hours worked, resulting in less than a 10 per cent reduction in the effective number of hours worked (Bloch-London, 2004). Thus, while subsidies could provide an incentive to adopt a 35-hour standard workweek, to be effective the subsidies must be offered widely and on terms employers will accept—either because the terms are agreeable or because employers believe they must acquiesce to them in order to receive the subsidy or to comply with the law, conditions absent in France.

Negotiated Solutions

Other approaches to negotiated solutions attempt to solve compliance problems by using a careful mix of government punishment and persuasion, and marshalling third-party monitors. The responsive regulation model developed by Ian Ayres and John Braithwaite, for example, posits a pyramid of enforcement in which compliant parties are rewarded, but non-compliance moves them up a pyramid of sanctions toward a 'big gun' aimed at the most serious offenders (1992). Additionally, recognising and seeking to avoid capture of regulatory agencies, Ayres and Braithwaite propose empowering public interest groups to monitor compliance and, especially in situations where unions or employee groups serve as monitors, to ensure internal accountability (Ayres and Braithwaite, 1992). Building on this tradition, Cynthia Estlund proposes a new approach to protect workers' rights in the face of insufficient union strength or agency resources. Questioning the ability of employees, who face collective action problems or fear of reprisal, to serve as adequate monitors, and asserting that US agencies have

---

[8] Loi No 2000-37 du 19 janvier 2000, Journal officiel, 20 janvier 2000, 975.

insufficient 'big guns' to pose a credible threat, Estlund proposes a hybrid model where outside consumers serve as monitors, targeting multinational corporations which fail to comply with regulations or which buy from non-compliant suppliers (2004).

A number of countries, including France and Australia, have turned to negotiated solutions to reduce working hours (Berg *et al*, 2004; Bloch-London, 2004). In France, the parameters of Aubry II, which guides implementation of the 35-hour workweek, were determined in negotiations between employers' and employees' unions and representatives. Because of strong opposition to the reduced workweek and threats of non-compliance from employers, the government allowed the second law to be weakened in many aspects in comparison to the first law. As discussed above, the method of calculating working time was relaxed, working time was measured for managerial and professional staff in days rather than hours, limits on total use of overtime hours were relaxed, computation of hours was annualised, and the amount paid for overtime hours was decreased. The newer French government further relaxed the overtime regime, allowing more use of overtime at a lower cost (Bloch-London, 2004).

The relaxation of overtime use and the annualisation of hours gave French employers considerable flexibility to organise workers' hours, in a phenomenon known in Europe as 'flexibilisation', which has also occurred in Australia, Germany, and other countries that have reduced the workweek through negotiated solutions (Berg *et al*, 2004). For some employers, flexibilisation works similarly to comp time systems discussed above, in which they can shift labour to peak times and away from slow times. For example, in France, workers at Samsonite agreed, through negotiation, to work 42 hours per week in the summer, when demand for luggage is high, and 32 hours per week in the winter (Trumbull, 2001). In other work settings, flexibilisation is imposed on a more transitory basis, often to the detriment of employees. One author describes companies in which lower-paid workers have had to make themselves available for work anytime between 6 am and 10 pm, five days a week, as well as Saturday mornings, with little prior notice. Their time off is often dictated to them, at the last minute, in a process called 'demodulation' (Pélisse, 2004a).

The French negotiated regime resulted in some job creation and working time reduction, with estimates ranging from three to 10 hours' reduction depending on the setting. Some employees, especially women in professional jobs, said they appreciate the fact that the new law provided them more time for family and leisure. Other employees, particularly lower-wage employees, reported inadequate control over their working hours and vacation time, which may be mandated by their employers (Bloch-London, 2004; Pélisse, 2004a). Unfortunately, the law left regulation of part-time work completely to company-level negotiations, a process that effected little change for most part-time workers. Nonetheless, there is some evidence of an overall reduction in part-time work, especially for workers with hours near 30 per week, who were able to transition into full-time work (Bloch-London, 2004).

Some of the shortcomings of the French negotiated solution are due to the relative strength of employers over labour unions or other groups representing employees—a condition that would be even more problematic in the United States. France attempted a weak version of legislated representation in Aubry I, in which companies without union representation could choose a designated employee to participate in the negotiation process (Bloch-London, 2004). While this process created wider employee representation in initial working time negotiations, studies indicate it was often used as a tool by management to validate a decision that was already made and has not created lasting new links to trade unions (Bloch-London, 2004). More positively, in Germany, employee works councils have been successful in helping to enforce collective agreements; working time has been estimated at 0.6 fewer hours per week in companies that have works councils compared to companies that do not have them (Lehndorff, 2004).

Experiences in France and other countries point to a number of conditions that would need to be ensured before the United States could take a negotiated approach to a 35-hour workweek standard. Most importantly, any proposal would have to incorporate a stronger structure to bolster representation of employees' interests for purposes of designing and enforcing corporate compliance. Legislation guiding the policy could create negotiating committees that would include diverse employee representatives (including women and minorities, low-wage and part-time workers). In addition, consumers or public interest groups could be charged with protecting workers by monitoring multinational corporations. Finally, it would be necessary to increase the monitoring capacity of agencies to detect and punish non-compliance. Agencies would need the power to impose stronger penalties for repeated violations of regulatory guidelines. With a fairly strong civil rights litigation-based regime in the United States, it might also be possible to bolster compliance by providing employees a private right of action backed up by punitive damages if they are fired for trying to enforce workplace standards or rights (Estlund, 2004). With more of these conditions in place, a negotiated approach could be effective.

Collective Bargaining

In some unionised settings, it might be possible to achieve new working time standards through collective bargaining. A collective bargaining approach might, in many ways, look like responsive regulation without government incentives. Assuming some unions have sufficient strength to bargain for the necessary reforms, their achievements might pave the way for broader adoption of a 35-hour standard.

Reductions of working time through collective bargaining have occurred in Germany and the Netherlands. German unions have long negotiated for a reduced workweek, mostly in order to preserve predominantly male manufacturing jobs (Figart and Mutari, 1998). For example, a prominent agreement between IG Metall and Volkswagen in 1993 implemented a 28.8-hour week over four days with a pay cut in order to preserve employment. By the mid-1990s, printing and metalworking unions had negotiated 35-hour weeks with flexibilisation, which allowed extended workweeks in peak periods or unusual circumstances, with time off usually given at a later time (Fajertag, 1999). Similar agreements have been arranged at Dutch companies (Fajertag, 1999).

The strength of collective bargaining in Germany may be weakening. Coverage by collective agreements fell from 69 per cent to 63 per cent in the former West Germany and from 56 per cent to 44 per cent in the former East Germany between 1996 and 2001 (Lehndorff, 2004). IG Metall suffered a significant defeat in East Germany in trying to bring work hours down to 35, to match those in West Germany (Fajertag, 1999). Furthermore, actual working time appears to be longer than collectively bargained time, reflecting insufficient enforcement, and pressure to increase hours despite efforts to negotiate otherwise. Flexibilisation can provide the mode for the workweek to stretch beyond the negotiated hours (Fajertag, 1999). With efforts to reduce working hours through collective bargaining failing in a country with strong union presence, such a strategy is likely to face serious difficulties in the United States. Unions would have to see a surprising upsurge, and stronger structures to enforce agreements would have to develop, before a collective bargaining approach to a 35-hour workweek could succeed on any significant scale.

Private Industry Initiatives

In light of the difficulties in achieving a reduced workweek through legislative and collective bargaining approaches, private industry initiatives may provide a way for change to begin. Employees could press individual employers to restructure the workweek, and some companies might comply in order to retain or to attract qualified employees or to achieve other efficiencies. By doing so, these employers would create best-practice models that provide success stories and impetus for larger change.

In the United States during the Great Depression, many companies reduced working hours in order to maintain employment. Under the leadership of its visionary founder and Chief Executive Officer, WK Kellogg, the Michigan cereal manufacturer Kellogg's maintained a 30-hour week for many years after the depression abated (Hunnicutt, 1998). WK Kellogg asserted that, with the reduction in hours, employees' efficiency and morale increased so much that the company could pay them the same wages for six hours as they had previously paid them for eight (Hunnicutt, 1998). When Kellogg left a direct management position, the six-hour days began to disappear. But they remained, to some degree, until the mid-1980s, when a new management team, as part of a strategy to trim the payroll to meet a loss in market share, threatened to relocate its headquarters if the workers and unions did not agree to end the remaining six-hour shifts (Hunnicutt, 1998).

Even today, some companies have reaped tangible benefits by reducing working hours in the current economy. SAS, a North Carolina software company, has a written policy allowing a standard 35-hour week; although not all employees take advantage of the policy, it is perceived as an option. SAS also provides a full range of on-site benefits to employees, including health care, a fitness centre, on-site car service, and guidance for children choosing colleges and parents seeking nursing homes (Bankert *et al*, 2001; Safer, 2003). This employee-centred, private company, run by co-founder and Chief Executive Officer Jim Goodnight, is highly profitable, partially due to its 3 per cent employee turnover in an industry that averages closer to 20 per cent (Safer, 2003).

In the recent past, some consultants advised companies of the benefits of reduced workweeks. Companies who followed such advice, such as Metro Plastic Technologies, found they attracted better workers and were able to fill empty positions more easily, while producing a higher-quality product with fewer defects (Saltzman, 1997). Such an approach may not apply as easily for some firms with highly skilled workers who require substantial training, where paying overtime can be less expensive than hiring additional employees (Saltzman, 1997). Reduced working time initiatives are more likely to be adopted by firms who face labour shortages and need to attract workers, companies that gain efficiency by increasing utilisation of capital, or companies that can reap the benefits of government incentives.

Nonetheless, industry efforts can provide individual models of success for later legislative and negotiated solutions. Furthermore, in industries where companies compete for highly skilled workers—such as SAS—a domino effect may take hold. As some employers reduce required work hours, others may have to follow suit or be at a comparative disadvantage.

CONCLUSION

At the dawn of the twenty-first century, the old breadwinner/caregiver model has become obsolete. Americans need a new social policy that recognises and provides greater support for the complex, simultaneous involvements in paid work, family caretaking, and civic affairs in which men and women are already engaged. In order to succeed, this new policy should reduce and restructure working time.

In the current political and economic climate, it will be difficult to reorganise working time in a way that genuinely improves workers' lives inside and outside of the workplace. Sustained public education and attention must be focused on the growing problems of overwork and underwork and on the lack of choice Americans face. Women's rights activists must join forces with domestic and international labour movements, civil rights groups, and other social activist groups to articulate a programmatic agenda and to press for change. Together, these groups can lay the foundation for a shift to reduced working time with greater benefits and protections for all workers. Preconditions include stronger employee representation and voice, government monitoring and enforcement capacity, and norms that enable and encourage all men and women to work more moderate, manageable hours.

Sustained academic attention and activism are developing in a number of countries, including the United States, to study and resist the growing time demands that threaten the integrity of family life, the fulfilment of personal goals, and the viability of civic and political engagement. At one level, groups like the Sloan Foundation are funding research on family-friendly initiatives, such as the path-breaking book by Jacobs and Gerson quoted in this chapter. On another level, activist groups have also begun to gain momentum for resisting increased pressures to work longer and harder and for ensuring enforcement of any legislation that succeeds. In the United States, the 'Take Back Your Time' movement, organised by the Center for Religion, Ethics, and Social Policy at Cornell University, has garnered national attention and support from academics, leaders of the labour movement, religious leaders, and non-profit organisations. Its stated role is as a 'nationwide initiative to challenge the epidemic of overwork, over-scheduling and time famine that now threatens our health, our families and relationships, our communities and our environment' (Center for Religion, Ethics, and Social Policy). A similar movement in Canada, 32 Hours: Action for Full Employment, seeks 'to achieve full employment and a high quality of life for all, through a legislated standard work week of 32 hours across Canada' (32 Hours).

As such activism spreads, we are beginning to witness progress in forming and fostering international norms at both the national and global levels. For example, the European Union (EU) has issued directives creating binding labour regulation on member states, including a 1993 Working Time Directive[9] that restricts and regulates working time for all employees (Murray, 2001b)[10] and a 1997 Part-Time Work Directive[11] mandating

---

[9] EC Council Directive 93/104 of 23 November 1993 concerning certain aspects of the organization of working time, [1993] OJ L 307.

[10] See also European Commission, 1998.

[11] EC Council Directive 97/81 of 15 December 1997 concerning the Framework Agreement on part-time work, [1998] OJ L 14.

pro-rata benefits for part-time workers. Recently, the International Labour Organization (ILO) has also begun to advocate a range of measures to upgrade non-standard and other forms of unregulated labour, and to ensure the creation of more secure forms, in the global 'Decent Work' programme of action (Murray, 2001, 208–12; ILO, 2002; Fudge and Owens, chapter 1 in this volume). A 2001 Report prepared for the European Commission, entitled *Beyond Employment*, explicitly addresses the need to reduce and restructure working time in ways that will broadly protect workers, rather than benefiting only traditional male head-of-household employees (Supiot *et al*, 2001: 90–93, 180). In particular, the Report advocates 'a model where men and women would share working time and keep enough free time for both without forfeiting social rights' (Supiot *et al*, 2001: 181). Such international initiatives may provide valuable resources for activists as they work to advocate for and develop policies at the national level. Although much more remains to be done, these types of efforts offer promise for mobilising support for policies that give Americans more power over the one resource that should truly be theirs to control: their time.

7

Gender and the Legal Regulation of Employment Breaks

CLAIRE KILPATRICK[*]

WHAT IS AN EMPLOYMENT BREAK?

IN THIS CHAPTER, I explore how employment breaks have been conceptualised by contract and statute, with a special focus on the gender implications of those conceptualisations. Because women's employment is more broken up than men's in order to accommodate maternity and caring responsibilities, how law analyses these broken employment patterns has important practical repercussions for women's employment security. The legal treatment of breaks for family reasons is also an important barometer of the value given by public policy to lives which combine paid work with unpaid care and reproductive work. The chapter first sets out a conceptual and social framework within which to analyse employment breaks for family reasons. It then examines the evolution of the legal position in the United Kingdom in order to elucidate and elaborate this framework.

However, first, I need to explain what I mean by the word 'break' and why I have chosen this particular word to organise my argument. It is not easy to find a neutral word to discuss the legal regulation of periods in which either the worker is not performing work or the employer is not paying wages or in which both parts of the wage–work bargain are not performed. While the phrase 'uninterrupted employment' successfully conveys a sense of employment in which the wage–work bargain is constantly afoot, its opposite, interruption, seems to suggest a temporary cessation of employment rather than a final and definitive rupture of the contractual relationship. However, what we need is a word that allows us to discover, rather than to prejudge, whether, in between two periods of wage–work bargains with the same employer, the pause button rather than the stop

[*] I am very grateful to the organisers of the workshop, the participants in the workshop, the anonymous referees, and Hugh Collins for helpful comments on an earlier version of this chapter.

button has been pressed on the employment relationship between the parties. The word 'break' seems to capture both these possibilities; it can mean both a temporary respite and a definitive ending. I will use 'break' on its own when both these possibilities are present, and 'temporary break' and 'definitive break' when I wish to indicate either more specific meaning.

TWO WAYS OF THINKING ABOUT EMPLOYMENT BREAKS

In this section, I consider two ways of thinking about employment breaks. The first is as a measure of the longevity of a particular labour market engagement. The second concerns those situations in which the standard wage–work bargain is disrupted. My aim is to show that different ways of constructing and conceptualising labour market engagements affect whether we classify periods in which wages are not exchanged for work as definitive or temporary breaks in a worker's contractual relationship with her employer. The more that breaks are construed as definitive, the more precarious a worker's position on the labour market becomes.

Employment Breaks as a Measure of the Longevity of a Particular Labour Market Engagement

A first sense in which we can think about uninterrupted employment is as *a measure of the longevity of a particular labour market engagement*. The longer the time between definitive breaks, the greater the longevity of a particular labour market engagement. In a recent book, *The Personal Employment Contract*, Mark Freedland (2003: 313) has provided a very useful typology of four different ways in which the longevity of particular labour market engagements can be characterised:

(1)   long-term career engagement (more than 10 years);
(2)   medium-term career engagement (between one and 10 years);
(3)   temporary engagement (less than one year, but measured in months or weeks)
(4)   very short-term or occasional engagement (for periods of less than one week).

I should be clear about the fact that I use this typology in ways which significantly diverge from the ways in which it is used by Freedland. He uses this typology to suggest that precariousness cannot in fact easily be read off the identification of a particular kind of engagement so that, for instance, a long-term career engagement can be *contractually analysed* as being less precarious than, for instance, a temporary engagement. This is because the notice term in employment contracts means that even long-term career engagements can quickly be ended by the employer in a contract-compliant fashion. In other words, from a legal-contractual point of view, all employment contracts are precarious. From this starting-point, he develops a further argument that the *implicit norms and expectations*, according to which engagements on contracts of indefinite duration terminable by notice are perceived to be more secure than, say, fixed-term contracts, are out of alignment with the actual contractual analysis of these engagements (2003: 305–18).

This is a useful reminder both of the contractual precariousness of almost all employment contracts and of the mismatch between legal-contractual analysis and the implicit norms and expectations brought to employment relationships by workers and employers. However, I interpret the implications of that mismatch differently. My view is that the type of engagement offered to a worker matters immensely, *despite* the fact that in legal terms it is generally very easy to terminate all of these engagements in a contract-compliant fashion. This is precisely because the type of engagement offered enormously affects the *implicit norms and expectations* that the parties bring to the employment contract, and this heavily conditions their contractual behaviour. When the parties agree to an indefinite contract terminable by notice in order to create what is envisaged as a long-term career engagement, they evidently view that engagement as such. This makes it much less likely that the power to terminate the contract, or even to consider the end of the contract, will be frequently at the forefront of the parties' minds, at least when times are good. The implicit norms and expectations are very different when it comes to fixed-term contracts, even those for a considerable number of years, where both parties are always *aware* of the contract's term. When it comes to short-term engagements, the message being sent out by the employer is that there is no deep commitment to a continuing relationship with the worker. So that workers who accept employment on these terms may not expect to have contractual continuity or statutory rights dependent on contractual continuity and may act accordingly, *even if legally they do have such rights*.

From this quite different perspective, the typology of four kinds of engagement can be probed in a number of ways in order to consider who engages in different patterns of labour market participation. A first set of issues arises from considering whether these patterns vary over the life-course. For instance, we could read the list as a ladder which workers can hope to ascend (but which they may also descend) as they grow older. A second set of issues asks whether different labour market engagements are in vogue at different periods because different choices about how to structure work are made by workers and employers. For instance, it could be argued that medium-term and short-term engagements are currently more prevalent than the long-term and temporary engagements that were more fashionable in other recent decades.

Most importantly for present purposes, do these patterns vary according to gender? This is discussed further in the next section. However, for now we can note that a disproportionate number of female workers are clustered in the forms of arrangement at the bottom of the list, temporary or occasional engagements, normally on fixed-term contracts or as casual workers. In addition, there would seem to be an important correlation between part-time work and very short-term or occasional engagements. Freedland is absolutely right to identify the long-term and medium-term engagements as being *career* engagements,[1] offering opportunities for skill enhancement and career progression, whereas temporary engagements and occasional engagements are not so viewed. If employers are reluctant to allow career engagements to be pursued on a part-time basis, this will tend to push workers who wish to work part-time down the ladder towards temporary engagements (usually on fixed-term contracts) and short-term or occasional engagements.

Employment Breaks as a Lack of Interruption in a Worker's Employment with the Same Employer

However, there is a second sense in which we can think about breaks in employment. This concerns those situations where there are *breaks in a worker's employment with the same employer*. In other words, the standard wage–work bargain between worker and employer is disrupted in some way or other. Again Mark Freedland's recent book provides an exceptionally useful way of considering how law analyses what happens to employment when it is disrupted in this way (2003: 106–8). He suggests that the employment contract can exist in four modes:

(1) Pre-Employment mode
(2) Full-Employment mode
(3) Sub-Employment mode
(4) Post-Employment mode

Standard continuous employment is what happens when the contract is in *full-employment mode*, that is, when there is a current set of obligations for the exchange of work and remuneration. It is important to recognise that the obligations to exchange work and pay do not exhaust the content of the employment contract in full-employment mode; those obligations are necessary but not sufficient elements of a characterisation of employment in that mode. The existence of other obligations in the contract beyond the wage–work bargain means that that even when the wage–work obligations are not fully operational, it may still be possible realistically to speak of the existence of an employment contract (albeit possibly one existing in a different mode) between the parties to that contract.

---

[1] However, it follows from my argument, although not from his, that medium-term engagements structured as fixed-term contracts are less likely to be seen as career engagements than medium-term engagements structured as indefinite contracts terminable by notice.

Indeed, the great contribution made by Freedland's typology of the four modes in which the employment relationship can exist is that it makes it clear that the employment contract has an existence and identity which extends beyond the full-employment mode. While the set of contractual obligations pertaining in other modes will not be the same as those pertaining when the employment contract is in full-employment mode, that does not mean that no contractual obligations exist when the contract is in one of its other three modes.

For present purposes, we are interested in the specific issue of how breaks in employment are characterised. It is possible to consider periods when the worker is not currently working in one of three ways. First, the employer may continue to pay the worker although the worker does no work, and the contract may be considered to continue in full-employment mode.[2] Alternatively, the period may be considered to be one when the employment relationship continues to exist but has simply passed into *sub-employment mode*, and this may mean that both employer and worker have a degree of contractual commitment to resume the employment in full-employment mode and/or that a set of obligations distinct from those which would apply in the post-employment mode continue to exist. Generally, this will concern situations in which neither side of the wage–work bargain is currently operating, that is, there is no current obligation on the employer to pay wages or on the worker to provide work. However, it is also possible to characterise precisely this type of bilateral break of the wage–work bargain as moving the contract from full-employment mode to post-employment mode, so that the contractual relationship is terminated (subject, of course, to any post-employment obligations which may apply). Here, even if the worker *in fact* goes back to work for the same employer, this will be seen as a brand new employment contract, and there will be *no contractual continuity* between the employment before the break and the employment after the break.

Again, I need to clarify a divergence between the approach taken by Freedland and the approach I wish to develop in this analysis. I wish to use this typology of employment modes for different purposes to those for which it is used in *The Personal Employment Contract*. In that work, this typology is utilised to provide a very illuminating analysis of a number of situations which in different ways sit uneasily between the full-, sub-, and post-employment modes: disciplinary suspension, industrial action, sickness, lay-off, and casual work (Freedland, 2003: 464–84). However, my suggestion is that if we consider the gendered nature of employment breaks, we can considerably expand the categories of breaks worth taking into

---

[2] Although the worker may wish to challenge the employer's refusal to supply work as being a breach of contract by the employer. This occurs in 'garden leave' situations: *William Hill Organisation Ltd v Tucker* [1999] ICR 291 (CA). In other words, in certain employment contracts, full-employment mode will require not simply payment of wages by the employer but will also entail an obligation on that employer to supply work.

consideration. At the risk of oversimplification, we can do this by considering the employment modes of, respectively, a model male and a model female worker.

The model male worker of the twentieth century did not interrupt his employment: while he worked for an employer, ideally he should consistently be in full-employment mode. Of course, in reality, the male workers to whom this model was addressed had employment breaks for very many reasons, some pleasant and desired, others much less so: lay-off by the employer, disciplinary suspension, illness and injury, strikes, holidays, births, marriages, and deaths all disrupted employment. The real male worker hoped that some of these breaks, such as a few days of illness, would not be seen as breaks at all so that the employer would continue to pay wages, and the employment would be considered to remain in full-employment mode. Alternatively, he could hope that the break would be characterised as placing the employment in sub-employment mode, that is a temporary break during which the employment contract continued to subsist albeit not in full-employment mode. The worst-case scenario was that the break would be considered to have terminated the employment, a definitive contractual break.

Now the reasons for breaks identified in the previous paragraph evidently also affect women workers, who also get sick, go on strike, and so on. However, for twentieth-century women, this model of uninterrupted labour market engagement tended to be presented, more or less strongly at different times and places, as a default model: what happened *faute de mieux* (that is, a husband and children). Hence, while for men breaks in work have been viewed as limited exceptions to a general pattern of uninterrupted employment, for women, a pattern of employment breaks was expected. Even if a woman continued to work for the same employer, large expanses of time taken up by maternity and child care were expected to break that employment. Whether time away from work for maternity and caring responsibilities is considered to move the employment into sub-employment mode (a temporary break), on the one hand, or into post-employment mode (a definitive break), on the other, is an absolutely critical element in an assessment of the precariousness of women's work.

It is of the greatest interest that very significant shifts are occurring in the construction of the model male and model female worker. These are particularly apparent in those countries, like the United Kingdom, where, as we shall see, breaks in employment for family reasons have been treated as definitive to a much greater extent for much of the twentieth century than in other European Union (EU) member states such as France and Italy. Three particular shifts can be highlighted.

First, it is now a public policy priority across the EU to encourage women to stay in employment and to retain their skill-levels after breaks for family reasons. This public policy priority interacts, on the one hand, with the implicit norms and expectations of female workers and employers, and, on the other, with the pre-existing legal position of how breaks for family reasons are conceived in the individual member states.

Turning to male workers, it is unclear the extent to which their implicit norms and expectations, and those of their employers, with regard to men taking breaks for family reasons have shifted. However, public policy has certainly shifted towards providing options for parents (sometimes even a much broader category of carers) and not simply mothers to take temporary breaks for family reasons.

Finally, the *grundnorm* of consistent employment in full-employment mode is being more broadly challenged as part of a general questioning by workers of the appropriate balance between the employment they are in and the rest of their lives. Many of the demands resulting from this simply require an adjustment of the timing, place and number of weekly hours of work rather than *breaks* from work. However, undoubtedly part of this broader shift in work–life balance expectations is a desire to have a flexible but secure method of taking a break from work with an employer in order, for instance, to travel, to set up a new business venture, or to carry out voluntary work. These demands have as yet had a more limited impact on the *legal* responsiveness of public policy-makers, although public policy initiatives to encourage employers of the benefits of adapting to these new worker norms and expectations have been undertaken.[3] However, because this chapter analyses the legal regulation of employment breaks, and their gender impact, it focuses principally on breaks for family reasons, rather than broader work–life balance initiatives.

I have used Freedland's two typologies to investigate two axes along which employment breaks can be measured: the longevity of a particular labour market engagement and breaks of employment with the same employer. However, the overall picture can only be obtained by investigating the interactions between these two typologies.

If breaks for family reasons (maternity or care) are conceptualised as temporary (a move from full- to sub-employment mode within a subsisting employment contract), then women and men can maintain a long- or medium-term career engagement at the same time as taking those breaks.

However, where breaks for family reasons are conceptualised as definitive, terminating the worker's relationship with the employer, those taking breaks cannot have long- or medium-term career engagements until they stop taking those breaks. Such a situation makes it less likely that an equal number of women and men will have long- or medium-term career engagements with an employer. Just as importantly, if a view that breaks are definitive is combined with a view that career engagements are more compatible

---

[3] See, eg, in the United Kingdom, the Work–Life Balance Campaign, analysed in Kilpatrick and Freedland, 2004.

with full-time work, women who wish to continue work on a part-time basis while their children are young could find it difficult to obtain a long-term career engagement at the same occupational level which they held prior to having children. This creates propitious conditions for the spawning of a whole sub-category of kinds of non-career labour market engagements especially suitable for family carers: easier to interrupt and with a shorter daily duration, but with few opportunities for skill enhancement or progression. These 'family carers' form a substantial proportion of workers in the short-term or occasional engagements category.

It is this last category of engagement which creates the greatest trouble for the interaction between the two typologies, one focused on the longevity of a particular engagement with an employer and the other on the characterisation of breaks occurring within a relationship with an employer. We can see this easily if we consider three different working patterns of women working for an employer for two years before ceasing to work for that employer again.

If a woman is engaged during that two-year period on an indefinite contract terminable by notice or on a two-year fixed-term contract, and works regularly during that time, we would confidently characterise this as being a single engagement for two years because the employment is generally in full-employment mode during that period.

Now imagine instead that a woman agrees to work during that two-year period on frequent but regular short periods of exchanges of wages and work. We would be more hesitant about characterising this two-year period in the same way, that is as a single engagement for two years, because (a) the frequency of employment in full-employment mode is not the same; and (b) the parties have structured the relationship as one of short-term engagements.

We would feel even less confident about characterising as a single contractual engagement a woman working for two years for the same employer on frequent and irregular short periods of exchanges of wages and work. Both short-term engagement patterns share the feature that the employment frequently dips out of full-employment mode in which wages and work are exchanged. The latter adds the additional feature that those dips out of full-employment mode are erratic.

Hence, short-term engagements are more difficult contractually to characterise as a single engagement because the contractual mode is often not that of full employment. However, it is equally the case in our two examples of short-term engagements over a two-year period that it is very difficult to categorise each of the breaks in wage–work bargains as being definitive, an ending of the relationship with that employer. Because the fact is that it is not. The relationship ends after two years, not after each wage–work bargain. This suggests that the most appropriate way of characterising the contractual status of the women on the short-term engagements for two years is to say that they work in an on-going contractual engagement in which the employment frequently dips between the full- and sub-employment modes. Evidently, however, it remains possible to argue that the close of each short-term engagement signals a definitive contractual break so that any on-going relationship is of purely social or, at any rate, of non-contractual, relevance (compare Collins, 2000 with Freedland, 2003: 100–4, 477–78).

This illustrates the broader point that comes out of this discussion of two ways of thinking about employment breaks: while a worker continues to have a relationship with an employer, there is no inevitable or a priori way of characterising any of these breaks as being by nature definitive or temporary. Instead, choices about how to characterise each of these breaks have to be made by judges and legislatures. Moreover, those legal choices can affect the implicit norms and expectations of women, men, and employers. That is to say, whether breaks are generally legally categorised as (a) definitive or (b) temporary can, especially if a clear legal stance is adopted, make a difference to how workers, especially women workers, and employers orient themselves to the labour market.

THE LEGAL RELEVANCE OF CONTINUOUS EMPLOYMENT: CONTRACTUAL AND STATUTORY CONTINUITY

In legal terms, why does it matter if breaks are seen as temporary or definitive? The employment contract law issues relating to continuity were discussed in the previous section. It matters if the employment contract subsists during a break, albeit in sub-employment mode, because employers and workers may owe each other certain obligations during that period which the parties can invoke or enforce. However, the incentive to establish contractual continuity is more often linked to the enjoyment of statutory employment rights. In many employment law systems, employment counted as continuous is an important gateway both to qualify for statutory employment rights and to determine the extent of a successful claim of one of those statutory employment rights. So, for instance, one year's (52 weeks') continuous employment is required to qualify for the right not to be unfairly dismissed in the United Kingdom. And to obtain the maximum statutory redundancy payment in United Kingdom law one needs inter alia to have clocked up 20 years' continuous employment.[4]

As Davies and Freedland note, when it comes to working out what continuous employment is for the purposes of *statutory rights*, 'the most obvious basis for such measurement should be the contract of employment' (1984: 570). And indeed the primary measurement of a week that 'counts' as a week of continuous employment in UK law is that:

---

[4] Employment Rights Act 1996 (ERA 1996), s 162(3).

> Any week during the whole or part of which an employee's relations with his [sic] employer are governed by a contract of employment counts in computing the employee's period of employment.[5]

In other words, an uninterrupted contractual pattern of a certain kind is required to have a week which counts for the purpose of statutory 'continuous employment'. Note, however, that the contract of employment in each of these weeks, although it will have to be with the same employer, does not have to be the same contract of employment. So while, for statutory purposes, there must be *a* contract of employment in existence with sufficient regularity (every week), an employee could qualify for unfair dismissal protection provided she could show 52 separate contracts of employment, each one occurring in a consecutive week. Therefore, even when statutory continuity takes the contract of employment as its yardstick, the statutory contract-based continuity test does not necessarily produce the same analysis as that forthcoming from a purely contractual analysis of continuity. For instance, a weekly pattern of short exchanges of wages and work would suffice to satisfy the statutory continuity test, even if the breaks between each of those engagements were viewed as constituting a definitive break in the contract. But workers with a pattern of short but sporadic exchanges of wages and work would struggle to satisfy this test, again, if the breaks between wage–work exchanges were regarded as (contractually) definitive. Hence the incentive for workers employed in such arrangements to try to establish the *contractual* continuity of a single engagement in order to enjoy employment rights requiring a long period of continuous employment.

Moreover, while statutory continuity rules, perhaps unsurprisingly, take their main lead from the identification of an employment contract, legislation can depart further from the need to find an employment contract. Statute can provide that employees qualify for employment rights even when a contract would not be regarded as subsisting between the parties in each week. Two main legislative techniques can be used to achieve this outcome. The first technique involves the legislature deeming a contract to exist during a definitive (contractual) break, and specifying which contractual obligations remain in force during that break. The second technique entails the legislature providing that, despite the absence of contractual employment, continuity is nonetheless established for statutory purposes in defined situations. The latter has been the primary technique used in UK law. Currently, UK law provides that statutory continuity exists for any week, even in the absence of a contract, in which the employee is:

---

[5] *Ibid*, s 212(1).

- incapable of work because of sickness or injury;
- absent from work on account of a temporary cessation of work;
- absent from work in circumstances such that, by arrangement or custom, she is regarded as continuing in the employment for any purpose.[6]

Hence, there is no shortage of techniques available to judges and legislatures to establish, or conversely to deny, contractual and statutory continuity. What is most interesting then is to trace how approaches taken by courts and legislatures to these employment breaks have changed over time. I focus on the United Kingdom as it provides an excellent demonstration of the significant shifts made by judges and legislatures in their thinking about employment breaks, as well as the important challenges that remain. I have suggested that casual working arrangements can in part be seen as a way of having frequent breaks for family reasons and outlined the issues this kind of employment pattern raises for contractual and statutory continuity. In the sections that follow, I focus on analysing formal and extensive (at least one-week) periods of leave for family reasons.[7] In my concluding remarks, I consider the implications of this analysis of formal periods of leave for family reasons for the casual working arrangements offered to women with family responsibilities.

STATUTORY LEAVE PERIODS AND CONTINUOUS EMPLOYMENT

Pre-New Labour

Before 1975, there were no statutory rights to leave for maternity reasons in the United Kingdom, let alone a broader range of rights to leave for family reasons. Maternity departures were viewed as signalling a definitive break of the contractual relationship with the employer. The antithesis of a family-friendly employment law regime, it made mothers' employment as precarious as possible.

In 1975, the first right to maternity leave was introduced. This granted qualifying employees (those with two years' continuous service of over 16 hours per week) a period of maternity leave and a 'right to return' to work thereafter. The 'right to return' regime, in place until its replacement by the New Labour Government in 1999, is a fascinating guide to how legally to construct a precarious employment break. Its precarious design feature was

---

[6] *Ibid*, s 212(3). Sickness/injury absence only counts for up to 26 weeks. Before 1999, this included absence on account of pregnancy or confinement up to a maximum of 26 weeks or absence on the longer period of leave connected to the statutory right-to-return maternity regime. See further below.

[7] This also means that I exclude 'time off' for, eg, family emergencies or ante-natal appointments from my analysis.

that the employee's actions could easily tip the break from being a temporary one to being a definitive one.

The legislation did not use the first technique described above, that is, deeming contractual continuity to subsist during the period of maternity leave. Instead, the legislation used the second technique identified, by providing that, even in the absence of a contract of employment, statutory continuity would be conferred on those enjoying the right.[8] The problem with this formula was that the right to return could be lost in a bewildering variety of ways progressively elaborated by the courts and Conservative Governments in the 1980s and 1990s. In terms of legislative design, the most important way that an employee could lose the right to return was by failing to fulfil notification requirements, which were ratcheted up during Mrs. Thatcher's first administration in the Employment Act 1980. At least 21 days before an employee wanted the period of absence to begin, she had to notify the employer in writing of the commencement of her leave.[9] She had to inform the employer at this point (before childbirth) whether she intended to exercise her right to return.[10] Whilst away from work, she was obliged to reply to the employer's request for written confirmation that she intended to exercise her right to return.[11] She was further obliged to notify her employer in writing 21 days in advance of her anticipated return to work.[12] Failure to fulfil any of these notification requirements meant losing the right to return.

Just how difficult the statutory construction of the right to return made the status of the woman's employment, as a matter of contract and of statute, during this maternity break was highlighted in a number of cases where women had been unable, normally because of postnatal depression, to return to work on the last possible date permitted by the right-to-return regime. The employer informed them that by failing to return on that date they had lost their right to return (that is, they had lost their job). The women challenged this outcome as being an unfair 'right-to-return' dismissal as UK law provided:

> Where an employee has the right to return to work ... and has exercised it in accordance with [the notification requirements] but is not permitted to return to work, then ... she shall be treated for the purposes of this Part [that is, the set of provisions related to the right to return] as if she had been employed until the

---

[8] Above n 6.

[9] See old ERA, ss 74–75. The requirement that this notification be in writing was added by the EA 1980. Old ERA signifies the position under the ERA 1996 before New Labour. Prior to consolidation in 1996, the law was contained in the Employment Protection Act 1975.

[10] Old ERA, s 80(1).

[11] *Ibid*, s 80(2). This requirement was inserted by the EA 1980. The woman had 14 days to reply.

[12] *Ibid*, s 82. This was originally one week (Employment Protection Act 1975 (EPA 1975), s 49(1)), and was changed to 21 days by the EA 1980.

notified day of return, and, if she would not otherwise be so treated, as having been continuously employed until that day, and as if she had been dismissed with effect from that day for the reason for which she was not permitted to return.[13]

In the alternative, the women argued that it was ordinary unfair dismissal, a wrongful dismissal (that is, dismissal in breach of contract) or prohibited discrimination under the Sex Discrimination Act 1975 not to allow them to return to work.

For practically all of its existence, the courts found that successful exercise of the right to return depended on the woman not only fulfilling all of the notification requirements but actually physically returning to work on the required date of return.[14] Accordingly, failure to do so automatically ended the woman's relationship with the employer so that she had no statutory claims of any kind against the employer. In 1998, the Court of Appeal in the *Kwik-Save* case radically departed from this stance by stating that a woman had successfully exercised her right to return once she had fulfilled correctly all of the notification requirements.[15] However, the House of Lords in *Halfpenny*, an appeal decided after the right to return had already been replaced by a new regime introduced by New Labour in 1999, decided that neither of these alternatives was the correct reading of the right to return.[16]

The House of Lords decided, unlike the pre-*Kwik-Save* decisions, that Ms Halfpenny did have a right to return which she had not been permitted to exercise because her employer failed to allow her to return. However, contrary to the view of the Court of Appeal in *Kwik-Save*, this right to return did not arise simply because she had notified properly. It arose because, on the notified date of return, she was unable, *for a reason consistent with her contractual rights and duties*, to physically attend work. As Lord Clyde put it, '[h]er position should be the same as if during the ordinary course of her contract of employment she had not attended for work.'[17] The employer's action therefore was deemed to constitute a dismissal for the purposes of the right-to-return regime in accordance with the statutory provision set out above.

However, the House of Lords also found that the contract of employment had been revived only by, and only for the purposes of, the right-to-return regime. Accordingly, Ms Halfpenny *was not employed* for the purpose of any other claim: 'The effect then is as if the refusal had occurred on the notified day before the whole contractual provisions had fully revived.'[18] It is very instructive to see how the House of Lords construe the maternity

---

[13] Old ERA, s 96.

[14] See eg *Kelly v Liverpool Maritime Terminals Ltd*, [1988] IRLR 310 (CA); *Crouch v Kidsons Impey*, [1996] IRLR 79.

[15] *Kwik-Save Stores Ltd v Greaves* and *Crees v Royal London Mutual Insurance*, [1998] IRLR 245 (CA) (*Kwik-Save*).

[16] *Halfpenny v IGE Medical Systems Ltd*, [2001] ICR 73 (HL) (*Halfpenny*).

[17] *Ibid* at 86E.

[18] *Ibid* at 86H (per Lord Clyde).

break under the right-to-return regime for the purposes of Ms Halfpenny's two other claims, one under contract; the other under statute. This gives us a very clear picture of how maternity breaks were conceptualised both as a matter of contract and as a matter of statute during the quarter-century of operation of the right-to-return regime.

Ms Halfpenny claimed that the employer had wrongfully dismissed her by dismissing her in breach of contract. The House of Lords found that it was not clear what the status of her contract was during the maternity break. However, its view, expressed by Lord Browne-Wilkinson, was that even if such a contract existed, all rights under it had been suspended, save possibly a free-standing contractual right to permit return separate from the statutory right. And even if such a contractual right to return existed, by choosing to enforce her statutory rights instead, under the terms of the right-to-return regime,[19] Ms Halfpenny had chosen not to exercise the lone contractual right she possessed while on her maternity break.[20]

She also claimed that the employer had discriminated against her on grounds of sex contrary to the Sex Discrimination Act 1975. Again, the House of Lords found that all her contractual rights were in abeyance during the break because '[n]one of the normal indicia of a contract of employment were present: there was no obligation to provide work or to do work: no obligation to pay.'[21] And the contract was never revived because the employer did not allow that to happen. Therefore, she was not 'a woman employed by' her employer as required for a claim under the Sex Discrimination Act 1975.

Two points of great interest for the conceptualisation of maternity breaks emerge from this authoritative judgment of the House of Lords. First, from a statutory point of view, it should now be clear why the right-to-return regime can be viewed as a legal blueprint for a precarious maternity break. Failure by the employee to fulfil any of a number of stringent requirements turned the break from being temporary to being definitive.

Second, from a contractual point of view, it is worth examining more closely how the House of Lords envisaged the content of any employment contract that does exist during a maternity break. They made clear their view that once the obligations to work and to pay had been suspended, no other meaningful contractual obligations existed between the parties during the break. It is useful to compare this thin view of a contract in sub-employment mode with the statutory renderings of contracts in sub-employment mode which we shall consider in the next section.

---

[19] The relevant statutory provision (old ERA, s 85(1)) stated:

> An employee who has the right to return to work under [statute] and a right to return to work after absence because of pregnancy or childbirth under a contract of employment or otherwise may not exercise the two rights separately but may, in returning to work, take the advantage of whichever right is, in any particular respect, the more favourable.

[20] *Halfpenny*, above n 16 at 83B–D (per Lord Browne-Wilkinson).
[21] *Ibid*, at 83G.

Women in the United Kingdom were rescued from sole reliance on the right to return in 1993 because the United Kingdom then had to transpose an EC Directive on pregnant workers.[22] This required all employees (that is, no qualifying period of continuous employment could be imposed) to have 14 weeks' maternity leave and two weeks of compulsory maternity leave around the birth. Unlike the right-to-return regime, the contract was deemed to exist during this 14-week leave period (that is, the first of the techniques described above). The relevant provision of the transposition legislation simply stated that the employee's terms and conditions, apart from remuneration, would be as though she had not been absent on maternity leave. However, as maternity leave provided only 14 weeks' leave whereas women could get a maximum total of 44 weeks away from work under the right-to-return regime (11 before birth plus 29 after birth plus a possible extension of four weeks), the right to return, with all its defects, continued to be important until its replacement in 1999 under legislation introduced by the New Labour Government.

New Labour

Family-friendly employment rights have been the defining feature of New Labour's employment law agenda. Its activity in this area can be characterised as an ongoing programme of rationalisation, improvement, and extension. This is evidently in very sharp contrast to the pre-existing legal position in the United Kingdom which was explored in the previous section.

There have been two central stages in this programme so far: the Employment Relations Act 1999 and the Employment Act 2002, each accompanied by a piece of secondary legislation. In relation to the complex mess of maternity legislation it inherited, the government rationalised this by creating three periods of leave: Ordinary Maternity Leave (OML), Compulsory Maternity Leave (CML), and Additional Maternity Leave (AML).[23] OML is the successor to the maternity leave introduced to transpose the Pregnant Workers' Directive; AML is the successor to the right-to-return regime. Improvement went hand-in-hand with rationalisation: between 1999 and 2002 OML was 18 weeks long and AML was 29 weeks long; from 2002, each is 26 weeks long. In 1999, the qualifying period for AML was reduced from two years to one year; in 2002, it was further reduced to six months. Statutory Maternity Pay is available during the OML period, although this does not provide full income replacement.

---

[22] EC Council Directive 92/85 EC of 28 November 1992 on the introduction of measures to encourage improvements in the safety and health of pregnant workers and workers who have recently given birth or are breastfeeding, [1992] OJ L 348/28 at 1.

[23] ERA 1996, ss 71–73.

However, rights for family reasons have been extended well beyond bio-logical mothers. In 1999, a right to parental leave was introduced, giving 13 weeks' leave per child under the age of five to employees with one year's continuous employment and parental responsibility.[24] The Employment Act 2002 introduced adoption leave and paternity leave. Adoption leave is modelled on maternity leave so that there is Ordinary Adoption Leave (OAL) of 26 weeks and Additional Adoption Leave (AAL) of 26 weeks.[25] It is also modelled on a birth event in two other ways. First, only one adoptive parent has the right to adoption leave. Where it is a joint adoption, one of the adopters must elect to take the leave.[26] Second, because it is modelled on the regime now applied to birth in UK labour law, the other adopter will have the right to paternity leave. In relation to biological mother births, paternity leave gives the father or the husband or partner of the child's mother the right to two weeks' leave.[27] So, for example, the female partner of a woman giving birth can take paternity leave. In relation to adoption, the paternity leave entitlement is given to the partner of the adopter of a child.[28] So, for instance, the partner of a man adopting a child, whether that partner is female or male, is entitled to paternity leave.[29] For any partner or father to qualify for paternity leave, they must be employees with 26 weeks' continuous employment.[30]

Many valid criticisms can be made of the new raft of family-friendly leaves. For instance, there has been a failure to provide adequate income replacement during these leave periods. This means both that too few men will take leave and that women will suffer financially and be financially insecure when they take leave. To give another example, not enough women will have access to the right to take leave because the new family rights are currently restricted to the narrow category of 'employees', thereby excluding many who tend to fall outside that definition such as casual workers, agency workers and home workers (see Fredman, chapter 8 in this volume). I am not focusing on those important criticisms here (see McColgan, 2000a; Conaghan, 2002).

---

[24] *Ibid*, s 76; Maternity and Parental Leave etc Regulations 1999, SI 1999/3312 (MPL Regs 1999), regs 13 and 14.

[25] ERA 1996, ss 80A (paternity leave), 75A (OAL), and 75B (AAL). See also the Paternity and Adoption Leave Regulations 2002, SI 2002/2788 (PAL Regs 2002).

[26] This results from the definition of 'adopter' in reg 2(1) of the PAL Regs 2002.

[27] *Ibid*, reg 5.

[28] *Ibid*, reg 8.

[29] The wide range of those who can take paternity leave results from the definition of 'partner' in reg 2(1) and (2) of the PAL Regs 2002. The definition includes a person, whether of a different sex or the same sex, who lives with the mother or adopter and the child in an enduring family relationship but is not a close blood relative of the mother or adopter (ie a parent, grandparent, sibling, aunt, or uncle).

[30] PAL Regs 2002, regs 4(2) and 8(2).

Instead, my point is simply that it is also important to evaluate the degree of employment security given to those workers, who will disproportionately be women, who take these breaks from employment. From that perspective, what interests me here is how these new periods of family leave have been constructed, bearing in mind the distinctions between definitive and temporary breaks and between contractual and statutory continuity. These are the building-blocks which can be assembled in different ways so as to increase or diminish the precariousness of workers taking breaks from employment for family reasons.

We can look at three specific dimensions of the construction of these leave periods: the status of the contract during the leave period; guarantees of employment security on the return from a break; and accrual of seniority and pension rights during a break. The legislation in effect creates a two-tiered system of family leave rights. In the first tier are rights connected with the arrival of a new child into the home: this concerns OML, OAL, and paternity leave. In the second tier are rights concerned with the on-going care of a young child or an older child who is disabled: AML and Additional Adoption Leave (AAL). Interestingly, parental leave moves from the second to the first tier as we move through these three dimensions.

Turning to the first dimension, in the first tier the contract of employment is deemed to subsist during the break. While the employee continues to be entitled to the benefit of her terms and conditions—other than pay—while on OML, OAL, and paternity leave, that employee in turn 'is bound by any obligations arising under those terms and conditions' except in so far as they are inconsistent with being on one of these leaves.[31] Hence only the obligations to carry out work (on the employee) and to provide pay (on the employer) are suspended during the leave period. This may well be the fullest possible statutory rendering of the sub-employment contractual mode identified by Freedland. It stands in sharp contrast to the vision of the employment contract propounded by the House of Lords in *Halfpenny* where it was assumed, as we saw, that once the wage–work obligations had been suspended, the contract contained no obligations during a break worth talking about.

We can see the far-reaching position taken in relation to first-tier rights by looking at the second tier of leave rights involving AML and AAL and, in this dimension, parental leave. Here the legislature has instead chosen to deem only certain specified contractual obligations to exist during these leave periods. Therefore, this must be considered to be a smaller set of contractual obligations than those present in the sub-employment mode of the first-tier rights. Given that, it is noteworthy that it is nonetheless an

---

[31] MPL Regs 1999, reg 9(1) (OML); PAL Regs 2002, reg 19 (OAL); PAL Regs 2002, reg 12 (paternity leave).

impressively rich range of contractual obligations. Four obligations for the employer are matched by five obligations for the employee. The employee is entitled to the benefit of the employer's implied obligation of trust and confidence, any terms and conditions of employment relating to notice of termination of the employment contract by the employer, compensation in the event of redundancy, and disciplinary or grievance procedures. She is bound by her implied obligation of good faith, any terms and conditions relating to notice of termination of the employment contract by her, the disclosure of confidential information, the acceptance of gifts or other benefits, and her participation in any other business.[32] To put the contrast between the first- and second-tier rights along this dimension in another way, in the former, the sub-employment mode is even closer to full-employment mode than in the latter. However, both renderings place the contract during the break much closer to full-employment mode than the characterisation as a matter of pure contractual analysis made by the House of Lords in *Halfpenny*.

Turning to the second dimension, employment security on return from a break, the first four weeks of parental leave are here placed by the legislature in the first tier, while the remaining weeks remain in the second tier. An employee on a first-tier leave has a right to have the same job after leave;[33] an employee on a second-tier leave has this right in principle but can be given another suitable and appropriate job for that employee if it is not reasonably practicable to give her back her old job.[34] An employee on a first-tier leave has therefore a strong guarantee not just of *employment* security but of *job* security.

Finally, an employee on OML, OAL, paternity leave, and parental leave (here moved fully into the first tier of leave rights) has a right to accrued seniority and pension while on leave.[35] Employees on AML or AAL do not accrue these rights during leave but the periods before and after leave are treated as if they are continuous, that is, the leave pauses but does not stop continuity of employment.[36] Overall, employees taking a break which is in the first-tier along all three dimensions are, again, leaving aside the important issue of income during the break, treated as though they have never been away. Were income replacement also to be assured, this would be as unprecarious as an employment break can get.

---

[32] MPL Regs 1999, reg 17 (AML, parental leave); PAL Regs 2002, reg 21 (AAL).

[33] MPL Regs 1999, reg 18(1) (OML, parental leave less than four weeks); PAL Regs 2002, reg 26(1) (OAL); PAL Regs 2002, reg 13 (paternity leave).

[34] MPL Regs 1999, reg 18(2) (AML, parental leave greater than four weeks); PAL Regs 2002, reg 26(2) (AAL).

[35] MPL Regs 1999, reg 18A(1)(a)(ii) (OML, parental leave); PAL Regs 2002, reg 14(1) (paternity leave).

[36] MPL Regs 1999, reg 18A(1)(a)(i) (AML); PAL Regs 2002, reg 27(1) (AAL).

EMPLOYER FAMILY LEAVE SCHEMES AND
CONTINUOUS EMPLOYMENT

From the end of the 1980s, growing numbers of UK employers have intro-duced child-break schemes in order to retain skilled female workers, although often these are limited to managerial employees. This evidently raises important questions as to how these new employer-led breaks will be legally conceptualised. Will the tools of contractual and statutory continu-ity be used to construct these as temporary or as definitive breaks in the relationship with the employer?

The Court of Appeal has recently analysed the child-break scheme of Marks & Spencer (M&S).[37] Ms Curr, who had worked for M&S from 1973 to 1990, decided, on the birth of her third child, to take advantage of a new child-leave scheme that had just been introduced. Her break lasted for four years. She signed an agreement relating to the leave. This required her to come and work for a minimum number of weeks each year and not to undertake any other paid employment during the break without prior consultation with her line manager. It also stated that she would be treated as having resigned, would receive no staff benefits, and would have her pen-sion frozen during the break. M&S undertook to offer re-employment in a managerial position, although not necessarily at the same level or in the same function on her return.

Ms Curr resumed normal work in 1994, having in fact worked for con-siderable tracts of time during the break (almost two years in total). She was dismissed on grounds of redundancy four and a half years later. M&S gave her a redundancy payment based on four and a half years' continuous employment, that is, it treated the child-break scheme as a definitive break. Ms Curr argued that as she had worked for M&S for over 20 years[38] she should receive the maximum statutory redundancy payment, that is, her time on the child-leave scheme should be treated as a temporary break.

The break could be seen as temporary on the basis of two different argu-ments, one based on establishing statutory continuity by showing contrac-tual continuity during the break, the other based on establishing statutory continuity despite the absence of contractual continuity (the second of the techniques for establishing statutory continuity identified earlier). Both these arguments that the break was temporary failed.

On the contractual argument, the Court of Appeal found that there was no contract of employment during the employment break. The Court of Appeal relied on the three-fold requirements for a contract of employment established

[37] *Curr v Marks & Spencer plc*, [2003] IRLR 74 (CA) (*Curr*).
[38] see above n 3.

in the earlier *Ready Mixed Concrete* case.[39] The court found the first two requirements to be satisfied: there was mutuality of obligation because of the requirements to work during the break and there was control of the employee's performance of that work. However, the third requirement, that the other provisions of the contract be consistent with its being a contract of employment, was not met. As Lord Justice Peter Gibson put it, 'The terms [of the child-leave agreement] are quite unlike a contract of employment that I have ever seen.'[40] This was because there was too much flexibility in when, where, and for how much money Ms Curr would work. Therefore, in Lord Justice Peter Gibson's view, the child-leave agreement was a master agreement which would provide the terms of any specific contracts of employment Ms Curr entered into during the child-break scheme, not a contract of employment.[41]

On the statutory continuity without a contract argument, Ms Curr argued that, in accordance with section 212(3)(c) of the Employment Rights Act 1996, her employment was continuous during the break because she was an employee 'absent from work in circumstances such that, by arrangement or custom, he is regarded as continuing in the employment of his employer for any purpose.' This argument, which had persuaded the Employment Appeal Tribunal, was rejected on the ground that, although there was clearly a continuing relationship between Ms Curr and M&S, it was insufficient for the purposes of the subsection. Both parties needed to regard the employee's employment as continuing. None of the features of Ms Curr's or the employer's obligations during the break, considered separately, sufficed. The fact that she had been required to resign pointed strongly against an arrangement or custom of continuing employment.

The Court of Appeal's reasoning shows just how difficult it will be for employees to persuade courts that an agreed break is temporary.

In relation to the contractual argument, this is because the courts assume that for a contract of employment to exist, it must exist in full-employment mode. They do not recognise in any real sense the existence of a contract in sub-employment mode during breaks. If they did so, it would make an immense difference. The statute does not require a contract of employment to exist in full-employment mode to be a week that counts in computing continuous employment: it suffices that an employee's relations with her employer are 'governed by a contract of employment'. That could very properly be a contract of employment in sub-employment mode.

In relation to the statutory continuity without contract argument, the judicial approach to breaks for family reasons seems to diverge widely from the current legislative and public policy stance being taken towards leave periods

---

[39] *Ready Mixed Concrete (South East) Ltd v Ministry of Pensions and National Insurance* [1968] 2 QB 497 (*Ready Mixed Concrete*).
[40] *Curr*, above n 37, at 80.
[41] For a similar argument in the context of the contractual analysis of casual work arrangements, see Collins, 2000.

for family purposes. In the previous section, we saw how New Labour has constructed a series of statutory breaks for family reasons in which a far-reaching set of contractual commitments are maintained between the parties during the break. Here, by contrast, the employer is in effect given the power to maintain the extensive benefits of a continuing relationship with the woman taking the break, while avoiding any of the costs of being an employer simply by dint of stopping the employee's benefits during the break, and requiring her to resign as a condition of taking up the break. In so doing, the employer here was able to convert an extremely long-term career engagement into a much shorter career engagement. Small wonder then that Ms Curr protested that 'morally' her period as a temporary employee should be taken into account in calculating the redundancy payment.

PRECARIOUS WORKING LIVES AND FAMILY BREAKS

The recent spurt of family-friendly activity by the UK legislature has created a disparity in the treatment of employment breaks for family reasons. This disparity is closely related to which of the two statutory continuity techniques is applied to a period or pattern of broken employment. Where the first technique is applied, deeming the contract to subsist during a break, the break is certainly temporary. This is the technique applied to the wide range of statutory breaks for family reasons created by the New Labour Government. However, where the second technique is applied, deeming statutory continuity to be established in certain situations (a temporary cessation of work, an arrangement or custom for continuing employment), despite the absence of contractual continuity, the courts are very likely to find the break to be definitive. This is the technique upon which those with casual working arrangements and contractually agreed career-leave schemes have to rely. Indeed, casual workers and career-leave workers such as Ms Curr find themselves in the same double bind. They are unable to establish contractual continuity for two main reasons. First, the courts are reluctant to accept the existence of any on-going contractual obligations when the worker is not actually working for the employer; they maintain a narrow focus on the wage–work bargain. Second, the UK courts defer to any signs in the contractual arrangements that the employer regards the break as definitive, although in practice it continues to benefit from its on-going relationship with the worker and will normally be in a position to dictate the contractual arrangements. The double-bind arises because the courts then refuse to apply the statutory technique of establishing continuity outside the contract *for precisely the same reason*, that is, the employer did not intend the cessation to be temporary or did not intend to enter into an arrangement or custom for continuing employment.[42]

---

[42] See *Booth v United States of America* [1999] IRLR 16, and *Curr*, above n 37.

The result is that, with few exceptions, unless the UK legislature tells the courts that a contract subsists despite the non-exchange of wages and work, or the parties have expressly agreed it, the UK courts assume that there is no continuity between the parties. Breaks are definitive and the position of women taking these breaks is thereby rendered very precarious indeed.

It might be argued that for the courts to construct continuity, either by saying that a contract exists in sub-employment mode during the periods when wages and work are not exchanged or by using the second statutory continuity technique to find that the break is a 'temporary cessation of work' or an 'arrangement' to keep the employment going, would simply be a regulatory own-goal. Employers would either contract around whatever the courts say or, alternatively, would simply cease to offer casual working arrangements or career breaks to women with family responsibilities.

With regard to the evasion argument, UK law, like other labour law systems, contains a perfectly good, although underused, technique which can be used to prevent employers contracting out of statutory obligations. UK law provides that, '[a]ny provision in an agreement (whether a contract of employment or not) is void in so far as it purports to exclude or limit the operation of any [statutory] provision.'[43]

As to the latter argument, that should casual workers or workers on contractually-agreed leave breaks accrue continuity in between wage-work bargains, employers would cease to offer contractual arrangements conducive to work–family reconciliation, this is the ever-green argument that labour law seriously affects how employers structure their jobs and to whom jobs are offered. No doubt sometimes this is true, though much less often than many would have it. One would have to establish that the costs to employers of casual workers and career-leave workers accruing continuity are high enough to exclude such workers from work–family-compatible contractual arrangements. In the meantime, the costs of the current legal analysis of casual workers and career-leave workers are much more tangible and most definitely gendered. More broadly, it is to be hoped that the courts will replace their twentieth-century male worker paradigm of employment patterns with contractual and statutory analyses attuned to new workers, men and women, with different priorities in a new economy.

---

[43] ERA 1996, s 203(1).

Part IV

A Matter of Status? Protecting Precarious Workers

8

Precarious Norms for Precarious Workers

SANDRA FREDMAN

F LEXIBILITY IS THE golden word of modern labour market policy. In the current era of globalisation, information technology, and the 'knowledge' economy, flexibility is said to achieve 'the highest levels of efficiency' (Collins, 2001: 18). In principle, flexibility seems to deliver the best of all worlds: for employers, to match labour supply and skills with rapidly changing demands; and for workers, to achieve a work–life balance, particularly where they have substantial child care responsibilities. Hugh Collins paints a rosy picture of the flexible worker, who uses a high level of knowledge and experience and is vested with a wide discretion not just to ensure that the job is done well, but also to redefine the tasks, goals, and the work itself (Collins, 2001: 24).

The real life experience is very different. 'Flexibility' itself is a flexible term, and its users are often not precise as to which meaning is being referred to. Whereas 'functional' flexibility consists in the employer's ability to require employees to adjust their skills to match the demands of changes in technology or workload, 'numerical' flexibility involves adjusting labour inputs to meet fluctuations in the employers' needs (Atkinson, 1984). Numerical flexibility is usually achieved by utilising part-time, temporary, and agency workers, altering the working-time patterns of shift or full-time workers, or contracting out. It is numerical flexibility that yields the precarious workforce: characterised by low pay, low status, and little by way of job security, training, or promotion prospects. The gains to employers in matching supply and demand have been translated directly into costs to workers. This shift of the costs is true across the European Union (EU): more than two thirds of those involuntarily in part-time work are in low-quality jobs—for example, low-paid, low-productivity jobs that do not offer job security, access to training, and career development opportunities (Commission of the European Communities (CEC), 2002b). This chapter is concerned with flexible workers in the numerical sense, and, to avoid confusion, the term 'non-standard worker' is used, referring to primarily to part-time, casual, agency, home, and temporary workers.

It is no accident that the non-standard workforce is made up predominantly of women. Women's continued primary responsibility for child care, together with intense pressure to provide or contribute to the household income, leaves them with comparatively few options for paid work. This dilemma is exacerbated by the United Kingdom's long-hours culture: the greater rewards open to men working long hours simply reinforce the gendered patterns of paid work and child care. While the rosy picture might be true of an ideal of functional flexibility, the real challenges for labour law lie in addressing numerical flexibility.

Non-standard work has been a feature of the UK labour market for many years, much longer than in many of its EU counterparts. This is largely because, while non-standard working was closely regulated in other jurisdictions, the policy of successive UK governments (often for differing rationales) has been to regard non-standard forms of work as outside the sphere of legitimate employment protection. Flexibility first gained currency as a labour market tool while the Conservative Party was in power from 1979 to 1997. Drawing on neoliberal economic dogma, the Thatcher and Major Governments legitimated exclusion on the grounds that non-standard workers could only be cost-effective to employers if their terms and conditions of employment were kept low (Fredman, 1997b).

Since 1997, a 'Third Way' has been in the ascendant, both in the EU and under New Labour in the United Kingdom (Fredman, 2004b). Rejecting the neoliberal view that employment standards impede job creation by creating burdens on business, the 'Third Way' views employment rights as facilitating productive and committed non-standard workers. Thus the EU employment strategy has consistently emphasised 'quality [in work] as the guiding thread of the Social Policy Agenda, and in particular quality in work as an important objective of the European Employment Strategy' (CEC, 2002b: 9). Indeed, Simon Deakin and Jude Browne have recently argued that such rights are essential to market creation (Deakin and Browne, 2003). The ideal of a flexible worker has been a key component of the Lisbon strategy to make the EU the most dynamic and competitive economy in the world (Ashiagbor, chapter 4 in this volume).

However, there remains a deep ambivalence on the part of policy-makers as to the extent to which the benefits employers gain from flexibility should carry with them social responsibilities. Much rhetoric is expended within New Labour ideology on the mutuality of rights and responsibilities, and on the importance of family-friendly norms, but the more powerful voice is that of competitiveness; and the apparent match between 'family-friendly' and flexibility soon evaporates. The result has been that diluted EU norms have been further diluted in their transposition into domestic law. The position of non-standard workers remains precarious.

The aim of this chapter is to examine the development of these precarious norms for precarious workers from a specifically gendered perspective. Women have always formed the bulk of the precarious workforce, and even now the numbers of men in this form of work are small. The chapter critically evaluates the contribution of the 'Third Way' policy objectives and the ways in which these objectives are refracted through the prism of the courts. The first part of the chapter examines the gendered dimension of precarious work through workforce statistics. The second part briefly rehearses legal developments, before turning more specifically to New Labour's attempt to refashion labour law to be more inclusive of precarious workers. The third part focuses on the legal understandings of the concept of a 'worker', examining particularly mutuality of obligation and the requirement for personal service, while the final section considers the ways in which the equality concept has been used, and its interaction with substantive rights.

WOMEN ON THE MARGINS: PRECARIOUS WORK AND GENDER

Distribution of wealth, power, and resources in modern Britain remains highly gendered. In 2003, women in Britain were still 14 per cent more likely than men to be living in poverty, that is, in a household with incomes below 60 per cent of the median (Bradshaw *et al*, 2003). These figures, moreover, probably significantly understate the problem, since there is an implicit assumption that women in households with incomes above this level have access to a male partner's income. In fact, women's poverty may well be hidden by unequal distribution of income within the household. Crucial to the alleviation of women's poverty, therefore, is access to their own income through paid work. However, as John Bradshaw *et al* point out, 'women in paid work are not free from the risk of poverty. This is because for women more than for men, labour market does not guarantee an adequate income' (Bradshaw *et al*, 2003: 15).

The reasons for this have not changed in decades (Fredman, 1997a). Women remain primarily responsible for child care, while men in the United Kingdom work excessively long hours. In fact, figures from 2002 show that UK fathers work an average of 46 hours a week, compared to the average of almost 28 hours for UK mothers. As many as one in eight fathers work 60 or more hours a week, compared to less than 2 per cent of mothers (O'Brien and Shemitt, 2003: 11). Women, under increasing pressure to contribute to the income of the family as well as care for children, therefore, resort to part-time or non-standard work, entering the workforce on the very margins. Part-time work is thus profoundly gendered. In 2002, 43 per cent of female employees in the United Kingdom worked part time compared with only 9 per cent of male employees. Moreover, most of the male part-time employees were under 25 years old, reflecting the fact that for men part-time work is a transient feature of their lives. Women, however, work part time at all stages of their lives. These figures are larger than the average in the EU as a whole, where 34 per cent of women employees work part time as against only 7 per cent of men (EU, 2004).

Part-time and non-standard work carry obvious benefits for employers, permitting them to match staffing levels to peaks in demand. In addition, non-wage costs, such as national insurance payments and training costs, are low. In principle, too, part-time working has substantial advantages for workers, who can combine paid work with participative parenting. In fact, however, working part time carries with it significant detriments, as employers' costs are transferred to workers. For women in particular, part-time work tends to be poorly paid and undervalued. In 2003, women working part time earned only 59 per cent of the average hourly earnings of men working full time, a pay gap that has hardly changed since 1975 (Equal Opportunities Commission (EOC), 2003). Statistics showing a narrowing of the pay gap between men and women reflect full-time work only; reflecting the general invisibility of part-time work.

The long-hours culture for men, by contrast, brings with it substantial rewards, particularly in the form of overtime pay and other bonuses. The result is that, if we shift the focus from hourly pay to gross income, we find that, for 2003 women's gross individual income, including income from employment, pensions, benefits, investments, and so forth, was, on average, a startlingly low 51 per cent of men's (EOC, 2003). A key component of this disparity is the relative lack of access of part-time workers to performance-related pay.

Particularly problematic is the effect of non-standard working on pensions. Non-standard working carries with it all the factors associated with low pension income: low earnings, time not spent in full-time work, low or irregular private pension contributions, and earlier retirement. In particular, larger reductions in pension income arise from caring and part-time work (EOC, 2003: 8). Moreover, disadvantage is cumulative. As well as being less likely to have a current private pension arrangement, women are less likely to make regular contributions to a pension. Of those aged 25 to 59 in work in 2001–02, 44 per cent of men but only 26 per cent of women had made pension contributions in each of the previous 10 years (EOC, 2003: 15). Recent reforms will have some impact in offsetting lower earnings, partially offsetting fewer private pension contributions, but there are still significant reductions in state and private pension income through time spent out of paid work, and in part time work. According to the EOC, 'the close link between eventual pension income and standard labour market participation in the current pension system means that many women will continue to receive low individual pension incomes' (2003: 24).

It has been argued by neoliberal economists such as Richard Posner that the focus on women's pay ignores the fact that the division of labour within the household produces an overall income stream, whereby the father contributes the bulk of the income and the mother the bulk of the family work (Posner, 1989). Apart from the dubious assumption that all family units are composed of father and mother, this assumes that the income is equitably shared within the household. In fact, research shows that part-time work simply reduces the pressure on the husband's wage without increasing the wife's influence over finances. It is also widely demonstrated that relatively more of a woman's earnings is used on household necessities; often simply allowing their partner to spend more of his earnings on his own consumption (Bradshaw *et al*, 2003: 21). Where the woman is the only earner in the household, the position is clearly even worse.

Other types of non-standard work display similar patterns of disadvantage. Workers on temporary and fixed-term contracts by definition have little or no job security, but added to this are their relatively low income levels, lack of access to vocational training, and exclusion from occupational pension schemes. Women and men are fairly evenly balanced within agency work but a higher proportion of women than men work on fixed-term contracts (European Foundation for the Protection of Living and Working Conditions, 2002: 93–94). This seems to reflect the underlying job segregation, with the largest percentage of agency workers in banking and finance where women predominate. Even if non-standard working of some types is not gendered in its composition, it is often gendered in its rewards. The gendered nature of rewards is particularly striking in relation to evening and night working (as opposed to regular day work). Although a higher proportion of men than women work nights (17 per cent of men compared to 9 per cent of women employees), recent evidence shows that while men usually receive a wage premium for working at night or in the evenings, women do not. Such premiums enable low-skilled men to avoid low pay by working at night. Thus, full-time working men received a 3 per cent pay premium for working during the evening, and 7 per cent for working at night. Women, on the other hand, received a 3 per cent pay premium for working evenings but only if they worked full time. No premium was attached to part-time women workers during the evening; and full-time female employees receive no pay premium for night work (Harkness, 2002).

It is not only in respect of their direct pay packet that non-standard workers are disadvantaged. In addition, those who earn below the lower earnings limit (LEL) for national insurance contributions (£79 a week in 2004) are effectively excluded from the national insurance system. Workers earning below the LEL are not required to pay contributions, nor are employers required to pay contributions on their behalf. The result is that they do not acquire rights to key contributory benefits, including incapacity benefit, retirement pensions, contribution-based jobseeker's allowance, statutory sick pay, statutory maternity pay, statutory paternity pay, and statutory adoption pay. Currently, as many as one-and-a-half million, or one in eight, working women earn less than the LEL (Pensions Policy Institute, 2003: 12). The vast majority (94 per cent) of employees who earned below the LEL in 1998 worked part time, and more than a third of all part-time women employees earned below the LEL. Workers earning below the LEL are more likely to be employed in temporary jobs than those earning above the LEL, although a higher proportion of women than men who earn below the LEL are in permanent jobs (McKnight *et al*, 1998).

Of most concern is the effect of the LEL on retirement pensions. State pension rights require contributions above the LEL for at least 44 years for men and women born after 1955.[1] None of those women earning below the LEL will therefore qualify even for basic state pension. Nor will the almost one-and-a-half million women currently of working age who have, at some time during their lives, paid the reduced rate for married women (EOC, 2003). It is no surprise that elderly women are amongst the poorest in society. Women's pension income is only 59 per cent of that of men, with 50 per cent of women pensioners receiving less than £103 per week (EOC, 2003).

PRECARIOUS NORMS: HISTORY AND CONTEXT

Legal responses in the United Kingdom to non-standard forms of work have varied markedly over recent decades, reflecting wide divergences in the function attributed to labour law.[2] For the first half of the twentieth century, the prevalent ideology was that of collective laissez faire, the term coined by Otto Kahn Freund to describe the primacy of collective bargaining over direct legal regulation of terms and conditions of employment (Davies and Freedland, 1983: 18). The primacy of collective bargaining meant that, unlike most continental systems, there was little if any legal regulation of standard work. Instead, terms and conditions were determined by collective bargaining. Only in areas of work which collective bargaining failed to reach was legal regulation justified. Paradoxically then, it was in the areas of non-standard work that such 'special' protection applied. Thus, protective legislation regulated the hours of work only of children and women, and minimum wages legislation applied only to pockets of employment with exceptionally low pay and no collective bargaining. Notably, protective legislation specifically included workers under a contract for services, provided the contract was personally to execute work or labour.

---

[1] For women born before 1955, the pension age is 60 and the number of years of contribution is 39.

[2] This section is derived from Fredman, 1997b.

It was, however, in the context of social security that the 'binary' divide was instituted (Deakin, 2002). It was only on behalf of 'subordinate' workers that employers could be expected to pay national insurance contributions, thus sharing the risk of unemployment. Self-employed workers or independent contractors were considered to be responsible for themselves, paying lower contributions and excluded from the unemployment compensation scheme. Thus, as Simon Deakin demonstrates, it was the National Insurance Act of 1946, drawing on the Beveridge Report on social insurance (Beveridge, 1942), that first instituted the 'binary' divide between employees and the self-employed (Deakin, 2002: 185).

During the 1960s and 1970s, collective laissez faire was gradually under-pinned by a floor of rights, such as notice, protection against unfair dis-missal, and redundancy compensation. Unlike the special protection of the earlier period, however, these rights were not intended for those on the mar-gins. Indeed, those on the margins were rendered invisible by the division between workers who needed and deserved protection, and independent entrepreneurs, who could stand on their own two feet. Workers in turn were subdivided into those under a contract of service, and those under a contract of personal services. The latter were only entitled to protection against sex and race discrimination,[3] while the former were entitled to a range of employment rights.

The task of differentiating between these two categories was left to the courts, whose focus on legalistic notions of contract made it impossible to frame the category according to the social purpose of redressing the imbal-ance between employer and worker.[4] The growing body of non-standard workers found themselves outside of the scope of both collective bargain-ing and employment protection, without having the genuine economic inde-pendence of the entrepreneur. These divisions were deepened by the social insurance system, which followed a similar distinction between employed, self-employed, and non-employed workers. The self-employed, initially excluded from national insurance, were later admitted, but only partially. They remain excluded from unemployment and industrial injury benefits, and maternity benefits are lower. Contributions are only payable by the employer on behalf of 'employed earners'; the self-employed pay a single flat-rate contribution.

The exclusion of non-standard workers from employment rights was ele-vated into an ideology by the neoliberal government in power from 1979 to 1997. Conservative labour law policies were driven by the view that a low-cost and highly flexible workforce was essential to increased competitiveness and lower unemployment. Part of the project of decreasing the 'burdens on

---

[3] Sex Discrimination Act 1975 (UK), s 82; Race Relations Act 1976 (UK), s.78.

[4] This may be contrasted with the Canadian court's purposive approach: see Fudge, chap-ter 9 in this volume.

business' was consciously to remove employment protection rights from non-standard workers. These included abolition of minimum wage laws, and increasing eligibility thresholds for unfair dismissal and redundancy rights. Employers were encouraged to classify workers as self-employed or to keep pay below the national insurance threshold in order to avoid having to pay employers' national insurance contributions. The process of exclusion was augmented by creating both duties and incentives on employers to transfer workers out of standard employment into non-standard working. Thus, local authorities and other public bodies were required to move from in-house employment to outsourcing under the Compulsory Competitive Tendering programme, and private employers followed suit.

These policies, particularly measures undermining rights for part-time workers, had a disproportionately serious impact on women. During this period, the only bulwark against the onslaught was the sex discrimination laws, supported by EU directives on the same subject. Crucially, the courts accepted that imposing a detriment on part-time workers in fact excludes substantially more women than men, thus breaching the indirect discrimination provisions.[5]

New Labour came to power in 1997 committed to an ideology of the 'Third Way', which characterises employment rights, not as a burden to business, but as a positive business asset. The Third Way sets itself apart both from neoliberalism and from its social welfare predecessors in four main respects (Fredman, 2004a). The first concerns the nature of the state. Instead of the neutral, non-interventionist state to which neoliberals aspire, and the highly interventionist social democratic state, the Third Way proposes a facilitative role for the state. Second, the Third Way stands for civic responsibility, according to which individual rights carry with them important social responsibilities. Third, the Third Way stands for participative democracy, aiming to create a socially inclusive society. The fourth characteristic of the Third Way is its emphasis on equal opportunities. Instead of the egalitarian emphasis on outcomes, the Third Way stands for equal opportunities. 'We favour true equality,' writes Tony Blair, 'equal worth and equal opportunity, not an equality of outcome focused on incomes alone' (Blair, 2002: 2). Equal opportunity frequently means more than the removal of demand-side obstacles. In addition, it requires the provision of strategic goods, such as education, child care, and income that make it possible for individuals to utilise available opportunities (White, 2001: 4).

These principles point to a state that facilitates the integration of all into the paid workforce, so as to ensure that all participate in the life of the community. Therefore, a central policy of New Labour has been to counter unemployment and tackle poverty and social exclusion. Welfare has been

---

[5] *R v Secretary of State ex parte Equal Opportunities Commission* [1995] 1 AC 1 (HL).

reshaped to provide a bridge between unemployment and paid work, the central aim being to facilitate a move away from welfare and into paid employment. In principle, this has meant not just creating more low-paid jobs, as had been the case under Conservative policy, but making paid work more attractive. A key to this policy then is the provision not just of social benefits but of 'social investment', the creation of greater opportunities by investing in individual human capital through education, training, and other supply-side means. This matches current EU policies that focus not just on quantity, but also on quality of work.

Several key policies have been put in place in furtherance of this objective. On the 'push' side have been the welfare-to-work programmes centred on the New Deal; while on the 'pull side' have been the minimum wage, working families tax credit (now child-tax credit and working-tax credit), and the national child care strategy. In addition, measures to alleviate child poverty have put more money in the hands of those primarily responsible for children, namely women (Bradshaw *et al*, 2003). However, gender inequalities have not been addressed directly, with the result that disparities in provision remain, for example, in the provision of resources for various New Deal programmes.

The 'pull side' measures have the potential to enhance the benefits of working part time or for low earnings. Women, and non-standard workers in particular, have been the prime beneficiaries. However, many of the labour law measures, under the guise of creating a synthesis between fairness and efficiency, have in fact been primarily driven by efficiency considerations. The result has been the dilution of the norms.

The minimum wage is a good example of such a dilution. Since women are over-represented amongst the poorest paid workers, it is not surprising that they are amongst its chief beneficiaries. The minimum wage on its introduction benefited one-and-a-half million workers, of whom about 70 per cent were women. Annual increases of the wage have shown similar patterns: the increase in 2002 benefited about one million workers, 70 per cent of whom were women and about two thirds of whom worked part time. The minimum wage has also had some effect on the gender pay gap, but only at the bottom of the earnings distribution (Low Pay Commission, 2003).

In fact, however, the number of beneficiaries has been lower than that predicted by the Low Pay Commission (Low Pay Commission, 2003). Since the Low Pay Commission sets the rate at a level which it believes will be easily absorbed by the labour market, this suggests that it could have been set at a level which benefited more workers without negative effects on the labour market (Simpson, 2004). As Bob Simpson argues, this demonstrates that the aim of the minimum wage is not to produce a living wage, but to set a threshold for benefits (Simpson, 2004). Setting the minimum wage at such a level means that the many women who work in precarious jobs will continue to find that, while paid work is a necessity, it is by no means a guaranteed route out of poverty. Indeed, despite the promises of New Labour, it is not intended to be.

A similar pattern is evident in respect of the regulation of working time, where 'flexibility' has come to mean employers' freedom to increase working time as and when their operational requirements suggest. The UK government achieved this by making maximal use of the exception permitted by the EC Directive for individuals to make agreements with their employers to opt out of the 48-hour limit to weekly working hours.[6] The use of the opt-out is very widespread indeed: a Confederation of British Industry (CBI) survey found that 33 per cent of UK workers have signed an opt-out agreement.[7] Indeed, the ability to opt out has been portrayed as an important element in ensuring that the British labour market remains more 'flexible' than its European counterparts. As has been cogently argued, 'flexibility' in this sense seems to mean 'freedom from external constraint' (Barnard *et al*, 2003: 249), quite the opposite of the ideals of New Labour. It is not surprising that the Working Time Directive has had so little impact on the long-hours culture in the UK. In fact, the number of people working above the maximum limit has increased from 15 per cent at the beginning of the 1990s to 16 per cent in 2004.

Also an important part of the strategy of providing equal opportunities has been the bundle of 'family-friendly' rights. As well as the national child care strategy, there have been improved maternity rights,[8] and new rights to parental[9] and paternity leave.[10] In addition, employees with children under the age of five have the right to request a change from full-time to non-standard working.[11] But, as with the minimum wage and working time, all these rights are subservient to employer's interest. Thus, parental leave is unpaid and the employer can postpone it for business reasons; paternity leave is very brief; and the right to request flexible working is no more than a right to request, and to be given reasons if refused. Most importantly, all of these rights and the opportunity to request flexible working time depend on a worker having the status of 'employee',[12] which, as we shall see below, excludes a significant number of non-standard workers. It is to this issue that I now turn.

---

[6] Working Time Regulations 1998, SI 1998/1833, art 18(1)(b).

[7] Communication from the Commission from the Commission to the Council, the European Parliament, the European Economic and Social Committee and the Committee of the Regions and the social partners at Community level concerning the re-examination of Council Directive 93/104 concerning certain aspects of the organization of working time (2003), COM (2003)843 final/2.

[8] Employment Rights Act 1996, ss 71–75.

[9] *Ibid*, s 76.

[10] *Ibid* at ss 80A, 80F.

[11] Employment Act 2002, s 47.

[12] Self-employed workers have some maternity rights.

THE ROLE OF THE COURTS

The above discussion has shown that the legal framework, while showing plenty of promise, has been considerably weakened by the tenacity of the underlying assumption that employment rights are a burden on business. The resulting norms have been further diluted in the hands of the courts, which are responsible for defining the concept of worker and, therefore, the scope of statutory rights. As will be shown below, the courts' fixation with the principle of contract has not just marginalised workers but made them invisible. This topic is explored below.

Definition of 'Worker'

Non-standard workers pose particular challenges for contract-based labour law because their services are not wholly at the disposal of the employer. This arrangement gives them a semblance of autonomy and independence, which appear to be the hallmarks of the independent entrepreneur or micro-enterprise. But this appearance is only because the relationship is seen from the perspective of the employer. From the perspective of the worker, the absence of a full-time commitment to one employer is evidence of the instability and precariousness of their role in the labour market. The independent entrepreneur actively assumes the risks and benefits of the market. For non-standard workers, by contrast, the position is reversed. The advantages of flexibility to the employer lie primarily in passing some of the risks of the enterprise onto the worker. Far from transforming the non-standard worker into an independent entrepreneur, this adds to the vulnerability and precarious status of the worker.[13]

It is this difference in power relations between the entrepreneur and the non-standard worker that UK labour law, with its fixation on contract as a means of defining work relationships, finds so difficult to grasp. Instead, the assumption is that the employer can only be expected to have certain social responsibilities or duties towards the worker where the employer has the power to demand that the worker accepts work. Any choice on the part of the worker to refuse to do the work, however formal, appears to give him or her sufficient autonomy to relieve the employer of its social responsibilities. This assumption is expressed through the notion of mutuality of obligation, explored further below. Similarly, the employer cannot, on this view, be expected to have obligations to those who are employers in their own right. It is this assumption that is expressed through the requirement of personal service. The potential for the worker to substitute another person appears to turn the worker into an employer in her own right. In fact, as

---

[13] For a helpful typology of self-employment, see Fudge, chapter 9 in this volume.

will be argued below, the substitution requirement more often represents a shifting of the risk of unavailability for work from the employer to the worker. Instead of the employer having to find substitutes for the worker, the employer requires the worker to do so.

Some of the problem lies in the characterisation of the employment relationship as bilateral, existing between the worker and the specific employer. Flexibility challenges this bilateral characterisation because non-standard workers are frequently in relationships with more than one employing entity; or are only partially occupied in the labour force at all. From the perspective of the individual employer, it may seem that the relationship with the worker does not warrant social duties being placed on that particular employer. But the implication of adopting this perspective is that no single employer has any duties towards the worker. This implication is particularly problematic for women, whose family responsibilities may make it impossible for them to make themselves available to the employer to the extent seen to justify reciprocal obligations on the part of the employer.

Instead, the new flexible labour market requires an acknowledgement of the shared responsibility of all employers within the labour market as a whole. The Third Way ideology contains the potential to make this move. Third Way ideology emphasises corporate civic responsibility as one of the key pillars of the philosophy. Responsibility is not seen as a burden on business, but as an aspect of citizenship. More pragmatically, Third Way ideology characterises flexible working as contributing in a central way both to the individual employer and to the economy as a whole. The responsibilities attached to the employment of flexible workers are viewed as incentives to employers to invest in flexible workers' human capital because of their potential to enhance performance and hence competitiveness. This perspective contrasts strongly with previous views that saw such responsibilities as adding to the cost of workers and therefore only justifiable if the employer had access to the worker's services at all times.

However, this perspective requires a move away from the strictly bipartite notion of contract that continues to dominate the area of employment law in the United Kingdom. With the significant and salient exception of the *Dacas* case (discussed below),[14] the courts have so far refused to do so. From the perspective of contract, the precarious worker simply does not exist. There has been some attempt to change this at legislative level. Statutory protection against discrimination has always extended beyond the contract of service to the contract to provide personal services. This concept has been refined under New Labour legislation, to exclude contracts for services where the relationship is one between a professional or business and a client or customer.[15]

---

[14] *Dacas v Brook Street Bureau* [2004] EWCA (Civ) 217 (CA).
[15] *Clark v Oxfordshire Health Authority* [1998] IRLI 125 (CA) (*Clark*).

The attempt here is to capture two distinct sets of power relationships: one between employer and worker, where the former is clearly dominant, and one between a service provider and a client or customer, where relationships are on a basis of market equality. This definition has been attached to the rights introduced under the influence of the Third Way, in particular minimum wage laws,[16] working time,[17] and part-time workers' rights.[18]

However, as will be seen below, the courts have tended to ignore this aspect of the definition, focusing instead on the questions of personal service and mutuality of obligation. Since these are questions relating to the very existence of the contract, they apply to both contracts of service and contracts for services. Recent cases have rarely proceeded to the next stage, which requires a classification of the contract as one for services or of service. The result has been significantly to diminish the importance of the distinction.

A somewhat different way of conceptualising the distinction is to consider economic dependence instead of subordination (European Commission, 2003a). Economic dependence can arise without subordination where a worker provides a service to an employer, but instead of having a diversity of 'clients', it is wholly or largely dependent on a single source. This conceptualisation could capture some non-standard workers, particularly, agency workers within the scope of employment protection legislation.[19] But many of the most vulnerable workers would, almost by definition, need to be only partially dependent on a single employer, needing to look to other employers, social security, or family members to supplement earned income.

These general principles are expanded below, with particular emphasis on the way in which the statutory definitions are refracted in the prism of the court.

Mutuality of Obligation

For non-standard workers, the fact that they have only a fragmented relationship with a particular employer makes it very difficult for the courts to conceive of a contractual framework encapsulating that relationship. There is typically no problem in characterising the period in which work actually takes place as a contract, and in general the contract has all the trappings of control and subordination of a contract of service. However, the courts

---

[16] See, eg, National Minimum Wage Act 1998, s 54(3)(b).

[17] Working Time Regulations 1998, above n 7, reg 54.

[18] Part-Time Workers (Prevention of Less Favourable Treatment) Regulations 2000, SI 2000/1551, reg 2.

[19] *Motorola Ltd v Davidson* [2001] IRLR 4 (EAT) (*Motorola*).

have declined to see these individual contractual fragments as part of an on-going contractual relationship (see Kilpatrick, chapter 7 in this volume). Instead, where an employer structures the relationship so that the worker may choose whether or not to carry out a particular assignment, the courts have refused to make the employer responsible for the worker in between contracts. The employer's corresponding right not to offer work is seen to reinforce this approach.

This pattern can be clearly seen in the series of decisions on mutuality of obligations that have been issuing from the courts since the *Trusthouse Forte* decision in 1995.[20] For a spectrum of workers, ranging from casual waiters[21] to dockworkers,[22] bank nurses,[23] and casual tour guides,[24] the courts have refused to find that a series of individual contracts could be characterised as part of an on-going relationship. The employer's freedom to choose whether to offer work, the essence of flexibility, is seen to be simply a reflex of the worker's freedom to choose whether to accept work on each occasion. However, far from transforming a worker into an equal partner in the labour market, the absence of mutuality increases the precariousness of the worker's situation.

The courts are quick to point out the ideal combination of flexibility on both sides: that of workers, predominantly women, to fulfil their domestic commitments, and that of employers to respond to fluctuations of demand.[25] These advantages to women are seen to legitimate the employer's lack of on-going responsibility. However, what is lost in this contractual focus is the fact that work becomes doubly precarious for the women: not only can they not rely on a constant source of work, but the on-going relationship with the employer (which clearly exists as a social reality) does not bring with it any social responsibilities by the employer towards the worker. This result is particularly problematic when the effect is to permit race or sex discrimination by the employer.

This is well illustrated by the House of Lords in *Carmichael*,[26] in which the House of Lords was required to consider whether casual tour guides at British Gas were employed under a contract of service and were therefore entitled to a statement of their particulars of employment. Lord Irvine had no difficulty in pointing out that when actually working as guides, they

---

[20] See *Franks v Reuters* [2003] IRLR 423 (CA) (*Franks*); *Hewlett Packard Ltd v O'Murphy* [2002] IRLR 4 (EAT) (*Hewlett Packard*); *O'Kelly v Trusthouse Forte* [1983] IRLR 369 (CA) (*Trusthouse Forte*).
[21] *Trusthouse Forte*, above n 20.
[22] *Hellyer Bros Ltd v McLeod* [1986] ICR 122
[23] *Clark*, above n 15.
[24] *Carmichael v National Power plc* [2000] IRLR 43, [1999] 1 WLR 2042 (HL) (*Carmichael*).
[25] *Ibid.*
[26] *Ibid.*

were clearly under contracts. However, the fact that the employer did not have the contractual right to insist on the worker's services on all occasions made it impossible for the court to envisage a contractual relationship. Instead, it was held, the documents provided by the employer detailing their responsibilities 'provided no more than a framework for ad hoc contracts of service or services which [the applicants] might make with [the employer] in the future.'[27] Such flexibility, Lord Irvine pointed out, suited both the employer's needs and those of the workers, who were, not surprisingly, women with domestic commitments.

However, the result, when looked at in the round, is strange. On the one hand, British Gas advertised for, selected, and then trained the women. It then made them an 'offer of employment as a station guide on a casual as required basis.' But, according to the court, by accepting the offer,

> Mrs Leese and Mrs Carmichael were doing no more than intimate that they were ready to be invited to attend for casual work as station guides as and when the [employer] required their services. Just as the [employer] was not promising to offer them any casual work, but merely intimating that it might be offered, so also they were not agreeing to attend whenever required.'[28]

On the face of it, the courts seem driven by the contractual concept to insist on mutuality of obligations. However, it is not clear why contract should require such mutuality. In all the cases in question, there is no doubt of the fact that there was a continuing relationship between the employer and the worker, and this was encapsulated in documentation such as that in *Carmichael*, where workers expressly accepted 'employment'. Reading this arrangement as constituting no more than an intimation that work might be offered is at odds both with the wording of the document and the social reality. The result, too, is at odds with the purpose of statutory employment rights.

The rationale from an employment protection perspective is difficult to discern. Casual waiters were denied the right to belong to a trade union;[29] long-standing dockworkers were denied redundancy compensation despite having worked on a series of separate contracts for up to 25 years;[30] bank (or agency) nurses were denied protection against unfair dismissal;[31] and casual tour guides were denied the right to a statement of particulars of employment.[32] The Third Way promises a happy marriage between flexibility and fairness, where fairness to the worker is not a burden but a positive asset to the employer. The structure of the law, far from creating incentives

---

[27] *Ibid.*
[28] [1999] 1 WLR 2042 at 2047
[29] *Trusthouse Forte*, above n 20.
[30] *Hellyer Bros*, above n 22.
[31] *Clark*, above n 15.
[32] *Carmichael*, above n 24.

to employers to invest in workers to this end, encourages the opposite. Neoliberal assumptions that employment rights are burdensome and unfair costs on business remain dominant in the outcome.

Most difficult to justify is the application of the doctrine of mutual obligations to discrimination. There is no ready rationale for permitting discrimination against others in the labour market, regardless of the nature of the interrelationship. But where there is a relationship of dependence, however it is constituted, there is nothing to explain the legitimation of sex, race, or any other form of discrimination. Given the increasingly complex web of interrelations and dependence, the ways in which demarcation lines are drawn become more and more indefensible.

This is strikingly illustrated by the recent Court of Appeal case of *Mingeley*,[33] in which a taxi-driver brought a race discrimination claim against the proprietors of Amber Cars, which allocated calls to drivers. His claim failed. Although he wore the Amber Car uniform, and was wholly dependent on them to provide paying passengers, he was free to work or not to work as he pleased. The court concluded that there was no mutuality of obligation. The Tribunal accepted that in the real world, the applicant would make himself available to work, so that he could earn a living. But they insisted that the test was not the commercial reality but the strict contractual position. The result was to block his claim of race discrimination without ever considering the merits. The use of this criterion in relation particularly to discrimination makes the statutory purpose difficult to defend. As both Buxton and Maurice Kay LJJ stated in *Mingeley*,[34] it is doubtful whether Parliament intended the emphasis on dominant purpose, but they held that the line of authority was too strong to disrupt.

Personal Service

The criterion of 'personal service' tries to capture the difference between a service provider who is herself an employer, and therefore falls into the category of a micro-enterprise, and one who provides a service in a relationship of imbalance of market power, captured by the notion either of subordination or economic dependence. However, this criterion has proved to be far from an accurate gauge of the distinction between equal market relationships and the imbalance of power between employer and worker, because the employer can take advantage of its position of power in respect of the worker and insist that the worker be responsible for providing substitutes in the event of absence. The result is, again, a double reinforcement of the

---

[33] *Mingeley v Pennock and Ivory (trading as Amber Cars)* [2004] EWCA Civ 328 (CA) (*Mingeley*).
[34] *Ibid.*

imbalance of power. The contractual term serves to pass the risk of absence to the worker, which, in turn, functions to absolve the employer of a range of responsibilities towards the worker, including that of non-discrimination.

The limiting influence of this criterion has been exacerbated by judicial interpretations, which have insisted that the contract should not just be personally to execute work or labour, but that this should be the dominant purpose.[35] This is clearly open to manipulation by employers. Thus, in *Express & Echo Publications Ltd v Tanton*,[36] the employee was made redundant, and re-engaged under an 'agreement for services', which required him to arrange for a substitute should he be 'unable or unwilling' to do the work. The Court of Appeal held that where a contract allowed services to be provided by another person, it had to be construed as a contract for the supply for services rather than a contract of service. Accordingly, Tanton could not be considered an employee and therefore had no right to claim unfair dismissal.

The potential limiting consequences of the personal services criterion were fortunately stemmed in *MacFarlane*,[37] where gymnastic instructors, who were previously employees, were issued with new contracts changing their status to self-employed contractors, and which included a clause requiring them to arrange for a substitute, at their own expense, on any occasion on which they were unable to work. The risk of absence was, therefore, clearly passed from the employer to the worker. Fortunately, the court distinguished the case from *Tanton*, on the basis that the clause only applied if they were unable to work, rather than, as in *Tanton*, when they were 'unable or unwilling' to work. The court dubbed the *Tanton* clause as 'extreme', but it is clearly not beyond the wit of a well-advised employer to include a clause of that nature.[38] Although *MacFarlane* is a welcome acknowledgement of the social realities, it stands alone against a strong line of Court of Appeal authority, as has already been demonstrated.[39]

Agency Workers

It is only with respect to agency workers that the courts have very recently been willing to expand contractual concepts. Agency workers are workers who are not employed directly by the end-user or principal, but supplied by an agency to do the work, typically under a contract between the end-user and the agency. Agency workers pose a particular challenge, because the

---

[35] *Mirror Group Newspapers v Gunning* [1986] IRLR 27 (CA).
[36] [1999] ICR 693 (CA).
[37] *MacFarlane v Glasgow City Council* [2001] IRLR 7 (EAT).
[38] *Dacas*, above n 14.
[39] *Staffordshire Sentinel Newspapers Ltd v Potter* 2004 WL 1060637.

managerial function is triangulated, so that the entity that has control over the worker is different from the entity that is responsible for remuneration. Courts have found this so difficult to disentangle that they have, on occasion, held that the worker is an employee of no one.[40] However, a series of cases,[41] culminating in the important Court of Appeal case of *Dacas*,[42] has suggested that a contract of service should be implied between the end-user and the worker where this was a necessary inference from the conduct of the parties and the work done. This was fully compatible with the existence of contracts along the other two sides of the triangle, namely between the worker and the agency, and between the agency and the end-user.

This result was strongly contested by Mr Justice Munby in dissent. He argued that the fact that the obligation to remunerate and the right to control are located in different parties has previously been 'relied on by the industry as necessarily producing the happy outcome happy that is, both for the agency and the end-user, though, not of course, for the worker that the worker has no contract of service either with the agency or with the end-user.'[43] In particular, he held that there was no mutuality of obligation between the end-user and the worker, because the end-user was under no obligation to either provide work or provide remuneration. Particularly illuminating is his analysis of the nature of the employer's obligation, which he envisaged as consisting only of the obligation to provide work or the obligation to remunerate.[44] This failure to recognise that employers (including end-users) ought to have a range of responsibilities consequential on their power to control the worker epitomises the narrowness of the judicial approach, and the inevitability that the very precariousness of non-standard workers' position will be used as a reason for the courts to refuse them social rights. Fortunately, both Lord Justices Mummery and Sedley emphasised that the contractual situation should be made to accord with common sense and practical reality.

EQUALITY AND PRECARIOUS WORKERS

For many years, the only source of protection for non-standard workers was anti-discrimination law. This is because the coverage of discrimination law is somewhat wider, including not only workers under a contract for personal services, than the scope of other employment-related legislation, and because principals who make work available to individuals not

---

[40] *Ibid.*
[41] *Franks*, above n 20; *Hewlett Packard* above n 20; and *Motorola* above n 19.
[42] *Dacas*, above n 14.
[43] *Ibid.*
[44] *Ibid* at para 84.

employed by them are also covered by anti-discrimination law. In addition, there is no service qualification for anti-discrimination legislation. Sex discrimination and equal pay laws have been particularly important for part-time workers, where the overwhelming over-representation of women has meant that it is indirect discrimination to provide fewer rights for part-timers in a range of situations.[45] However, discrimination law has its limits. In order to prove indirect discrimination, a court must be convinced that there is sufficient coincidence with gender, and in particular that substantially more women than men are excluded. To prove this gender-based impact, an applicant faces a minefield of complex issues: which two groups should be compared, how large the disparity should be, and how stable should the pattern be year by year? While this strategy has generally been relatively successful for part-time workers,[46] it has proved impermeable for fixed-term workers.[47]

Even if these hurdles can be surmounted, the employer still has the opportunity to justify the claim. Although courts were initially relatively strict as to the standard of justification,[48] more recently, courts have lowered the standard, particularly where the justification is offered by governments.[49]

Another potential source of relief for discrimination against non-standard workers is equal pay laws. However, equal pay legislation is premised on a particular model of employment, which requires a rigid bipartite relationship between employer and employee as a precondition for the imposition of social responsibilities. This requirement is manifested in the circumscribed nature of the comparison which can be drawn: a woman can only claim equal pay with a man who is not only employed by the same employer but also works at the same establishment, or is employed under common terms or conditions. These limitations in equal pay laws create incentives for employers to avoid the equal pay laws by fragmenting the employing entity, either by contracting out[50] or by transforming employees into agency workers.[51] The result has been that workers find that they cannot bring equal pay claims on the basis of a comparison with colleagues whom they work with at the same establishment, because their employer has been changed. Courts, accustomed to regarding the employing institution as a 'given', have been unwilling to look behind the reconfiguration of the

---

[45] *Case 1007/84 Bilka-Kaufhaus* [1986] IRLR 317 (ECJ).

[46] *R v Secretary of State for Employment ex parte Equal Opportunities Commission*, above n 5.

[47] *R v Secretary of State for Employment ex parte Seymour Smith and Perez* [1997] IRLR 315 (HL).

[48] *Case 10007/84 Bilka-Kaufhaus*, above n 45.

[49] *R v Secretary of State ex parte Seymour Smith and Perez*, above n 47.

[50] *Lawrence v Regent Office Care Case C-320/00* [2002] ECR I-7325 (ECJ).

[51] *Allonby v Accrington & Rossendale College* [2004] IRLR 224 (ECJ) (*Allonby*).

employment relationship. Thus, the process of flexiblisation has itself undermined the efficacy of equal pay laws.

The way in which flexiblisation functions to limit the reach of equal pay laws is clearly seen in the recent European Court of Justice (ECJ) cases of *Lawrence*[52] and *Allonby*.[53] In *Lawrence*, the process of flexibilisation involved contracting out the provision of school dinners to an outside contractor, so that women working as 'dinner ladies' found themselves employed by an outside contractor and therefore unable to contest their diminished pay packet by comparing themselves to the male employees whom they worked alongside but who remained employed by local authorities. In *Allonby*, higher education colleges decided to transfer their part-time lecturing staff from direct to agency employment. Contracts with part-time lecturers were terminated, and instead, lecturers were required to register as self-employed workers with an agency. By the device of splitting up the employment function, moving from a bipartite to a tripartite relationship, the employer made it impossible for women to compare their pay to that of directly employed male colleagues, despite continuing to work alongside them. They thus successfully prevented non-standard workers from bringing equal pay claims.

This myopic focus on the individual employer is widened slightly in EU law, where the ECJ has held that it is not necessary for both the claimant and the comparator to be employed by the same employer. However, the ECJ has closely circumscribed the range of comparison, holding that a claim can be brought only where the difference in pay can be attributed to a single source (such as legislation or a collective agreement). Otherwise, there is no body responsible for the inequality that could restore equal treatment.[54]

In insisting that a body must be found that is responsible for the inequality, the ECJ in both *Lawrence* and *Allonby* assumes that liability arises only if fault can be established. It is now widely recognised that inequality of pay is frequently a consequence of institutional arrangements for which no single actor is 'to blame'. In *Allonby* itself, the court demonstrated a disturbingly narrow understanding of fault, a direct result of the refusal to acknowledge the nexus between the college and the employment agency (ELS). This emerges strikingly from the opinion of the Advocate-General where he stated: 'On any other view, ELS would have to bear the consequence attributable to another employer without there being any connection between the body responsible for the inequality and the body required to restore equal treatment.'[55] This focus meant that the court was unable to

---

[52] *Lawrence*, above n 50.
[53] *Allonby*, above n 51.
[54] *Lawrence*, above n 50.

locate fault despite the acknowledgement by both the Advocate-General and the Commission that the institutional arrangements had been deliberately manipulated. What is not explained is why the loss should fall on those who are least at fault, the part-time lecturers themselves (see also Stone, chapter 11 in this volume).

This narrow view of responsibility is further limited by the refusal to see the contractual nexus between the end-user and the agency as sufficient to create a dual set of responsibilities. In *Allonby*, the ECJ held that the fact that the level of pay received by Ms Allonby was 'influenced' by the amount paid by the college to ELS was not a sufficient basis for concluding that there was a single source for the purposes of the *Lawrence* test. This rigid view of the demarcation of each enterprise leaves the court wholly deferent to the employer's self-definition of the boundaries of its responsibility. Yet the clear contractual nexus between ELS and the college meant that it could not only easily ascertain the level of pay of the appropriate comparator, but also pass on the extra cost to the college.

More recently, the trend has been to provide rights specifically to non-standard workers rather than on the basis of the gendered nature of such work. Thus the Part-Time Workers Directive[56] and the Fixed-Term Workers Directive[57] will, it is to be hoped, in due course, be followed by an agency workers directive. These directives overcome some of the difficulties of relying on indirect discrimination. Instead of the claimant having to prove that a woman suffers disproportionate detriment in respect of the terms and conditions of non-standard work, it is possible to make the claim as a non-standard worker in her own right.

However, instead of giving substantive rights per se, these new provisions have operated through the principle of parity between non-standard workers and standard workers (see also Vosko, chapter 3 in this volume). In other words, a part-time or fixed-term worker has a claim only if she can prove that she is less favourably treated than a full-time equivalent in the same employment. Not only is she required to show that she is employed by the same employer at the same establishment doing broadly similar work, in addition, she must be engaged under the same 'type of contract' as well as performing duties of a broadly similar nature.[58]

The limited case-law so far has shown courts interpreting this requirement restrictively. Thus part-time or retained firefighters were held not to

---

[55] *Allonby*, above n 51.

[56] EC Council Directive 97/81 of 15 December 1997 concerning the framework agreement on part-time working, [1997] OJ L 009/14.

[57] EC Council Directive 99/70 of 28 June 1999 concerning the framework agreement on part-time working, [1999] OJ L 175/43.

[58] Part-Time Workers (Prevention of Less Favourable Treatment) Regulations 2000, above n 18; Fixed Term Employees (Prevention of Less Favourable Treatment) Regulations 2002, SI 2002/2034.

be comparable to full-time firefighters for the purposes of a claim under the Part-Time Workers Regulations[59] because of the additional duties required of full-time firefighters when they were not fighting fires. Although the Court of Appeal took a more generous view of the 'type of contract' category, its approach to the question of whether duties are of a broadly similar nature was restrictive. Thus it rejected the argument that the fact that both full-time and part-time firefighters performed the core function of firefighting was enough to render the work in each category as broadly similar. The rejection of this argument meant that the part-time workers lost their claim despite the fact that, as the Tribunal found, they were treated less favourably on the grounds that they were part-time workers and that such unfavourable treatment could not be justified. This limitation is likely to constitute a significant handicap for claims by part-time or fixed-term workers, who may well find that there is no equivalent full-time worker at their establishment.

In domestic law, this restriction is further narrowed by the definition of worker itself. The Fixed-Term Employees Regulations have restricted claims to those who are employees in the narrowest sense of being employed under a contract of employment.[60] Under the Part-Time Workers Regulations, even the wider definition of a worker under a contract for service[61] is still likely to fall foul of the mutuality of obligation principle.

MINIMUM WAGE AND MAXIMUM WORKING TIME

The two main sets of new substantive rights, introduced under the influence of the Third Way, have both expressly extended beyond the standard employee paradigm. Both minimum wage and maximum working time cover workers under a contract of personal service (subject to the client/customer exception) and both expressly refer to agency workers,[62] home workers, contract workers, and others.[63] However, non-standard workers still pose significant challenges, again because their working hours are often a combination of apparent autonomy and controlled commitment. This challenge is particularly difficult for workers who are on call, either from home, or at their employer's premises. For the purposes of calculating the minimum wage or maximum hours due to them, it is necessary to quantify their hours

---

[59] *Matthews v Medway Towns Fire Authority* [2004] EWCA (Civ) 844 (CA).

[60] Above n 58, reg 2(2)–(4).

[61] Part-Time Workers (Prevention of Less Favourable Treatment) Regulations 2000, above n 18, reg 1(2).

[62] Working Time Regulations 1998, above n 6, reg 1.

[63] *Clark* above n 15, Working Time Regulations 1998, above n 6, reg 36; National Minimum Wage Act 1998, above n 16, ss 34–35.

of work. Should these include only hours actually working, or all the available hours (see Kilpatrick, chapter 7 in this volume)?

The key question, as Simpson puts it, is whether the employer has to bear the cost of maintaining labour available (Simpson, 2004). The answer to this question, in turn, depends largely on which category the courts choose to use to describe the working time. In some cases, they have been prepared to recognise that workers are in fact 'at work' in that, although not occupied all the time, they have no personal independence or freedom of choice during the period. This finding of lack of choice was true for duty nurses to whose homes calls about emergencies were diverted,[64] and for a night watchman who was required to be on the employer's premises to respond to an emergency alarm, but was entitled to sleep, read, or watch television when not occupied.[65] Had the court classified these workers as being 'on call' rather than 'at work' the workers would have been entitled to be paid only for the time spent working.[66]

A very different approach can be detected in the Court of Appeal's judgment in *Walton*,[67] where a caregiver who looked after an ill person by living in at her house for three days out of six claimed that her working time should be calculated for the full 24 hours. Instead of classifying her work as time work, on the ground that she had to be available to her employer all the time during her three days on, the court held that her work was 'unmeasured work', which could be specified by a daily average agreement. As Simpson argues, the effect of this is to allow an agreement to displace rights—a result that should not be acceptable, given the worker's inequality of bargaining power (Simpson, 2004: 31).

CONCLUSION

The statistics show clearly that women form the vast majority of non-standard workers and that their labour market position remains precarious, despite the framework of social rights created since the mid 1970s. The main reason for this is the failure to address the gendered dimension of the issue. For women, the dual obligations of paid and unpaid work make it essential that the boundary between home and market remains permeable. Non-standard working is the only way many women can navigate this boundary. However, from the legal perspective, the ability to move in and out of the employment relationship is portrayed as an autonomy or

---

[64] *British Nursing Association v Inland Revenue* [2003] ICR 19 (CA).

[65] *Wright v Scottbridge Construction Ltd* [2003] IRLR 21 (Court of Session).

[66] National Minimum Wage Regulations 1999, SI 1999/584, regs 3, 15(1), 6.

[67] *Walton v Independent Living Organisation Ltd* [2003] ICR 688 (CA); Working Time Regulations 1998, above n 6, regs 3 ('time work'), 15(1) ('on call'), and 6 ('unmeasured work').

independence, which makes it both unnecessary and illegitimate to impose social duties on the employer. Again, courts have found it difficult to envisage that a social commitment arises on behalf of the employer for hours over which the employer chooses not to make use of the worker's services.

The inability to distinguish between real autonomy and the results of dual obligations or shared commitments has led to the exclusion of the most vulnerable workers from the protection of labour law. Even the broader definitions of worker have been subverted by this unquestioning imposition of a 'male breadwinner' model on all paid workers.

For those non-standard workers who are able to squeeze into the contractual model, equality laws have held some promise. But they too are limited by a fault-based model of the employer, who can only be held liable for inequalities for which it can be found to be directly responsible. This underlying assumption has meant that any comparisons can be drawn only between employees of the same employer, a stricture that has been extended and tightened by the regulations specifically aimed at protecting non-standard workers.

It is only by recognising that employment rights are owed to all who participate in the paid labour market, regardless of how peripherally, that the status of the non-standard worker will become less precarious. Duties fall on employers, not because of their immediate power to command the time and commitment of an individual worker, but because of their labour market power and the civic responsibility that attaches to those with power (Hutton, 2002). Such responsibilities have been shown to yield important benefits to employers themselves, and to enhance their efficiency and competitiveness. But they are also intrinsic to the status of employer. The importance of ensuring that individuals can navigate the boundary between paid and unpaid work without undue cost cannot be overstated. It is only then that men will be in a position to move away from the male breadwinner model and share the dual responsibilities of paid and unpaid work. However, this ideal seems further away than ever. The rise of the flexible worker has brought women into the paid workforce, but has not lessened their home responsibilities. While men are no longer the main breadwinners, the 'male breadwinner' model remains intact, and women enter the paid workforce on vastly unequal terms.

9

Self-employment, Women, and Precarious Work: The Scope of Labour Protection

JUDY FUDGE*

INTRODUCTION

A KEY FEATURE OF the new economy was the 'partial renaissance' (OECD, 2000b) of self-employment in the 1980s and 1990s, an important component of which was the participation of women. This feminisation of self-employment was celebrated as evidence of women's entrepreneurship and the spread of enterprise culture, and some governments, such as those in Canada and the United Kingdom, promoted self-employment as providing economic independence and autonomy for women (Felstead and Leighton, 1992: 16; Hughes, 1999: 6; Prime Minister's Task Force on Women's Entrepreneurs, 2003: 113). However, researchers have questioned whether the feminisation of self-employment is evidence instead of the spread of precarious employment and the deterioration in the quality and conditions of self-employment. Much of women's self-employment differs along a range of important dimensions from that of men, and it challenges the prevailing stereotype about self-employment and its association with independence and entrepreneurship (Burchell and Rubery, 1992; Hughes, 1999; Vosko and Zukewich, 2005).

Women's self-employment also challenges basic legal norms that determine the scope of employment and labour protection. The distinction between employees and independent contractors is the boundary between

* This chapter draws on research conducted with Eric Tucker and Leah Vosko, which was supported by the Law Commission of Canada and the Social Sciences and Humanities Research Council, and it was initially written during my tenure as Law Foundation of Saskatchewan Chair at the College of Law, University of Saskatchewan. Thanks to all of the workshop participants and, especially, Rosemary Owens for very helpful comments on an earlier draft, and to the two reviewers for useful suggestions. As always, all shortcomings are my own.

employment and labour law, which among other things (Collins, 2001), provides a range of rights and entitlements, on the one hand, and civil and commercial law, which emphasises competition, on the other. In common law and civil law systems, subordination (lack of control) is what divides employees from independent contractors (Pedersini, 2002). But as employment relationships have changed with the growth of 'market-mediated' work arrangements and networks of firms (Abraham, 1990), the simple dichotomy between subordination and autonomy is not a very effective way of determining entitlement to labour protection under the law. The border between paid employment and self-employment has blurred, and false self-employment (or disguised employment) has grown (ILO, 2000a: 7; OECD, 2000: 163, 177).

Defining the scope of employment, in particular distinguishing between dependent workers and the self-employed for the purpose of labour and social protection, has been a matter of some contention at the international level. In 1990, the International Labour Conference adopted a resolution calling for the protection of workers who are nominally self-employed from exploitative subcontracting arrangements and labour contracts (ILO, 1990a). However, employer representatives have been keen to preserve self-employment as a sphere of independent contracting free of labour regulation, and they have refused to participate in International Labour Organization (ILO) processes if this boundary is not respected (Prügl, 1999: 133). As a compromise, the focus of the international standard has been softened from a binding Convention to a promotional Recommendation and narrowed to self-employed workers who are actually disguised employees and to those whose classification as dependent workers or independent contractors is truly ambiguous (ILO, 2003b).

Canada is a good case study to explore what the growth in women's self-employment reveals about the legal norms of employment and independent contracting, and the fit between contemporary work arrangements and the scope of legal protection. Women's share of self-employment is larger in Canada than in any other member of the OECD, and the federal and some provincial governments promote self-employment for women (Hughes, 2003a). There is also a significant body of empirical research that demonstrates the gendered nature of self-employment, and the relationship between women's self-employment and social reproduction (Hughes 1999, 2003a, 2003b; Rooney *et al*, 2003; Vosko and Zukewich, 2005).

This chapter begins by examining the stereotype of self-employment and how it is distinguished from employment in order to develop a more complex and accurate typology of subordination and autonomy in employment relationships. The next section turns to the ILO, and traces its approach to self-employment. Since 1990, the ILO has attempted to fashion an *entente* between employees' representatives, employers' representatives, and governments around the scope of employment protection and the coverage of self-employed workers. The next section begins the case study and presents some of the recent Canadian data on self-employment, and examines it along the dimensions of subordination and dependency identified in the typology. It also explores the extent to which women's self-employment is precarious, and how women's self-employment is shaped by their responsibility for domestic labour. The scope of employment in labour-related law and legislation in the common-law jurisdictions in Canada is mapped in the next section, and it is compared to the reality of women's self-employment.[1] A key question is whether the scope of legal protection of employment contributes to the precarious nature of self-employment for women. The chapter concludes by considering what effect the ILO's approach is likely to have on access to labour and social protection for self-employed women in Canada. Women's self-employment demonstrates the need to go beyond employment to consider self-employment *and* unpaid caring labour in order to develop policies and laws that promote women's equality.

A TYPOLOGY OF SELF-EMPLOYMENT

The growth of women's self-employment challenges the traditional stereotype of self-employment, which is linked to ownership, autonomy, and control over production, clearly distinguishing craftspeople, independent professionals, and small business proprietors from waged workers (Eardley and Corden, 1996: 13). Historically, men have made up the majority of the self-employed and self-employment has been associated with independence and contrasted with the dependent status of employees (Burchell and Rubery, 1992: 105; Hunter, 1992; Fraser and Gordon, 1994). Two key elements that have traditionally defined the self-employed are their ownership of the means of their own production, and self-direction or autonomy in their work (Dale, 1986). In the stereotype, self-employment is linked to entrepreneurship and men's experience is taken as the norm (Mirchandani, 1999: 225; Hughes, 2003a: 5; Vosko and Zukewich 2005).

But the problem with this stereotype is that it does not reflect either the diverse range of employment relationships that fall within the broad category of self-employment or the changing nature of self-employment. British researchers recorded an increase in consultants, professionals, and contractors, especially in the service sector, and a decline in small business

---

[1] Jurisdiction over labour law in Canada is split between 10 provinces, three territories, and the federal government. The provinces and territories have jurisdiction over labour relations within their territory, with the exception of labour relations pertaining to federal undertakings, such as banks, railways, airlines, and so on, over which the federal government has authority. In Canada, the legal system of every jurisdiction except Quebec's is based on the common law.

owners who employed other workers (Dale, 1986; Hakim, 1987; Eardley and Corden, 1996). They also discovered that a sizeable portion of the self-employed included home workers and labour-only contractors, as well as franchisees, freelancers, and outworkers. The employment situations of these workers differ dramatically from the stereotype of the self-employed, since they do not own much by way of means of production, exercise little control over production, and do not accumulate capital (Dale, 1986, 1991; Felstead, 1991; Meager, 1991; Rainbird, 1991; Bryson and White, 1996; Eardley and Corden, 1996; Stanworth and Stanworth, 1997; Brodie, Stanworth, and Wotuba, 2002).

Several researchers have concluded that the simple dichotomy between subordination and independence does not capture the heterogeneity of self-employment, and advocate a multi-dimensional approach to classifying self-employment (Felstead, 1991; Burchell and Rubery, 1992). Instead of finding the best discriminating factor for identifying the self-employed, Brendan Burchell and Jill Rubery (1992) argue that it is better to develop a typology of the self-employed that involves looking at a range of discriminating factors for both overlapping and contradictory classification. They identify a number of dimensions to analyse the extent of subordination or dependency among the self-employed, which includes direct measures of autonomy and other measures that are indirectly associated with dependency. The first group includes determining whether a self-employed person regards himself or herself as running a business, provides goods and services to a number of different clients, or hires employees. The indirect indicators of dependency include the location where the self-employed person works (home, a separate business establishment, a client's office), why the person became self-employed, how the self-employed person is paid and/or determines price, the amount of capital needed to set up the business, and the extent of income variation. Using these dimensions to measure subordination and independence among the self-employed in the United Kingdom, Burchell and Rubery (1992: 108) found that 'a higher proportion of the self-employed are affected by at least some aspects of subordination than would be implied by dividing the sample using a multi-dimensional classification.' They also discovered that gender was an important dimension of self-employment, and that it was linked to subordination (Burchell and Rubery, 1992: 109).

THE ILO AND THE SCOPE OF THE EMPLOYMENT RELATIONSHIP

The dramatic increase in self-employment during the 1980s caught the ILO's attention, and in 1990 it released a report on self-employment. The report described the heterogeneity of self-employment; at best it allowed workers to be autonomous, to realise their potential, and to reap financial rewards, while at worst it was a marginal and precarious form of employment (ILO, 1990a). It also indicated that there was no clear distinction between employment and self-employment and that there had been a growth in both nominal self-employment and dependent workers. Noting that the Convention on Freedom of Association (No 87) already applied to the self-employed, the report recommended that efforts be made to ensure that the self-employed enjoy the same level of protection as other categories of workers regarding social security and conditions of employment (ILO, 1990a: 66, 69). At the 1990 session, the International Labour Conference adopted a resolution calling for the protection of workers who are nominally self-employed from exploitative subcontracting arrangements and labour contracts (ILO, 1990b; Benjamin, 2002: 81). However, the employers' group has vigorously resisted this expansive approach to the scope of employment, and the legal status of self-employment has tested the limits of tripartism, which is the basis of the ILO's structure and source of its legitimacy (Prügl, 1999: 133).[2] In order to maintain social dialogue between employers' and workers' organisations, the ILO narrowed its focus to dependent workers and adopted a 'soft' approach to setting standards. During the lengthy discussions and negotiations on the scope of employment protection, the gender dimension rarely surfaced as an issue of sustained concern.

The degree of contention between the social partners over the scope of labour protection became apparent in 1995 during the International Labour Conference discussion of a Convention on Home Work (Prügl, 1999; Sankaran, 2002; Vosko, 2002). The employment status of home workers—whether they are employees or self-employed—lay at the heart of the debate.[3] The gender dimension of this form of employment was impossible to ignore, and women's groups played an important role at the Conference (Prügl, 1999). The following year, the employers' group refused to

---

[2] The International Labour Conference functions as an international parliament of labour, and it has a tripartite membership structure (each member state has two government delegates, and one delegate representing employers and another representing workers), which is designed to enhance the legitimacy and viability of the rights and standards that it adopts. These rights and standards take the form of Conventions and Recommendations. The Conventions are created through an elaborate and lengthy process of consultation with representatives of governments, employers, and workers; and the final text of a Convention must receive two thirds of the votes cast by the delegates to the general Conference of the ILO. Conventions are international treaties that, once adopted by the Conference, are open to ratification by member states. Once a member state ratifies a Convention it is legally bound by the Convention. By contrast, Recommendations are intended as guides only and are not legally binding.

[3] The legal status of intermediaries and subcontracting chains was also a contentious issue in these discussions, and in subsequent discussions on the draft convention on contract labour, workers in situations in need of protection, and the scope of the employment relationship (Sankaran, 2002: 867–69; Vosko, chapter 3 in this volume).

participate in the Conference Committee on Home Work, which was finalising a draft Convention, and abstained from the vote on the Convention because it was unhappy with its scope. Despite the decision of employers' representatives to abstain, the Convention was adopted by the Conference, although very few countries have ratified it (Prügl, 1999; Sankaran, 2002: 863; Vosko, 2002).

The withdrawal of the employers' group from the ILO process over the Convention on Home Work was unprecedented. It suggested that the limits of social dialogue had been tested by the attempt to extend labour protection beyond employment. The discussions on contract labour, which was the next time that the scope of employment protection was raised, confirmed the extent to which this was a contentious issue.

In 1997, the International Labour Conference began a preliminary discussion on a Convention on Contract Labour. The draft Convention defined contract labour as 'all situations in which work is performed for a person who is not the worker's employer under labour law but in conditions of subordination and dependency that are close to an employment relationship under the law' (ILO, 1998b: 2). The employers' group was concerned that the draft Convention extended the scope of employment too far into the ranks of the self-employed and jeopardised the sanctity of independent contracting as a form of commercial contracting free from labour regulation (ILO, 1998c: para 13). During the 1998 discussion on the Convention by the Conference, the Committee on Contract Labour tabled the Convention and abandoned the term 'contract labour'. However, it resolved that further study be given to 'workers in situations needing labour protection' and that the issue be brought back to the Conference (ILO, 1998c, 2003a: 4; Vosko, 2002: 37).

The ILO commissioned 39 country studies and five regional meetings by legal experts to identify 'those categories of situations where workers are in need of protection, as well as the problems resulting from the absence or inadequacy of such protection, and the means of action adapted to such situations and guidelines for possible international standard setting action' (ILO, 2000a: para 9; 2003a: para 14). To avoid confusion over terminology and to provide a basis for comparing the different country reports, the experts were instructed to focus on four situations in which workers might need protection: dependent employment, self-employment, triangular employment (where intermediaries are involved), and self-employment in conditions of dependency. They were also asked to pay particular attention to the situation of women (ILO, 2003a: paras 10, 11).

In May 2000, the ILO released a technical document (which was based on the national reports and regional meetings) on workers in situations needing protection and a meeting of experts was convened. The technical document concluded that there is a category of workers who appear to be excluded from the protection provided by the employment relationship, but who in fact carry out work within the framework of concealed or disguised employment relationships. At the same time, there are objectively ambiguous situations, which are on the increase, which merit protection, since the workers involved are placed in situations of dependency, but in respect of which the scope of legislation may be too narrow, in that it does not allow an identification of the employer or the persons who should assume responsibility vis-à-vis the worker. In addition to this situation, there is also the significant phenomenon of the non-application or poor application of labour legislation.

(ILO, 2000a: para102)

It also found that women faced a worse situation than did men when it came to disguised and ambiguous employment (ILO, 2000a: para 90).

At the experts' meeting, the employers' group emphasised the need to combat fraudulent employment and to step up enforcement of labour legislation while at the same time preserving independent contracting (ILO, 2003b: para 44). Despite the position of the employers' experts that there was no need for an international standard, the experts' meeting issued a common statement, which noted the discrepancy between the legal scope of the employment relationship and the reality of working relationships. The statement also stressed the need for countries 'to review and, if appropriate, clarify or adapt the scope of regulation of the employment relationship in the country's legislation in line with current employment realities' (ILO, 2000b: para 107, point 5). However, there was hardly any discussion of the gender dimension of the scope of employment at the experts' meeting.

In March 2001, the Governing Body considered the common statement of the meeting of experts. It noted the problem of 'the existence of a growing sector of workers who perform services for other parties in conditions of dependency and to whom labour legislation is not applied in practice,' and scheduled the issue for general discussion at the 2003 Conference (ILO, 2001: para 36). A Report on the Scope of the Employment Relationship was submitted to the 2003 Conference, and a Committee on the Employment Relationship was constituted in order to discuss the possibility of adopting an international standard. The Report characterised the issue as one of refocusing the law to better adjust with reality, and it was careful to emphasise that the concern was not self-employed workers per se, but those self-employed who were dependent workers—either disguised employees or ambiguously self-employed (ILO, 2003a: 10, 22). It also emphasised, although it did not elaborate upon, the gender dimension of the scope of employment (ILO, 2003a: 10, 13).

The Committee managed to achieve a consensus on adopting an international standard relating to the scope of employment. But it did so by settling on a Recommendation (which is advisory) instead of a Convention (which is binding once ratified by a member state), and by dropping any reference to triangular employment relationships (ILO, 2003b: paras 1, 9).[4] The Committee agreed that the

> Recommendation should focus on disguised employment relationships and on the need for mechanisms to ensure that persons with an employment relationship have access to the protection that they are due at a national level. Such a Recommendation should provide guidance to member States without defining universally the substance of the employment relationship. The Recommendation should be flexible enough to take account of different social, legal and industrial relations traditions and address the gender dimension. Such a Recommendation should not interfere with genuine commercial and independent contracting arrangements.
>
> (ILO, 2003b: para 25)

In its conclusions, the Conference Committee noted that the 'lack of protection of dependent workers exacerbates gender inequalities in the labour market' (ILO, 2003b: para 15) as well as the 'need to have clearer policies on gender equality and better enforcement of the relevant laws ... so that the gender dimension of the problem can be effectively addressed' (ILO, 2003b: para 16). However, this attention to gender came over the objections of the employers' group; the employer vice-chair of the Committee claimed that the 'gender aspect of the issues under discussion ... was not fully understood' (ILO, 2003a: para 53; Vosko, chapter 3 in this volume).[5]

In March 2004, the Governing Body placed a Recommendation on the Employment Relationship (based upon the conclusions of the Committee on the Employment Relationship) on the agenda for the 2006 session of the International Labour Conference (ILO, 2004c). The goal of the standard is to refocus the employment relationship in order to bring the scope of labour better in line with the reality of employment. Dependent workers, who are either disguised employees or objectively ambiguous self-employed, are the target of regulation and developing a clear and transparent method for determining the scope of employment that preserves the autonomy of genuine self-employment is a key objective. Significantly, the Recommendation is supposed to address the gender dimension of the scope of employment. However, the price for proceeding with the Recommendation on the scope of employment was steep; triangular employment relationships and self-employment were dropped from the scope of the standard-setting process. The 2005 Report (ILO, 2005) focuses on dependent workers. It does not

---

[4] Triangular relationships, which typically involve an employee, employment agency, and a user firm, challenge the bilateral employment norm, and have been very contentious (Vosko, chapter 3 in this volume).

[5] The General Conference of the ILO adopted the Committee's conclusions, and sent the matter to the Governing Body.

take a precise position on the scope of the employment relationship, but it does suggest a methodology and indicate criteria to allow countries to define and establish an employment relationship. This is the outer circle of labour protection. However, there is also an inner circle of more restricted protection (Marin, 2005) that covers all workers without distinction.

There are already a number of key ILO standards that apply to the self-employed. Convention No 87 (1948) concerning Freedom of Association and Protection of the Right to Organise guarantees the right of 'workers and employers, without distinction whatsoever' to establish and join organisations of their own choosing without state authorisation, and, according to the Freedom of Association Committee of the ILO's governing body, self-employed workers in general should enjoy the right to organise, and the existence of an employment contract should not determine whether a person is covered by the right (Benjamin, 2002: 80). Similarly, Convention No 111 (1958) on Discrimination (Employment and Occupation) applies to all people who work (Sankaran, 2002: 862).

WOMEN AND SELF-EMPLOYMENT IN CANADA[6]

Self-employment has been a significant source of job growth in Canada; it grew at a faster rate than paid employment between 1979 and 1998 (OECD, 2000: 157; Hughes, 2003a: 2).[7] In 2000, the self-employed represented 16 per cent of all workers, down from a high of 19 per cent in 1998 but up from 11 per cent in 1976. Women's self-employment outstripped men's in the 1990s; however, historically women have had low rates of self-employment. Whereas nearly 14 per cent of men were self-employed in 1976, this was the case for just 6 per cent of women. By 2000, 19 per cent of men and 12 per cent of women were self-employed—about one in six of all of the working people in Canada (Fudge, Tucker, and Vosko, 2002: 22).[8]

Self-employment is conventionally divided into two major forms of self-employment: own-account or solo (Hughes, 2003a), in which the self-employed person does not employ other workers, and employer self-employed, in

---

[6] This section is based on Fudge, Tucker, and Vosko, 2002.

[7] Mode of remuneration is the basis for distinguishing between paid employees and the self-employed, and it underpins the International Classification of Status in Employment (Elias, 2000: XI) as well as the majority of Statistics Canada's survey instruments. On the basis of these definitions, in Canada and elsewhere, total employment is divided into two broad groupings: paid employees and the self-employed. For a brief discussion of some of the problems with statistical measures, see Loufti, 1991; Fudge, Tucker, and Vosko, 2002: 12–14.

[8] Nadja Kamhi and Danny Leung (2005) note that after rising steadily for almost two decades and reaching a peak of 17.3% in 1998, the self-employment rate in Canada fell back to 15.2% in 2002. Both the increase and decrease in the self-employment rate was primarily driven by the own-account (or solo) self-employed.

which other workers are employed. This distinction is important because it is employer self-employment that generates other jobs and more closely conforms to the stereotype of entrepreneurship and the male norm of self-employment. However, this distinction is more porous than conventionally understood. There is significant movement between solo and employer self-employed. In the Survey of Self-Employment, those self-employed with paid help in a given reference year are classified as employers, while the self-employed who do not hire others are considered as own-account self-employed. Based on this definition, in 2000, 46 per cent of the self-employed in Canada were employers. Yet, when the same group was asked whether they had paid help during a particular reference week, only 38 per cent fell into this category (Delage, 2002: 12).

The majority of the increase in self-employment in the 1990s was in the solo category, which grew from 6 per cent to 10 per cent of total employment between 1976 and 2000. In contrast, the employer category grew from 5 per cent to 6 per cent of total employment, yet it declined every year from 1995 to 2000. In 2000, 65 per cent of the self-employed were own-account self-employed (Fudge, Tucker, and Vosko, 2002: 5).

Women now make up one third of the self-employed, compared to one quarter in the mid-1970s. However, when men's and women's shares of self-employment relative to their share of total employment are compared, women are still under-represented in self-employment. Women comprise 40 per cent of the solo self-employed but only 25 per cent of employers (Hughes, 2003a). Only women in the solo category are nearing their representation in the employed population. Women are three times as likely as men to be solo self-employed (31 per cent versus 10 per cent) (Vosko and Zukewich, 2005).

Like their counterparts in paid employment, self-employed women are also confined to a limited, albeit expanding, number of industries and occupations. Much of the recent growth in self-employment has come from various service industries. In the last 25 years, men in solo and employer self-employment have shifted to services, reflecting expansion in this sector. Although the intense concentration among solo self-employed women in the mid-1970s in personal services has also changed, they remain crowded in personal services, other services, and the retail trade. Solo self-employed men are still spread across a much broader set of industries (Fudge, Tucker, and Vosko, 2002: 25).

Trends by occupation mirror what has happened regarding industry. In 2000, the largest segment of the self-employed were in managerial/professional occupations (42 per cent), followed by service occupations (25 per cent), blue-collar occupations (21 per cent), and occupations unique to the primary sector, which includes forestry, logging, mining, fishing, and trapping (12 per cent). By sex, fully 92 per cent of the self-employed in blue-collar occupations and 84 per cent in occupations unique to the primary sector are men. The only occupational grouping where women constitute a larger share (56 per cent) of the self-employed than men is services. Women in self-employment are concentrated in two groups of occupations: management/ professional occupations and services. Solo women remain concentrated in a few areas—21 per cent of whom are child- and home-support workers (versus 0.8 per cent of men), and women's share of this occupational group was 95 per cent compared to 5 per cent for men in 2000 (Fudge, Tucker, and Vosko, 2002: 26).

In the 1990s, there was a rise in part-time self-employment, especially among the solo self-employed, such that one in four workers in this category worked part time by 2000. That year, fully 42 per cent of women and 16 per cent of men in the solo category worked part time; rates almost double those of women and men in paid employment. Part-time work is much less common among employers such that women employers have lower rates than their counterparts in solo self-employment and paid work (Fudge, Tucker, and Vosko, 2002: 29). Differences in hours of work account for a large part of the wide range in income among the self-employed.

Immigrants are generally as likely as people born in Canada to choose self-employment upon arriving in Canada, except for the cohort that arrived between 1991 and 1995—they were 30 per cent more likely to enter self-employment than those born in Canada (Frenette, 2002). One explanation for this shift to self-employment by recent immigrants concerns the declining success of immigrants in the paid workforce. Marc Frenette suggests that immigrants from non-English-speaking countries, a rising portion of immigrants, may face difficulties integrating into paid jobs and thus may choose self-employment (Frenette, 2002: 13). Other studies indicate that immigrant workers are, increasingly, people of colour who face systemic discrimination when searching for employment (Galabuzi, 2001; Jackson, 2002). In 1999, 20 per cent of men in the employer category and 19 per cent of those in the own-account category were born abroad, versus roughly 8 per cent of men in the total population. While data for immigrant women employers are unavailable for that year, 20 per cent of women in the solo category were born abroad, versus roughly 7 per cent of women in the total population. Moreover, in 1999, 13 per cent of self-employed people were members of 'visible-minority groups' (the term used by Statistics Canada) (versus roughly 9 per cent of the whole population), fully 16 per cent of self-employed men, and 9 per cent of self-employed women.[9]

In Canada, we see the most significant income differences among the self-employed when we look at type of self-employment—in 1999, the average annual incomes of self-employed employers and the solo self-employed

[9] Statistics Canada. 2000, *Survey of Labour and Income Dynamics* (Public Use Micro Data, Special Run).

were $46,825 and $16,918, respectively. Income differences are also related to gender—in 1999, female and male employers had average annual incomes of $39,920 and $49,470, respectively, and women and men in the own-account category had average annual incomes of $13,032 and $19,769, respectively.[10] The comparable figures for all female and male wage and salary employees were $26,015 and $40,183, respectively, indicating that the average annual incomes of men and women in wage and salary employment tend to be less than those of their counterparts working as self-employed employers, but significantly more than their counterparts in solo self-employment. When income is examined by immigration status, gender, and type of employment, among the solo self-employed, where insecurity is greatest, the average annual income of men born in Canada is highest ($20,188), followed by men born abroad ($18,476), women born in Canada ($12,918), and women born abroad ($11,929).

The income of the self-employed is extremely polarised; in 2000, 25 per cent of the self-employed had incomes of $20,000 or less and 22 per cent had incomes above $60,000 (Delage, 2002: App B.4). The largest percentage of self-employed women (47 per cent) had incomes of $20,000 or less, while self-employed men were much more evenly distributed across income groups (Fudge, Tucker and Vosko, 2002: 32). This polarisation reflects earnings differences between employers and the solo self-employed. A sizeable proportion of the solo self-employed had incomes under $20,000 (35 per cent), but only a small percentage had incomes greater than $90,000 (around 3 per cent). In contrast, 18 per cent of employers have incomes over $90,000 (Delage, 2002: App A.4).

In 2000, fully 55 per cent of all visible minorities in employer self-employment earned less than $20,000 annually, while only 30 per cent of non-visible minorities in employer self-employment earned less than that amount. Moreover, 71 per cent of visible-minority own-account self-employed earned less than $20,000 annually, whereas only 57 per cent of non-visible-minority own-account self-employed earned less than that amount. Immigrant self-employed, whether employers or own-account self-employed, also earned less than their counterparts who were born in Canada; 46 per cent of all immigrants in employer self-employment earned less than $20,000 annually, versus 30 per cent of non-immigrants, and the

---

[10] Obtained from the Survey of Labour and Income Dynamics (SLID), the data in this paragraph refer to net income. Data on earnings are not available for the self-employed. Statisticians routinely argue that, for the self-employed, income is a better indicator of economic status than earnings, since they derive a range of benefits from their employment status invisible in earnings data (Fudge, Tucker, and Vosko, 2002: 26). There are concerns about the reliability of income data for the self-employed because of the belief that under-reporting of income is prevalent (Miras *et al*, 1994). But even with this caveat, income data tell an important story. All of the amounts are expressed in Canadian dollars, which are about par with the Australian dollar and worth about 65% of the US dollar.

equivalent figures for own-account self-employment are 64 per cent and 57 per cent. Regardless of whether they are employer or solo, visible-minority self-employed, as a group, fare worse in terms of income than their non-visible-minority counterparts, and self-employed visible-minority women earn the least of all groups of self-employed. The same is true for immigrant self-employed (Fudge, 2003). These data suggest that the distinction between types of self-employment, while critical for determining the income of the self-employed population as a whole, is less important for immigrants and visible minorities. At the same time, the data indicate that, along with gender, race and immigrant status are key axes of differentiation within both categories of self-employment.

The work arrangements of the self-employed indicate that there is no clear-cut distinction between paid employees and the self-employed. In 2000, a considerable proportion of the self-employed worked in either client locations (20 per cent) or locations supplied by clients (4 per cent); fully 30 per cent of the solo self-employed worked in such situations (Delage, 2002: App B.6). Furthermore, 37 per cent of the self-employed (35 per cent of men and 46 per cent of women) received support from their clients; 24 per cent (20 per cent of men and 37 per cent of women) received equipment, tools, or supplies from their clients; and another 21 per cent received support in the form of other office equipment such as a fax or photocopier. The day-to-day business operations of many self-employed mirror those of paid employees. Data on the proportion of the self-employed with a former employer as a client, and on the importance of the revenue obtained from this client, illustrate the difficulty in distinguishing between the self-employed and paid employees. In 2000, 15 per cent of the self-employed (18 per cent of the own-account self-employed) reported that their last employer was one of their clients, of whom 51 per cent obtain more than half of their annual revenue from work done for their last employer. In their survey, Graham Lowe and Grant Schellenberg (2001, Table 4.2) found that 41 per cent of the self-employed (51 per cent in solo self-employment) had fewer than five clients in 2000.

The self-employed in Canada give a number of reasons for choosing self-employment. While independence, freedom, and the ability to be 'one's own boss' are the foremost reasons given by men (42 per cent), women are equally likely to choose self-employment to balance work and family obligations (23 per cent) as they are for independence and freedom (24 per cent) (Delage, 2002: 27). Many women, although not all, use self-employment as a way to accommodate the demands of balancing the need for remuneration with family, especially child care, responsibilities (Hughes, 1999; Arai, 2000; Hughes, 2004; Vosko and Zukewich, 2005).

There has been an increasing polarisation and feminisation within the ranks of the self-employed in Canada. Not only has the range of self-employment that women engage in begun to widen, men's self-employment has deteriorated. Despite this convergence in women's and men's self-employment, significant patterns of gender segregation in self-employment have remained. Moreover, immigrant and visible minority women are over-represented at the low end of the income range among self-employed women.

Much of the self-employment that women engage in has many dimensions of subordination identified by Burchill and Rubery (1992). Self-employed women are less likely than men to hire employees, and a larger majority of women than men are solo self-employed. They are more likely than men to depend upon a few clients and to depend upon work from a former employer. Self-employed women are more likely than men to work at home (Gurstein, 2001) or in a client's location. Women choose self-employment for reasons that differ from those given by men (Delage, 2002; Hughes, 2003b; Vosko and Zukewich, 2005). They also have less employment stability than men (Vosko and Zukewich, 2005). There is little data in Canada on how the self-employed are paid, how they determine their prices, and the amount of capital needed to set up business. However, the income data indicate that most solo self-employed women have a very low income, and their income is, on average, lower than that of their counter-parts in paid employment. Thus, although self-employed women have greater autonomy along some dimensions than employees (Hughes, 1999), in many respects they are dependent. The majority of self-employed women do not conform to the stereotype of the independent entrepreneur—which is a full-time employer (Vosko and Zukewich, 2005).

A great deal of women's self-employment in Canada is precarious, and, as with women's paid employment, the further women's self-employment departs from the male norm the more likely it is to be precarious (Vosko, Zukewich, and Cranford, 2003; Vosko and Zukewich, 2005). Leah Vosko and Nancy Zukewich identified degree of regulatory protection and benefits, job certainty, control over one's employment situation, and income adequacy as dimensions of whether or not self-employment is precarious, and they developed a range of empirical measures for these dimensions. According to these measures, they found that a large portion of women's self-employment, especially the solo variety, is precarious (Vosko and Zukewich, 2005). Most significantly, few solo self-employed women earn sufficient income to sustain a household without relying on another adult earner. Most women who are solo self-employed have a spouse, and the majority of them obtain important benefits through a male breadwinner.[11]

---

[11] Self-employed women (77%) are much more likely than self-employed men (44%) to obtain extended benefits coverage through a spouse. Twice as many men (14%) as women (7%) acquire extended benefits through an association. Men's higher rates of benefits through an association reflect the higher percentage of self-employed men in professional and managerial occupations, in the employer category, and in higher income earning groups.

Part-time self-employed women (both the employer and solo categories) are more likely than men to have a spouse and at least one child under the age of 16 at home. Women employers who most closely resemble the male norm of self-employment are slightly less likely than their male counterparts to have either a spouse or a child under 16 (Vosko and Zukewich, 2005).

Although women's self-employment is polarised, the majority of women's self-employment, especially that of the solo variety, is precarious. For women, solo self-employment in particular is often a strategy that they use to accommodate the unequal burden of social reproduction and the need to earn income; in effect, solo self-employment is a strategy for balancing work and family responsibilities.[12] But the question is whether this is an optimal strategy (Hughes, 1999: 29). Self-employment has negative consequences for women's income especially during retirement (Hughes, 1999: 28), and it assumes that households are stable and income is shared between the members throughout their lifecycle (Vosko and Zukewich, 2005).

THE LEGAL BOUNDARY OF LABOUR PROTECTION

With the rise of the standard employment relationship and the post-World War II Fordist-regulatory regime (Fudge and Vosko, 2001a; Supiot *et al*, 2001), the distinction between employees and independent contractors became crucial for determining the scope of labour protection (Deakin, 1998). Employment standards and collective bargaining legislation across Canada was confined to employees; however, very few statutes provided a specific definition of the term. Labour boards, tribunals, and minimum standards adjudicators resorted to the common law test of employment, which focused on control, to distinguish between employees and independent contractors. The importance of control, understood as authority to direct the labour process, is attributed both to the historical legacy of master and servant law with its emphasis on subordination and to the nature of early production processes in which masters could directly supervise workers (Carter *et al*, 2002). But the problem of applying this test to the range of actually existing contractual relationships for the performance of work grew as the nature of employment changed.

Although employment is considered to be a contractual relationship (Fredman, chapter 8 in this volume), the contracting parties' characterisation does not determine their legal status. Employment status is a question

---

[12] Research in the United Kingdom and the United States also supports this finding (Boden, 1999; Hundley, 2000; Baines and Gelder, 2003).

of law to determined by the adjudicator because of concerns about inequality in the contracting parties' bargaining power and the possibility that they might collude in order to avoid public obligations. How the contracting parties characterise their relationship is simply one of the factors that a decision-maker may consider when determining employment status for legal purposes (England *et al*, 2005: paras 2.21, 2.30).

Courts developed a variety of new legal tests for determining employee status in a variety of different legal contexts and they consider a range of different factors in applying the tests. These tests have tended to widen the scope of employment, as the emphasis has shifted from direct subordination to include economic dependence as the basis for extending labour protection to working people. Control continues to be a factor in determining employee status, but what is meant by control changes with the nature of the work. Recently the Supreme Court of Canada, having reviewed the jurisprudence on determining employment status in the context of vicarious liability, concluded:

> there is no one conclusive text, which can be universally applied to determine whether a person is an employee or an independent contractor. The central question is whether the person who has been engaged to perform the services is performing them as a person in business on his own account. In making this determination, the level of control the employer has over the worker's activity will be a factor. However, other factors to consider include whether the worker provides his or her own equipment, whether the worker hires his or her own helpers, the degree of financial risk taken by the worker, the degree of responsibility for investment and management held by the worker, and the worker's opportunity for profit in the performance of his or her task.[13]

The court continued: 'It bears repeating that the above factors constitute a non-exhaustive list, and there is no set formula as to their application. The relative weight of each will depend on the particular facts and circumstances of the case.'[14] The court also articulated a set of policy justifications for vicarious liability to assist in the process of weighing the factors in the case.

While it is likely that this purposive, or policy-based, approach to determining employment status will continue to expand the boundaries of employment by emphasising economic dependence, it is not obvious that it will generate greater certainty than the earlier tests. A new judicial test, particularly one that is so open textured, does not address one of the key problems with determining the personal scope of employment and labour legislation

---

[13] *67122 Ontario v Sagaz Industries Canada Inc*, [2001] 2 SCR 983.

[14] *Ibid* at para 48. Contrast the situation in the United Kingdom, where the courts still take a very formalist, contractualist approach to determining employee status (Fredman, chapter 8 in this volume).

in Canada: its complexity. Different tests are applied in order to distinguish between employees and independent contractors, extended definitions of 'employee' have been added to particular statutes, and there have been some ad hoc extensions and exclusions that affect particular groups of workers under different legislative regimes. The personal scope of employment and labour legislation differs from jurisdiction to jurisdiction, as well as across different legal regimes. While there are some general patterns, for example, legal regimes that are designed to promote social justice such as human rights and occupational health and safety legislation have the broadest coverage and income tax legislation has the narrowest, the scope of coverage for economic governance regimes that regulate the terms and conditions of employment, and social wage regimes varies widely (Commission on Labor Cooperation, 2003; Fudge, Tucker, and Vosko, 2003a). It is possible to have two different employment statuses simultaneously, for example, to be an employee under collective bargaining law but an independent contractor for income tax. The complexity of the legal landscape makes it very difficult to navigate the boundary between employees and independent contractors.

The recent growth of self-employment exacerbates the problems with the traditional methods of determining the scope of labour protection. Much of the recent self-employment does not fit easily into either the employee or independent contractor category. A significant proportion of the solo self-employed, whose ranks, especially among women, have swollen, may be either disguised self-employment or dependent workers who have an objectively ambiguous employment status. But the growth in self-employment not only contributes to the problem of mapping legal definitions onto the reality of self-employment, it also raises the crucial normative question: is it justifiable to limit labour protection to subordinate employees and to exclude the self-employed? This question is particularly pressing given the gendered dimension of much of the growth of self-employment.

By failing to provide either a clear or a principled distinction between employees and independent contractors, Canadian law creates a climate that is conducive to the growth of disguised self-employment. In British Columbia in the mid-1990s a task force appointed by the provincial government to review employment standards legislation noted a problem with de facto employees who were falsely classified as independent contractors (Thompson, 1994). The traditional tests of employment have proven not to be of much help for workers who fall outside the traditional norm of employment in their attempts to avail themselves of labour protection. For example, the legal status of home workers, who are predominantly women, is very difficult to determine, and the traditional control test tends to result in their classification as independent contractors (Bernstein *et al*, 2001: 13–14, 36–38; Gurstein, 2001, 32–36). Although women who provide child care in their home have successfully established through litigation that they are employees for the purpose of pay equity, collective bargaining, and employment standards legislation (Cox, 2005),[15] governments (in Canada and Australia) have been willing to deny employment rights to women who perform traditional domestic work such as caring for others for remuneration (Hunter, 1992; Cox, 2005; Bernstein, chapter 10 in this volume). And tax courts seem unwilling to hold intermediaries who help to regulate and organise the provision of child care services in women's homes to be employers for the purpose of requiring them to make Canada Pension Plan or Employment Insurance contributions for the women who provide child care in their homes.[16]

The ILO has noted that women's predominance in certain occupations and sectors, such a domestic work, nursing and care professions, and home work, is linked to their high prevalence in ambiguous and disguised employment relationships in Canada (ILO, 2003b: para 15). Historically there has been a resistance to characterising women's domestic labour as employment (Owens 1995; Fudge 1999; Bernstein, chapter 10 in this volume). Fredman (chapter 8 in this volume) illustrates how contemporary courts in the United Kingdom are unable to distinguish between real autonomy and the results of dual obligations (to earn an income and care for others) in distinguishing between employees and independent contractors. Women's domestic work, whether paid or unpaid, does not fit well with legal categories that historically have reflected men's experience of employment.

Evidence regarding the work arrangements of many of the women who are self-employed in Canada suggests that some are only nominally self-employed (Hughes, 1999: 29; Hughes, 2004). But assessing the extent of disguised employment among the self-employed using survey data is a problem and it is necessary to develop proxy measures for determining employment status at law. Graham Lowe and Grant Schellenberg identified disguised employees among the ranks of the self-employed by focusing on control. They combined using a client's tools or equipment and working alongside client's staff as one measure and then looked at the extent to which there was also a close financial relationship (50 per cent or more of total revenue) with the portion of self-employment that is likely to be disguised employment. They found that 15 per cent of the solo self-employed and 8 per cent of those who were employers were subject to control that was similar to that of employees. However, they were careful to emphasise that this group of self-employed could be either disguised employees or they could 'occupy a distinct location between truly independent self-employed workers and the traditional "dependent" employee' (Lowe and Schellenberg, 2001: 15).

---

[15] *Wellington (County) v Butler*, [1999] OPED no 9 (Pay Equity Hearings Tribunal); *OPSEU v Cradleship Creche of Metropolitan Toronto v CUPE*, [1986] OLRB Rep 3351-84-R; *Re MacAulay Child Development Centre*, [1993] Can Rep Ont 1202, ESC 3157 (*Wacyk*).

[16] *Cambrian College v Minister of National Revenue* (2004), 36 CCEL (3d) 83 (Tax Court of Canada).

Disguised employment is difficult to distinguish from objectively ambiguous self-employment, which is the second problem for defining the scope of labour protection. A 'grey zone' of self-employment, inhabited by dependent workers, has grown (Deakin, 2002).[17] The complexity of the Canadian approach to the scope of labour protection creates problems for determining the rights and entitlements of these workers. In Canada, dependent contractors, who reside in the grey zone of dependent workers who are not classically subordinate, are already treated like employees for certain purposes, such as collective bargaining (Fudge, Tucker, and Vosko, 2003a). The issue is whether they should enjoy the full range of employment rights and standards (Saunders, 2003: 8). This issue is particularly important for women who become self-employed to balance household obligations such as caring for children or ill family members and who because of their self-employed status are not entitled to maternity or parental leave and benefits in Canada (Fudge, Tucker, and Vosko, 2003a).

The precarious situation of many of the self-employed squarely raises the question of whether the exclusion of self-employed workers from labour and social protection can be justified. One of the central purposes of labour law is to protect vulnerable workers and it is clear that many self-employed workers are vulnerable and in need of protection (ILO, 2003a). Fairness requires that similarly situated individuals be treated equally. People who are dependent upon the sale of their labour should be treated similarly regardless of the legal form that the transaction takes. From a normative perspective, there is no compelling reason for excluding self-employed workers who perform work personally from labour and social protection (Sen, 2000; Egger, 2002). In fact, there are strong normative reasons, associated with combating discrimination against women in the labour market, for including the self-employed within the scope of employment protection. According to the Committee of Experts appointed by the European Commission to examine changing employment relations and labour law and social protection:

> It may be particularly detrimental to women to restrict the scope of application of labour law and its main guarantees to the field of subordinate employment and the traditional contractual form of such employment, namely the employment contract, without taking account of work performed for others that is channelled through other kinds of legal or contractual relations: known as independent, autonomous, or self-employment or similar. The continued identification of labour law with the regulation of the prototype of labour relations associated with the industrial model that gave rise to such relations – which, moreover, was never fully representative even of all dependent or subordinate work – limits the

---

[17] Estimates in the United Kingdom are that 8% of the self-employed who are classified as independent contractors are dependent workers or employees (Burchell, Deakin and Honey, 1999).

protection afforded to a smaller and smaller core of workers and leads to even greater segmentation of the labour market.

(Supiot *et al*, 2001: 180–81)

The exclusion of the self-employed from the scope of employment protection may function as a form of gender segmentation (and segregation) of the labour market. Moreover, rising levels of self-employment jeopardise pay and employment equity initiatives that seek to address gender disparities in earnings and occupations (Hughes, 1999: 29). Because these initiatives do not apply to the self-employed, a greater proportion of women workers fall outside their scope. Expanding the scope of employment to include the precariously self-employed is an important component of any strategy to combat discrimination against women in the labour market.

CONCLUSION

Women's self-employment calls into question stereotypes about employment and entrepreneurship and poses a challenge to the traditional scope of labour law. However, the ILO's focus on dependent workers takes a relatively narrow approach to the scope of labour protection and does little to challenge the stereotype of self-employment as a form of entrepreneurship. By contrast, the Expert Committee appointed by the European Commission recommended that the scope of labour protection be extended 'beyond employment' to the self-employed (Supiot *et al*, 2001: 153). As part of the rationale for expanding the scope of labour protection, the Committee noted that limiting it to employment marginalised the necessary but unpaid care labour that women perform (Supiot *et al*, 2001: 53).

The ILO's modest approach to the scope of labour protection is likely to be more influential in Canada, where any attempt to expand the scope of employment protection to include the self-employed would be likely to run into strong opposition from employers' representatives. The Canadian employer's representative to the ILO, who played a prominent role at both the meeting of experts (ILO, 2000b) and the Conference Committee on the Scope of the Employment Relationship (ILO, 2003b), stressed the need to ensure that self-employment continues to be carved out of the scope of labour protection, and emphasised 'that the expansion of the scope of the employment relationship would be an obstacle to growth and opportunity' (ILO, 2003b: 4). For employers, it appears that confining the scope of employment protection to dependent workers and preserving a realm of independent contracting is sacrosanct—a boundary beyond which labour protection should not stray. Moreover, there are indications that the Canadian government's objectives are limited. During the discussion of the Report on the Scope of Employment by the 2003 Conference, a representative of the Canadian government agreed that there was a need for labour law reform in order to provide accessible and transparent processes for determining workers' employment status, especially in light of the complexity of the issue in Canada, and suggested that emphasis be given to the most vulnerable workers (ILO, 2003b: 6, 7).

But even this narrow approach to refocusing the scope of employment on dependent workers could have some important consequences for self-employed women in Canada. A clearer definition of employment and the extension of labour protection to dependent workers, who are not covered by employment standards, would help the 10 to 15 per cent of self-employed workers in Canada who are either disguised employees or ambiguously self-employed. Concentrating on the most vulnerable workers and effective enforcement of existing standards is an important starting point for law reform and it would assist self-employed women workers whose situation tends to be the most precarious.

In Canada, although little political attention has been devoted to extending *labour* protection to the self-employed, which imposes obligations on employers, the extension of *social* protection, which is a public responsibility, is a different matter. The situation of self-employed women who are excluded from maternity and parental benefits under the federal employment insurance legislation has begun to attract the attention of parliamentarians. In 2001, the Standing Committee on Human Resources Development and the Status of Persons with Disabilities recommended that the government consider developing ways to extend maternity and parental benefits (which can last up to 50 weeks) under the employment insurance system to the self-employed (Canada, House of Commons, 2001). Two years later the Prime Minister's Task Force on Women's Entrepreneurs (2003: 81) proposed extending employment insurance maternity and parental benefits to the self-employed. The odds of returning early to work after the birth of a child are eight times higher for self-employed women than women employees, and the main reason for early return was the lack of maternity and parental benefits (Marshall, 1999). The ILO Convention on Maternity Protection (No 183) (2000), which Canada has not ratified, covers all women workers, including those in atypical forms of dependent work, in the scope of maternity and parental leaves and benefits (Benjamin, 2002: 80; ILO, 2003b; Vosko, chapter 3 in this volume). Given that women often take up solo self-employment as a means of accommodating the dual demands of work and family responsibilities, it is not surprising that a key public policy issue is providing self-employed women with replacement income during periods of intensive childrearing. Quebec already has a system of maternity and parental benefits for the self-employed in place, although it does not come into effect until January 2006 (Rooney *et al*, 2003: 52–57; Hughes, 2004), and there has been some attention given to extending employment insurance benefits and other social safety-net programmes to the self-employed (Canada, House of Commons, 2001: Recommendation 8; Prime Minister's Parliamentary Task Force on Women's Entrepreneurs, 2003: 81–82). Extending maternity and parental benefits to these women seems a sensible public policy choice.

Women's self-employment challenges the male norm of independent contracting (Hunter, 1992). However, precarious self-employment is regarded as a trade-off that women are willing to make in order to have children. But the problem is that this bargain does not allow women to live autonomous lives; they are dependent upon men's earnings and benefits. It is only possible to improve the terms of precarious self-employment by going beyond employment and paid work to consider unpaid domestic labour. Women's self-employment demonstrates that it is impossible to separate the institutions of the labour market from the household and the social distribution of caring responsibilities. Under the current division of unpaid care labour, self-employment offers women limited choices. Solo self-employment does not enable women to be economically independent and employer self-employment does not allow women to balance domestic responsibilities unless they purchase domestic labour. The stereotype of the self-employed entrepreneur is, like the standard employment relationship, based upon a male norm. It is time for labour law to challenge this norm too.

10

The Regulation of Paid Care Work in the Home in Quebec: From the Hearth to the Global Marketplace

STÉPHANIE BERNSTEIN

INTRODUCTION

FROM A REGULATORY perspective, the work of caring for children, the elderly, the sick, and people living with chronic disabilities in the home has been marginalised in relation to 'traditional' employment. Socially constructed as women's work in the 'private' sphere[1], its legitimisation as paid employment has been arduous and is far from complete. In Quebec, after many years of debate and successive reforms, many care workers employed directly by individuals in private homes have finally been clumsily integrated into existing regulatory schemes based on an increasingly obsolete industrial model. At the same time, after gaining recognition and legislative protection, including collective bargaining rights, workers in some other forms of care work have been losing ground and rendered increasingly precarious. Those care workers who depend on state-controlled and funded agencies, such as early childhood centres and social service agencies, for work have seen their working conditions worsen and their employment situation become more uncertain with the externalisation[2] of these services, including to temporary employment agencies, and their transformation into 'independent' contractors.

---

[1] This social construction emerged with the Industrial Revolution and eventually served to shore up the male breadwinner model (Boydston, 1990; Lewis, 2001). See also Armstrong and Armstrong (2004) on women's roles in unpaid care and on the overlapping of the 'private' and 'public' spheres in relation to care.

[2] With externalisation, legal obligations and many costs and financial risks related to the traditional employment model are shifted to another employer (through subcontracting and temporary employment agencies) or directly to the worker, who is no longer an employee but a dependent or independent contractor (Dif, 1998).

The work/care debate—whether women's equality would best be served by promoting the need for restructuring the labour market and work generally to enable women's full and equal participation or by providing them with an income while performing care for their family members—has dominated feminist policy analysis in Canada and the United States, and it has tended to obscure the huge amount of paid care work performed by women. This debate also fails to appreciate how a woman's social location influences her choices about care and employment. Policies designed to enhance women's employment tend to rely on an increase in paid care employment, ignoring the fact that this reliance may increase conflicts of interest between women who perform paid care in the home and women who work for wages outside the home. If women who work outside the home for wages have to absorb the full costs of paying women who perform the care, they will be very constrained in supporting improvements in these workers' pay and conditions. Promoting women's full and equal participation in the workforce while at the same time providing for legal recognition of the economic and social value of paid care work is challenging, and while these two goals are not mutually exclusive, this case study from Quebec illustrates how they may conflict.

This chapter traces the path leading full circle from the exclusion of paid care workers who perform work in the home from labour legislation to their recognition and inclusion back to their precariousness in a context of deinstitutionalisation and privatisation. In the first part, this type of care work is defined, described, and situated in relation to the law. In the second part, some of the tensions in the work/care debate are highlighted. In the third part, the treatment of paid care workers under Quebec labour legislation serves to illustrate how paid-care work has been compartmentalised leading to the inclusion and exclusion of care workers on the basis of their place of work, the type of work being performed, and the employer's identity. Next, the tenuous nature of some care workers' situations is illustrated by their recent exclusion from labour legislation through the technique of deeming provisions. Finally, the relationship between paid care work and the global care market is briefly examined, bringing to the fore the fact that care work is definitely not just a 'family matter'.

PORTRAYING PAID CARE WORK IN THE HOME

Care work can be defined broadly as 'the work of looking after the physical, psychological, emotional and development needs of one or more other people' (Standing, 2001: 17). In this chapter, the term is used to designate paid work involving caring for children, the sick, the elderly, and people living with disabilities, as well as the related work of managing households and housework that takes place within the confines of the home.[3] All of this work has a key characteristic in common: it takes place in the home, either in the employer's home or, in some cases, the worker's home (in what has long been called the 'private sphere' as opposed to the labour 'market'). The focus here is not on unpaid care within the family and the community, but on the paid care worker who works in the home, and on her marginal status in the labour market and in labour law.

Care work is heterogeneous and, depending on the tasks performed and the situations of persons receiving care, diverse skills are called upon. This work is also shaped in Quebec and elsewhere by complex policies that have evolved under strategies of deinstitutionalisation and privatisation in the health and social services sectors and in response to a dearth of affordable and adapted child care (AFÉAS *et al*, 1998; MSSS, 1999; Anctil *et al*, 2000; Armstrong 2001; Linda White, 2001; Gilmour, 2002; MESSF, 2003). Decreased financing and increased privatisation of home care, as well as a renewed reliance on unpaid care provided by family members (women), have had a negative impact on the quality of care and contributed to the social exclusion of many people who are not able to pay for 'extra' home care beyond what the state provides (Aronson and Neysmith, 2001). The goal here is not to minimise the differences among care workers, care delivery programmes, financing schemes, and above all, the realities of people who receive care; rather, the objective is to look at paid care work performed in the home through the lens of the law to examine the categories it creates and the premises on which they are built. Despite the multiple dimensions of care work with respect to the skills required, the place of work, the employer's identity, the persons being cared for, and the modes of financing, the law has tended to relegate this work to the 'private sphere' and to contribute to its non-recognition.

One of the dominant characteristics of paid care work that is performed in the home is that it is often precarious (Cranford *et al*, 2005). When the direct employer is the person requiring care or a member of his or her family, the employee–employer relationship is often fraught with ambiguity. The employer may be a relatively vulnerable person and dependent in many ways on the care worker (Aronson and Neysmith, 2001). At the same time, the care worker's employment security is based on maintaining a good personal relationship with the employer and, often, acceptance of difficult working conditions. Care work is also characterised by its fragmentation and diverse employment forms; irregular work hours, multiple job-holding, work via temporary employment agencies (when the person requiring care

---

[3] Paid care work can be performed in institutions such as hospitals and long-term care facilities. Some forms of paid care work, such as nursing and midwifery, may also be performed in a home. Forms of paid-care work that are officially recognised and organised as a profession are outside the scope of this chapter.

is not the direct employer), and false self-employment are commonplace.[4] The pay is generally low, with few, if any, benefits (Morris *et al*, 1999), even state-mandated ones such as access to workers' compensation.[5] Also, the place of work, the home, is mistakenly assumed to be safe, which is reflected in the limited protective scope of health and safety legislation (Bernstein *et al*, 2001). Home-care workers, however, report a wide variety of work-related health concerns, such as back injuries from lifting, emotional stress related to working with the terminally ill, burn-out, infections, and physical aggression (Morris *et al*, 1999). Legislative exclusion from standards applicable to other workers leads to working conditions based on the worker's capacity to negotiate and often, on the employer's capacity to pay. The prevalence of the industrial male breadwinner standard employment relationship as the basis for the development of labour laws is at odds with the home as workplace and caring as work (Smith, 2000).

Since the Industrial Revolution, the value put on waged labour outside the home and the development of the cash economy has rendered the work that takes place in the home invisible and given it the label of 'unproductive', creating a dichotomy between the market and the family, the 'public' and the 'private' (Olsen, 1983; Silbaugh, 1996). This perception then permeates the law and the legal system (Taub and Schneider, 1982). The result has been that 'market, wage-based domestic labour is treated much more like unpaid housework than like any other paid labor', and has led to the legal stigmatisation of care work (Silbaugh, 1996: 27; Young, 2001; Ramirez-Machado, 2003). In Canada and elsewhere (Blackett, 1998; Ramirez-Machado, 2003), legal definitions of what is generically called 'domestic' work, including or excluding the care of other people, are more often than not characterised by a simplistic vision of the actual skills involved in caring. The profound gendering of these skills has undervalued them socially and in comparison to other types of employment, leading to the further marginalisation of these groups of care workers in an already sexually divided labour market (Fudge and Cossman, 2002: 7).

---

[4] The confusion surrounding care workers' employment status is widespread. To illustrate this, the Canadian 2001 National Occupational Classification, which contains standardised definitions and descriptions of jobs in the Canadian labour market used for research, analysis, and statistical purposes, characterises most care workers who work in their employers' homes as 'self-employed', even though they may not be under the law (see Government of Canada, 2001). Citizenship and Immigration Canada's directives on foreign workers also state that 'a "Live-in Caregiver" is considered to be "self-employed" and as such is totally responsible for taxes and other salary deductions required by law', even though this is not the case under provincial labour laws (Citizenship and Immigration Canada, 2004).

[5] In Quebec, for example, complex legal categories exist based on whether or not the worker lives in and on the tasks performed. In some cases, the worker is completely excluded, while in others she has to pay her own premiums to be protected. See Industrial Accidents and Occupational Diseases Act, RSQ c A-3.001, ss 2 and 18.

Indeed, the continued use of the antiquated term 'domestic' is in itself emblematic. It serves conceptually to restrict the care worker to the private sphere of the home and the family, distancing her from the wider labour market and the social policies in which she is an important actor. Also, specific sociological and historical connotations surround the term. *Fowler's Modern English Usage* (1996), under the term 'domestic', comments that '[c]hanges of attitude in the 20 c have largely driven [this term] out of use, and [it has] been replaced by a range of terms that are intended to reduce the social divisions once taken for granted ...'. Yet, use of the term 'domestic', reminiscent of the days of paternalistic 'master–servant' relations, is perpetuated through legislation. In Quebec civil law, for instance, the term was only eliminated in 1994 with the repeal and replacement of the 1866 Civil Code of Lower Canada by the new Quebec Civil Code. Despite successive reforms and repeated demands[6] to eliminate the term 'domestic' from the law, it continues to be used in several provincial labour and social protection laws: in Quebec, this includes minimum employment standards legislation.

THE WORK/CARE DEBATE

According to Joan Williams, 'the major issue for feminist jurisprudence is whether to fight the sacralization of care work, to embrace it – or both' (Williams, 2001: 1447). Labelling care work as a 'commodity', or an economic good provokes ambivalent reactions. Care work in the home has, however, been commodified for centuries, and the women doing the caring for pay have, on the whole, been poor women, including women who migrate from rural areas to the city and from poor countries to richer ones (Macklin, 1992; de Groot and Ouellet, 2001; Langevin and Belleau, 2001; Salazar Parrenas, 2001). The debate over the commodification of care work therefore includes the implications of paying women to do this work, so that other women—those who, with or without the aid of other family members or the state, can afford to pay others—can have access to the broader labour market, calling into question how care work, paid and unpaid, is valued in economic terms.

In theory, ascribing an appropriate economic value to this work would lead to its recognition as 'real' work. Refusing to recognise the economic value of unpaid care work keeps care workers' wages low and shapes social and labour policy (Silbaugh, 1996: 73; Cahn, 2001). The undervaluing of paid care work in turn has an impact on the value, both social and economic, attributed to unpaid care work (for example in family and tax law) (Silbaugh, 1996: 79). But is there a virtuous circle such that valuing unpaid care work

---

[6] See, eg, Association des Aides Familiales du Québec (AAFQ), 2002.

will translate into valuing paid care work and vice versa? One of the under-lying assumptions in this debate is the realisation of women's full and equal access to the labour market through policies that recognise the intrinsic social and economic value of unpaid care work. Yet, public subsidies for unpaid care workers, for instance, have been found not to enhance gender equality in or out of the labour market (OECD, 1999). The question is how to value care work without further entrenching gender roles (Ungerson, 1997).

Women, who remain the primary caregivers for their families, face many hurdles to full and equal access to the labour market. Labour policies that aim to better balance work and family rarely call into question the overall structures of the labour market and the organisation of work outside the home. Many women adapt their participation in the labour market to their caregiving role by working part time or at home (Bernstein *et al*, 2001; Cancedda, 2001). As Vicki Schultz (2000) points out, formal equal access to the labour market is not sufficient, as it is also a locus of gender inequal-ity, and must be accompanied by a modified view of citizenship, care, and work itself. Indeed, policies intended to increase women's access to the labour market have fallen short in many respects. Paid parental and family leave policies do not necessarily redistribute the burden of responsibility for care work between men and women or between different groups of women. The overwhelming majority of workers who receive parental benefits (which are available to both men and women) are women.[7] Moreover, not all women who work have access to income replacement during such leaves, even if they have contributed to the Employment Insurance scheme that provides these benefits. Since many women who work for wages occu-py precarious jobs, their access to leave and decent benefits is limited (Zeytinoglu and Muteshi, 2000; Fudge and Vosko, 2001a), as is their capacity to pay for others to perform care work.

This environment shapes the complex relationship between women who employ other women in their homes to care for their families and the women who perform care work for pay in other women's homes. This rela-tionship raises troubling questions for feminists. Women who employ other women to perform care work may reinforce gendered care roles by arguing with others against the full recognition of paid care work in labour law and social policies. Indeed, the legal treatment of workers who perform care work for pay in the home both illustrates and contributes to the broader marginalisation of these workers.

---

[7] In 2003, women made 86.3% of parental benefits claims. Men who claimed these bene-fits during the same period received them for on average just under 14 weeks, compared with women, who received them for an average of 30 weeks (in addition to 15 weeks of maternity benefits). During the same period, 93.7% of full-time workers were eligible for maternity, parental, and compassionate leave benefits, compared to 61.2% of part-time workers (64.5% of women and 52.9% of men). Although benefits represent 55% of workers' gross salary, the Family Supplement increases the benefit rate from 55% to 80% for parents with net family incomes of $25,921 or less (Canada Employment Insurance Commission. 2004).

(DE)COMPARTMENTALISING CARE WORK:
THE QUEBEC LABOUR STANDARDS ACT

The recognition of care work as *work* in labour law has been a long, laborious, and not always successful process. Indeed, law has been much slower than other disciplines, such as sociology, economics, and history, in reconceiving unpaid care work as work, which in turn affects how paid care work is perceived (Silbaugh, 1996: 17). The treatment of care workers in minimum employment standards legislation in Quebec is a case in point. In 1979, the 1940 Quebec Minimum Wage Act[8] became the Labour Standards Act,[9] establishing a floor of rights for almost all workers, unionised or not, regarding such norms as wages, vacations and holidays, maternity leave, and protection against unjust dismissal. Through successive reforms, particularly two major rounds in 1990 and 2002, the scope of the law was widened to include parental and family leave, timid equal treatment for part-time workers, and unremunerated sick leave. The coverage of the law was also broadened and the Act is today considered a main pillar of labour market regulation in Quebec (Bernstein, 2005). But the ambivalence towards care workers remains: the law has always made a distinction between care workers and other workers by denying or limiting the coverage of care workers. Whether or not a worker who performs care work for pay is covered by protective labour legislation depends upon how her work fits into different compartments: the place of work, the kind of work, and the type of employer.

Quebec is not alone in attaching legal significance either to the type of paid work in the home or to how it is slotted into different compartments. Multiple legal compartments or categories have been created in Canada to distinguish people who do one kind of care work from another: looking after children versus cooking and cleaning, and so forth. In some cases, these divisions among care workers serve to include, and in others, to exclude them from legal coverage.[10] In Ontario, employment standards legislation defines three types of paid care worker: 'domestic worker', 'residential care worker', and 'homemaker'.[11] Similar legislation in British Columbia includes five different categories of care workers: 'domestics', 'live-in home support workers', 'night attendants', 'residential care workers', and 'sitters' (the term 'domestic servant', a distinct category, was recently removed from the legislation).[12] These categories appear to be the

---

[8] SQ 1940, c 39.
[9] RSQ, c N-1.1.
[10] Most workers in Canada (90%) are exclusively covered by provincial labour legislation.
[11] Exemptions, special rules and establishment of minimum wage, Ont Reg 285/01, ss 11, 19, 20; Employment Standards Act, 2000, SO 2000, c 41.
[12] Employment Standards Regulation, BC Reg 396/95, s 1; Employment Standards Act, RSBC 1996, c 113.

result of a never-ending political compromise between the state's, care recipients', and care workers' claims regarding the cost and the value of care. In Quebec, employment standards legislation has distinguished workers on the basis of their place of work, whether or not they do housework and the identity of their employer.

The first, and perhaps most problematic, category is that of people who work in their employer's home. These women who work for their direct employer are then subdivided into two other categories: those whose *main* function is housework and who may also care for people in the household, defined in the law as 'domestics', and those whose *exclusive* function is caring for a person in the household, and who only do housework *directly* related to the care of the person. Until 1990, women whose main function was looking after people but who also did housework unrelated to the care of the person, were excluded from the definition of 'domestic' in the Labour Standards Act and hence from labour protection. Women whose exclusive function was looking after children, the elderly, the sick, or people living with disabilities in their employer's home were completely excluded from the Act until mid-2004.[13] They remain excluded from overtime pay provisions, and care workers who 'sit' (that is, who care for children, typically) on an occasional basis are also excluded. Litigation and the subsequent case-law will determine the scope of this last exclusion; the legislative intention appears to have been the exclusion of adolescents who take care of children on an irregular basis.

The Labour Standards Act still refers to two categories of care workers who work in their employers' homes: the 'domestic' and the 'employee whose exclusive duty is to take care of or provide care to a child or to a sick, handicapped or aged person, in that person's dwelling, including, where so required, the performance of domestic duties that are directly related to the immediate needs of that person'.[14] Depending on which slot the care worker fits into, she will have more or less rights under minimum employment standards legislation. If the worker does not fit into one of these definitions, but does some form of paid care work (for example, an educator in an early childhood centre), she is a regular 'employee' and not subject to particular treatment under employment standards legislation. This category is usually the case for care workers who do not work directly for the person requiring care or for his or her family. Outside the law,

---

[13] Bill 143, An Act to Amend the Act Respecting Labour Standards and Other Legislative Provisions, 2nd Sess, 36th Leg, Quebec, 2002 (assented to 19 December 2002), SQ 2002, c 80) [Bill 143], s 74.
[14] Above n 9, ss 1, 3(2). The definition of the term 'domestic' in s 1 is:
an employee in the employ of a natural person whose main function is the performance of domestic duties in the dwelling of that person, including an employee whose main function is to take care of or provide care to a child or to a sick, handicapped or aged person and to perform domestic duties in the dwelling that are not directly related to the immediate needs of the person in question.

care work has most often been categorised according to the 'clientele' needing care: children, the elderly, people with disabilities, and the sick.

In reality, it is hard to distinguish between the worker whose main function is ensuring the well-being of another person, but who also does housework unrelated to the care of this person, and the worker whose exclusive function is looking after other people in the home. When is a household task unrelated to the care of the person? Is vacuuming the apartment related to the care of the person if he or she lives alone and is not able to vacuum? What if this person lives with someone else who is capable of vacuuming? Does the vacuuming then become unrelated to the care? Does the care worker have to wash the parents' as well as the children's breakfast dishes to be considered a 'domestic' and be entitled to the payment of overtime? The distinction between the two is thus often artificial and has served as fodder for contesting these workers' rights before the courts.[15] An overview of minimum employment standards legislation in Quebec, as well as of some other laws such as workers' compensation legislation, reveals that housework has been valued as work, while caring for people has not by the exclusion of workers whose exclusive function is ensuring the well-being of others from the purview of labour legislation.[16]

Until recently, 'domestics' covered by the law were further divided into those who did not live with their employer and those who did, the latter having a lower minimum wage and longer workweek. Modifications to the Labour Standards Act in 2002 eliminated the distinction between live-in and live-out workers, which had created a system whereby migrant care workers were treated differently from non-migrant workers (Bakan and Stasiulis, 1997). At the end of the nineteenth century, labour shortages of women willing to 'live-in' as 'domestics' led to the establishment of various temporary migrant workers' networks and then specific programmes. This led to the creation of the Foreign Domestic Movement Programme in 1981, replaced by the Live-In Caregiver Programme in 1992,[17] which allows these migrant workers, generally from poorer countries, to ask for permanent residency after two years of 'live-in' service (Macklin, 1992; Langevin and Belleau, 2001). These workers face obstacles that are not only gender-based, but that also stem from their national origin, race/ethnicity, and class (Macklin, 1992; Salazar Parrenas, 2001).

The potential for exploitation of migrant 'live-in caregivers' is high and Audrey Macklin (1992: 751) suggests that 'some Canadian women's access to the high paying, high status professions is facilitated through the revival of semi-indentured servitude ... one woman is exercising class and citizenship

---

[15] See, eg, *Dary v Nocera*, [1999] DTE 482 (caregiver determined to be an employee).

[16] Industrial Accidents and Occupational Diseases Act, above n 5, s 2; Labour Standards Act, above n 9, s 3(2), as rep by Bill 143, s 74.

[17] Immigration and Refugee Protection Regulation, SOR/2002-227, ss 110*ff* ('Live-in Caregivers').

privilege to buy her way out of sex oppression.' The question of whether state-sponsored migration programmes to fill labour shortages of 'live-in' 'help' should be abolished is a thorny one (Langevin and Belleau, 2001; Young, 2001). On the one hand, for some women it is the only avenue allowing them to emigrate to Canada. On the other, evidence of exploitation and abuse exists and feminists (and others) have to question the ethics of bringing women to Canada to fill jobs that no one else wants because of mediocre and substandard working conditions.

In addition, the identity of migrant care workers as mothers and family providers has also been denied. Until 2004, many of these workers were excluded from legislation granting them maternity and parental leave, as were many non-migrant care workers, since these entitlements are provided for in the Quebec Labour Standards Act. The Live-In Caregiver Programme (which is administered by the federal government since it has jurisdiction over immigration) requires that women work 24 months as live-in caregivers over a period of 36 months in order to apply for their permanent residency. These women may be (illegally) dismissed if they become pregnant, or their employers do not want to house their children as well. If this occurs, they are not able to work as 'live-ins' for the required period. The possibility of attaining permanent resident status is thus jeopardised if they have a child while they are temporary workers (Macklin, 2002). They must also complete the required two years of live-in service before they can bring their own children—who are usually being cared for by other women in their country of origin—to Canada.

By eliminating the distinction between 'live-in' and 'live-out' care workers and by including all care work under the purview of the legislation, the Quebec legislature has taken a step toward remedying the existing imbalance in rights between the two groups. When it presented the Bill to amend the Labour Standards Act in 2002, the government undertook an economic impact analysis of the proposed amendments, including the amendments concerning care workers (CNT and Ministère du Travail, 2002). Despite the paucity of information regarding employers' incomes, the analysis concluded that those who employed 'live-in' care workers were in all likelihood higher income earners and that the impact on them of extending legal coverage to care workers would therefore be negligible. The requirement to 'live in' nevertheless remains under Canadian immigration legislation and contributes in large part to the imbalance of power between these workers and their employers. The employment of migrant women as live-in 'domestic' workers in Canada illustrates a further dimension of the increasing polarisation among women surrounding the issue of care.

Another dimension of this polarisation is the difficulties underlying the promotion of 'family-friendly' policies that allow women to participate in the labour market while keeping the related economic costs relatively low for these women, for families generally, and for the state. This was clearly illustrated in some of the briefs presented to the Quebec Minister of Labour during the process to reform minimum employment standards legislation that occurred in 1990 and 2002. Perhaps the most telling representations were those of the Quebec Council for the Status of Women, a government-appointed body whose mandate is to promote women's rights and address their concerns. In 1990, while recognising the importance of guaranteeing at least some minimal rights to care workers not covered by the Labour Standards Act, the Council recommended maintaining their exclusion from standards that would cost their employers more money, especially a minimum wage, overtime, and paid holidays. The Council maintained that it would be unrealistic to apply standards that would increase the costs of care work for employers, for example, families unable to assume the financial burden, and would impede other women from pursuing their professional activities outside the home. During the preliminary ministerial consultations on the review of the Act in 2002, the Council presented the same position in its initial submission.[18] In its brief, the Council recognised that the excluded care workers should be considered 'real' workers and covered by the law, but maintained that their employers were not prototypical. With an increase in cost for employers through the application of provisions on pecuniary advantages such as a minimum wage, the Council contended that more care workers would accept undeclared work or would lose their jobs, and that women who would no longer be able to pay for the care provided would have to withdraw from the labour market. When the Bill was presented, the Council had changed its position and applauded the government for proposing much fuller coverage of these workers, including with regard to minimum wage provisions.[19] For the government, this was no doubt made politically possible by the implementation of $5-a-day (now $7-a-day) daycare in Quebec, making childcare more affordable for a growing number of parents, and some, albeit insufficient, economic and fiscal measures to help families pay for care work.[20]

---

[18] See Conseil du Statut de la Femme (CSF), 1990; CSF, 2002a.

[19] See CSF, 2002b. See also Quebec, National Assembly (Permanent Commission on the Economy and Labour), 2002: 21-7 (6 December 2002) (intervention by Diane Lavallée, President of the CSF).

[20] On subsidised daycare programmes in Quebec, see MESSF, 2003. The Quebec government does, however, recognise that many workers, particularly those occupying non-standard employment have particular daycare needs that are not being met (Rochette, 2003). On the Quebec government's home support strategy for people living with disabilities and the elderly, see MSSS, 2003. This strategy relies heavily on unpaid family and community caregivers (who are, in the majority, women), while at the same time includes a series of programmes involving paid care workers in home support, funds available for adapting homes to the needs of people living with disabilities, and a series of fiscal measures for unpaid caregivers and persons requiring care (eg the Quebec Tax Credit Respecting Home Support Services for Seniors). See also Nancy Guberman (2002), who analyses the differential impact of such policies in Quebec on women.

The Council's initial position seems rather tenuous if one looks at the artificial divide created by the legislator between looking after other people's well-being and 'housework'. Many workers that the Council had recommended should be excluded from such provisions as the minimum wage, were in all likelihood covered since, despite their job title, they did housework not directly related to the care of the person. The Council's position also tacitly confirmed the view that the commodification of care work in the broader marketplace, regardless of the status of the employer (whether a temporary employment agency, private daycare, publicly funded daycare, etc), is what legitimises it as work worthy of being covered by labour laws. As soon as the employer is the person needing care or a member of his or her family, care work is relegated once again to the private sphere and invisibility.

Many people, in particular, many living with disabilities, prefer being able to choose and directly pay care workers, thereby retaining a modicum of control over how their needs are being addressed (Cranford *et al*, 2005; Ungerson, 1997). At the same time, the idea that adults requiring care should be considered employers for the purposes of labour laws may meet opposition because of the often onerous administrative requirements of managing employees (tax deductions, pay slips, and so forth) (Vaillancourt and Jetté, 1999). For instance, in a recent unanimous Federal Court of Appeal decision on the insurability of care workers' remuneration under the Employment Insurance Act, the court refused to recognise the employer status of a man who had become severely disabled following an automobile accident. The court reasoned:

> [g]iven the applicant's physical condition and the consequences that result from employer status, [the court does] not think it is reasonable to infer that the applicant intended to enter into a contract of employment with the three workers that would make him their employer.[21]

This decision is disquieting for two reasons. First, the court's reasoning contradicts much of the case-law with respect to the weight to be given to the parties' intention as far as employment status is concerned. The court furthermore appears to determine that the intention of the person requiring care is implicit because of his physical limitations. Second, the lack of support for people needing care in their dealings with care workers led the court to deny rights to workers who would otherwise probably be considered employees and covered by the law. At the same time, the court underlines some of the dilemmas of conferring employer status on certain people requiring care.

---

[21] *Daniel Poulin v Minister of National Revenue* (30 January 2003), Ottawa A-526-01, 2003 FCA 50 (Federal Court of Appeal), para 30 (*Poulin*).

The needs and limitations of some people require the state and other actors to lessen the burden associated with being an employer.[22] Some solutions have been found in Quebec such as the 'chèque emploi–service' (literally 'job-service cheque', modelled on a similar initiative in France),[23] whereby the allowance paid by the state to the person requiring some forms of home care is administered for payroll purposes by a private or public entity. This system also serves to counter tax evasion on the part of paid care workers and their employers. The particular situations of some people requiring care do not, however, justify (or explain) a history—or a future—of legislative exclusion. When care work of a similar nature is performed outside or inside the home with a firm (for example, a temporary employment agency or even a not-for-profit organisation[24]) or the state as the employer, variations to and exclusion from labour laws, with some limited exceptions, do not apply. When the relationship between the employer and the care worker is perceived to most resemble a family-type relationship, the law ceases to include the worker within the scope of regulation and protection. Resistance to state intervention in the home and threats to family privacy have thus also shaped the regulation of care work (Taub and Schneider, 1982; Silbaugh, 1996).

Where the employer or a member of his or her family is not the person requiring care, care workers are not explicitly excluded by legislation. This is not to say that the existing labour law framework provides these care workers with adequate coverage and that their employment situations are not becoming increasingly precarious, a phenomenon which is also gendered (Vosko *et al*, 2003; Cranford, 2005). Care work does not become 'de-gendered' by virtue of its commodification in the wider marketplace. On the contrary, the undervaluing of care work in terms of skills and, in turn, of remuneration, remains, forming part of the overall segregation of women and men into different occupations (Folbre, 2001; Fudge and Vosko, 2001; Comeau, 2003). As part-time workers, multiple job-holders, and temporary agency workers, they face the same legal obstacles as other workers in precarious employment in Quebec (Bernstein, 2005; Lippel, 2005). Their situation

---

[22] See Chantier de l'Économie Sociale, 2000.

[23] See Ministère de la Santé et des Services Sociaux, *Vous recevez de l'aide ... Les services d'aide à domicile et le chèque emploi-service*, online: <ftp.msss.gouv.qc.ca/publications/acrobat/f/documentation/2004/04-513-05.pdf> (date accessed: 15 August 2004); Ministère du Travail, *Dossiers pratiques: chèque emploi-service, Ministère du Travail, France*, online: <http://www.travail.gouv.fr/infos_pratiques/ch_emploi-service.html> (date accessed: 15 August 2004). See also Ungerson (1997) and OECD (1999) on different forms of 'direct payment' schemes in different countries.

[24] In Quebec, many not-for-profit 'social economy' or 'third sector' corporations and cooperatives provide domestic help services (AFÉAS *et al*, 1998; Vaillancourt and Jetté 1999). For a profile of the sector, see Ministère du Développement Économique et Régional, 2002. On the working conditions in the 'social economy', see Comeau, 2003; Guay *et al*, 2003. On the 'third sector' in Europe, see Cancedda, 2001.

is further exacerbated given their place of work—the home—which complicates the enforcement of applicable labour standards, renders other norms such as health and safety standards inapplicable, and severely limits their capacity to organise. Moreover, even existing coverage is being eroded: recent legislative initiatives have targeted specific care workers and introduced new exclusions.

LEGAL FICTION: CARE WORKERS AS BUSINESSWOMEN

Soon after coming into power in the spring of 2003, a new Liberal provincial government introduced legislation to exclude certain care workers who work in their own home from labour laws by deeming them to be independent contractors. The workers targeted by these two Bills are home childcare providers and intermediate resources in private dwellings in the social services sector,[25] both recently determined by the courts to be employees of state-controlled and funded agencies.[26] While this legislation was implicitly directed at unionisation and collective bargaining, recognition of employee status is precluded under all labour and social security laws since these Bills state that these workers cannot enter into a contract of employment with their provider of work.[27] The legislation creates an irrefutable presumption that they are independent contractors. Not only do these laws eliminate all possibility of having the courts determine that they are 'employees' by applying the traditional tests developed by the case-law, they also reverse administrative, quasi-judicial, and judicial decisions to the contrary rendered before the amendments came into force at the end of 2003, and in effect cancelled the certification of existing unions.[28]

[25] Bill 8, An Act to Amend the Act Respecting Childcare Centres and Childcare Services, 1st Sess, 37th Leg, Quebec, 2003 (assented to 18 December 2003) SQ 2003, c 13 (Bill 8); Bill 7, An Act to Amend the Act Respecting Health Services and Social Services, 1st Sess, 37th Leg, Quebec, 2003 (assented to 18 December 2003) SQ 2003, c 12 (Bill 7). An intermediate resource is a resource (a person or persons) attached to a public social services institution that provides a person requiring care with a living environment appropriate to his or her needs, while maintaining this person's access to public support or assistance. Such resources are normally located in private dwellings. The objective of the establishment of these resources is to maintain or integrate the person requiring care into the community.

[26] See, eg, *Centre de la petite enfance La Rose des vents v Alliance des intervenantes en milieu familial Laval, Laurentides, Lanaudière (CSQ)*, [2003] DTE 763; *Centre du Florès v St-Arnaud*, [2001] R.JDT 1228, [2002] DTE 309 (Sup Ct). The previous government had also introduced a Bill shortly before the end of its mandate providing for such a deeming provision in the case of intermediate resources, but it died on the order paper: Bill 151, An Act to Amend the Act Respecting Health Services and Social Services, 2nd Sess, 36th Leg., Quebec, 2002 (introduced on 13 December 2002).

[27] In the case of workers' compensation, see *Simard v Centre de réadaptation en déficience intellectuelle de Québec* (26 January 2004), Quebec 191174-32-0209, CLPE 2003LP-267 (CLP).

[28] Bill 7, above n 25, ss 1 and 7; Bill 8, above n 25, ss 1 and 3. Quebec's four main union centrals have contested the constitutionality of these amendments under ss 2(d) and 15(1) of the Canadian Charter of Rights and Freedoms, Part I of the Constitution Act 1982, being Sch B to the Canada Act 1982 (UK, 1982, c 11), and under ss 3 and 10 of the Quebec Charter of Human Rights and Freedoms, RSQ c C-12 regarding freedom of association and equality

These workers, the vast majority of whom are women, have thus become 'entrepreneurs' under the law, despite the extensive control state agencies wield over how they do their work, when they do their work, and how much they can charge (Cox, 2005; Fudge, chapter 9 in this volume). Economic rationale and increased demand, particularly with the popular '$5 a day' childcare programme, were the main motivating factors behind denying employee status to these workers. In 2003, almost half of daycare places subsidised by the government in Quebec were offered by home child-care providers, who are under the control of early childhood centres (MESSF, 2003: 11). Most daycare places are subsidised in Quebec: these include places in not-for-profit early childhood centres, home daycares (of which most are under the control of early childhood centres), and for-profit private daycare centres. With the implementation of the reduced $5-a-day (now $7-a-day) parental contribution to subsidised daycare in 2000, government subsidies per child per day are considerably less for home child-care providers than for places in early childhood centres ($21.83 versus $37.54 in 2002–03), which makes encouraging the development of the for-mer far more attractive in economic terms (MESSF, 2003: 19). Tensions among workers in these sectors regarding a preference for either independent contractor or employee status further complicated the issues underlying the Bills.[29] The denial of employee status to intermediate resources and home childcare providers through legislation is yet another manifestation of the misfit between the logic of existing labour law and care work. It is also another form of commodification, redolent of notions of free enterprise and free choice: women are not only carers but now businesspeople as well.

GLOBALISATION AND REDEFINING COMMODIFICATION

While paid care work is portrayed as belonging to the intimate sphere of the home, it has had global implications for a long time. The informal and then institutionalised migration of women from poorer countries to work in Canadian homes is one important manifestation of how women are differently situated in the care work debate. Global economic forces that negatively affect poorer countries and their inhabitants provide the impetus for this migration. Women who are able to emigrate for economic reasons, often leaving behind their own children, then compensate in part for labour

---

rights. They have also filed complaints with the International Labour Organization's Committee on Freedom of Association. Governing Body, *Eighth Item on the Agenda: 336th Report of the Committee on Freedom of Association*, GB.292/8 (Part 1), 292nd Session. Geneva: International Labour Office, March 2005 (Cases nos 2314 and 2333).

[29] See, eg, the brief presented by the Association des Éducatrices et Éducateurs en Milieu Familial du Québec Inc during the parliamentary hearings on Bill 8, supporting their recognition as self-employed workers (AÉMFQ, 2003).

shortages of care workers in wealthier countries, responding to the needs of families who can accommodate a live-in caregiver (Salazar Parrenas, 2001: Young, 2001). However, despite high demand for live-in care workers, the laws governing this migration, and the historical treatment of these workers under labour law reflect once again the little value placed on the skills of these workers and on the work itself. This is evident when their treatment is compared, for instance, with that of 'highly-skilled' workers allowed into Canada within the framework of the North American Free Trade Agreement[30] (Macklin, 2002).

Another facet of the international commodification of care work is the transnationalisation of firms that offer care services, including the temporary employment agency industry (Peck and Theodore, 2002; Hankivsky *et al*, 2004). The expansion of this transnationalisation is the subject of much debate, as uncertainty grows over which health and social services will succumb to the rules of free trade under the NAFTA and the General Agreement on Trade in Services (Blacklock, 2000; Hankivsky *et al*, 2004). In addition to the questions this raises concerning the privatisation of and public control over such services and democratic choice, it also raises the issue of the ability of policy-makers to address the work/care dilemma through publicly funded and managed programmes.

Global phenomena may also generate global responses. On a regional level, the European Commission has begun looking at paid care work as an emerging avenue for job creation. Questions remain, however, regarding the quality of these jobs in many countries of the area, the need to improve working conditions, and the risks of further entrenching gender segmentation in the labour market (Anderson, 2001; Cancedda, 2001). It remains to be seen whether this interest in care work will lead to further standard-setting at the European level. At the international level, the International Labour Office has timidly been proposing that paid care workers (what it still calls 'domestic workers') be fully recognised and protected under national legislation (Blackett, 1998; Ramirez-Machado, 2003). Few standards address the particular aspects of 'domestic work', while others are universal in nature and, in theory at least, apply to all workers (Ramirez-Machado, 2003: 73*ff*). The latter is true of international standards on freedom of association and discrimination in employment, for example. However, some international conventions, explicitly or implicitly, allow 'domestic' workers to be excluded from their purview (for example, the ILO Convention Concerning Termination of Employment at the Initiative of the Employer (No 158) (1982)). Yet other standards have been adopted to address some of the issues generated by the worldwide proliferation of

---

[30] North American Free Trade Agreement Between the Government of Canada, the Government of Mexico and the Government of the United States, 17 December 1992, Can TS 1994 No 2, 32 ILM 289 (entered into force 1 January 1994) (NAFTA).

'non-standard' forms of employment such as part-time work, temporary work, and home work, all of which can be of significance to precarious care workers (Vosko, chapter 3 in this volume).

CONCLUSION

Historically, the law has marginalised paid care work in the home, reaffirming a much criticised divide between what goes on inside and outside the home. The context of care work in the home has changed since the nineteenth century, yet the law has been very slow to reflect these changes. Even today, the closer paid care work is to the family, the less likely it is to be given legal protection. In the absence of a prototypical employer, the legislator has chosen to deny care workers the legislative and social protection afforded those who work for more typical employers, and to make them bear the burden of inadequate policies to balance work and family life. In Quebec, a particular social and political context made the inclusion of formerly excluded care workers in the Labour Standards Act possible as of 2004. Yet, legal coverage for care workers remains fragile as demonstrated by the use of deeming provisions to transform such workers into independent contractors.

The law also reflects years of political compromise and conflicting interests in the work/care debate. Lack of affordable childcare and eldercare and policies of deinstitutionalisation and privatisation over the years have not only put pressure on women generally as primary caregivers, but also created an increased demand for paid care work in the home. However, reconciling the claims of the state, care recipients and their families, and paid care workers has been difficult. In addition, women situated in different social locations have been polarised over the legal treatment of paid care work. This has served to justify and legitimise maintaining legislative exclusions. This polarisation divides not only different groups of women in Canada, but also women from poorer and richer countries.

Indeed, labour law and immigration law have contributed to the creation of pools of precarious women workers who care for others. International tendencies in the trade arena, including the prospect of a transnationalisation of the care industry, pose new risks for precarious women workers in this sector, whether they work in the home or not. At the same time, paradoxically, perhaps the trend toward global commodification of paid care work will lead to its increased visibility as the treatment of care workers gets discussed in wider fora.

Part V

Old Laws/New Workers

11

The New Face of Employment Discrimination

KATHERINE VW STONE[*]

INTRODUCTION

O VER THE PAST 10 years, the employment relationship in the United States has undergone a profound transformation. We see evidence of this change all around us. For example, employees are no longer called 'workers' or even 'employees'—they are professionals in a particular skill or line of work. Cafeteria workers are now termed 'Members of the Culinary Service Team', salespeople are now 'Sales Associates', clerical workers are 'Administrative Assistants', cashiers are 'Cash Register Professionals', and bank loan officers are 'Personal Bankers'. These new-breed professionals have their own web pages, magazines, and trade conferences in which they network with others like themselves to keep abreast of opportunities and developments.

At the other end of the spectrum, business consultants talk about the 'talent wars' of recruitment. They advise firms to restructure human resource policies in order to attract the top talent by offering learning opportunities, lifestyle perks, and performance incentive compensation. To retain valued employees, they need to permit people to customise their jobs to suit their own ambitions and lifestyles. Thus, they counsel firms to let their employees select their work tasks, work location, schedule, and learning opportunities. Employees are free agents operating in a free talent market, so they should be offered whatever it takes to attract and keep them—whatever it takes except job security (Tulgan, 2001: 155–57).

These observable trends reflect what management theorists and industrial relations specialists call the 'new psychological contract', or the 'new deal

---

* This essay is a condensed version of Chapter Eight of Katherine VW Stone, *From Widgits to Digits: Employment Regulation for the Changing Workplace* (Cambridge: Cambridge University Press, 2004), and is reprinted here with permission of the author and publisher.

at work'. In the new deal, the long-standing assumption of long-term attachment between an employee and a single firm has broken down. No longer is employment centred on a single, primary employer. Instead, employees expect to change jobs frequently. And employees no longer derive their identity from a formal employment relationship with a single firm; rather, their employment identity comes from attachment to an occupation, a skills cluster, or an industry. At the same time, firms now expect a regular amount of 'churning' in their workforces. They encourage employees to look upon their jobs as short-term arrangements and to manage their own careers. Employees no longer expect long-term or career-long job security. In its idealised form, the new deal is a move to a free agency model of employment, in which each individual operates as a rational economic actor in a labour market unmediated by institutions, customs, and norms and without regard for long-term ties or mutual loyalty.[1]

THE NEW EMPLOYMENT RELATIONSHIP

The new employment relationship is a vast departure from employment relationships of the past. Roughly one hundred years ago, the employment relationship underwent a transformation that persisted throughout most of the twentieth century. On the basis of the scientific management theories of Frederick Winslow Taylor, most large corporations organised their workforces into job structures that are termed 'internal labour markets'. In internal labour markets, jobs were arranged into hierarchical ladders, and each job provided the training for the job on the next rung up. Employers who adopted internal labour markets hired only at the entry level, and then utilised internal promotion to fill all of the higher rungs.

Taylorism became the dominant type of human resource policy within large US manufacturing firms throughout most of the twentieth century. Throughout corporate America, management reduced the skill level of jobs—a process termed 'deskilling'—while at the same time they encouraged employee–firm attachment through promotion and retention policies, explicit or de facto seniority arrangements, elaborate welfare schemes, and longevity-linked benefit packages. Because employers wanted employees to stay a long time, they gave them implicit promises of long-term employment and predictable patterns of promotion. While these systems had their origins in the blue-collar workplace of the smokestack industrial heartland, by the 1960s they were adapted to large white-collar workplaces such as insurance companies and banks.

Sometime in the 1970s, employment practices began to change. Since then, there have been widespread reports that large corporations no longer

---

[1] I describe the elements of the new employment relationship in detail in Stone, 2004.

offer their employees implicit contracts for lifetime employment. Work has become contingent, not only in the sense that it is formally defined as short term or episodic, but in the sense that the attachment between the firm and the worker has been weakened. The recasualisation of work has reportedly become a fact of life both for blue-collar workers and for high-end professionals and managers. This trend was expressed eloquently by Jack Welch', the miracle-maker CEO of General Electric Company (GE), in an interview with *Harvard Business Review* in 1989 when he said:

> Like many other large companies in the United States, Europe, and Japan, GE has had an implicit psychological contract based on perceived lifetime employment. People were rarely dismissed except for cause or severe business downturns, like in Aerospace after Vietnam. This produced a paternal, feudal, fuzzy kind of loyalty. You put in your time, worked hard, and the company took care of you for life. That kind of loyalty tends to focus people inward. But given today's environment, people's emotional energy must be focused outward on a competitive world where no business is a safe haven for employment unless it is winning in the marketplace. The psychological contract has to change.

As employers dismantle their internal labour market job structures, they are creating new types of employment relationships that give them flexibility to cross-utilise employees and to make quick adjustments in production methods as they confront increasingly competitive product markets. They do not want to create expectations of long-term career jobs because they want to be able to decrease or redeploy their workforce quickly as product market opportunities shift. As a result, a new employment relationship is emerging through theoretical writings and experimental programmes of organisational theorists and management practitioners. Despite differences in emphasis, the approaches share several common features. One is that employers explicitly or implicitly promise to give employees employability, rather than job security. They promise to provide learning opportunities that enable employees to develop their human capital but do not promise long-term employment. Thus, employers no longer promise to, nor are they are expected to, keep employees on the payroll when demand for the product fluctuates downward. Rather, in the new employment relationship, the risk of the firm's short-term and long-term success is placed squarely on the employee.

The new employment relationship also involves compensation systems that peg salaries and wages to market rates rather than internal institutional factors. The emphasis is on offering employees differential pay to reflect their different talents and contributions.[2]

---

[2] See eg 'Pay Attention!'; 'How to Reward Your Top Employees'; 'Sleep Well Last Night?', online: *Perspectives.on Total Rewards*, January 2000, http://www.towers.com/publications/ publications_frame, in which the leading management consulting firm, Towers Perrin, urges its clients to 'reward results, not tenure, even at the hourly level.'

Another feature of the new employment relationship involves providing employees with opportunities to network with the firm's customers, suppliers, and even competitors so that they can raise their social capital. It also involves a flattening of hierarchy, the elimination of status-linked perks, and the use of company-specific grievance mechanisms. The workplace is becoming boundary-less as employees move frequently across departmental and firm boundaries.

THE CHANGING NATURE OF EMPLOYMENT DISCRIMINATION

The changing work practices have had a significant effect on the nature of employment discrimination and on the effectiveness of current anti-discrimination laws to redress it. Over the past three decades, the civil rights laws in the United States have made major advances in reducing employment discrimination in the workplace. Despite the success of civil rights efforts, however, discrimination still exists in the workplace, although it now often takes new forms. The diffused and decentralised authority structure of the new boundary-less workplace can give rise to subtle forms of bias and favoritism. Women and minorities in formerly white male workplaces often encounter overt hostility and subtle harassment from co-workers as well as glass ceilings and other de facto barriers to advancement. The civil rights laws were designed to eliminate discrimination as it was manifest in the old employment relationship, and have been less effective to redress new forms of discrimination. In particular, the new workplace practices make liability for discrimination difficult to establish and render many of the old remedies ineffective. Further, contemporary human resource practices that involve delegation of important decisions to peer groups intensify the problem of co-worker harassment and raise the spectre of discrimination without a discriminator, an injured plaintiff without a legally accountable defendant.

Changes in workplace practices force us to rethink conceptions of liability and the remedies that should be used to eliminate employment discrimination as it is manifest in the new workplace. Historically, employment discrimination has been linked to internal labour markets. Internal labour markets have played an important role in the creation and perpetuation of employment discrimination in the twentieth century. Arguably one of the most important causes of women's disadvantaged position in the labour market has been the internal labour market structure of American industry throughout much of the twentieth century.

Internal labour markets operated to keep jobs in the primary sector predominantly male and predominantly white. One of the ways in which internal labour markets have fostered discriminatory employment practices has been through the use of statistical discrimination. Statistical discrimination occurs when two groups vary on average in terms of some relevant characteristic, and an employer treats all members of each group as if they all possess that average characteristic. For example, if employers assume all women will have short job tenure and treat all women on the basis of that belief, then employers will avoid hiring women for jobs for which they value longevity (Blau, 1984: 122–23; Oppenheim Mason, 1984: 165; Arrow, 1998: 96–97). In particular, they will not hire women for jobs that require on-the-job training or that are organised into job ladders (Blau, 1984: 345).

Under the internal labour market employment system that dominated US industry in the early twentieth century, employers valued longevity; they wanted to hire employees who would stay on the job a long time. Yet, for most of the twentieth century, women as a group had a pattern of short job tenure relative to men (Goldin, 1990: 101). Labour economist Claudia Goldin found, on the basis of available data, that in around 1900, males had almost three times the job duration that women had in their current occupations, and one-and-a-half times the number of years with their current employer compared to women. According to Goldin (1990: 116) 'firms often used sex as a signal of shorter expected job tenure.' Thus, by operation of statistical discrimination, employers avoided hiring women for jobs with internal labour markets (Thurow, 1975; Bulow and Summers, 1986: 401). Instead, women tended to be placed in jobs that required few skills and were provided little or no on-the-job training (Goldin, 1990). In this way, the system of job ladders, internal promotion, and limited ports of entry operated to keep women out of the best jobs.

Throughout most of the twentieth century, women were not hired by large corporations with internal labour markets. Rather, the dominant labour relations practices, based on the theories of early twentieth-century scientific management theorists, kept women out of the better jobs in manufacturing. Jobs occupied primarily by women or minorities almost invariably have offered lower pay, fewer benefits, and lesser status than jobs occupied by white males (Committee on Women's Employment and Related Social Issues, 1986: 49–50; Jacobs, 1989: 28–30: 1756–57; Schultz, 1998; Schultz, 2000: 1894–95). The use of internal labour markets and the operation of statistical discrimination led employers to hire men for primary labour market jobs. When women finally were permitted in, union-negotiated promotion rights and job ladders ensured that they come in at the bottom.[3]

In the 1970s and 1980s, employment patterns began to change. First, women became more attached to the labour market so that employers had less reason to practise statistical discrimination. In addition, equal employment

---

[3] For example, Milkman (1997: 37) notes that women in General Motors auto plants do not get the highly desirable jobs because their average seniority is considerably less than that of men.

opportunity laws forced many firms to hire women (Blau, 1984: 125; 1986: 207–8) and blacks (Darity and Mason, 1998: 63–90) for previously all-white male jobs.

Early in its history, the Equal Employment Opportunity Commission (EEOC) took the position that Title VII prohibited statistical discrimination by declaring that it was unlawful for employers to make hiring decisions based upon real or perceived group characteristics.[4] Overt discrimination in hiring became unlawful unless it was pursuant to a 'bona fide occupational qualification', which was narrowly defined.[5] As a result, the sex segregation of jobs, as well as the pay gap between men and women, declined (Blau, 1984: 127–29).

Minorities also experienced a narrowing of the pay gap between blacks and whites from 1965 to 1975, but the trend flattened somewhat after that (Donaghue and Heckman, 1991: 1604). Nonetheless, the pay gap between black and white women narrowed substantially, so that by 1981, black women were earning 90 per cent of what white women earned—a dramatic increase from the mere 69 per cent of 1964. In the same period, the gap between the earnings of black men and white men narrowed from 66 per cent in 1964 to 71 per cent in 1981. Occupational segregation, which has not been as extreme for minorities as it has been for women, also declined (Blau, 1984: 126, 135–36).

Even after the most blatant pay differentials and explicit barriers to hiring women and minorities were broken, those groups continued to be disadvantaged within major corporations. Because jobs were arranged in hierarchical progression, latecomers came in at the bottom and had the furthest to rise. They did not have access to the higher rungs of the internal labour markets. Also, because they were at the bottom, the latecomers were the first to be laid off in times of cutbacks. Efforts by women and minorities to jump over established arrangements for hierarchical progression generated intense and bitter disputes about affirmative action. White male workers resisted because they felt that they were entitled to a certain sequence of advancement and that affirmative action was thus a violation of their rights.

THE NATURE OF DISCRIMINATION IN
THE BOUNDARY-LESS WORKPLACE

Because many aspects of employment discrimination originated in or were perpetuated by the hierarchical job structures of internal labour markets,

---

[4] See EEOC Guidelines, 29 CFR § 1604.2(a)(1) (1968).

[5] 42 USC §§ 2000e to 2000e-17. The bona fide occupational qualification (BFOQ) exception permits employers to make hiring decisions based on otherwise prohibited reasons, if such decisions are necessary to the 'essence of the business': *Int'l Union, UAW v Johnson Controls, Inc*, 499 US 187, 203 (1991).

there is reason to believe that discrimination might subside in the future. The new workplace, with its rejection of implicit long-term employment guarantees and its repudiation of rigid job ladders, offers the possibility of creating new opportunities for women and minorities. To the extent that the old labour system locked them out, the demise of that system could be a major improvement. The new employment relationship could spell the end of labour market dualism and the beginning of more egalitarian job structures. However, there are new impediments to the achievement of equal opportunity for women and minorities in the new workplace that need to be addressed.

Today the workplace does not have as much formal hierarchy as in the past, so women and minorities face fewer formal impediments to advancement. In the boundary-less workplace, everyone makes lateral movements, but some move in circles, while others spiral to the top. Because there are not defined job ladders and the criteria for advancement are not clearly specified, it is difficult for someone to claim that she has been bypassed for advancement because of her gender or race. That is, the diffuse authority structure of the new employment relationship makes discrimination hard to identify and difficult to challenge.

In addition to the hidden nature of the decision-making process, there is also a hidden element to the decision criteria in the modern corporation. The decentralisation of authority and the flattening of hierarchy mean that decisions are delegated to a wide range of people who are permitted to use their individual, often idiosyncratic, discretion. Furthermore, when jobs are defined in terms of competencies and employees are valued for their varied skills and flexibility, it is difficult for firms to articulate clear criteria for advancement. Often social credentials are used in lieu of objective performance measures. These social credentials include such things as prestigious education, membership of social clubs, participation in certain sports–all activities that have traditionally excluded women and minorities. Thus, under a system that rewards social credentials, women and minorities are disadvantaged (Edward S. Adams, 2002: 167–68).

A growing number of employment discrimination class action lawsuits allege that informal and decentralised promotion practices foster covert discrimination against women and minorities. For example, in a suit filed in 2001 against Johnson & Johnson, the plaintiffs alleged that the giant conglomerate knowingly engaged in racial discrimination by maintaining promotion policies that allowed supervisors to 'handpick white candidates, resulting in fewer promotions for African-Americans and Hispanic-Americans and perpetuating a glass ceiling and glass walls,' thereby blocking advancement of these employees into 'visible and influential roles within the organization' (Mantz, 2001: 40). Similar complaints against informal promotion policies are becoming widespread.

In addition, the new non-hierarchical workplace makes power and lines of authority less visible. Thus, it is often difficult to know to whom to make appeals, with whom to lodge complaints, or how to bring about change. For example, there are numerous cases in which an employee experiences sexual harassment and wants to complain, yet loses her discrimination claims because she did not know to whom to report the offensive conduct, or because she reported to the wrong person.

When there is no visible power structure, the invisible structures rule. In the new workplace, these invisible power structures may well turn out to be more remote and impenetrable for women and minorities than the old power structures. Responsibility for discriminatory decisions has become difficult to assign and even more difficult to remedy. The difficulties of identifying discrimination and locating the responsible party in the face of decentralised and dispersed decision-making structures are recurrent themes in contemporary employment discrimination litigation, as will be seen below.

A related problem for women and minorities in the new workplace stems from the trend toward delegating major employment decisions to peers. The new workplace exacerbates the age-old problem of cliques because it involves empowering peer-based decision-making. Many of the new organisational theories call for using peers to decide issues such as hiring, evaluation, job allocation, and pay (see, for example, Lawler, 1994). While peer-based decision-making may work well in some situations, it can also promote cliquishness, patronage systems, bigotry, and corruption. In such a workplace, women and minorities could again find themselves excluded.

In addition, the new workplace relies on teamwork and cooperation to function well. Employees are expected to interact with each other to learn the tricks of the trade, share necessary information, assist in tasks, and coordinate performance (Granovetter, 1974: 45–48; Jacobs, 1989: 182). Yet incumbent white males often refuse to include women and minorities in their informal networks, thereby compromising their ability to succeed (Jacobs, 1989: 181–82; Sturm, 1998: 642). Many sociologists and journalists have documented the phenomenon of women being shunned, ignored, and frozen out of the loop when they enter predominately male workplaces (see the case studies and other examples cited by Abrams, 1998: 1196–98). Clique members use the tools of ostracism, belittlement, verbal harassment, innuendo, nefarious gossip, and shunning—tools that are difficult to identify or remedy. Reports of such conduct are becoming increasingly prevalent.[6]

---

[6] See Jacobs, 1989: 181–82; Kanter, 1977; see studies cited by Roos and Reskin, 1984: 235–56; Tilly and Tilly, 1998: 223; see examples of the ways in which gender dynamics can sabotage women's ability to function on the job in Schultz 1998: 1704; see first-person accounts in Schultz, 1990: 1832–39, and Yamada, 2000: 477–78.

APPLYING TITLE VII TO THE BOUNDARY-LESS WORKPLACE

Title VII embodied an approach that was appropriate to discrimination as it occurred in employment relationships made up of long-term, stable work-forces and well-defined, hierarchical paths of advancement. As will be shown below, today's flexible work practices make it difficult to establish liability under the conventional Title VII approaches. In addition, the new workplace practices foster forms of discrimination that elude existing Title VII remedies.

Establishing Liability

For a plaintiff to prove an allegation of discriminatory treatment under Title VII, she must show that the employer made an adverse decision or took an adverse action with a discriminatory intent. The employer's intent can be established with direct or indirect evidence. Direct evidence of discrimination means overt statements such as a supervisor saying, 'I did not hire you because you are black,' or 'You cannot be promoted because we only give managerial jobs to men'. Such direct evidence is rare today because most employers have trained their supervisors to disguise any overt discriminatory motives they might harbour.[7]

Because of the difficulty of finding direct evidence of disparate treatment the US Supreme Court, in *McDonnell Douglas Corp v Green*, established a method of establishing discriminatory motive with indirect evidence.[8] Under *McDonnell Douglas*, as elaborated in subsequent decisions, a plaintiff who is dismissed from a job or denied a particular job because of her gender or race, can establish a prima facie case by showing that: (1) she was a member of a protected class; (2) she was qualified for the job; (3) she applied for but was not given the job; and (4) the job was given to someone who was not a member of a protected class.[9] If she can establish these

---

[7] The requirement to show discriminatory intent is sometimes called the 'causation requirement'—for example, the requirement of showing that the employer took the adverse action against the plaintiff *because* of the plaintiff's race or gender: Schwartz, 1998: 1709–10. A plaintiff does not need to show that the employer had an intent to discriminate when she alleges that the employer engaged in a neutral practice that had a disparate *impact* on a protected class. See *Griggs v Duke Power Co*, 401 US 424 (1971). However, disparate impact theories are difficult to prove because an employer can defend by showing that the challenged practice was 'job related and consistent with business necessity': 42 US C 2000e-(2)(k). The business necessity requirement has been interpreted as a relatively light burden which an employer can satisfy by showing that the challenged practice serves its legitimate goals.

[8] 411 US 792 (1973) (*McDonnell Douglas*).

[9] *McDonnell Douglas* was modified in *Texas Dept of Community Affairs v Burdine*, 450 US 248 (1981); *St Mary's Honor Center v Hicks*, 509 US 502 (1993) (*St Mary's*); and *Reeves v Sanderson Plumbing. Products Inc*, 120 S Ct 2097 (2000) (*Reeves*).

factors, the burden switches to the employer to produce evidence showing that the action was taken for a legitimate non-discriminatory reason.

In practice, the essential factor in establishing liability under the *McDonnell Douglas* framework is the employer's reason, that is, its motive, for the adverse employment action. If the employer can convince the court that it acted from a legitimate rather than a discriminatory motive, it will prevail (McGinley, 2000: 448–65). Because, as Justice Souter stated, 'employers who discriminate are not likely to announce their discriminatory motive',[10] a Title VII plaintiff must usually establish her case by means of circumstantial evidence. One method to establish that an asserted motive is a pretext is to show that it is false. For example, if an employer refuses to promote a woman on the stated ground that she has only worked for the firm for five years and thus lacks sufficient experience, that claim can be refuted if it can be shown that the same employer routinely promoted men with four years' or less experience to the same position. Or, if an employer refuses to hire a black woman on the stated ground that she does not have a high school diploma, that reason can be impugned by showing that the employer routinely hires white males without a high school diploma for the same job.[11]

Proving a discriminatory motive is the single most important task of the Title VII plaintiff. However, the available techniques for demonstrating an unlawful motive only make sense in a world in which employers make employment decisions on the basis of uniform policies and practices that can be articulated. In such a world, if an employer departs from its uniform policy or pre-existing practices, then the plaintiff can use that fact to show that the employer's proffered reason is a pretext. When employers have uniform policies and practices, these policies establish a baseline against which an employer's actions can be measured and a pretext can be identified. Indeed, without evidence that an employer's practice is a departure from a uniform baseline, it is practically impossible for a plaintiff to prove that an employer's asserted motive is a pretext.

The *McDonnell Douglas* methodology of proof is undermined by many new employment practices. In the boundary-less workplace, employment decisions are decentralised. Rather than promoting uniform policies and centralised decision-making, many firms today delegate job assignment decisions to disparate, decentralised decision-makers. Sometimes these decision-makers are peers. In the boundary-less workplace, decision-makers are expected to exercise subjective, often ad hoc, judgements. In this setting, it is difficult to establish whether a particular decision is pretextual because

---

[10] *St. Mary's*, above n 9 at 534, Souter J, dissenting.
[11] In *Reeves*, above n 9, the Supreme Court stated at 147 that it is '*permissible* for the trier of fact to infer the ultimate fact of discrimination from the falsity of the employer's explanation' (emphasis in original).

there is no uniform baseline from which the employer's deviation can be identified. The baseline is constantly changing.

Under the *McDonnell Douglas* test, an employee cannot win simply by showing that the employer's reasons were inefficient, irrational, or even tyrannical. The court will not judge the reasonableness or sagacity of the business decisions. Rather, to prevail, the plaintiff needs to show that the reason was discriminatory—for example, a departure from a baseline because of the plaintiff's race or sex. Given today's world of work, in which employees are hired, reassigned, and laid off on a frequent and unsystematic basis, a plaintiff cannot easily refute an employer's asserted legitimate reason for its actions. Employers seek flexibility in their staffing decisions, and that flexibility often means the freedom to make ad hoc judgements that are not part of a uniform pre-established plan. This does not mean that the employer's decisions are arbitrary or random, but rather that they are made on the basis of factors that are difficult to articulate.

One example of the difficulties of disproving a pretext in the new workplace is found in the case of *Gentry and Whitley v Georgia-Pacific Corp*, in which Katherine Whitley alleged that the company discriminated against her by failing to promote her to a supervisory position.[12] Whitley began working as an hourly employee in the Shipping Department in 1991. In 1995, in response to a notice of vacancy, she applied for a position as shift supervisor. The selection process involved a structured interview, with numerical scores given by a mixed-gender panel. She did not get the position. In 1996, the company posted another shift supervisor position, for which she also applied. By then the company had changed its selection process. Under the new process, an application involved a test of basic education skills, a structured interview, and a creative expression exercise. Those that completed these requirements successfully were then required to participate in a workshop with other applicants, out of which a selection was made by a panel, which made recommendations to the superintendent of the Shipping Department. The panel recommended three male candidates. One was awarded the job at hand, and the other two were awarded the next available vacancies. In 1998, another vacancy was posted; again Whitley applied, and again a male candidate was selected and hired. Whitley then filed a discrimination complaint.

While the court conceded that Whitley had made out a prima facie case under *McDonnell Douglas*, it found that she had not shown that the employer's stated ground—merit as revealed in a non-discriminatory selection procedure—was a pretext. Because the selection process had multiple components, the court refused to give credence to evidence about how the

---

[12] 250 F3d 646 (8th Cir 2001). Bettye Gentry also sued for discriminatory failure to promote to supervisor positions, but the court dismissed her claim on the ground that she had not applied for the positions.

plaintiff's score compared to the other applicants on any particular component. In addition, the court disregarded affidavits from two former supervisors that reported that the superintendent designed the multi-component process as he did because, as he said, 'that is the surest way of getting the one I want and they cannot come back on me.' The court also refused to give weight to the fact that the Georgia-Pacific Corporation had never promoted a female production worker to a shift supervisor in the Shipping Department. Rather, the court held that Whitley had not met the burden of showing that the panel's recommendations were based on anything other than neutral criteria. In effect, the court imposed on the plaintiff an insuperable burden to prove discrimination in the face of the multi-component selection procedure and the subjective element in the final decision-making.

In the new workplace, claims of discrimination in promotion are particularly difficult to establish. A plaintiff who believes she has been passed over for a promotion on the grounds of her sex or race must show that the employer awarded the position to a male or white employee who was less qualified. That is, the plaintiff must show that the employer's claim that the successful applicant had superior qualifications was a pretext. Yet, courts are reluctant to decide cases based on the relative qualifications of candidates because they do not want Title VII to be used as a vehicle for second-guessing an employer's business judgement. Employers can make incorrect and even irrational decisions without violating Title VII—what they cannot do is make discriminatory decisions. Thus an employer's choice of an inferior candidate does not prove a discriminatory intent—it could merely demonstrate bad business judgement. As one court stated, 'the bar is set high for this kind of evidence because differences in qualifications are generally not probative evidence of discrimination unless those disparities are of such weight and significance that no reasonable person, in the exercise of impartial judgement, could have chosen the candidate selected over the plaintiff for the job in question.'[13]

In all these respects the change in work practices makes it more difficult than ever for a plaintiff to establish a case of discriminatory treatment. When employer decisions are decentralised, unsystematic, and ad hoc, it thus becomes difficult for many plaintiffs to survive a motion for summary judgement.

Class Action Certification

Because of the onerous burden on plaintiffs who bring individual employment discrimination claims, many are turning to class actions as a vehicle

---

[13] *Daniels v Home Depot Inc*, 2002 US Dist LEXIS 11990, *26–27 (ED La 2002), quoting *Celestine v Petroleos de Venezuela SA*, 266 F3d 343, 357 (5th Cir 2002). See also *Deines v Texas Dep't of Regulatory Services*, 164 F3d 277, 279 (5th Cir 1999).

for vindicating their claims of discrimination. In class actions, plaintiffs can allege either disparate treatment or disparate impact. Class-wide disparate impact claims are directed against seemingly neutral policies that have a disparate and disadvantageous impact on a protected group. Class-wide disparate treatment claims involve allegations of intentional discrimination against women or minorities. While such claims, like individual disparate treatment claims, require the plaintiffs to show that the employer acted with a discriminatory intent, class action plaintiffs can make a circumstantial case with statistics that demonstrate a pattern or practice of discrimination. In a class action, the use of statistics provides an evidentiary end-run around the problem of demonstrating pretext. However, the class action plaintiff encounters unique difficulties when the workplace has a diffuse and decentralised decision-making structure.

In practice, most class actions turn on the question of class certification. If the plaintiffs manage to obtain class certification, then the companies usually settle the claim in order to avoid a lengthy, expensive, and potentially embarrassing lawsuit. Because of the central role of class certification, the requirements for class certification are the crucial issue in the ability of class action plaintiffs to succeed. Under Rule 23(a) of the Federal Rules of Civil Procedure, to be certified as a class action, the moving party must show: (1) the class is so numerous that joinder of all members is impracticable; (2) there are questions of law or fact common to the class; (3) the claims or defences of the representative parties are typical of the claims and defences of the class; and (4) the representative parties will fairly and adequately protect the interests of the class. These necessary elements for class action certification are known, in shorthand, as requirements for showing numerosity, commonality, typicality, and adequacy.[14]

In the boundary-less workplace, the requirements of typicality and commonality are difficult to satisfy. When a claim involves individualised assessment of each class member's claim, then there is no typicality or commonality. Thus, allegations of discriminatory treatment that resulted from decentralised decision-making are particularly hard to aggregate into a class action. For example, in *Allen v Chicago Transit Authority*,[15] the court refused to certify a class action that sought to challenge the employer's promotion decisions as racially biased because it found that the company's promotion decision-making policy was not sufficiently uniform to satisfy the requirement that class actions must involve 'questions of law or fact common to the class.'[16] In that case, decisions concerning promotion to exempt positions were made at the department level, where departmental managers

---

[14] In addition, the moving party must show that one of the elements of Rule 23(b) of the Federal Rules of Civil Procedure is present.
[15] 2000 WL 1207408 (ND Ill) (*Allen*).
[16] Federal Rules of Civil Procedure, rule 23(a).

had wide discretion to decide how and whether to fill positions. The only uniform policy was a requirement that anyone selected for promotion ultimately had to be approved by the Vice President of Human Resources. A number of black employees brought suit, alleging that the decision-making was biased in that qualified blacks were repeatedly passed over for promotion to jobs that were given to less qualified whites. The court considered whether the claims could be brought as a class action, and concluded that the very decentralised nature of the decision-making meant that it could not be maintained on a class-wide basis. The court found that 'promotion and pay decisions are made at the level of individual departments by many different people using different methods with varying human resources involvement.'[17] It also found that the Vice President of Human Resources was involved in some departments' decisions, he had little to do with the personnel decisions in others. Because the company had neither a highly centralised nor an entirely subjective practice regarding promotions, the court held that the complaint failed to allege a uniform discriminatory practice that satisfied the requirement of common questions of law and fact.

The *Allen* case is typical of many courts' approach to the issue of class certification in the face of decentralised decision-making authority. Yet without class action certification, it is often impossible for plaintiffs to prevail on a race or sex discrimination claim.

Finding the Defendant

The new decentralised workplace, with its diffused authority structure, not only makes it difficult for victims of discrimination to prove their case, it also makes it difficult for them to bring suit against the people who are discriminating against them. The flattening of workplace hierarchies and the delegation of authority to peers in the workplace elevates and legitimates the power of the working group. Under contemporary human resource practices, peer groups are often used to allocate work tasks, evaluate individual performances, distribute rewards and perks, and impose punishments. In some cases, peers are called upon to make decisions regarding hiring, promotions, lay-offs, and discharge. And in an increasing number of firms, supervisor decisions can be appealed to a peer review appeal panel. All of these techniques enhance the power of the working group.

While the empowerment of the peer group can be an egalitarian development, it also can have deleterious consequences for women and minorities. As explained above, workers in traditionally all-male or all-white workplaces are often hostile to the integration of minorities and women. If the

---

[17] Above n 15.

integration occurs as a result of an affirmative action programme by which the women or minorities jump over the incumbent white males in rank or salary, the hostility can be intense. Moreover, in workplaces that are historically predominantly male or white, the incumbents often generate a culture that communicates to women or minorities that they do not belong. Through techniques of ostracism, bullying, shunning, or other means of exclusion, the predominant whites and/or males can make the newcomers feel unwelcome, insecure, and inadequate. Furthermore, the predominant group often refuses to share knowledge of the tricks of the trade, or to engage in customary forms of cooperation, thereby undermining the competence as well as the confidence of women or minorities. Thus, for example, there are numerous instances in which women fail to succeed in formerly male jobs for such simple reasons as not knowing where the tool room is or not knowing how to fix a particularly temperamental machine (Abrams, 1998).

The more an employer delegates power to peers, the more the 'old boy' networks can marginalise, penalise, and terrorise women and minorities. Many women who are victimised by these means give up in despair. Some bring discrimination claims, but the claims are difficult to win.

When a woman or minority worker encounters bullying, ostracism, informal sabotage, or failure to train by co-workers, her legal recourse is to sue for harassment. However, she cannot sue the co-workers directly—she must sue the employer. To establish a claim for co-worker hostile environment under Title VII, the plaintiff must show: (1) membership of a protected group; (2) that she was subject to unwelcome harassment; (3) that the harassment occurred because of membership of the protected group; (4) that the harassment was so severe and pervasive as to affect a term, condition or privilege of employment; and (5) that the employer knew or should have known of the harassment and failed to take adequate remedial action.[18] Several of these requirements are difficult to establish in the boundary-less workplace.

The first problem is that when a woman alleges that she suffered harassment that was not overtly sexual in nature, most courts find that it does not come within Title VII. Rather, they hold that informal bullying, ridiculing, shunning, or ignoring are not sufficiently tangible harms to come within Title VII. (Schultz, 1998).

In addition, the alleged harassing conduct must be 'because of sex' to be actionable. When there is no overtly sexual element in the conduct, courts are reluctant to find co-worker mistreatment, however egregious, to be 'because of sex'. Often workers experience mistreatment by co-workers—slights, snubs, rude remarks, hostile glances, and so forth. Someone can be excluded from a group for any number of reasons—because they wear the

---

[18] *Jacob-Mua, et al v Veneman*, 289 F3d 517, 522 (8th Cir 2002); *Scusa v Nestle USA Company, Inc*, 181 F3d 958, 965 (8th Cir 1999).

wrong clothes, listen to the wrong music, have the wrong hobbies, have an off-putting personal style. None of these workplace unpleasantries are necessarily 'because of' sex or gender. Someone can be different, or downright irritating, without being the victim of discrimination.

Finally, and most problematically, women and minority plaintiffs who complain of co-worker harassment must prove that the employer knew or should have known about the harassment and failed to take remedial measures. The plaintiff has the burden of proof on both issues, and the burden is formidable. If a worker fails to report co-worker harassment for fear of subtle and not-so-subtle retaliation, her failure to report makes it easy for a firm to deny knowledge of the harassment, and thus escape liability. Some courts find that the employer is on notice of harassment if other employees have reported similar incidents, but not all courts do so.[19] Similarly, some courts find that an employer is not on notice of harassment if the employee complains to the wrong supervisor. For example, in one case, an employee reported harassment to her immediate supervisor, but the court concluded that because that person was a low-level supervisor, it did not count as notification to the corporation (George, 2001: 153–54).

The heightened requirement of knowledge in the case of co-worker harassment makes it particularly difficult for Title VII to redress such claims. While Title VII is designed to prevent discrimination practised by employers, the contemporary workplace is structured to push much of the discriminatory conduct down to lower levels. In the face of this reality, a new theory must be devised to hold the employer responsible for the oppressive and discriminatory co-worker conduct that can result.

Crafting a Remedy

In addition to making it more difficult to establish liability, the new employment practices have made conventional civil rights remedies problematic. Civil rights enforcement efforts were initially directed at corporate hiring and compensation practices in order to obtain equal pay and access to jobs for women and minorities. But it quickly became apparent that women and minorities needed not simply jobs, but good jobs. They needed access to jobs in the primary sector that offered promotion opportunities, training, job security, and benefits—that is, jobs that were part of internal labour markets. Hence, Title VII plaintiffs sought not only hiring mandates, but also affirmative action to help women and minorities enter the primary labour market, and training and promotion programmes to help women

---

[19] Compare *Madray v Public Supermarkets, Inc*, 208 F 3d 1290 (11th Cir 2000) with *Jackson v Quanex Corp*, 191 F 3d 647 (6th Cir 1999); *Hurley v Atlantic City Police Dept*, 174 F 3d 93 (3rd Cir 1999).

and minorities move up once inside. Early on, the EEOC required companies that it found to be in violation of Title VII to develop goals and timetables for measuring their compliance with equal employment objectives. These remedies helped numerous women and minorities gain access to previously segregated workplaces and helped them move up within the firm.

The EEOC's remedial strategies assumed that there were identifiable job ladders that defined advancement opportunities within firms, and sought to move women and minorities up these ladders. They were also strategies that triggered bitter and divisive conflicts over affirmative action between incumbent senior white male employees and newly hired minorities and women who sometimes jumped over them in rank. However, these same remedies are problematic in firms with flattened job structures that provide lateral rather than hierarchical mobility. Affirmative action in promotion is meaningless when there is no promotional ladder by which advancement can be measured.

Today, most Title VII suits are brought by private parties rather than by the EEOC, and they seek monetary awards rather than injunctive decrees. While damage remedies such as back pay, front pay, and even punitive damages are available for victims of discrimination, these remedies provide compensation for harm done, not a correction of discriminatory conditions. Individuals can benefit from generous monetary awards, but such awards do not directly alter the working conditions for either the victims or others stuck in the same discriminatory situation. It is possible that large damage awards could shatter the glass ceilings, warm up the chilly climates, and help women and minorities break into the 'old boys' clubs by inducing corporations to change their practices, but runaway jury awards in Title VII cases are rare and random events. Furthermore, corporations can limit their liability for large damage awards through liability insurance or the use of mandatory arbitration (Sturm, 2001: 475–78). Given the availability of insurance, Title VII's monetary remedies become a cost of doing business or, at most, a weak inducement for change.

REDRESSING DISCRIMINATION IN THE NEW WORKPLACE

Employment discrimination in the new workplace is more subtle and intractable than in the old. As discussed above, sharply drawn legal tests for liability are difficult to apply in part because the legal wrongs themselves are difficult to identify. Women and minorities experience exclusion and encounter glass ceilings, yet it is not always clear how the employer has engaged in wrongdoing. The harms from such actions are far from trivial— cooperation of co-workers and access to grapevine information is often the key to success in today's workplace. Yet it is difficult to bring the objectionable conduct within conventional discriminatory doctrinal framework.

What is needed to redress discrimination in the new workplace are new conceptions and definitions of liability, new procedures for bringing claims, and new types of remedies.

Currently, Title VII is directed to harm caused by employers or their agents and assumes a hierarchical authority structure. Title VII reaches co-worker harassment only when the employer knew or should have known of the harassing conduct, and failed to take adequate remedial measures.[20] This is because the law prohibits those who have authority in the employment relationship from exercising their power in a discriminatory fashion.[21] While there is authority and power in the new workplace, it is often exercised through cliques and peer groups, defying traditional tools for assigning accountability. Yet, as courts frequently reiterate, Title VII is not a generalised code of workplace civility.[22] Therefore, to redress the new forms of employment discrimination, it is necessary to combine new concepts of substantive liability with new procedures and remedies that operate on horizontal as well as vertical power relations.

At present, employment discrimination claims are brought to a court or an administrative agency such as the EEOC or a state human rights agency. These fora have the virtue of placing decision-making authority in the hands of someone who is not part of the workplace that gave rise to the alleged discrimination, and who can apply neutral, non-discrimination norms. However, both courts and agencies are also remote from the workplace, circumscribed in the evidence they can hear and limited in the remedies they can issue. Furthermore, as Judith Resnik (2004) has pointed out, courts and agencies have constricted approaches to standing that prevent them from treating discrimination as the collective harm that it is. Rather, by requiring the individual targets of discrimination to bring an action, courts cannot address the ways in which a culture of harassment can arise that shapes power relationships among all individuals in a workplace.[23]

Furthermore, as discussed above, much of today's discrimination takes the form of co-worker conduct that marginalises a member of an outsider group. It is difficult to imagine a court imposing civil liability on a group of workers for ganging up on a co-worker or for spreading nefarious gossip unless the conduct constitutes a crime or tort, such as assault or rape. For a court to judge the subtle aspects of exclusion and marginalisation that

---

[20] See *Gunnell v Utah Valley State Coll*, 152 F 3d 1253, 1265 (10th Cir 1998); *Blankenship v Parke Care Ctrs*, 123 F 3d 868, 873 (6th Cir 1997); *Yamaguchi v United States Dep't of Air Force*, 109 F 3d 1475, 1483 (9th Cir 1997).

[21] See *Burlington Indus. v Ellreth*, 524 US 742, 761–62 (1998).

[22] See *Harris v Forklift Sys Inc*, 510 US 16, 21 (1993) (stating that Title VII does not make actionable conduct that is merely offensive).

[23] Susan Sturm (2001: 475–78) has also pointed out that the activities that produce exclusion of women and blacks are highly contextualised, and not amenable crisp, clear rules of right and wrong.

debilitate women and minorities in the workplace would involve it in micro-managing workplace etiquette, something courts are reluctant to do.

In addition, it is not always feasible for individuals to obtain redress from a court or administrative agency. Courts and agencies are inundated with complaints and have large backlogs. Thus, they are not always able to hear cases in a timely fashion. Litigation is expensive and many victims of employment discrimination lack the resources to enforce their rights.

Even if the courts were not backlogged and litigation was not expensive, there is an additional reason why these new forms of discrimination are not best handled in an adversary procedure. The adversary process gives each side a stake in proving the truthfulness of its claims and the falsity of the opposing party's claims, even when doing so inflicts damage on a continuing relationship. Where complaints involve allegations of exclusion, marginalisation, or subtle forms of harassment, the complaining party must either demonise her co-workers or risk demonisation herself. For example, if a plaintiff complains she has been shunned and denied access to informal know-how, her co-workers might defend themselves by claiming that they refused to socialise with her because they disliked her and found her to be obnoxious or paranoid. The complaining party then must counter by impugning the motives and good faith of the dominant group, accusing them of racism or sexism or worse. That is, the courtroom setting tends to make each side exaggerate its accusations and harden its position rather than seek conciliatory solutions. For all these reasons, conventional litigation is not always an appealing option for remedying employment discrimination. Rather, it is necessary to devise a workplace-based dispute resolution mechanism to supplement, not substitute for, existing procedural mechanisms.

A workplace-based alternative dispute resolution (ADR) mechanism could provide an accessible and flexible approach to workplace discrimination. However, as with any procedural mechanism, the key lies in the details. First and foremost, ADR procedures to redress employment discrimination must be designed to identify rather than obscure the existence of discrimination. Such a system cannot delegate responsibility for recognising and remedying discriminatory conduct to the work group, because the work group is often the source of the problem. Similarly, it cannot delegate those tasks to high management officials, because they have an interest in smooth operations, which often means condoning the discriminatory conduct. Instead, it is necessary to devise a system of workplace-specific ADR that utilises neutral outsiders to scrutinise workplace conduct, identify subtle as well as overt discriminatory practices, and fashion effective remedies. That is, the system must resemble arbitration or mediation, *not* peer review or open door policies.

The use of arbitration and mediation for addressing employment discrimination complaints has been growing at a rapid rate since 1991, when the

Supreme Court held, in *Gilmer v Interstate/Johnson Lane*, that an individual could be compelled to submit his age discrimination complaint to arbitration.[24] The use of arbitration to resolve employment discrimination disputes has been highly controversial. Many non-union arbitration systems are biased toward employers and serve to evade, rather than enforce, external norms. Also, under current interpretations of the Federal Arbitration Act (FAA), arbitral awards receive virtually no judicial review (Stone, 1999: 954–55). The result is that often employees are required to bring their employment discrimination complaints to decision-makers who are either biased in favour of the employer or simply lack knowledge of anti-discrimination law, and yet if the employee receives an adverse decision, she has practically no ability to appeal.[25]

Despite the potential abuses of arbitration, it should be possible to design an internal dispute resolution systems to address the subtle but powerful forms of discrimination in today's boundary-less workplaces. Such a system could seek to vindicate equality norms without the limitations imposed by current Title VII doctrine. For example, decision-makers could take into account many kinds of evidence, including the history of the individual workplace, to identify departures from past practices and consider whether or not an employer's stated reasons for an action was a pretext. Furthermore, claimants could impugn the plausibility of an employer's asserted reason by showing that the action was irrational or inconsistent with sound business judgement. Furthermore, workplace arbitration could embrace disputes between co-workers as well as disputes between employees and employers. While a court may not find a particular type of mistreatment to be sufficiently serious to be actionable under Title VII, an arbitrator may be better attuned to the contextualised nature of the harm done.

To identify and redress adequately subtle forms of employment discrimination that arise in the new workplace, courts would have to impose minimal standards of due process on the arbitration process. Thus, for example, a court would have to ensure that the complainant had a right to counsel, to take discovery, subpoena witnesses, obtain documents, and cross examine adverse witnesses. The arbitration procedure could not unduly shorten limitations periods, shift burdens of proof, or impose high costs on the party seeking to vindicate her discrimination claim. There would also have to be de novo judicial review for issues of law. Judicial review for arbitral rulings on issues of law would ensure that arbitrators did not merely defer to the rule of the clique, but rather applied Title VII and other employment laws to the workplace.

---

[24] 500 US 1 (1991).
[25] For criticisms of employer-designed arbitration systems in the non-union setting, see Grodin, 1996; Schwartz, 1997; and Stone, 1999.

CONCLUSION

This chapter has argued that existing employment discrimination laws do not adequately address the problems that women are facing in the changing workplace. As employment becomes increasingly precarious and as new work practices proliferate, women find themselves doubly disadvantaged. Workplace arbitration along the lines proposed might provide a mechanism for resolving discrimination disputes in the new workplace. It is a mechanism that would enable women and minorities to obtain redress for competency-sabotage, bullying, shunning, harassing, and other forms of gender-based or race-based conduct that undermines their employment prospects. The proposal does not provide a new test for liability, but rather a new mechanism for resolving discrimination disputes. It is hoped that a better procedure that could identify and remedy the new forms of discrimination would enable women and minorities to achieve true equality in the boundary-less workplace and enable them to pursue an unbounded career.

12

On the Gendered Norm of Standard Employment in a Changing Labour Market

JENNY JULÉN VOTINIUS

INTRODUCTION

THIS CHAPTER OFFERS a critical analysis of the problems associated with the working life norm of 'the standard employee' from a gender perspective, focusing on questions relating to working time and the form of employment in Sweden. I argue that the norm of permanent, full-time employment is gendered and that this norm has an impact on 'non-standard engagements', including fixed-term employment. As fixed-term employment has become increasingly prevalent in the Swedish labour market, it has begun to evince the gendered characteristics of permanent full-time work.

Images of the standard employee differ according to context, but there are certain basic assumptions that recur in the majority of descriptions. Primary among them are the assumptions that paid employment can and should be a full-time occupation and that the employee has permanent, not fixed-term, employment. This picture takes form and is mediated in many ways in society; in the mass media, in places of work, in the home, and in everyday conversation. But the description of employment as a full-time and permanent engagement accords only in part with the true situation. It corresponds to a much larger extent to men's employment situation than it does to that of women. Employees who do not fit the picture of the standard employee cannot take it for granted that their needs and interests will be met to the same degree. Employees with engagements that differ from the norm of the labour market are assigned in labour law to different categories of exception. These engagements which depart from the norm are usually given the generic title *non-standard engagements*. Part-time work and fixed-term employment are obvious categories falling under this heading.[1] Employees working for temporary-employment agencies are also normally counted among them. This chapter does not discuss the particular problems arising from employment with such agencies, but questions regarding the length of working time and the form of employment have the same relevance for employees who work for agencies as for those in other sectors of the labour market.

The proportion of non-standard engagements among different groups of employees in the Swedish labour market varies greatly. Part-time employment and fixed-term employment is more, indeed much more, common among blue-collar workers than among salaried employees.[2] It is, furthermore, significantly more common among those workers born abroad than among those born in Sweden, and significantly more common again among younger rather than among older employees. However, what stands out more than anything else is the uneven distribution of non-standard employment between men and women in the labour force. Whether we examine the breakdown among blue-collar workers and salaried employees, among those born abroad and those born in Sweden, or among the younger and the older age groups of employees, we find that women consistently account for by far the greater proportion of non-standard engagements (Statistics Sweden, 2004).

In labour law it is the norm relating to the standard employee which both governs the assessment of which employee needs should be accorded the status of rights and provides the foundation on which legal protection is constructed. The norm of full-time employment means that a worker who does not have full-time employment is typically perceived as less motivated, less responsible and hence also less worthy of the rights and privileges which are connected with labour (Tornes, 1994). The employee who diverges from the norm of an employee's expected performance is to some degree regarded also as having waived the moral right to make the same demands as other employees. This view may apply even when it is the employer who has decided that the work is not to be full time, but its manifestations are more apparent in relation to those who have themselves decided to work part

[1] However, it is important to underline that part-time employment does not always entail precariousness in the employment situation. Voluntary part-timers typically have a fairly secure employment situation, in contrast to the group of part-timers who wish to work full time (Numhauser-Henning, 2004).

[2] *Part-time employment* can be voluntary or involuntary on the part of the employee. Involuntary part-time work is also referred to as part-time unemployment. In *fixed-term* employment, the end of the employment relationship is determined by objective conditions such as reaching a specific date, completing a specific task, or the occurrence of a specific event. In this chapter special attention is paid to two forms of fixed-term employment: project employment and casual employment. In *project employment* the employee carries out either specific limited working tasks within the framework of a project or a consultancy task, or a task that is financed by special funds or in some other way can be distinguished from the rest of the business. The term *casual employment* is used to describe an employment situation where the employee works in a specified capacity from time to time when and if needed.

time. The norm of permanent employment, which is manifest in the Employment Protection Act,[3] is the very basis of the employee's rights. It limits not only the employer's managerial prerogative or right of decision, by preventing wrongful dismissals and excessive measures in reassigning the worker to different tasks. The effects of the law go far beyond that, because it is only with knowledge of the rules protecting employment that the employee can exploit all legally established rights without thereby risking job loss. In that way, employment protection is of decisive importance for the normative content of the employment relationship and for the mutual relationship of power between the two sides to the contract. The majority of the employee's rights have been designed against the background assumption that employment is protected. This means not only that employees who have inferior employment protection lack the same security of work and income, but also that they lack certain access to many other rights laid down in law. And the value of a right which cannot reliably be exploited is limited. The employer has very much the upper hand in relation both to those employees on fixed-term contracts who hope to be given new or extended employment and to the involuntary part-time employees who need income from overtime and who would prefer to work full time.

NON-STANDARD EMPLOYMENT IS INSECURE

Living with Non-standard Employment

The living conditions of part-time workers and temporary employees have been investigated in a series of studies in Sweden (inter alia, Båvner, 2001; Håkansson, 2001; Aronsson, 2002; Holmlund and Storrie, 2002, Wikman, 2002; Jonsson, 2003). There is no doubt that these employees very often find themselves in a more vulnerable or precarious position than those who correspond to the image of the standard employee. This exposed position concerns not only the employment relationship itself, but also the broader social context. The effect of the norm of the standard employee extends far beyond the limits of labour law.

When an employer, contrary to the will of the employee, decides that a job is to be fixed term or part time, the employee does not have the desired link with the labour market either as regards the duration or extent of the job. The nature of the link or connection to the labour market is of immediate relevance to income and family-maintenance, and hence to the standard of living. Because of their work-situation, many employees in fixed-term work have difficulties in planning for the future, since it is uncertain whether and

---

[3] (1982:80) [Employment Protection Act].

for how long they will be able to continue to work, and hence also how much money they will earn. This uncertainty puts limits on their ability to raise loans, for example, in order to buy a house or flat. Even their opportunities to enter into other contracts, in which their financial situation is of importance, are diminished. For example, many landlords require that would-be tenants have a permanent job. Moreover, money already earned must be managed with great caution because the future income situation is uncertain.

The situation is particularly insecure for casual workers. It is the employer alone who dictates the terms of casual employment. The employer offers work if and when a need arises in production, which entails that the employee is employed afresh on each occasion. Casual work can therefore be described as the absolute opposite of permanent employment. In practice, casual workers live in a state of unemployment that, at irregular intervals and in unforeseeable ways, is interrupted by work when the employer happens to require it. This form of employment not only leads to financial insecurity but also puts a serious mental and physical strain on these workers, in the sense that they must constantly be available and within reach of the employer in order not to miss any offer of work. If they do, there is a great risk that further offers will not be made to them in future. In recent years casual employment has increased more than any other form of work, having shown a threefold growth since the beginning of the 1990s, and still continuing to increase since 2000. Today, almost a quarter of all fixed-term employment is in that form. Roughly twice as many women as men are employed on a casual basis. For women this form of employment is now, by a wide margin, the most common form of fixed-term employment, after work standing in for absent employees (Nelander and Goding, 2003).

Involuntary part-time work can in practice show considerable similarities with casual work. Involuntary part-time workers have shorter working-time, and hence lower income, than they would like. Many of these employees experience the same uncertainty as casual workers and other fixed-term employees as to how much time and money they will have at their disposal in the future. In order to meet an irregular need for labour, certain branches of industry have developed the strategy of having a corps of part-time workers to match low levels of demand for labour in their business. Every chance increase in the demand for labour is met by requiring these employees to work overtime. The fact that the organisation of the work is largely based on overtime means that these employees learn only at the last minute how much work and what income they will have per month (Jonsson, 2003). This strategy is widely developed in the retail trade, in the hotel and restaurant industry, and in the health and social care sector. In all these branches, which are heavily dominated by women employees, part-time work has gradually become an important part of the organisational structure of business, and hence the possibility of obtaining permanent work in these sectors has dwindled. Almost 30 per cent of the female part-time workers in these occupations would prefer to have longer working hours (Nelander and Goding, 2003).

The form and extent of employment can also affect the employee's social security protection. The purpose of social security is to give the employee financial recompense during periods of temporary loss of income and when the employee is no longer active in the labour market. As a complement to paid employment, social security is constructed with its point of departure in the working-life norms of permanent and full-time employment. In social security, as in working life, the criteria for benefits are linked with this norm. The right to benefits deriving from social security is in certain cases directly related to the extent of working time and the length of employment. However, the fact that those who correspond with the working-life norm of the standard employee also enjoy the greatest social security protection depends equally on the fact that the level of social insurance benefits is based on income from paid employment.

Alongside the practical and social security effects of the norm of the standard employee, purely labour law effects also operate. The fact that the full-time and permanent employee constitutes the norm does not prevent the general labour law legislation from often giving equally good protection to employees with other forms of employment. But there are also examples in which the general labour law protection is expressly inferior for employees who deviate from the normative description of the person in paid employment. This applies especially to rules imposing qualification provisions according to which the employee must have been employed for a certain length of time in order to be entitled to employment rights.

The norm of full-time permanent employment is not only, nor even in the first instance, expressed in the shape of direct provisions of the law and collective agreements. More often this norm functions as a tacit and self-evident point of departure in the structure of rules. That can lead to the perception that the problems that arise for part-time workers and temporary workers can be ascribed to these employees personally, when instead the problems have to do with the fact that their employment situation does not correspond with the norm on which the labour law is based. Instead of problematising the norm, employees in non-standard forms of employment are then described as divergent cases with particular labour market-related problems. This perception can to some degree be reinforced by the fact that the terms of employment for part-time workers and temporary workers are now regulated by a special Act on discrimination.[4] On a legally systematic

---

[4] The Act on Prohibition of Discrimination against Part-Time Workers and Workers with Fixed-Term Employment (2002:293), implementing EC Council Directive 97/81 of 15 December 1997 concerning the Framework Agreement on part-time work concluded by UNICE, CEEP and the ETUC, [1998] OJ L 14/9, and EC Council Directive 1999/70/EC of 28 June 1999 concerning the Framework Agreement on Fixed-term Work concluded by ETUC, UNICE and CEEP, [1999] OJ L 175/43.

plane, this legislation partly places part-time and temporary workers in the broader labour law context which includes the proscription of discrimination with regard to the employees' sex, ethnic background, sexuality and disability—grounds of discrimination that all relate to the person of the employees. However, even if the purpose of this regulation is to improve the terms of work for part-time and temporary employees, it also means that these employees are once again described as diverging from the norm. By introducing a special Act on discrimination without at the same time improving the general labour law protection, the legislation does not challenge the norm of the standard employee. The fact that there is a major imbalance in the distribution of standard employment across the labour market, and that this imbalance has particular gender aspects, is a matter which remains hidden from sight.

Legal Protection takes the Norm of the Standard Employee as its Starting-Point

As we have seen, certain labour law rules are so constructed that they cannot be exploited on equal terms by an employee who deviates from the norm of the full-time and permanent employee. But the employment situation experienced by many part-time and temporary workers, which is uncertain and difficult to cope with in practice, is not immediately related to the design of any particular provision or right. The explanation is to be found at a significantly more basic level. In a normative context in which 'employment' is synonymous with 'permanent employment' and 'work' is synonymous with 'full-time work', work in non-standard forms of employment implies that non-standard employment is *per se* a precarious position. This derives from the fact that non-standard employment rests on premises other than standard employment, which is the foundation of the structure of labour law. The sphere in which the employer exercises authority has been determined on the basis of the assumption that the employee is in permanent employment, and the employee's rights have been designed with full-time work as the self-evident criterion of remuneration. This is something which fundamentally influences the legal position of non-standard employment.

The general legal principle about the employer's right to manage and assign work means among other things that it is the employer who alone determines how the business is to be organised and run. The employer's right of decision, or managerial prerogative, is matched by an obligation on the part of the employee to obey, within fairly broad limits, the employer's decisions about which working tasks are to be carried out and how they are to be done.[5] The employer's right to decide and the employee's obligation

---

[5] AD 1997 No 74 (Lab Ct).

to obey together constitute the foundation of the employment relationship and distinguish this relationship from other contractual relations. The employer's right of decision is limited by other labour law principles and through legislation. While labour law legislation is generally of importance in balancing the interests of employer and employee, of particular importance is the discrimination legislation and the Employment Protection Act.

However, the particular prohibition of discrimination aimed at protecting part-time and temporary workers cannot be said to place any great limitation on the employer's right of decision, since this prohibition operates only in relation to pay and employment conditions. Moreover, the prohibition does not apply if the employer can show that the application of special terms of treatment is justified on objective grounds. While this Act is so recent that there has not yet been time for any case-law to grow up around it, it is nonetheless clear that the rules leave considerable room for the employer to favour employees with a strong connection to the place of work. It is also clear that this happens, and that it is to the detriment of large groups of employees who are covered by the Act on the prohibition of discriminatory terms of work. Many studies have shown that part-time and temporary workers have inferior career development, receive less training, and have less influence over their working situation than those employees in permanent and full-time employment (Håkansson, 2001; Aronsson, 2002; Wikman, 2002; Jonsson, 2003). The research also shows that employees with fixed-term employment suffer what is known as a 'wage penalty', that is to say that on average they earn less than permanent employees who do the same work (Holmlund and Storrie, 2002).

There are no rules limiting the possibilities for the employer systematically to engage part-time workers with a view to creating a labour force that has a strong economic incentive to accept overtime work at short notice, in order to meet an increased demand for labour. A number of trade unions and political representatives have long pursued the question of a legally established right to full-time employment, but so far no such right exists. In accordance with the Employment Protection Act a part-time employee who so wishes has a priority right to a position with longer working time. This is, however, only on condition that the employer's demand for labour is satisfied by recruiting the part-time employee with longer working-time *and* that the part-time employee has sufficient qualifications for the new working tasks. The assessment of whether these conditions are met ultimately lies with the employer.

With regards to fixed-term employment, the situation is different. The legislation contains a clear indication that such employment shall exist only in exceptional cases, but at the same time there are very extensive possibilities for exception. Thus, despite the fact that the Employment Protection Act indicates that permanent employment is to be the normal form of employment, the Labour Court has long made it clear that the employer has no obligation to choose permanent employment solely for the reason that the enterprise has a documented continuing demand for labour.[6] Within the framework established by the Employment Protection Act, employers are free to engage workers in the form of employment they find most appropriate. Moreover, the employer need not always state what type of temporary employment applies to the employee.[7] This has been referred to as a special problem, because it reduces the possibilities for checking whether the employer lives up to the few demands established for fixed-term recruitment by the Employment Protection Act.[8]

The Swedish National Institute for Working Life recently published a study, at the behest of the government, examining the extent to which Swedish labour legislation meets the demands for security and influence of employees in a flexible and efficient labour market. The terms of reference for this study included shedding particular light on the situation of fixed-term employees. The Institute noted in its report that there are currently manifest lacunae in the employment protection for fixed-term employees. These gaps have arisen because the list of permitted forms of fixed-term employment has been expanded without any accompanying comprehensive reinforcement of the legal protection for fixed-term employment.[9]

A CLOSER LOOK AT FIXED-TERM EMPLOYMENT

There are very few employees who have voluntarily expressed a wish to be engaged for a fixed term. Even though it is sometimes asserted that younger people value liberty rather than security and therefore prefer fixed-term employment, there are a number of extensive studies that show that, in principle, all employees would rather have permanent employment than fixed-term employment (Aronsson, 2002: 146; Holmlund and Storrie, 2002; Nelander and Goding, 2003). The young are no exception in this regard. Permanent employment reinforces the employee's position in relation to the employer. But despite the fact that the norm of permanent employment is the basis of labour legislation, its impact in practice is relatively weak.

The Norm of Permanent Employment has been Weakened

The central provisions relating to the form of employment are to be found in the Employment Protection Act. This Act rests on the basic principle that

---

[6] AD 1984 No 64, AD 1984 No 66, AD 1994 No 22, and AD 2002 No 3 (Lab Ct).
[7] AD 1999 No 7 and AD 2000 No 6 (Lab Ct).
[8] Government reports Ds 2002:56 at 218.
[9] Government reports Ds 2002:56 at 215.

fixed-term employment should exist only in exceptional cases, since it does not meet the employee's need for security of employment.[10] This principle is expressed directly in the text of the Act and it forms the basis of the formulation of the rules on protection. The norm of permanent employment thus constitutes a significant part of the legislative scheme of employment protection itself.

Originally, the Employment Protection Act recognised only a few cases of fixed-term employment, permitting such appointments only for work experience, substitution, and for specific work either for a specific season or having regard to the special nature of the working tasks. But as a result of amendments to the Act made during the 1980s and 1990s the list of situations in which fixed-term employment is permitted has been successively extended.[11] The Labour Court's interpretation of the existing legal rules has also contributed to a much greater tolerance of this form of employment.[12] The evolution that has occurred both in the law itself and in the case-law means that, taken as a whole, there are now considerably greater possibilities to enter into a fixed-term employment contract than was intended when the Employment Protection Act was introduced. Consequently, a large group of employees are left without the basic protection that the legal rules are intended to guarantee. During the 1990s, fixed-term employment increased as a whole by about 50 per cent (Nelander and Goding, 2003).[13] Today, fixed-term employment embraces over half a million employees, or one in six persons employed on the Swedish labour market (Wikman, 2002; Statistics Sweden, 2004).

Step by step, the centre of gravity in the content of the law has been shifted from the employee's need for security of employment to the employer's need for freedom of manoeuvre. From the legislator's side the explicit purpose of the amendments to the Act has been to meet the employer's need for a labour force which can readily be adapted to meet rapid changes in a market in which production is organised on the basis of principles concerned with customer needs and economic efficiency even in the short term. The

---

[10] Government Bill, prop 1973:129 and Government Bill, prop 1981/82:71. If the employee is hired on a fixed-term contract even though no such exceptional case exists, the court can at the request of the employee declare that the contract shall apply until further notice: Employment Protection Act, § 36.

[11] The introduction of the current Employment Protection Act 1982 already entailed extension of the possibilities for fixed-term contracts. The most palpable amendments occurred, however, in the mid-1990s. The rule concerning temporary employment by agreement, which is the latest in a series of such amendments, was introduced in 1996 and entered into force in 1997: Government Bill, prop 1996/97:16. Fixed-term employment is also permitted in collective agreements.

[12] Government Bill, prop 2001/02:97 at 52. Government reports Ds 2002:56 at 223–25.

[13] In 1990, 378,000 people were in fixed-term employment, and in 2003, the number was 511,000.

legislator has emphasised industry's need to be able readily to recruit additional labour and then, as occasion demands, to reduce the labour force without any obligation to observe the rules of the Employment Protection Act.[14]

One of the forms of fixed-term employment that already existed when the Employment Protection Act was introduced was the recruitment of substitutes, in which an employee is engaged to replace a person who is absent from work. At the outset there was a strict requirement that the replacement should be linked to the absent employee and should cease when that person returned to work or ceased employment. The Labour Court has in practice completely abandoned that requirement.[15] In the same way, in its application of the Act, the Labour Court has extended the scope of permitted exceptions, so that they now include several consecutive replacements.[16] Since 2000, there has, however, been a legal rule protecting against excessively long replacement employment. The Employment Protection Act now states that an employee who has been employed as a replacement by the same employer for at least three of the last five years shall be regarded as having transferred into a position of permanent employment. The explicit purpose of this provision was the need to deal with the over-exploitation of replacement employment and, hence also, with the unsatisfactory state of affairs in which a large number of employees had long periods of employment without employment protection.[17] Long periods of insecure employment can still, however, arise despite this protective rule, since fixed-term employment can also occur on the basis of rules other than those concerning replacement employment.

Among these other provisions are, first, that which is applied in the case of what is known as 'project employment', where employees carry out specific limited working tasks within the framework of a project or a consultancy task. The rule is also applicable when the task is either financed by special funds or can be distinguished in some other way from the rest of the business, even if the work in itself lies within the framework of the ordinary business of the enterprise. Project employment ceases when the project or the limited tasks have been completed. There is no rule on how long employment on this basis may last, nor is there any bar to appointing the same person an unlimited number of times for different projects or defined tasks. The possibility for the employer to take on labour for projects is limited only by the requirement in the Act that it must relate to defined work. But this requirement for definition of the work has been considerably weakened in recent years through the case-law of the Labour Court.[18]

---

[14] Government Bill, prop 1996/97:16 at 32.
[15] AD 1985 No 130, AD 2002 No 3 (Lab Ct).
[16] See Government reports Ds 2002:56 at 223 for a detailed account of this development.
[17] Government Bill, prop 1996/97:16 at 38.
[18] Government reports Ds 2002:56 at 225.

With regard to tasks that form part of the day-to-day business of an enterprise and thus are not defined, the Act permits fixed-term employment for relatively short periods in situations where the employer encounters a temporary peak in the workload.[19] Probationary employment is also normally counted as fixed-term employment. During the period of probation, the maximum permitted length of which is six months, the employer may terminate the employment at any time and without stating the reason. If the probationary appointment is not terminated, it is automatically transformed into permanent employment after six months.

The employer's ability to enter into contracts for fixed-term employment has, for a number of years now, also extended beyond the special cases enumerated here. On the basis of a rule in relation to what is called 'agreed temporary employment', the employer may enter into such a contract without any specific reason for making it fixed term.[20]

In summary, the employer today has many opportunities to enter into contracts for fixed-term employment. When a fixed-term engagement expires it can also be renewed. Since the Act contains no limitation as regards the number of consecutive fixed-term appointments that may be made, chains of temporary appointments can be created in a manner that is wholly compatible with the requirements of the Employment Protection Act. The basis of the Act itself, the norm of permanent employment, has been hollowed out.

Major Differences between Various Groups of Fixed-term Employees

As the possibility to employ labour on fixed-term contracts has been progressively extended by law, such arrangements have become ever more common. But equally significantly, statistical analysis of the various forms of fixed-term contract also reveals major changes. Now most prominent is the increased use of two forms of employment—project employment and casual employment. The number of contracts for project employment has more than doubled since the beginning of the 1990s. Of those in fixed-term employment, a significantly larger proportion of men than of women have a project-employment contract: indeed of those employees on fixed-term contracts, 22 per cent of the men and just below 14 per cent of the women are on project-contracts (Nelander and Goding, 2003). During the same period, casual employment has more than tripled. As already noted, currently a quarter of all fixed-term employees are engaged in this insecure form of employment, the great majority of them being women.

---

[19] In addition, the Act permits fixed-term contracts for seasonal employment.

[20] At any given time an employer may have a maximum of five employees engaged on the basis of this rule. Their contracts may extend for no more than 12 months in any period of three years.

The chief argument for the change in labour law in the field of security of employment has been that fixed-term contracts meet employers' needs for an economically efficient organisation of labour. But in some contexts it has also been maintained that fixed-term contracts may also entail advantages for employees. This argument is based on the idea that a looser relationship with the employer is in itself an incentive to the employee to seek new challenges by making frequent changes of employer or work. An employee who can offer services in short-term employment and sell skills in a labour market exposed to competition can also attain a higher income. The changing working tasks provide opportunity for personal development and by changing the place of work the employee builds up a valuable network of contacts. That is roughly how the argument goes. It is a way of thinking that may be valid for certain employees, but only for small proportion of fixed-term employees.

Fixed-term appointments can occasionally be advantageous, from the point of view of remuneration and working conditions, for highly qualified employees on high incomes. Fixed-term employment contracts—on projects, say—create recurrent opportunities for negotiation with different employers. That implies greater opportunities for these attractive employees, for example to raise the level of their salary or wages.[21] However, taking the labour market as a whole, there is nothing to substantiate the idea that fixed-term employment is more advantageous for employees. On the contrary, there are indications that fixed-term employment tends to be at lower rates of remuneration than permanent employment, by a margin of about 10 per cent (Holmlund and Storrie, 2002). There are a number of studies that show that the overall quality of fixed-term engagements varies significantly, depending on the branch of industry to which the employee belongs, the level of education and the sex of the employee (Aronsson, 2002). Studies of the state of health of fixed-term employees, the possibilities for development, and transition to permanent employment, show that this type of working situation functions best for employees engaged on projects, and that the group that is most at risk is that comprising workers in casual employment. Employees on project contracts have a working situation that in many respects reflects that of permanent employees—their appointment is not as a replacement in someone else's position but in a new position with its own tasks, and they are often appointed because they can contribute skills of which employers have particular need. Casual workers, on the other hand, have a working situation that is so far divorced from that of permanent employment that comparison is scarcely meaningful.

In contrast to project contracts, casual work very rarely leads to permanent employment. Project employees are recruited because the employer needs the employee's particular competence, and on that basis the employee

---

[21] Government reports Ds 2002:56 at 209.

often has an opportunity to obtain a permanent engagement. In the case of the recruitment of casual labour, it is not the employee's competence but the loose form of the employment that is attractive to the employer. The very reason for the employer taking on casual workers is that permanently employed labour does not satisfy the enterprise's interest in being able to respond very rapidly to market changes. The argument that employees can improve their salary or wages through competition on the basis of competence does not apply in the case of casual workers. Indeed, on the contrary, in order to obtain any offer of work this group of employees may have to compete by being ready to accept *lower* pay. Casual workers are recruited not on the basis of any particular competence but on the basis of their availability, and other workers can readily be taken on instead of those who are unavailable when required. Availability cannot therefore function as a competitive advantage but is instead a basic condition without which there is no question of recruitment at all. A reduction in the level of remuneration sought is therefore the only thing that can make one casual employee more attractive than another. Since casual labourers are in practice recruited exclusively to do unqualified work, they also have no opportunity to develop skills. Even if the work tasks can vary on occasion, they still do not provide the opportunity for any meaningful improvement.

Competence and qualified working tasks also bear the main weight in the argument that fixed-term contracts can give an employee an opportunity to build up a network of contacts which promote development. The idea is that the employee is a mobile participant in the labour market who constantly makes her abilities available to various employers. But casual workers, who are primarily women employed in the retail trade, in the field of social and health care, and in the hotel and restaurant sector, are, as a rule, bound to a single employer.

In general, women are over-represented in fixed-term employment—approximately 60 per cent are women (Statistics Sweden, 2004). Furthermore, significantly more women than men have fixed-term contracts that are characterised by particularly unfavourable conditions. The labour market for fixed-term employees, like the rest of the labour market, is segregated as regards both the gender and the class aspects.

THE NORM OF THE STANDARD EMPLOYEE IS NOT GENDER-NEUTRAL

The Male Employee Constitutes the Norm of the Standard Employee

The working-life norm of the standard employee as being permanently employed full time reflects the situation of male employees much better than it does that of women employees. As we have seen, there are more women than men who lack permanent employment and, among fixed-term employees, women often have worse conditions than men. As regards the question of full-time work, it is even clearer that the norm of the standard employee refers to male employees and does not reflect the situation of women.

One Swedish employee in four works part time, and the great majority of such employees are women. This is important, because it is the standard employee's needs that determine the substance of the legal rules. The point of departure for labour law is that employees have a series of human needs and the ambition is that the demands of working life must be compatible with these needs. The provisions of labour law are formulated by weighing the interests of employers against those of employees. There is no great difficulty in identifying the employer's interests in this balancing process. Every rule which guarantees employees certain rights against their employers limits the employer's freedom to determine the content of the working relationship. It is therefore reasonable to assume that the typical interest of employers is that there shall be as little regulation as possible.

In contrast, when the interests of employees are to be established the point of departure is less obvious. Since not all employees live under the same conditions, it is impossible in the same simple fashion to determine what needs an employee has. In this situation, it is necessary for the legislator to determine the conditions of life and the important needs which are to be considered as so universally valid that it is right to resort to legislation in order to provide for them. These decisions are founded on conscious choices of a pragmatic and ideological nature, but they also embrace less conscious perceptions about employees—perceptions that are treated as if they were truths and that are seldom problematised or in any way questioned. This process of decision, which must distinguish the general from the special case, general rules from exceptions, involves questions about what kind of person an employee is and what needs an employee has. These questions are posed in a social and intellectual context that is characterised by the image of the standard employee, that image which in labour law finds expression in the description of a person who is employed on a full-time and permanent basis. The fact that this is a norm that broadly reflects the reality of male rather than of female employees can most clearly be seen in the provisions that relate to full-time work. Forty per cent of women employees work part time, but only 10 per cent of men have part-time work.[22] And nowhere is the difference between working time in paid

---

[22] There is a major difference between non-salaried workers and salaried employees—almost every other woman in non-salaried occupations works part time, just under every third woman in the salaried employee sector, and one in five female academics (Statistics Sweden, 2004).

employment for men and for women as great as it is in regard to employees with small children. Of those employees who have freely taken the decision to diverge from the norm of full-time work and to take up paid employment on a part-time basis instead, the great majority are women, and the great majority have taken that decision in order to look after their children (Båvner, 2001; Handelstjänstemannaförbundet, 2003). For women employees there are clear statistical links between part-time work and family circumstances (Nelander and Goding, 2003). This shows that there is at least one basic need that is not met within the framework of the norm of the standard employee—time for the responsibility of care that is the consequence of parenthood.

The Norm of the Standard Employee Consolidates Structural Gender Patterns

It is women who, in the first instance, take the practical and financial consequences of the birth of children in the family. This is both a consequence and an expression of the great sexual inequality that reigns in the division of household work. But it results also from the way in which the norm of the standard employee ignores the fact that a large proportion of employees must share time and commitment between paid employment and the duties of care as parents. A 40-hour working week has been regarded as reasonable in relation to the employee's capacity and need for time outside working life, time for participation in the community, for further education and training, and for social life with family and friends.[23] The necessary time that is allotted for these activities is regarded as being so fundamental that it cannot be subordinate to the demands of the labour market. Therefore, the law on working-time states that ordinary working-time should not exceed 40 hours per week. This is an example of the way in which the rules of working life reflect current perceptions of both the needs and interests of the employee deserving protection, and good working conditions.

But the function of rules is not only to reflect the situation. They contribute also to *forming* perceptions of working life and society at large. These include perceptions of what is an acceptable working situation and what are the fundamental needs of an employee. But they also concern perceptions of what needs are *not* to be considered as fundamental, or what in any event are not to be universalised, as general needs of employees. And even if labour market regulation is not always followed in practice, it nonetheless sets the standard for views of work and of employees—a normal working week comprises 40 hours and is assumed to give sufficient

---

[23] Government Bill, prop 1970:5 at 96.

time for the employee's needs in other areas of life. When the parents—read mothers–of small children reduce their working-time in order to have time for the work of running a home and caring for children, the consequent financial and career disadvantages are regarded as legitimate (Julén, 2001: 192). Full-time work functions as a norm of paid employment and those who, on their own initiative, diverge from this norm are regarded to some extent as having voluntarily accepted an inferior position (Markus, 1987; Tornes, 1994). This way of thinking is represented not only in the social security system and in the career structure of working life, it is also to be found among employees themselves. This is particularly clear among employees who have children. Inquiries show that, to a large extent, these employees themselves assume a sense of responsibility for the financial and organisational consequences to the enterprise when they have children. It is noted that many parents of small children have feelings of guilt towards their employers and it is quite common for pregnant women to regard themselves as having caused disruption at their place of work (Elvin-Nowak, 1999; Office of the Equal Opportunities Ombudsman, 1999). These feelings of guilt lead many working parents to downplay demands for their employers to respect their rights.

CHANGED WORKING LIFE—A NEW GENDER DIVISION

In this chapter, the principal discussion about how non-standard employment relates to the underlying norms of the labour market has been conducted around two central questions. The first question relates to who constitutes the basis for the image of the standard employee. Every provision that accords employees certain rights vis-à-vis employers also expresses percep-tions about who constitutes the typical individual in paid employment and what fundamental needs that individual has. But such regulation also con-tributes to *forming* perceptions about employees and about their fundamental needs. Those employee needs that are not identified within the framework of the rules of working life are perceived as being of less importance. The question of whose life situation is the basis of the description of the funda-mental needs of employees is therefore of key significance. As we have seen, the working-life norm of the standard employee as being in permanent full-time employment is a male norm. And it is a norm that only to a limited extent respects the basic need for time for the responsibility of care that fol-lows with parenthood. This is an important reason why many women on their own initiative decide to work part time, a decision which consequently means that they diverge from the working-life norm.

The second question that has been the object of discussion concerns the legal position of non-standard employees, and how legislation deals with those employees who do *not* correspond to the picture of the standard employee. In its terminology and system, the legislation contributes to separating out those employees who diverge from the labour law norm. These employees have a form of employment that rests on assumptions other than the standard form of employment that is at the basis of the formation of labour law. And the divergent employees therefore find themselves as a matter of principle in an inferior position compared with those who correspond to the description of the standard employee. At the same time as labour law regulation rests on a norm of the standard employee, it extensively permits employment agreements diverging from this norm. Due to this construction, the regulations create a space for employment relations in which the established labour law rules of protection cannot be guaranteed for the employee in practice. For fixed-term employees and for many part-time employees this entails essential parts of labour law not coming into play.

The question of working conditions also has clear gender aspects and acquires increased relevance in step with the increase in the extent of non-standard employment. Of the total Swedish labour force, today almost one third either work part time or do not have a permanent position (Statistics Sweden, 2004). More than 200,000 women who work part time would like to increase their working time, and discussions are currently in progress about setting up an official committee of inquiry into the situation of involuntary part-time workers.[24] The total number of part-time workers is at a relatively fixed level and has even fallen somewhat in recent times. In contrast, the number of fixed-term jobs has gradually increased since the beginning of the 1990s, and today approximately one employee in six is engaged on a fixed-term contract. Above all, it is project employment and casual work which have increased.

Throughout this period the proportions of men and women in fixed-term employment have remained more or less the same, but as fixed-term employment in total has increased so too has the proportion of men in fixed-term employment increased in absolute terms. There are in fact more men in fixed-term employment today than there were in 1990. Perhaps the greater number of men in fixed-term employment will gradually change the working-life norm of a standard employee, in such a way that fixed-term employment will be considered at least as typical as permanent employment, perhaps even as more typical. This conceivable change in the fundamental norms of working life could lead to a general improvement for employees who are today in non-standard positions. Such a development can today be discerned in demands for equal working conditions for non-standard and standard employees. One can, however, also imagine a development in the completely opposite direction. If the general demands and expectations in the matter of working conditions and security of employment are lowered,

[24] Government Bill, prop 2002/03:100 at 26.

this could also worsen the conditions for those in permanent positions. Such a development is also compatible with the principles of equality of treatment!

One clear and significant tendency is that fixed-term employment is beginning to form a male A-team and a female B-team in step with the process by which such appointments are becoming more common for men too. Formerly it was virtually only women who had fixed-term employment. Women have been in paid work as long as men, but they have in many respects been regarded as workers of an inferior class (Oakley, 1976; Frangeur, 1998; Florin and Nilsson, 2000). Even though the description of the female labour force as a reserve, which is called upon when the demand for labour increases but which is not allowed to work when there is a downturn in the economy, is somewhat simplistic, it squares to a certain degree with the facts.[25] A convenient way of calling up this 'reserve' has been to recruit labour on a fixed-term basis. The predominance of women that formerly distinguished fixed-term recruitment now seems to be in the course of disappearing. Both men and women are today to be found in fixed-term employment. But what is now growing up is a gender division resembling that to be found on the labour market in other respects. Men and women are in different places and work on different terms. Thus a significantly greater proportion of men are engaged on project employment, while it is very largely women who are in casual labour. And casual recruitment reproduces precisely the perception of women as a less-qualified reserve working force. The fact is that the present legal development is going in the direction of an improvement in protection for employees in the relatively long fixed-term appointments in which a particularly large proportion of men are to be found.[26] In contrast, there is nothing to suggest that there will be a similar development as regards short-term appointments. These latter appointments are represented not least by casual recruitment in which women predominate.

[25] The understanding of the female workforce as a reserve is not to be taken literally, especially not with reference to the Nordic countries. For a discussion on this subject and for a balanced description of women's position in the workforce, see Anttalainen, 1985, Bradley, 1989, and Walby, 1990.

[26] Government reports Ds 2002:56 at 254–82.

13

The Legal Production of Precarious Work

ROSEMARY HUNTER*

INTRODUCTION

A S THE VARIOUS chapters in this volume document, all industrialised
countries have experienced a rise in 'non-standard', 'contingent', or
'precarious' forms of employment over the last two decades.
However, the precise kinds of precarious work differ between countries—an
indication that the local regulatory regimes have played a role in mediating
and channelling the effects of global economic restructuring. This chapter
examines the role of Australian labour regulation in producing particular
kinds of precarious work, and it also looks at the timing of these changes.
The chapter argues that Australian labour law[1] has been a large part of the
problem in relation to precarious work for at least the last 15 years, and
there are few signs that it has much to contribute by way of solutions.
However, labour law has interacted with several other factors in the production of precarious work in Australia, including entrenched gender divisions
of labour in both the public and private spheres. Among other things, these
factors have given precarious work its particular gender dimensions.

THE INCIDENCE AND DISTRIBUTION OF PRECARIOUS WORK

The major forms of precarious work in the Australian labour market are casual employment, certain part-time jobs, home work/outwork, dependent contracting, and agency work. There is a considerable degree of overlap between
these categories. For example, part-time work may also be undertaken on a

---

* I would like to thank Anna Harrop for her invaluable research assistance on this chapter.
[1] I am using the term 'labour law' here to refer broadly to both the individual (employment)
and collective (industrial) aspects of labour regulation.

casual basis, outworkers may also be dependent contractors, and agency workers may also be casual employees or dependent contractors. Casual employment is the most prominent of these categories. Home workers and dependent contractors each make up around 3 per cent of the Australian workforce (Burgess and Campbell, 1998: 14; Watson *et al*, 2003: 64; O'Donnell, 2004: 25), but casual workers constituted 28 per cent of Australian employees in 2003.[2]

The incidence of precarious work has been rising in Australia, while that of standard employment has declined. For example, between 1988 and 2003, the proportion of employees engaged on a full-time permanent basis fell from 75 per cent to 61 per cent.[3] While the Australian labour force grew by two-and-a-half million between 1985 and 2001 (Watson *et al*, 2003: 53), employment growth has been in forms of precarious employment, at the expense of full-time permanent employment (Brosnan and Walsh, 1998: 12). Casual jobs accounted for two thirds of the increase in total employment in the period 1990–2001 (Watson *et al*, 2003: 48).[4] As a result,

in spite of high 'headline' employment rates, many sections of the community now have limited access to jobs paying a substantial wage (Borland *et al*, 2001: 4).

There have been clear gendered patterns in the growth of precarious employment.

Men's employment growth since 1987 has been concentrated in casual jobs, whether part-time or full-time. Women's employment growth has been concentrated in part-time jobs, whether casual or permanent (Junor, 1998: 78).

The rate of jobs growth for women has also considerably exceeded that for men, particularly in low-skilled occupations such as sales and personal services. '[W]omen accounted for three quarters of all the new jobs in the low-skilled occupations' since the late 1980s (Watson *et al*, 2003: 59). In a study based on 1995 data from Australia and New Zealand, Brosnan and Walsh found that women in both countries had less employment security than men, and the least secure employment in Australia was in the industries of cultural and personal services, trade and food (1998: 32, 35)—industries in which women predominate.

---

[2] ABS, 2004b. This statistical series defines 'casual' workers as those without entitlements to paid holiday and sick leave. As O'Donnell notes, it tends to overestimate the number of casual workers because it includes owner-managers of incorporated enterprises (who constitute around 2% of employees), and uses employees as its denominator rather than all employed persons. However, it is the only series to provide significant trend data on casual employment, and more recent surveys using different definitions of casual employment have introduced their own problems of under-estimation (O'Donnell, 2004: 4–7).

[3] ABS, 1988a; ABS, 2004b.

[4] At the other end of the scale, there was also a substantial increase in professional jobs (Watson *et al*, 2003: 55–57), resulting in increased income inequality and a so-called 'hollowing out' of the middle of the employment ladder.

Casual Employment

Casual workers have traditionally had no entitlements to annual leave, sick leave, parental leave, redundancy pay, protection against unfair dismissal, or other benefits available to permanent employees. They have only limited access to superannuation accumulation, and virtually no access to training or career paths. Few casual employees belong to a union (Campbell, 1996: 586), and casualisation has in fact been one of the contributing factors to the decline in union membership in Australia (Creighton and Stewart, 2000: 215).

The various disadvantages of casual employment are supposedly offset by a casual 'loading', that is, a higher hourly rate of pay than that available to permanent employees. But the casual loading does not adequately compensate for the multiple benefits foregone and extensive 'disamenities' of casual work (Smith and Ewer, 1999: 35–41). Moreover, this assumes that the casual loading is actually paid, something that cannot necessarily be relied upon (Campbell, 1996: 581).

Although the traditional justification for casual employment was to enable employers to fill short-term, temporary job vacancies, there is in fact wide variation in the duration of casual employment. At one end of the spectrum are 'long term casuals', who are used in the same way as permanent employees, but are 'deprived of the standard rights, benefits and entitlements associated with permanency' (Campbell, 2000: 72). At the other end of the spectrum are those casual workers who 'cycle in and out of work without finding a long-term secure job,' in the phenomenon known as 'labour market churning' (Watson *et al*, 2003: 41). A recent study has demonstrated a close alignment between the demographic characteristics of self-identified casual employees and the unemployed, suggesting that these two groups have much in common, and are often the same people (Parliamentary Library (Australia), 2004: 1–4).

The number of casual employees in the Australian workforce doubled between 1988 and 2003, from 1.1 million to 2.2 million.[5] The major period of growth in casual employment was in fact between 1988 and 1996, when casual employees as a proportion of all employees rose from 18.9 per cent to 26.1 per cent. Since 1996, the proportion of casual employees has risen only marginally to 27.6 per cent.[6] This timing is significant, since it shows that the burgeoning of casual employment occurred *before* the introduction of new, deregulatory labour legislation at federal level in 1996.[7] Casual work is still more likely to be found in part-time than in full-time

[5] See above n 2.
[6] *Ibid.*
[7] Workplace Relations Act 1996 (Cth).

employment, but the major growth has been in full-time employment. In 1988, full-time casuals constituted only 5.8 per cent of full-time employees, but by 1996 the proportion had almost doubled to 10.8 per cent, rising again to 13.8 per cent in 2003. By contrast, part-time casuals made up 68.3 per cent of all part-time employees in 1988, falling to 60.4 per cent of part-time employees in 2003.[8]

The occupational groups in which casual employment has grown are those at the lower end of the occupational scale. Almost all new permanent full-time jobs in the 1990s were created in managerial, professional, and associate professional occupations. Trades and advanced sales and service occupations saw an overall decline in employment. All other occupations experienced an increase in casual employment (Borland *et al*, 2001: 12–13). Borland *et al* argue that such a striking pattern across a range of occupations cannot be explained by supply-side factors (eg by employee choice) alone (2001: 17).

It has been widely observed that over the last 15 years 'the net of casual employment [has spread] and [drawn] in a wider range of social groups' (Campbell, 2000: 87). In particular, casual employment has gone from being a female ghetto area to one increasingly shared by men. In 1988, 11.7 per cent of male employees were employed on a casual basis. By 1996, that figure had almost doubled to 21.2 per cent, rising again to 24.0 per cent by 2003. By contrast, female casual employees as a proportion of all female employees remained fairly stable at around 30 per cent.[9] The main employer of both male and female casual workers is the retail industry, accounting for 25 per cent of all casual employees. Beyond that, however, female casual employees are clustered in the accommodation, cafe and restaurant, and health and community services industries, while male casuals tend to be found in property and business services, construction, and manufacturing.[10] The 'apparent shrinking of the gender differential in participation in casual employment' (Campbell, 2000: 87) is, therefore, a phenomenon observable only at the aggregate level. The gender segregation of the labour market continues to place women and men in different kinds of casual jobs and, in particular, to place women far more often in part-time casual jobs. This has significant economic consequences.

Part-Time Work

As noted above, part-time work is primarily the domain of women. Thus any discussion of women and precarious work must take account of part-time work as a form of precarious employment, and particularly its failure to

---

[8] See above n 2.

[9] *Ibid*. Female casual employees made up 28.8% of all female employees in 1988 and 31.9% in 2003.

[10] *Ibid*.

deliver the feminist goal of economic independence for women. Belinda Probert has noted the fact that women's participation in full-time employment in Australia has barely changed since the 1930s. In 1933, 25.2 per cent of Australian women were in full-time employment, and that figure had only risen to 27.1 per cent in 1994. By contrast, only 8.4 per cent of women were employed part time in 1966, rising to 20.1 per cent by 1994 (Probert, 1997: 186). Rather than improving their economic status over the course of the twentieth century, therefore, women have increasingly moved into part-time employment, in a context in which by 2000, average earnings in part-time jobs were only 37.5 per cent of average earnings from a full-time job (Borland *et al*, 2001: 10). Probert argues that part-time work for women does not challenge the domestic division of labour:

> We might conclude that the massive expansion in part-time work for women has been the vehicle through which major forces for change (both economic and cultural) have been contained. Women have been incorporated into the labour force, but have manifestly failed to seriously challenge the culture of work that rests on a traditional sexual division of labour at home.
>
> (Probert, 1997: 187)

In the 1980s in Australia, full-time jobs grew by 19 per cent while part-time jobs grew by 77.5 per cent accounting for 43 per cent of all new positions created. In the 1990s, full-time jobs grew by only 5.5 per cent while part-time jobs grew by 60.8 per cent. These figures contrast with those from the United States, where full-time employment grew much more rapidly than part-time employment during the 1980s and 1990s, for both women and men (Borland *et al*, 2001, 10).

Like casual work, part-time work also exists on a spectrum of precariousness. In the Australian context, part-time casual work carries with it many of the disadvantages of casual employment outlined above, combined with very low earnings. In 2000, average weekly earnings in part-time casual jobs were only around 30 per cent of average weekly earnings in full-time permanent jobs (Borland *et al*, 2001: 4). In relation to permanent part-time work, Anne Junor draws a valuable distinction between such work that is 'employee-initiated'—often a temporary Equal Employment Opportunity (EEO) measure designed to enable professional women to balance career and family responsibilities—and 'employer-initiated' permanent part-time work, which offers security of tenure, but less than a living wage and no career prospects. This kind of part-time work, Junor argues, 'may present the façade of standard employment, without the substance' (1998: 91).

Home Working, Dependent Contracting, and Agency Work

Home-based work or outwork is a familiar concept with a long history. Outworkers are usually paid at piece rates rather than receiving a regular wage, and have little or no control over the amount of work they receive. In slow periods, their income may drop dramatically, while in periods of high demand, they may be compelled to recruit family members and friends to finish the work provided within the required time. The piece rates paid are unlikely to reflect the full value of the work performed.[11] In addition, home workers bear all their own overhead costs, are required to regulate their own health and safety, and have no access to training or skills development. They are unlikely to belong to a union, and such legal protections as may exist 'on the books' are notoriously difficult to enforce. If their work arrangement is structured in terms of dependent contracting rather than direct employment, they are exposed to a range of additional costs, including for equipment and insurance. Home working is a traditionally gendered phenomenon, like part-time work, employing particularly women with childcare responsibilities. In a case study of outworkers in south-east Queensland, Brosnan and Thornthwaite observed that 'people with disabilities, those from ethnic minorities, and non-native language speakers are also often used as homeworkers' (1998: 98).

Dependent contractors are those who are theoretically self-employed, or working on their 'own account', but who are in fact dependent upon the provision of work by a single organisation or entity. The attachment of a range of employment protections to the status of 'employee' but not to other kinds of workers has enabled the exploitation of the common law distinction between 'employees' (those employed under a 'contract of service') and independent contractors (those employed under a 'contract for services'), to create a category of workers who are deprived of basic employment conditions such as payment at award rates, workers' compensation coverage, employer superannuation contributions, and protection against unfair dismissal. Where contractors own their own tools of trade, and can tender for business or perform work for a range of buyers at rates which they set to reflect their expenses, this is a perfectly legitimate arrangement. But where a contractor is in a position to sell services to only one buyer, who dictates the terms of engagement, the result is a distinctly precarious form of employment. As noted above, dependent contractors may also be home workers; however, those who are not home workers tend to be found in male-dominated areas of the labour market, particularly labourers in the construction industry, IT professionals in property and business services, and drivers in the transport and storage industries (Watson *et al*, 2003: 71–72).

Agency work involves engagement by a labour hire agency rather than directly by the ultimate consumer of labour. Agency work resembles casual employment in many ways, including a spectrum of practices ranging from

---

[11] New South Wales Industrial Relations Commission, 1998: 536–611.

instability, insecurity, and irregularity of work at one end, to quite stable arrangements whereby an agency supplies a pool of workers to a particular enterprise on a regular and long-term basis at the other. Agency workers may be permanent or casual employees of the agency, or may be engaged as dependent contractors, with the benefits and protections available to them varying according to the relevant status. Like casual work, too, the gender distribution of agency work has undergone a change from being predominantly female (for example, clerical and nursing) to more mixed gender (spreading to male-dominated industries such as construction and mining) (Watson *et al*, 2003: 73–74). Agency work also connects directly to the global economy, as large corporations increasingly attempt to source cheaper labour from offshore labour hire agencies (Watson *et al*, 2003: 74)—an area that remains beyond the scope of domestic labour regulation.

LEGAL REGULATION ENCOURAGING PRECARIOUS WORK ARRANGEMENTS

One of the arguments of this chapter, as noted above, is that the particular kind(s) of precarious work found within a national labour market owe much to the features of national labour regulation. I take a broad view of national labour regulation, to include not only laws regulating employment per se, but also industry, trade and competition policy, taxation regimes, rules relating to pensions and benefits, and welfare provisions. For example, it is clear that the much-vaunted reduction in unemployment in Australia over the past eight years is directly related to the increasingly disciplinary and punitive nature of social security legislation in Australia, which has, on the one hand, produced discouraged job seekers, who cease looking for work and thus disappear from the unemployment statistics, and, on the other hand, driven people into precarious, low-value, temporary jobs as a condition of the receipt of unemployment benefits (Burgess and Campbell, 1998: 17). In addition to local regulatory regimes, the particular kinds of precarious work created are also a product of gendered assumptions made by employers, historical gender segregation in the labour market, and ongoing gender divisions of labour in the family.

As discussed in the previous section, much of the striking change in the labour market in relation to precarious employment occurred between the advent of economic restructuring and the determined pursuit by employers of a flexibility agenda, dating from the late 1980s (Junor, 1998: 77), and the introduction of the Workplace Relations Act 1996. There was a Labor government in power at federal level in Australia from 1983, which by the later 1980s had thoroughly embraced a restructuring agenda, involving corporatisation and privatisation of state-owned enterprises, deregulation of the financial system, the dismantling of trade barriers and tariff protection for manufacturing industries, and increased exposure of Australian companies and products to (global) competition. This in turn produced demands for reduced labour costs and increased flexibility of labour utilisation (Owens, 1993: 405; Burgess and Campbell, 1998: 16), as well as the significant decline of some areas of employment (particularly manufacturing) and the rise of others (particularly services).[12]

The Workplace Relations Act 1996 can be seen to have confirmed and cemented the shifts that occurred in the previous decade. While it introduced a range of new measures that were conducive to the increased precariousness of employment (see Owens, chapter 15 in this volume), most of the legal structures facilitating growth in insecure part-time jobs, casual employment, dependent contracting, and agency work were already in place. These included award restructuring to break down rigidities in the classification, organisation and skilling of labour; a shift from centralised wage-fixing to enterprise-level bargaining; and long-established distinctions between permanent and casual employment, and between employees and independent contractors, that were able to be exploited.

Casual Employment

As O'Donnell has observed, 'the category of casual employment in Australia is largely the creation of the award system' (2004: 13). Awards at once invoked and restricted the employment of casual workers as an exception to the norm. They often contained proportional limits or quotas on the employment of casuals, placed restrictions on how casual employees could be used (Campbell, 1996: 579), or specified time limits on their engagement (such as a maximum of three months) (Weller *et al*, 1999: 4). In the 1980s and early 1990s, however, the value of casual workers increased, while award restrictions on their use were gradually stripped away.

While pursuing an economic restructuring agenda, federal and state Labor governments also introduced new protections and benefits for permanent employees in the 1980s, such as parental leave entitlements, redundancy payments, unfair dismissal regimes, and mandatory employer superannuation contributions. These new entitlements made permanent employment more costly. By contrast, casual employment did not attract the same range of entitlements, and also enabled a lower level of investment in recruitment and training.

---

[12] Allan explains why personal service work tends to produce more precarious jobs: production and consumption occur simultaneously in personal services, resulting in 'strong cost pressure on employers to ensure that labour-use patterns directly correspond to consumer-demand patterns' (1998: 3).

For example, 'short term' casual employees are excluded from the coverage of much unfair dismissal legislation.[13] A group of textile, clothing and footwear employers interviewed in 1995 'attributed their preferences for casual labour to the inflexibilities of labour market regulations, particularly unfair dismissal laws' (Weller *et al*, 1999: 28):

> Employers were not certain whether or not relying on casual employment produced a cost saving ... Overall managers did not emphasise cost advantage as a primary motive for casual recruitment. ... The consensus seemed to be that the direct cost difference between casual and permanent employees is insignificant, but that the indirect costs – the costs of staff turnover and recruitment, absenteeism, redundancy and carrying ineffective or disruptive workers—are important.
>
> (Weller *et al*, 1999: 28)

Across the manufacturing sector, according to Weller *et al*: 'The rise of casual work represents a substantial shift in approaches to recruitment stemming partly from employers' unwillingness to commit to permanent employment until they are certain that a potential recruit meets their expectations, and partly from unstable business conditions' (1999: 30–31).

Weller *et al* contend that the growth of casual employment is constrained by labour market conditions, labour market regulations, and union activity (1999: 31). However, in Australia in the 1980s and 1990s, labour market conditions and labour market regulation did not act as constraints on, but rather as accelerators of, the growth of casual employment. And as a result, the possibilities for union activity became constrained. Creighton and Stewart (2000: 215) have observed more generally that:

> In theory, the [casual] loading is meant to discourage employers from hiring casuals. However, even if the loading does constitute adequate compensation for the full value of the non-wage benefits foregone, most employers seem happy to pay the additional amount in return for what they perceive as the flexibility of being able to hire and fire at will. For some workers too, the loading may seem an attractive substitute for benefits they are unlikely to access, or whose true value they do not appreciate. For many though, the question of choice is simply irrelevant when the only alternative to accepting casual work is unemployment.

As well as casual employment becoming more attractive to employers in the 1980s and 1990s, limitations on casual employment were eased or traded off in award restructuring and enterprise bargaining processes. The process

---

[13] See, eg, Workplace Relations Act 1996 (Cth), s 170; Industrial Relations Act 1996 (NSW), s 83; Industrial Relations (General) Regulations (NSW), cl 6; Industrial Relations Act 1999 (Qld), s 72; Fair Work Act 1994 (SA), s 105A. Each of these provisions defines (differently) what constitutes 'short-term' casual employment for the purposes of exclusion.

was completed by the Workplace Relations Act 1996, which specifically deprives the Australian Industrial Relations Commission (AIRC), in making or varying industrial awards, of the power to 'limit the number or proportion of employees that an employer may employ in a particular type of employment.'[14] Campbell also argues that a significant effect of labour market deregulation has been to widen the gaps in award coverage, so that there is a wider sphere of unregulated contracting, providing greater opportunities to designate employment as 'casual' (1996: 584).

The desire to avoid liability for unfair dismissal does not appear to be the primary motivation for 'long-term casual' employment, since casuals employed for more than 12 months are covered by the federal and most state unfair dismissal legislation.[15] But it still presents other cost advantages, for example in relation to recruitment, (non-) training, redundancy, and (non-) unionisation. In two case studies of private hospitals, Cameron Allan identified another advantage of long-term casual employment, to achieve flexibility of labour supply and thus to reduce labour costs, while at the same time ensuring quality control, familiarity with structures and systems, and continuity of personnel (1998: 61, 70). The hospitals in the case studies targeted their recruitment of regular casuals towards:

> middle-aged, married local women, a group that the hospital identified as the most stable labour market segment ... less likely to quit and more prepared to tolerate working shortened shifts, to attend work at short notice, and go without work for reasonable periods.
>
> (Allan, 1998: 71)

This strategy exploited women's domestic arrangements, in that they were likely to be primary carers of children and to prefer working locally, and unlikely to be primary breadwinners. This is consistent with statistics for New South Wales showing that for 25.2 per cent of women, but only 1.4 per cent of men, undertaking casual, part-time, or temporary employment was dictated by family reasons[16] (see also Owens, 1993: 425).

Part-Time Work

Legal restrictions in awards on part-time work were more extensive than those relating to casual work (Probert, 1995: 7). These restrictions were a legacy of the union movement's concern to protect the wages of male

---

[14] Workplace Relations Act 1996 (Cth), s 89A(4).

[15] *Ibid*, s 170CBA; Industrial Relations (General) Regulations (NSW), cl l.6 (six months); Industrial Relations Act 1999 (Qld), s 72(8); Fair Work Act 1994 (SA), s 105A (nine months).

[16] ABS, *Part-time, Casual and Temporary Employment, New South Wales* (Cat No 6247.1) (Canberra: ABS, 1998), cited in Smith and Ewer, 1999: 22.

breadwinners. Where part-time work was created, it thus tended to be casual rather than permanent.

In 1988, the Business Council of Australia argued that award restrictions on part-time work encouraged casualisation, and hence that award revisions to allow for more flexible working time could lead to increased permanent part-time employment (Campbell, 1996: 583). In introducing the Workplace Relations Act 1996, the federal Liberal–National Coalition Government made the same argument—that preventing the Commission from including in awards either limitations on the number or proportion of employees that an employer may employ in a particular type of employment, or specifications of maximum or minimum hours of work for regular part-time employees, would enable employers to offer more permanent part-time work. Neither of these predictions has eventuated, and casualisation has continued apace (Campbell, 1996: 583). Where the regulatory regime allows for both permanent and casual part-time employment, the casual option appears to be preferred, for the kinds of reasons outlined in the previous section.

Home Working, Dependent Contracting, and Agency Work

The common law distinction between 'employees' and 'independent contractors' has been compounded in Australia by the fact that virtually all employment benefits and protections provided in industrial awards or industrial legislation have attached only to the status of 'employee.' Thus 'contracting out' work to supposedly independent (but in reality dependent) contractors can be even more advantageous to employers than engaging casual employees. Employers can avoid any form of paid leave *and* the casual loading, any requirement to pay award or minimum wages or penalty rates for unsociable hours, any liability for unfair dismissal, redundancy payments, or superannuation contributions, the need to administer PAYE tax deductions and the obligation to pay payroll tax. In addition, employers can externalise the costs of production onto contractors (particularly if they are home workers), externalise responsibility for supervision and quality control (often by means of penalties for sub-standard work), and externalise occupational health and safety risks, thereby avoiding the costs of providing a safe workplace, as well as the need to pay workers' compensation premiums (Brosnan and Thornthwaite, 1998: 100). It is then hardly surprising that employers in highly competitive industries with low profit margins make use of dependent contractors and, as discussed earlier, this is even easier where the domestic division of labour presents limited choices to the workers themselves. For example, clothing outworkers in Australia were classified as independent contractors until the late 1980s, and consequently worked for low pay under appalling conditions. Family daycare workers engaged by local councils (women providing child care to a small number of children in their own homes) have also been found to be independent contractors rather than employees, and thus not entitled to award pay and conditions.[17]

Brosnan and Thornthwaite's illuminating case study (1998) gives an insight into contemporary home work and dependent contracting. The home workers they interviewed had previously been employed directly by the same company and paid at piece rates, but in 1991 the company moved to a contracting system, thereby avoiding training levies, superannuation contributions, workers' compensation premiums, and payroll tax. It invited its current home workers to tender for the work, but only accepted tenders at the existing piece rate of 5.5 cents per unit. Home workers were required to re-tender for business each year, but only at the rate determined by the company. Pay rates for home workers remained fixed for four years, and those who attempted to increase their rates simply did not have their contracts renewed. Home workers could be underemployed for part of the year, overworked in busy periods, and easily dismissed by the company providing no further work. The company attempted to justify the low rates of pay by arguing that the workers could minimise income tax by claiming their costs as business expenses, but this assumed that their earnings were above the tax-free threshold—something that did not necessarily occur (Brosnan and Thornthwaite, 1998: 103–6). Here, a legal regime providing overwhelming cost and flexibility advantages of contracting out to home workers, combined with a ready supply of labour with little choice but to accept work on that basis, produced an inevitable shift to precarious employment.

Obtaining workers through a labour hire agency provides all the advantages for the employer of contracting out, together with the administrative simplicity of contracting only once with an agency, as opposed to multiple times with individual contractors. In structuring the relationship with their workers, agencies have made the same kinds of choices as those of direct employers outlined above, preferring to engage workers on either a casual or dependent-contracting basis rather than as permanent employees. While considerations such as the casual loading and tax advantages—combined with an absence of real choices—may induce workers to enter into casual or dependent-contracting arrangements, a further factor in agency arrangements is the complexity and ambiguity of the legal relationships involved in agency work. These may lead workers to misunderstand and overestimate their employment status (see, for example, Gryst, 2000), the implications of which may only become clear when they find themselves dismissed.

---

[17] *Re Municipal Association of Victoria* (1991), 4 CAR 35.

COUNTERVAILING MEASURES—(LIMITED) PROTECTION FOR PRECARIOUS WORKERS

It must be acknowledged that labour law has not uniformly and consistently worked in the direction of increasing precarious work. Some state governments have enacted legislation and some industrial tribunals have made decisions designed to extend protection for precarious workers; some courts have interpreted legal provisions and common law principles to the benefit of workers; and some unions have sought to shift the legal status of workers to less precarious forms, and to increase the costs of precarious employment for employers. Nevertheless, these efforts have been piecemeal, and in some instances unsuccessful or counterproductive. At best, they have mitigated the status of precarious workers, within an overall policy and legal setting which continues to respond to employer demands for flexibility by facilitating the spread of precarious employment.

Improved Conditions for Casual Workers

Increased Casual Loading

In *Re Metal, Engineering and Associated Industrial Award 1998 – Part I*,[18] the Australian Metal Workers Union sought a variation of the metal industry award to increase the loading to be paid to casual employees. In its decision, the Full Bench of the AIRC took the view that the casual loading should compensate for the lack of standard award benefits, primarily paid leave, long service leave, lack of notice of termination, and the effects of employment by the hour.[19] However, it considered that disadvantages relating to underclassification, lack of access to training, and limited access to superannuation were more appropriately dealt with otherwise than via the casual loading,[20] although it did not specify how or where this was to occur. Looking at the value of the benefits forgone, the Full Bench took the view that the existing 20 per cent loading covered only the absence of paid leave, while permanent employees had gained access to additional forms of personal leave since the last adjustment to the casual loading, and the other factors listed above remained uncompensated.[21] It determined, therefore, that the casual loading should be increased to 25 per cent.

---

[18] (2002), 110 IR 247 (AIRC) (*Re Metal Award*). See also *QCU v Crown & Ors*, [2001] QIR Comm 43 (QIRC) in which the Queensland Industrial Relations Commission made a general ruling increasing the minimum casual loading in all Queensland State awards to 23%.
[19] See *Re Metal Award* above n 18 at 306, 318.
[20] *Ibid* at 318.
[21] *Ibid* at 319.

In the course of the decision, the Full Bench expressed the view that casual employment 'should not be a cheaper form of labour, nor should it be made more expensive than the main counterpart types of employment'.[22] Actual deterrence of casual employment would be inconsistent with the rationale for its existence,[23] that is, employers' need for labour flexibility. The decision, however, maintained the status of casual employment as at least indirectly a cheaper form of labour, by not addressing the issues of classification, training, and superannuation, or that of ease of termination (at least for the first 12 months). Since employers appear to have been more attracted to these indirect benefits, while being undeterred by the casual loading, it is at least questionable whether a 5 per cent increase in the loading would have any effect on the growth of casual employment (while rendering casual employees marginally better paid but no more secure in their jobs). As noted earlier, it is also questionable whether the full casual loading is actually paid in all cases.

Protection Against Unfair Dismissal—For Some

As discussed previously, most industrial legislation provides access to unfair dismissal provisions for casual employees other than short-term casuals, and some industrial tribunals have taken a narrow view of short-term casual employment, so as to maximise the extent of protection against unfair dismissal for casual employees.[24] Such coverage may be of very little value for at least some casual employees, however. For example, in *Jeanine MacKenzie and RMF Group Pty Ltd*,[25] the applicant was engaged as a casual employee, but was covered by the unfair dismissal provisions in the Queensland Industrial Relations Act since she had been employed on a regular and systematic basis for more than one year. However, under the award, casual employees could be legally terminated on one hour's notice. Given this provision, the Commissioner found that the applicant's termination was not harsh, unjust, or unreasonable.

Parental Leave (and Other Entitlements)—For Some

The New South Wales Industrial Relations Act extends entitlement to parental leave to 'regular casual' employees but not to other casual employees.[26] The

---

[22] *Ibid* at 307.
[23] *Ibid* at 316.
[24] See, eg, *SDA v Dymocks* (2001), 103 IR 390 (NSWIRC).
[25] [2001] QIR Comm 39 (QIRC).
[26] Industrial Relations Act 1996, s 53(1). Section 53(2) defines a 'regular casual' employee as one who 'works for an employer on a regular and systematic basis and who has a reasonable expectation of on-going employment on that basis'. Section 57 of the Act stipulates that parental leave is available only to employees (of whatever kind) who have more than 12 months' continuous service with their employer.

Queensland Industrial Relations Act has also recently been amended to extend family leave, carer's leave, and bereavement leave to 'long-term casual' employees.[27] By contrast, the federal, South Australian, and Western Australian legislation specifically excludes casual employees from access to parental leave,[28] although casual employees covered by federal awards do enjoy the benefit of the 2001 parental leave test case,[29] in which the AIRC extended the award standard parental leave clause for permanent employees to those casual employees 'employed on a regular and systematic basis ... during a period of at least twelve months' who have 'a reasonable expectation of ongoing employment'. A union campaign to extend redundancy protection and severance pay to long-term casuals was rejected in Queensland[30] and at federal level,[31] on the basis that these matters are already covered by the casual loading.

As Owens points out, however:

> In every instance ... these protections operate, through the use of qualifications of continuity and length of service, by assimilating casual workers to the traditional image of the worker with ongoing employment. Incorporated into the legal regime then is the view that it is acceptable to exclude some casual workers from the rights and entitlements which are the marker of the dignity of the worker as a human being.
>
> (2002: 222)

She goes on to argue that the legal divide between short-term and long-term workers is as potentially dangerous as that between permanent and casual employment (Owens, 2002: 230), or, one might add, as the legal divide between employees and independent contractors: '[s]uch a divide creates an opportunity to structure inequality into the workplace by providing business with incentives to organise patterns of employment in ways that avoid the duty to accord workers' rights and entitlements' (Owens, 2002: 230). In this context, it is encouraging to note that the Australian Council of Trade Unions' (the ACTU's) current *Family Provisions Test Case* seeks to extend entitlements to all casual employees,[32] and this campaign has recently resulted in an agreement to allow all casual employees under federal awards access to short periods of unpaid leave to care for family members in situations of

---

[27] Industrial Relations Act 1999, ss 16, 39(2), 40. Section 15A defines a 'long term casual employee' as one who is 'engaged by a particular employer on a regular and systematic basis, for several periods of employment during a period of at least one year'.

[28] Workplace Relations Act 1996 (Cth), sch 14; Fair Work Act 1994 (SA), sch 5; Minimum Conditions of Employment Act 1993 (WA), s 33.

[29] *Re Vehicle Industry Award* (2001), 107 IR 71.

[30] *Queensland Council of Unions v Queensland Chamber of Commerce and Industry Ltd & Ors*, [2003] QIR Comm 383 (QIRC).

[31] *National Union of Workers & Ors v Australian Industry Group & Ors*, (26 March 2004) No PR032004 (AIRC).

[32] *Family Provisions Test Case 2004*, ACTU Outline of Contentions, 30 April 2004.

illness or emergency.[33] But the balance of the claim remains undecided at the time of writing.

Moreover, as with casual loadings and protection against unfair dismissal, the legal situation with regard to parental and family leave for casuals still leaves a problem of enforcement—another potential gap between the law in the books and the law in action. In the case of *Tapuvae v Vetob Pty Ltd t/a Browse About*,[34] the New South Wales Industrial Relations Commission found that a regular casual employee had not been advised of her maternity leave entitlements as required by the legislation, and had been refused work when she wished to return after having her third child. In the circumstances, this refusal constituted a harsh, unjust and unreasonable termination of employment, and the employee was awarded compensation. One wonders, however, how often this factual scenario is repeated without the employee having any knowledge of, or ability to assert, her legal rights.

Permanent Part-Time, rather than Casual Part-Time

Permanent part-time (PPT) work has been perceived by feminist and union advocates as providing higher quality jobs than casual part-time work, since permanent part-timers have pro rata access to the full range of legislative and award benefits denied to casual employees.[35] Based on their studies of PPT employment, however, both Probert and Junor have been highly critical of PPT work as a panacea for women with family responsibilities.

First, the kinds of jobs in which the majority of PPT work is available have, in practice, turned out to be low status and low paid. In terms of Junor's distinction between the 'individual EEO' model and the 'employer initiative' model of PPT work, most PPT jobs conform to the 'employer initiative' model—they are 'not fractions of full-time jobs but different jobs altogether' (Junor, 1998: 91). These jobs enable more efficient time utilisation by service industry employers 'by making possible more sophisticated forms of rostering than can be achieved through casualisation.' They also allow employers to avoid overtime payments, since PPT workers can be asked to work up to full-time hours at ordinary-time rates (Junor, 1998: 86). Importantly, such jobs tend to be 'base grade jobs given to mature-aged women re-entering the workforce' (Junor, 1998: 77). They are 'explicitly

---

[33] ACTU Media Release, 'Two million casual workers win new right to time off for families' (5 July 2004).

[34] (2002), EOC 93-241 (NSWIRC).

[35] Conversion from casual part-time to permanent part-time work is an aspect of the broader strategy of conversion from casual to permanent employment (see Owens, chapter 15 in this volume).

female, graded at entry level and located outside the career track, although maturity and experience [are] recruitment criteria' (Junor, 1998: 80). Similarly, Probert notes that PPT work in the retail industry is identified with married women with children, who are thought to have a different attitude to work, which is used to justify the lack of career structure and low pay (1995: 31–32).

Second, the benefits attaching to PPT work may turn out to be illusory, and the switch from casual to PPT may actually involve losses for the workers involved. According to Junor, 'when employers initiate a switch to permanency in formerly casualised industries, particularly where hours are very flexible, they may be pursuing the removal of casual loadings in exchange for a rather tenuous form of job security' (Junor, 1998: 83). For example, in one agreement between the shop assistants' union and a large supermarket chain, casual workers were converted to part time, with the loss of casual loadings, together with an extended spread of hours attracting the ordinary time rate of pay, hence reducing the incidence of overtime payments. 'According to one account, a 19 year old casual worker … [would] lose about half of his wage packet' (Probert, 1995: 40). In another agreement concerning hotel maids and cleaners, the company (Sheraton) believed it would save money by shifting from casual to PPT employment arrangements, because it would not have to pay the casual loading, it could achieve flexibility by means of rostering, and it gained a more highly trained and multi-skilled workforce than it would have done with casual employees. Time flexibility was accompanied by 'functional flexibility'—total flexibility of jobs and duties, and the total elimination of 'normal' hours and penalty rates (Probert, 1995: 20–21).

This kind of flexible rostering can in fact be extremely family unfriendly, thus negating the supposedly major benefit of part-time employment (Junor, 1998: 84). According to Belinda Probert (1995, 41), the new agreements in many cases greatly increase the range of hours within which a part-timer may be expected to work. Such a range of hours is particularly problematic for women with family responsibilities.' In the Sheraton case, for example, the flexibility requirements disadvantaged women with children, who had to deal with the inflexibilities of childcare arrangements, school hours, and school holidays, and the company ended up with the majority of its workforce aged under 25 (Probert, 1995: 22–23). In light of such outcomes, Probert criticises the assumptions behind the strategy of casual to PPT conversion:

[I]t has generally been assumed that making women's work more like men's work will benefit women, so that reducing casual employment, giving part-timers access to pro-rata benefits and increasing full-time standard employment opportunities are seen as progress. Since, however, women are not like men in their freedom to exploit employment opportunities, these changes may have the unintended consequences of reducing women's access to certain kinds of employment, or at

least of excluding older married women in favour of improving the employment
conditions of younger single women.

(Probert, 1995: 34)

Third, where the potential benefits of PPT for workers are real, employers
are less likely to be interested in providing it. Junor refers to an industrial
campaign on behalf of Technical and Further Education teachers, which
attempted to convert their status from casual to PPT. However, this would
have resulted in considerably increased salary and other costs for TAFE
employers (and hence ultimately for the government), and they refused to
agree to the change (Junor, 1998: 83).

Fourth, under some circumstances, PPT may drive out permanent full-
time as well as, or instead of, casual part-time employment. In 1991, the
former Victorian Industrial Relations Commission sought to discourage
casualisation and increase permanent employment in the retail sector, and
it amended the relevant state award to allow more part-time employment,
to increase the span of normal working hours, and to reduce penalty rates.
Retail employers responded by increasing the number of part-timers at the
expense of full-timers, rather than at the expense of casuals (Probert, 1995:
27–28). This should have been a predictable outcome, according to Probert,
since the casual and part-time workforces in the retail industry have been
long recognised to be 'derived from different and non-substitutable social
groups' (Probert, 1995: 31). In the Sheraton case, where substitution
between casuals and permanent part-timers did occur, management adopted a practice of replacing full-time jobs with two part-time jobs, since part-
timers offered much greater flexibility than full-timers (Probert, 1995: 21).

Thus, PPT appears to represent a 'win–win' solution for both workers
and employers in only a small proportion of cases that conform to Junor's
'individual EEO' model. Otherwise, casual-to-PPT conversion at best substitutes one form of precarious employment for another, and at worst renders jobs inaccessible to their previous incumbents.

Deemed Employees

The remaining set of measures discussed in this section attempts to mitigate
the more deleterious effects of dependent contracting and agency work
arrangements. One strategy in this context is to redefine as employees
groups of workers who would be defined at common law as independent
contractors. For example, in the 1987 *Clothing Textile and Footwear
Award 1982* decision,[36] the AIRC reclassified clothing outworkers as

---

[36] (1987), 19 IR 416 (AIRC).

employees, which brought them under the protection of the award and the other entitlements attached to being an employee (Hunter, 1992; Owens, 1995: 47–48). The current Clothing Trades Award 1999 contains explicit and extensive protections for outworkers, including employer registration, agreed hours of work, and awards rates of pay, and entitlement to paid annual leave (Pittard and Naughton, 2003: 76). The difficulty of enforcing this legal position, however, is widely acknowledged.

Two state Labor governments have included in their industrial relations legislation provisions that deem certain workers to be employees, or enable applications to be brought for groups of workers to be deemed employees, and hence to gain access to legislative and award conditions and benefits attaching to the status of employee.[37] The list of deemed employees under the New South Wales legislation includes milk vendors, bread vendors, cleaners, carpenters, joiners and bricklayers, painters, plumbers, drainers and plasterers, blinds fitters, outworkers in the clothing trades, timber cutters and suppliers, ready-mixed concrete drivers, and Road Transport Authority lorry drivers. It is interesting to note that only two of the specified occupations involve typically women's work—cleaners and clothing outworkers. Home working dependent contractors in other industries are not covered.

The Queensland Industrial Relations Act allows the Full Bench of the Queensland Industrial Relations Commission to make an order declaring a class of persons to be employees.[38] There has only been one reported order made to date, concerning security guards who were engaged as independent contractors on terms falling far short of the entitlements they would have enjoyed even as casual employees under the company's certified agreement.[39] The fact that there have not been more cases under the Queensland legislation may be a reflection of the circumstances under which it can be invoked. Applications may be brought only by a trade union, a state peak council, or the Minister. Many groups of dependent contractors, particularly home workers, are unlikely to come to the attention of any of these entities.

Similarly, in New South Wales, extension of the groups covered by schedule 1 of the Act requires the government to pass regulations, something it is unlikely to do without at least significant union pressure. In other words, traditional mechanisms of enforcement and protection for full-time permanent employees, via unions, are assumed to be effective for unorganised workers in circumstances of deunionisation and enterprise-level bargaining

---

[37] Industrial Relations Act 1996 (NSW), s 5(3), sch 1; Industrial Relations Act 1999 (Qld), ss 5(1)(d), 275.

[38] In *Transport Workers' Union of Australia (Qld Branch) v Australian Document Exchange Pty Ltd*, [2000] QIR Comm 18 (QIRC), a Full Bench held that a 'class of persons' for the purposes of the section could be a class identified by reference to their employer/contractor.

[39] *ALHMWU v Bark Australia*, [2001] QIR Comm 22 (QIRC).

structures that make it difficult for unions to represent their traditional constituents, let alone extend their reach to new ones. In practice, it is likely that unions will act if proposed or actual dependent contracting arrangements threaten the position of current full-time permanent union members. Where this is not the case, deemed employee provisions are unlikely to have any effect.

Classification Cases

While deemed employee provisions represent an attempt (if ineffective) to tackle dependent contracting at a systemic level, there has also been a considerable amount of litigation over the question of whether, in the circumstances of a particular case, workers should be classified at common law as employees or as independent contractors. (There have also been some classification cases concerning the question of whether employees are casual or permanent[40]—interestingly involving women workers, whereas independent contractor cases have tended to involve male workers.)

The employee versus independent contractor cases often involve convoluted reasoning as the court attempts to reach its preferred result, and the outcomes of these cases are highly unpredictable. For example, the same bicycle couriers have been held by one court to be independent contractors and by another court to be employees;[41] agency workers in some cases have been classified as employees, while in others, agency workers with similar contracts have been classified as independent contractors.[42] The way in which the issue is framed, and the court's policy choices in relation to that framing, appear to have a large bearing on the decision. This legal indeterminacy renders the litigation strategy risky and unreliable, as it is impossible to predict which way the court will jump in any given case.

Unfair Contract Provisions

The federal, New South Wales and Queensland industrial relations legislation contains provisions allowing (in)dependent contractors to challenge contracts whose terms are unfair.[43] Again, these provisions are little used,

---

[40] See, eg, *Australian Municipal, Administrative, Clerical and Services Union v Auscript* (1998), 83 IR 38; *Julia Ross Personnel and Rebecca Wain*, [2001] QIC 8 (QIC).

[41] *Vabu Pty Ltd v Commissioner of Taxation* (1996), 81 IR 150 (NSWCA); *Hollis v Vabu Pty Ltd* (2001), 207 CLR 21.

[42] See, eg, *Forstaff Pty Ltd v Chief Commissioner of State Revenue*, [2004] NSWSC 573 (employees); *Building Workers Industrial Union of Australia v Odco Pty Ltd*, (1991), 29 FCR 104 and *Odco Pty Ltd v Accident Compensation Commission*, [1990] VR 178 (VSC) (independent contractors).

[43] Workplace Relations Act 1996 (Cth), s 127B; Industrial Relations Act 1996 (NSW), ss 105–106; Industrial Relations Act 1999 (Qld), s 276.

and such cases as have been brought have tended to be confined to male-dominated occupations such as truck driving, taxi driving, and insurance agency work.[44] Indeed, the federal jurisdiction incorporates a public/private distinction, excluding work for the private and domestic purposes of the principal.[45] Another deterrent is the fact that, under the federal legislation, applications must be brought in the Federal Court, although the New South Wales legislation allows for applications to the Industrial Relations Commission.

It appears that unfair contract cases are often brought after termination of the contract, perhaps indicating that contractors are unaware of their rights when performing work under the contract but tend to seek legal advice if it is terminated, or perhaps indicating an awareness that attempting to bring a case while a contract is on foot would soon result in termination. Nevertheless, it seems that, in some cases, contractors attempt to use the unfair contract jurisdiction as a de facto unfair dismissal remedy. This can involve some straining of the legislative provisions, which are intended to deal with the terms of the contract, not the manner in which it was terminated, and further illustrates the inequitable consequences of the legal distinction between employees and independent contractors (Brooks, 1994).

Thus, it can be seen that the various attempts via legislation or litigation to reverse the trend to precarious employment or to mitigate its effects have had limited success at best. At worst, as in the case of some casual-to-PPT conversions, they have been distinctly counterproductive.

CONCLUSION

This chapter has identified several factors interacting to produce the particular kinds of precarious employment now evident in the Australian labour market, including the notable increase in casual employment from the late 1980s to mid-1990s. Those factors are: the nature of the economy and economic policy—including job creation policies that give no emphasis to the quality of the jobs created; the state of the labour market; labour law and regulation (conceived broadly); and gendered practices both in paid employment and in the home. Attempting to change legal norms while the other factors remain constant can only have a limited effect. Even if legislation

---

[44] See, eg, *Buchmueller v Allied Express Transport Pty Ltd.* (1999), 88 IR 465 (FCA); *Jordan v Aerial Taxi Cabs Co-operative Society Ltd* (2001), 108 IR 263 (FCA); *Harding v EIG Ansvar Ltd* (2000), 95 IR 349 (FCA). The recent NSW case of *Masri v Nenny Santoso*, [2004] NSWIR Comm 108, however, did involve the recovery of a large sum of unpaid wages to an Indonesian housemaid.

[45] Workplace Relations Act 1996 (Cth), s 127A(1)(a)(ii).

were enacted that extended a minimum set of conditions and benefits to all workers, regardless of their status as permanent, casual, long-term, short-term, employees or contractors, pressures to minimise labour costs and maximise flexibility would still result in loopholes in the safety net being found and exploited, for example, by converting full-time jobs to part-time jobs, by extending the use of home workers, or by increased recourse to agency arrangements, including offshore agencies. Moreover, such a legislative outcome is highly unlikely from any Australian government in the foreseeable future.

Of the four factors identified, the one most likely to change in the medium term in Australia is the state of the labour market. Gender segregation in the labour market and the gender division of labour in the family have proved remarkably stable and resilient in the face of more than three decades of social change around the status of women. However, the demands of flexibility in the labour market appear to have had an adverse impact on the important matter of labour reproduction. Thus, the country faces significant demographic change, as the post-war 'baby boomer' generation starts to retire and the size of the working-age population shrinks. This chapter has discussed the fine line between precarious employment and unemployment for many Australian workers, and the limited choices available to low-skilled service workers, particularly women with family responsibilities. By contrast, conditions of relative labour scarcity would provide increased choices and bargaining power for workers, and may do more to reduce precarious employment than legal tinkering around the edges.

Part VI

The Challenge of Flexibility

14

Flexibility and Security, Working Time, and Work-Family Policies

SUSANNE D BURRI*

INTRODUCTION

S INCE THE END of the 1990s, the Dutch social partners have developed policies to enhance the flexibility of the labour market in order to improve competitiveness in a context of increasing internationalisation and globalisation. How to realise the flexibility of working time, of employment contracts, and of working conditions without giving up employment security and employees' rights, and thus how to reconcile divergent interests of employers and employees, became the main dilemma within the debate known as 'flexibility and security'. An important issue in this debate was from the very beginning how to realise a better work–family balance in view of women's increased labour market participation. Traditionally, women's share in employment has been small in the Netherlands, only growing strongly during the last couple of decades. The female employment rate (66 per cent) is still lower than the male employment rate (81 per cent).[1]

The Netherlands has a very high rate of part-time work, nearly one in two Dutch employees (45 per cent) held a part-time job in 2003. Part-time work is the standard working pattern for women (74 per cent work part time), but also a relatively high percentage of men work part time (22 per cent). For a number of years, the rates of part-time employment in the Netherlands have been the highest of all the countries in the European

---

* This chapter includes materials from the following publications: Burri, Opitz, and Veldman, 2003; and Burri, 2005.

[1] In 1992 the female employment rate in the Netherlands was 52% and the male employment rate, 76%. In 2003 the EU (15 member states) female employment rate was 56% (in 1992: 50%), the EU male employment rate, 73% (in 1992: 73%); (European Commission, 2004: 238, 255). These figures also include minor part-time jobs. In statistics provided by the Dutch Central Office for Statistics (CBS), jobs of less than 12 hours per week are not included.

Union.[2] No wonder that the Dutch economy has been described as the first part-time economy in the world (Visser, 2002). While women are over-represented in part-time work and casual work, temporary work and fixed-term work are less gendered.

The diverging demands of flexibility of employees and employers are not easy to reconcile. A better balance of work and care requires possibilities to adjust working time to the personal needs of employees during their career, flexible working time schedules and leave facilities. This also demands high-quality jobs and employment security, requirements that are not fulfilled with precarious jobs. In turn, employers are faced with demands of fluctu-ating or continuous production requiring a flexible deployment of the workforce, but with predictable working schedules. The Dutch Parliament has enacted several Acts with a view to improving the working conditions of employees with flexible employment contracts,[3] while at the same time trying not to disregard the needs of employers. Under this legislation the possibilities for adjusting one's working time have been enhanced and employees with family responsibilities can take various forms of leave such as parental leave. This chapter provides an overview of this legislation assessing it from a gender perspective.

EMPLOYMENT PATTERNS FOR MEN AND WOMEN IN THE NETHERLANDS

In the Netherlands most young men and women work full time at the begin-ning of their careers. The standard employment pattern for men is that they keep on working full time. If they work part time it is at the beginning of their career, combining work and study, or before retiring. The working-time pattern for women during their career is quite different. The imbalance in the division of paid and unpaid work between men and women becomes particularly manifest when employees become parents. When assessing the impact of parenthood on the employment rate of men and women, the employment rate of men increases while that of women decreases. Women either (try to) reduce their working time or (temporarily or permanently) interrupt their career. In the Netherlands, one out of ten (10 per cent of) working women give up their job when they have their first child, and one out of two (56 per cent) reduce their working time. Only one out of ten (13 per cent of) men quit or reduce their working time when their first child is

---

[2] The average part-time employment rate in the EU (15 member states) is 19%, the female part-time employment rate is 34%, and the male part-time employment rate is 7% (European Commission, 2004: 238).

[3] In the Netherlands precarious working relationships are usually called 'flexible working relationships', which are defined by the CBS as jobs without a fixed working time.

born (Sociaal Cultureel Planbureau (SCP) and Centraal Bureau voor de Statistiek (CBS), 2004: 100).

Traditionally, the breadwinner model has been dominant in the Netherlands among couples with children. The man worked full time during his whole career, while the woman took care of the household and the children. In 2000, nearly a third of all couples with children still had only one earner.[4] In the majority of couples with children, the man works full time and the woman works part time: this is called the one-and-a-half earner model.[5] Among couples with children it is quite uncommon for both men and women to work full time.[6] The number of hours spent on unpaid work is decreasing, both for men and women. But women still spend nearly twice as many hours taking care of the household, children, relatives, and so on.[7] For mothers, having children almost always means either the end of their career, a career interruption, or reduced working time. This pattern is less pronounced for women with a higher education, most of whom keep working with reduced working hours.[8]

Just as in other EU countries, the sex-segregation of the part-time labour market is very strong. Part-time jobs in the Netherlands are common in the health and education sector and in social services. Very few part-time jobs are found in industry, construction, and transport. The segregation of the part-time labour market between men and women is also strong, both horizontally and vertically. In higher and specialised functions, part-time work is still not common, especially in the private sector.

NON-STANDARD FORMS OF EMPLOYMENT

Part-Time Work

Part-time work is an accepted phenomenon in the Netherlands. The main characteristic of part-time work is that the (weekly) working time is less

---

[4] The one-earner model applied to 38% of couples without children in 1992, and to 29% in 2000. For couples with children the rates were 52% in 1992 and 32% in 2000 (Eurostat, 2002a).

[5] This model applied to 29% of all couples without children and 53% of all couples with children in 2000 (Eurostat, 2002a).

[6] This model applies to 38% of all couples without children and to 11% of all couples with children. In only 2% of the couples with children do both the man and the woman work part time. And in only 1% of couples with children does the woman work full time and the man part time (Eurostat, 2002a).

[7] In 2000, women spent on average 35.5 hours a week doing unpaid work, and men 20 hours a week (SCP and CBS, 2004: 93).

[8] Of higher-educated working women, 11% give up their job, 54% reduce their working time and 36% keep the same working time or extend it (SCP and CBS, 2004: 101).

than the usual working time.[9] Shift work and seasonal employment are generally not considered to be part-time work. The European Directive on Part-Time Work[10] defines the part-time employee as: 'an employee whose normal hours of work, calculated on a weekly basis or on an average over a period of employment of up to one year, are less than the average hours of work of a comparable full-time worker.' The collectively agreed average usual working hours in the Netherlands is 37 hours a week. The usual number of working hours for full-time employees is 38.9 hours, for part-time employees, 20.9 hours a week.[11] Contrary to most EU member states, where part-time work consist of jobs of more than 20 hours a week, half of the part-time employees in the Netherlands work less than 20 hours a week (Franco and Winquist, 2002). Due to the high levels of part-time employment, the equivalent in full-time jobs for women is quite low: 42 per cent, compared to 73 per cent for men (European Commission, 2004: 255).

The term 'part-time worker' does not provide any information on the nature of the employment contract or the number of hours worked. A part-time worker may work on a permanent or a fixed-term contract or do casual work. In practice, there is a huge difference in working conditions between stand-by contracts for a few hours a month and permanent employment contracts with nearly full-time work. To both types of workers, the current definitions of part-time work apply. The quality of part-time employment varies, depending on the number of hours worked, the nature of the employment contract, the flexibility of working hours, and the influence of the employees on working time schedules, and whether the part-time job is taken up voluntarily or not.

In the Netherlands, one out of three employees (30 per cent) works overtime (that is, more hours than stipulated in the individual employment contract), but fewer part-time employees work overtime than full-time employees. About 10 per cent of all employees working overtime are not paid (European Commission, 2003b: 144). Most part-time employees in the Netherlands voluntarily work less than the usual working time. But one out of four employees works part time involuntarily (European Commission, 2003b: 145). Education or training, family or personal responsibilities, and illness or disability are the main reasons given for having a part-time job.

The differences in working time between men and women influence incomes. Most men and women in the Netherlands have their own income. Indeed, in 2001, 71 per cent of all women and 79 per cent of all men had

---

[9] Less than 35 hours a week according to the definition of the CBS.

[10] EC Council Directive 97/81/EEC of 15 December 1997 concerning the Framework Agreement on Part-time Work concluded by UNICE, CEEP, and the ETUC, [1998] OJ L 14/9.

[11] The collectively agreed average number of hours of work in the EU is 38.5 hours a week. The average usual number of working hours for full-time workers in the EU is 40 hours, and that for part-time workers 18.8 hours a week (European Commission, 2003b: 143).

their own income (SCP and CBS, 2004: 134). But the average income of women amounts to only half of that of men (51 per cent). This is due to the high number of women working part time, and also to the fact that the average remuneration of women is lower than that of men. The gross hourly pay of women in 2002 was 81 per cent of that of men (SCP and CBS, 2004: 140). The difference in pay between women and men is highest amongst those working full time, and is less pronounced between those working part time. However, it is nearly non-existent between men and women working under flexible employment contracts. In 2002, the gross hourly pay for women working full time was €15.39, for men €19.07; for women working part time €15.24, for men €16.72; and for women working on flexible employment contracts €10.74, for men €11.05 (SCP and CBS, 2004: 140). Most women are still not financially independent. Only 41 per cent of all women aged between 15 and 65 years had an income higher than 70 per cent of the net minimum salary. In comparison, nearly seven out of ten men enjoy economic independence (SCP and CBS, 2004: 149).

Flexible Working Relations

The flexibility of the labour market increased in the 1990s, but recently the number of workers on flexible, or precarious, employment contracts has slightly decreased. This is particularly the case for casual work, such as work on demand or stand-by contracts. In 2002, more than eight out of ten employees had a permanent, either full-time or part-time, employment relationship, one out of ten workers was self-employed, and 7 per cent had a flexible working relationship, such as temporary work, a fixed-term contract or casual work (SCP and CBS, 2004: 77).

The term 'flexible working relationship', or 'flexible contract' or 'atypical contract', is usually applied to all those contracts and working relationships that differ from regular work on a permanent full-time contract. In the Netherlands, just as many men as women work in flexible working relationships other than part-time work: these include temporary work (more than a third), casual work (a quarter) and fixed-term contracts (41 per cent). But women are much more likely than men to have casual work with a share of 66 per cent (SCP and CBS, 2002: 81). Most workers with a flexible working relationship have that kind of contract because it corresponds to their availability for the labour market. However, one out of four employees with a flexible employment contract would prefer a permanent contract (Van der Toren, Evers, and Commissaris, 2002: 377). The reasons why employers make use of flexible working relations are to overcome insecurity, to substitute in cases where another employee is ill, or to respond to peaks during the production process. Employers also make use of flexible working relations to select new personnel.

For years, an appropriate balance between flexibility and job security has been seen as vital to enhance competitiveness in the EU, as well as in the Netherlands. Such a balance has been described by the term 'flexicurity'. Improving the quality of work is of great concern in relation to the flexibility of the workforce. In order to improve the working conditions of employees with flexible employment contracts, an Act on Flexibility and Security came into force in 1999.[12] This Act has reinforced the position of employees with stand-by contracts (a form of casual work). It has broadened the possibilities for prolonging fixed-term contracts, but at the same time limited the possibilities for successive fixed-term contracts. If certain conditions are fulfilled, a fixed-term employment contract becomes a permanent contract. Furthermore, two Acts have been enacted with a view to improving the working conditions of employees working on part-time and fixed-term contracts. Differences based on working time and/or between fixed-term and permanent contracts are prohibited, unless they can be objectively justified. Evaluations have been carried out in order to measure the effects of some of this legislation in practice.

LEGISLATION TO IMPROVE WORKING CONDITIONS

Flexibility and Security

The aim of the Dutch Act on Flexibility and Security is to contribute to a better balance on the labour market, in which flexibility and security go hand in hand. The law is based on an agreement at national level between the bipartite Joint Industrial Labour Council. In this forum, national employers' organisations and unions hold top-level consultations. Where agreement is reached, they can recommend that the social partners insert provisions in collective agreements at sector or enterprise level consistent with the national agreement. This is significant because in the Netherlands most employees are covered by collective agreements, even if they are not members of a union. Only one out of four employees belonged to a union in 2000 (Van Cruchten and Kuijpers, 2003). Some collective agreements are generally applicable; some apply to certain undertakings or to a specific sector.

The Act on Flexibility and Security enables the unions and the employers' organisations to conclude other collective agreements on some points and thus derogate from the national legal provisions. Most collective agreements provisions have been amended in order to comply with the new legislation. To date, only a few collective agreements provide more flexible arrangements.

---

[12] *Wet flexibiliteit en zekerheid*, Stb 1998, 300 (Act on Flexibility and Security). Note that all Dutch legislation in force can be found at: www.wetten.nl (in Dutch).

A collective agreement on temporary work has been adopted with specific rules that are declared to be generally binding.

The main changes which the Act on Flexibility and Security has introduced concern, in the first place, two rebuttable presumptions relating to the employment contract and the number of hours worked. Two new Articles have been inserted in the Civil Code (CC).

Article 7:610a CC stipulates:

> a person who, for the benefit of another person, performs work for remuneration by such other person for three consecutive months, weekly or for not less than twenty hours per month is presumed to perform such work pursuant to a contract of employment.

Article 7:610b CC reads:

> Where a contract of employment has lasted for at least three months, the contracted work in any month is presumed to amount to the average working period per month over the three preceding months.

An evaluation of the Act on Flexibility and Security shows that in practice there has been little litigation in the courts concerning these presumptions (Van der Toren, Evers, and Commissaris. 2002: vi). Nevertheless, on this point the law has had a preventative effect as employment contracts are now formulated more clearly. Furthermore, one out of ten employees working in fact structurally more working hours than agreed has invoked the presumption before the employer. This provision means that employees working more (or fewer) hours than stipulated in their employment contract have a legal tool to get the number of working hours indicated in the contract matched with the hours they really work. Conflicts about how many hours have been worked may therefore be prevented. Nevertheless, most employees have not invoked the provision because they did not want to be burdened with the duties corresponding to an employment contract.

The second major change that the Act has brought about is that the employer now has an obligation clearly to determine the hours of work of some groups of casual workers.

Article 7:628a CC reads:

> Where a period of less than 16 hours of work per week has been agreed and the times during which the work must be performed have not been fixed or, if the working time has not or not clearly been fixed, the employee shall be entitled to the remuneration to which he would have been entitled if he had performed work for three hours for every period of less than three hours in which he performed work.

Research shows that four out of ten employers offer stand-by contracts with a minimum of three working hours for every period of work (Van der Toren,

Evers and Commissaris, 2002: vii, 48). Employers have often replaced stand-by contracts by part-time contracts or fixed term contracts.[13] According to a third of employees still working on stand-by contracts without fixed working time, the provision regarding the minimum of working hours for every period of work is not yet applied in practice, perhaps because employers offering such contracts are still not aware of this provision.

Third, employers have more possibilities for prolonging fixed-term contracts. On the other hand, the signing of successive fixed-term contracts is limited (Article 7:668a CC). When fixed-term employment contracts have succeeded one another over a period of 36 months or more at intervals of, at most, three months, the last employment contract shall be deemed to have been entered into for an indeterminate term. This is also the case if more than three fixed-term employment contracts have succeeded one another at intervals of not more than three months. But there is no conversion to a permanent contract when a contract of employment is entered into for not more than three months which is immediately consecutive to a contract of employment entered into for 36 months or more between the same parties. Derogation to the detriment of the employee is possible by collective agreement. Most collective agreements have included the new legal provision on successive fixed-term contracts, with some providing more possibilities for flexible arrangements and others less (Van der Toren, Evers and Commissaris, 2002: vii). Since the Act came into force the number of fixed-term employment contracts has increased, while stand-by contracts have decreased. Many fixed-term contracts have been prolonged, and more permanent contracts have been agreed upon.[14] Fixed-term contracts are nowadays more often used as a period of probation (the legally fixed period of probation is a maximum of two months). In only 10 per cent of all cases do employers interrupt successive fixed-term contracts for a period of more than three months in order to avoid a permanent contract. The effect of the legislation seems to have strengthened the position of employees with successive employment contracts for a long period of time. In cases where the employee has been offered a permanent contract, this means, of course, an improvement especially with regard to employment protection. It remains to be seen to what extent social partners will make use of the possibility to derogate from the legal provisions in collective agreements with a negative impact on the employment conditions of workers on flexible contracts. The protection afforded by the Act on Flexibility and Security therefore depends on the

---

[13] After the Act on Flexibility and Security came into force on 1 January 1999, 25,000 stand-by contracts were ended in 2000, and 93,000 stand-by contracts were replaced by a temporary, part-time contract, or fixed term contract (Ministry of Social Affairs, news release no 00/160).

[14] Since the Act came into force, a permanent employment contract was agreed upon after the end of a fixed-term contract in 217,000 cases. Some 86,000 fixed-term employment contracts were not prolonged (Ministerie van SZW, 2004).

content of provisions in collective agreements. To date, it seems that the legislation has strengthened the position of most casual workers and workers on successive fixed-term employment contracts.

To some extent, the position of temporary workers has been strengthened as well. Temporary workers have an employment contract with an employment agency (Article 7:690 CC). Article 7:668a CC on successive fixed-term contracts applies to temporary workers only after they have performed work for more than 26 weeks. During this first period successive fixed-term contracts are allowed. After that period the legal provision concerning successive fixed-term contracts and fixed-term contracts of more than three years applies in principle. But unions and employers' organisations have agreed on less strict rules in the collective agreement on temporary work that is declared to be generally binding. According to this collective agreement, temporary workers are entitled to a permanent contract after longer periods of time than the legal provision stipulates. In many cases, successive temporary contracts are thus still possible. A positive effect of the Act on Flexibility and Security is that more temporary workers are now building up pensions than before. A proposal for an EC Directive on temporary work has been launched by the European Commission and is still under discussion.[15]

The Dutch Act on Flexibility and Security has—together with different collective agreements—broadened the possibilities for employers to make use of flexible working relations, more specifically the prolongation of fixed-term contracts. Since the new legislation came into force, permanent or fixed-term, part-time contracts have been substituted for casual work. In general, fixed-term and part-time employment contracts offer better employment conditions than casual work, and in that sense the Act has strengthened the position of workers with flexible employment contracts, reducing the precariousness of such contracts. For workers with stand-by contracts the effect of this legislation is sometimes a decrease in the flexibility of working time going hand in hand with increasing income security. Casual workers may sometimes perceive the decreased individual working time flexibility as a disadvantage. This could explain why only a quarter of all flexible workers assess the effects of the legislation as positive (Van der Toren, Evers, and Commissaris, 2002: xiii).

Prohibition of Discrimination against Part-Time Workers

All member states of the EU have to implement the principle of equal treatment between part-time and full-time workers in their national law according

---

[15] Amended Proposal for a Directive of the European Parliament and the Council on Working Conditions for temporary workers, CELEX 52002PC0701, (COM 2002, 701).

to the EC Directive on part-time work.[16] Furthermore, the development of the concept of indirect discrimination in relation to part-time work in the case-law of the European Court of Justice has meant an improvement in the working conditions of part-time workers, especially in relation to access to occupational pensions (Tobler, 1999; Burri, 2000; Traversa, 2003).

For years, the Dutch policy on part-time work has had a twofold aim: to improve the working conditions of part-time workers; and to stimulate part-time work. Since 1996, a specific law prohibits differences based on working time, unless such differences are objectively justified.[17] The points of departure in this regulation are the differentiation of working time—the full-timer is not always the point of reference—and high-quality part-time work.

According to the Dutch legal provisions, the employer (or the public service) may not differentiate between employees on the basis of a difference in working time in the conditions under which a contract is agreed upon, continued, or terminated, unless the difference is objectively justified. The test to decide whether a difference is objectively justified is the same as in the case of indirect sex discrimination. The aim has to be legitimate and the means of achieving that aim have to be appropriate and necessary.

The Dutch legislator has provided guidance as to which treatment has to be applied to various conditions in order to comply with the law. The starting point is that differentiated treatment is required. The nature of the treatment depends on the working conditions at stake. The application of the principle of *pro rata temporis* will mostly not amount to a breach of this law: pay, for instance, has to be proportionate to the hours worked. But sometimes the same treatment may be required. Compensation for travel costs, for example, should be identical for full-timers and part-timers: that is, the real costs have to be paid.

This law only concerns working conditions, just as in the EC Directive. In Dutch law, there are still some exclusions for specific groups of part-time workers in statutory social security schemes. For example, persons working within the household of a private person for less than three days a week do not receive some benefits. General exclusions of part-time workers in legislation have been abolished. A recent evaluation of the law shows that part-time contracts for a few hours did not fall within the scope of collective agreements in only 2 per cent of those agreements that were the subject to the research (Arbeidsinspectie, 2004; De Geus, 2004b). Instead of general exclusions, more specific provisions have been adopted in sectorial collective agreements applying a differentiated treatment to different groups of

---

[16] EC Council Directive 97/81/EC, above n 10.

[17] *Wet verbod van onderscheid naar arbeidsduur, Stb* 1996, 391(Act on the prohibition of a distinction based on working time). See Art 7:648 CC, and Art 125g of the Public Servants Act.

workers. The vast majority of part-time workers thus enjoy the rights laid down in collective agreements, but some rights may be specific or restricted. Research shows that employers, employees, and works councils generally support the equal treatment of part-time workers, irrespective of the hours worked. There is now more clarity concerning the principle of equal pay and equal treatment in relation to part-time work in the field of working conditions. Since the law came into force, two out of five employers have adapted primary or secondary working conditions of part-timers in order to comply with the law.

Prohibition of Discrimination against Workers with Fixed Term Contracts

The EC Directive on fixed-term work[18] was implemented in the Dutch Civil Code in 2002.[19] An employer may not differentiate working conditions between employees based on the temporary or non-temporary character of an employment contract, unless such a difference is objectively justified. This Act is modelled on the Act on Equal Treatment of Part-time Workers. A similar provision applies to civil servants.[20]

The Dutch Equal Treatment Commission is competent to investigate whether there is a breach of the provisions on equal treatment of part-time workers and workers with fixed-term contracts. The Commission issues opinions on the application of the principle of equal treatment on request. The procedure is expeditious, easily accessible and free of charge. Research by the Equal Treatment Commission shows that employers and organisations generally follow its opinions and adapt the working conditions or policy at stake in order to comply with the principle of equal treatment.

DIFFERENTIATION OF WORKING TIME DURING LIFETIME

The work–family policies of the Dutch government are aimed at the so-called 'combination scenario'. Men and women should both be able to combine

---

[18] EC Council Directive 1999/70/EC of 28 June 1999 concerning the Framework Agreement on Fixed-term Work concluded by ETUC, UNICE and CEEP, [1999] OJ L 175/43.

[19] *Wet tot uitvoering van richtlijn 1999/70/EG betreffende de raamovereenkomst voor arbeidsovereenkomsten voor bepaalde tijd, Stb* 2002, 560 (Act transposing Directive 99/70/EC regarding the framework agreement on fixed-term contracts). See Art 7:649 CC.

[20] *Wijziging Ambtenarenwet in verband met de invoering van een verbod van onderscheid in arbeidsvoorwaarden op grond van het al dan niet tijdelijk karakter van de aanstelling, Stb* 2004, 88 (Amendment of the Public Servants Act in connection with the introduction of a prohibition to make a distinction in the working conditions based on the temporary or not temporary character of the appointment).

paid work and care activities, and both work in part-time jobs of about 32 hours a week on average during their career. Therefore, men should work less, while women should work more hours than is actually the case. Some tasks would be contracted out. Part of this strategy is that, on the one hand, part-time work should be more attractive to both men and women, widespread in all sectors of the labour market and in all functions. In addition, possibilities for adjusting working time to the changing needs of workers during their lifetime should increase. In the Netherlands, legislation has been adopted to ease the differentiation of working time and to facilitate a better balance of work and family life.

In the first place, the Working Time Adjustment Act came into force in 2000. Employees and civil servants have been given the possibility of reducing or extending their working time, unless serious business reasons preclude this. The employer has furthermore an obligation to take the personal circumstances of workers into consideration when establishing individual working-time patterns, as far as this can be reasonably demanded. An Act aimed at facilitating the reconciliation of work and family life entered into force in 2001, according different kinds of (partially) paid or unpaid leave, such as short-term care leave, to workers with family responsibilities. A statutory right to parental leave had already been introduced in 1991. The working time preferences of workers in the Netherlands reflect the need for part-time work, but surveys show that labour market opportunities for part-time work do not yet match actual preferences (Fagan and Warren, 2001; De Geus, 2004b).

Working Time Preferences

Recent research shows that one out of four workers have wanted to reduce their working time during the last two-and-a -half years (MuConsult, 2003: V). More men (27 per cent) than women (24 per cent) wanted to work less. The main reasons for both men and women wanting to work less are to have more time for family responsibilities or household duties in their private lives (34 per cent) or to pursue hobbies and other private activities (30 per cent). Most employees wish to work either eight hours (37 per cent) or four hours (48 per cent) less per week. In 80 per cent of cases the desire to work fewer hours was combined with preferences concerning how the hours are spread over the days of the week.

Over the last two-and-a-half years, women (19 per cent) more often than men (12 per cent) wanted to work more hours per week. In almost 60 per cent of cases, these employees invoked financial reasons to explain their desire; 38 per cent wanted to increase the working time by eight hours a week, 33 per cent by one day a week. Half wanted to work more hours during the same number of days, and half wanted to work more days. These results roughly correspond with earlier research (Burri, 2000: 43–49, Fagan and Warren, 2001; Tijdens, 2002).

Larger companies can in general offer more opportunities to change working hours than smaller ones. In traditionally male sectors (industry, building and construction, agriculture), the possibilities for changing working hours are more limited. Small and large businesses in which part-time work is already very common offer the most opportunities for changing working hours (MuConsult, 2003: V).

Only half of the employees who wish to reduce their working time inform their employer of this. Most employees consider the financial consequences to be too great (60 per cent). Other reasons given for not requesting a working-time reduction are that employees expect that their request will be turned down by the employer (23 per cent) or believe that their position in the company will be jeopardised (17 per cent). Three quarters of the employees wishing to extend their working time had informed their employer of this (MuConsult, 2003: V–VI).

Working Time Adjustment Act

In the Netherlands, the adjustment of working time has been a matter of political debate concerning employment strategies and equal opportunities since 1993 (Burri, 2001; Burri, Opitz, and Veldman, 2003). As the right to part-time work was by no means politically uncontested, it took several Bills and a change of government before the Working Time Adjustment Act was finally enacted by Parliament at the beginning of 2000.[21] Since 1994, most Dutch public servants have had the right to reduce their working time, unless serious interests of the service preclude it. For them, the Working Time Adjustment Act is chiefly of interest because of the possibility of extending working time.

The starting point of the Working Time Adjustment Act is that the flexibility of working time can meet the needs of both undertakings and workers. The Act has three main objectives: first, to widen the workforce by making better use of the potential of part-time workers; second, to facilitate the reconciliation of work and family life; and third, to create possibilities for more differentiation in working time. A request for a working time reduction does not necessarily have to relate to family responsibilities, as the underlying reasons why a worker wants a change of working time do not have to be mentioned.

The Working Time Adjustment Act grants employees a restricted statutory right to reduce or extend their individual working time resulting in a

---

[21] *Wet aanpassing arbeidsduur, Stb* 2000, 114 (Working Time Adjustment Act).

change to the employment contract. The Act does not provide a right to a temporary reduction of working time. Employers who employ less than ten employees are exempt from the main obligations of the legislation. These small businesses have to determine their own rules regarding the employee's right to an adjustment of working time. The provision on the extension of working time is not imperative, derogations in collective agreements are allowed. However, no derogations putting at stake the right to reduce working time are permitted, except in the case of small businesses.

The Requirement for Lodging and Handling a Request

A worker has to have been employed by the employer from whom a request for an adjustment of working time is made for at least one year before such an adjustment may take place. The request has to be submitted at least four months before the beginning of the intended change in working time, and it must stipulate the intended number of working hours per week, the distribution of hours over the week, and when the adjustment is to take effect. The request may concern only the worker's own position or function, but the right to change working time is not limited to the employer's same establishment. A request may be made only once every two years, after the employer has agreed or opposed the request. But if circumstances change— for example, a vacancy becomes available—then the employer has to consider a renewed request as a good employer.[22] The employer has three months to grant or refuse the request. If the employer does not answer, then the employment contract is changed in accordance with the request. If more than one worker requests an adjustment of working time, the applications have to be considered in the order in which they are received. After a request has been made, the employer is obliged, after consulting the employee, to grant the requested change in working time so far as it concerns the desired number of working hours and the date of commencement, unless this is precluded by serious business reasons.

Granting or Rejecting a Request

The Act stipulates reasons which may be considered to be serious business reasons, but this list is not restrictive. In the case of a reduction of working time, serious business reasons would arguably be at stake when such reduction would lead to serious problems for the organisation with regard to filling the post for the resulting hours that become vacant, ensuring security, or scheduling the work. In the case of an extension of working time, serious business reasons would be at stake at least if the extension of hours would

---

[22] See above n 17, Art 7:611 CC. The legal concept of 'a good employer' is enshrined in Art 7:611.

lead to financial or organisational problems, or if there was a shortage of available work or an insufficient personnel budget.

During the debates in Parliament, a great deal of attention was paid to what could be considered to be serious business reasons. The employer cannot merely state that the request has been refused because of serious business reasons. The employer has to justify the refusal with concrete data, including information on efforts to accommodate the working time change, and an indication as to why the change is absolutely not possible. It is a burdensome test. The employer has to show a willingness to grant the request. No definition has been given, but some examples were discussed during parliamentary proceedings. If a shortage of candidates on the labour market prevents securing a replacement, and the hours remaining in case of a reduction of working time could not be filled, then this would constitute a serious business reason. The continuity of service is in itself not such a reason, unless specific circumstances are at stake. Obviously, a manager cannot fulfil his or her tasks working only one day a week. On the other hand, working five days a week is not always necessary. Scheduling problems may arise: for instance, in schools, too many teachers alternately teaching the same class is generally detrimental to the interests of the school.

If the request is granted, the employer determines the times when the worker has to work during the week in conformity with the wishes of the worker. The employer may amend the distribution of working hours, and the worker's wishes will be overridden if this amendment is reasonable. The burden of proof in this respect rests upon the employer. The employer has to justify, in written terms, any refusal or a compromise compared to the originally requested working time change or distribution of hours.

The criterion of serious business reasons is stricter than the test of reasonableness, which applies to the distribution of working hours over the week. In this respect, the employer has more discretion. This may be problematic in the case of a reduction of working hours in order to reconcile work and family life, for a fragmented allocation of hours over the week could hamper, or even rule out, taking care of family duties. The employer cannot terminate an employment contract or decide not to prolong a fixed-term contract due to the fact that an employee has requested an adjustment of working time.

Working Time Adjustments in Practice

An evaluation of the Working Time Adjustment Act has recently been carried out and discussed in Parliament (MuConsult, 2003; De Geus, 2004b). The main conclusion of the Dutch government is that the adjustment of working time has become easier since the Act entered into force. In practice most requests are handled by mutual consent between the employer and the employee, without having to resort explicitly to the law. Nevertheless, the

Act provides the framework within which agreements on working time adjustment can be realised. The Working Time Adjustment Act is not sufficiently well known among employers with small businesses and employees, and this is especially true in relation to the right of employees to extend working time.

Employers and employees agree that there has been an increase in requests for working time adjustment. Five out of six large businesses and one out of six small businesses have received requests to reduce working time. More than half of the requests for a reduction of working time were granted, and one in ten was partially granted. The partial grants almost always concerned the issue of the number of hours that the employee wished to work. In practice, the distribution of hours is hardly ever an issue. A quarter of the requests were rejected, generally in conformity with the serious business reasons listed in the Working Time Adjustment Act. One in ten employees requesting a reduction of working time had not received an answer from the employer at the time of the research, but almost all employees who had received a response from the employer received it within the legally prescribed period of three months (MuConsult, 2003: VI).

Requests to extend working time are granted less often; 39 per cent of such requests were accepted, 23 per cent were partially accepted and 14 per cent were still being considered at the time of the research (MuConsult, 2003: VI). Just as in the case of requests to reduce working time, the serious business reasons invoked to explain the decisions where the requests were denied were generally in conformity with the reasons listed in the Act.

There is relatively little litigation on working time adjustment. During the period between the Act coming into force on 1 July 2000 and 1 May 2003, only 22 cases had been lodged at the Dutch courts (Beek, Van Doorne-Huiskens, and Veldman, 2002; Ministerie SZW, 2004). Twelve requests were granted, seven rejected. In the other cases no decision had yet been taken. More recently, requests have been rejected more frequently, probably because the arguments of employers have become stronger as there is now more clarity as to which reasons are to be considered as serious business reasons, and which are not. The courts often take into account the experiences of employees and employers during parental leave when reaching a decision.[23]

Increasing Influence on Individual Working Hours

According to the Dutch Working Time Act (Article 4:1a) the employer has to take into account the personal circumstances and responsibilities of the

---

[23] Between 1 July 2000 and 1 October 2004, 27 cases have been lodged in the Dutch Courts (Burri, 2004). Twenty cases concerned requests to reduce working time, of which 12 were (partially) granted. Four cases concerning extension of working time were all granted. The other three requests did not fall within the scope of the Working Time Adjustment Act.

worker outside work, such as bringing up children, caring for relatives and other social responsibilities, unless it is reasonable for the wishes of the worker to give way. As far as possible, the employer also has to organise the work in such a way that the worker adheres to a stable and regular working schedule. This provision came into force on 1 July 2003; it is therefore too early to assess its significance in practice.[24]

Leave and Child-Care Facilities

In the Netherlands a comprehensive Act on Work and Care was adopted at the end of 2001.[25] This Act provides for temporary full-time and part-time leave facilities in cases of, inter alia, pregnancy and young parenthood. It allows a female employee to take pregnancy and maternity leave on full pay for 16 weeks in total. Fathers are entitled to two days' leave on full pay after the birth of a child. In cases of urgent personal reasons, like the sudden illness of a child, Dutch labour law provides for a short period of leave to allow the employee to fulfil any necessary responsibilities. In the case of a prolonged illness of a spouse or a child, this may be converted into a 70 per cent paid leave up to a maximum of ten days a year (part-time workers have a proportionate right). This leave may, however, be refused by the employer when serious business reasons are at stake. Research shows that employees seldom use these forms of short-term leave in a case of emergency. Rather, most employees take a few days' annual leave (Van Luijn and Keuzenkamp, 2004).

Since 1991, Dutch employees have enjoyed a statutory unrestricted right to (part-time) parental leave that can be taken until the child reaches the age of eight years. This leave may be up to half of the weekly working time for a maximum period of six months. Extended full-time leave or a more flexible leave may be agreed upon with the employer. This statutory parental leave is unpaid, but a small percentage of employees are entitled to leave on reduced pay pursuant to collective agreements. Such agreements are more common in the public than in the private sector. Research shows that one in five employees entitled to parental leave took such leave between 1991 and 1999 (Grootscholte, Bouwmeester, and De Klaver, 2000: I). More women (28 per cent) than men (12 per cent) have taken parental leave. In sectors in which parental leave is partially paid, such as in the public sector, its uptake is much greater both among women (69 per cent) and among

---

[24] *Wijziging Arbeidstijdenwet en Burgerlijk Wetboek ter verruiming van zeggenschap van werknemers over arbeidstijden, Stb* 2003, 141 (Amendment of the Working Time Act and the Civil Code to extend the control of employees over working hours).

[25] *Wet arbeid en zorg, Stb* 2001, 567 (Act on Work and Care).

men (44 per cent). The research shows that men also take parental leave more often when the possibilities for flexible leave are offered, especially when leave can be taken for a few hours during a period longer than six months.

In the Netherlands, the lack of appropriate child-care facilities renders the reconciliation of paid work with family responsibilities difficult. Capacity is insufficient to supply the demand and waiting lists are common. In 1998, only 16 per cent of all children up to three years of age could be placed in a professional and official child-care facility. This percentage drops to 2 per cent for children between four and 12 years old (SCP and CBS, 2000: 88). An Act on Child-care Facilities entered in force on 1 January 2005.[26] The state, parents, and employers have to contribute in equal measure towards the costs of child-care facilities, but the contribution of employers is not mandatory. Parents receive subsidies from the state directly instead of organisations providing child-care facilities. This should enhance the choice for parents and leave more room for the operation of market forces. Up to now it seems that the costs for large numbers of parents have increased.

ASSESSMENT AND PROSPECTS

Although the participation of women in the labour market has increased during the past decades in the Netherlands, this has had little impact on the gendered division of paid and unpaid work. In the Netherlands, many women still interrupt their career in order to be able to take care of children and domestic tasks. An even larger group of women reduce their working hours. Even more than in other countries, part-time work is a structural feature of the employment pattern for women. A career break certainly has disadvantages and entails certain risks for workers, some of which are similar to those connected to part-time work. The disadvantages and risks of part-time work are less evident than in the case of a career break, but are nevertheless undeniable and increase as the number of working hours decreases. The income gained from a minor, part-time job is generally insufficient to attain economic independence. Having such a part-time job means working more often on irregular schedules, on stand-by or on a fixed-term contract. Stand-by and part-time employees working less than 12 hours a week are sometimes not entitled to rights pursuant to collective agreements. Career possibilities for part-time workers and employees on fixed-term contracts are often limited. Research shows that temporary work arrangements,

---

[26] *Wet kinderopvang, Stb* 2004, 455 (Act on child care).

either on a full-time or part-time basis, decrease enjoyment of life. But part-time work seems to have positive effects on the quality of life. This holds especially true for women and older employees (Nierop, 2003).

A better balanced division of paid and unpaid work between men and women is not likely as long as lifelong full-time employment remains the norm in the labour market. A new organisation of work means enhanced possibilities for men and women through a differentiation in working time adapted to the changing needs of workers during their lifetime. This also requires high-quality part-time work with good working conditions, possibilities to adjust working time and long-term (paid or partially paid) leave that meets the needs of employees. Structural change requires that the standard itself, like the full-time norm, is challenged and changed. Thus the question is raised as to whether and how the law can contribute towards realising such a perspective.

The evaluation of the Act on Flexibility and Security shows that stand-by contracts have become less common. Employees are instead offered more part-time and fixed-term contracts, which entail, in general, more income security and better working conditions. On the other hand, the increase in the number of fixed-term contracts means that fewer employees enjoy employment protection and that their position is more vulnerable in times of economic recession.

The Act on differences based on working time has contributed to clarifying the principle of equal treatment in working conditions for part-time employees. In Dutch policy documents, problems relating, for instance, to minor part-time jobs are often described, but specific measures to resolve them are still lacking.

In the Dutch context, it is still important to prevent women from leaving the labour market involuntarily when they have children. In order to achieve a more balanced division of paid and unpaid work between men and women, the combination model seems to be the most promising in the Netherlands, where part-time work appears to be increasingly accepted as a normal phenomenon. Still, there are many sectors and functions where part-time work does not occur, especially in sectors dominated by men and in higher functions. In this way, the Working Time Adjustment Act may play a role during negotiations around the kitchen table and at work. Research has shown that not only women, but also, and to an even greater extent, men would like to reduce their working time. Because of the loss of income, and the fear of harming their career, men are less inclined than women actually to take steps to adjust their working time. On the other hand, women, especially those with minor part-time employment, would like to extend their working time. Potentially, the Working Time Adjustment Act may contribute towards weakening the dominance of the full-time norm and further differentiating working time. But depending on which groups are making use of the possibilities offered by the law and the underlying reasons for their choice, it remains to be seen to what extent the law can contribute to a change in the existing gendered division of roles. It is likely that as women still earn less than men, more women than men will continue to take the income risk that a reduction in working time entails.

A new organisation of work not only requires working time adjustments during one's lifetime, but also 'time sovereignty'. Organisations' working schedules and the extent to which workers may influence time arrangements at work—time sovereignty—have an impact outside the workplace. This impact differs for women and men. Workers with family responsibilities more often face time conflicts when confronted with obligations to work overtime and irregular or unpredictable schedules. Potentially the provision in the Working Time Act on the assignment of working time patterns can contribute to a better work–life balance, but it has to be seen how it will be applied in practice. Furthermore, the Dutch government has started a project on new daily routine arrangements, and different experiments are taking place all over the country.[27] This issue has reached the political agenda, even if the results of the experiments have to be awaited.

To date, however, little attention has been paid in policy documents to the structural risks relating to career interruption and part-time work as described above. Proposals in order to facilitate transitional labour markets and to address the emergence of new social risks have been developed in advisory opinions (SER, 2001; Leijnse, Goudswaard, and Plantenga, 2002;) and in the literature (O'Reilly, Cebrián, and Lallement, 2000; Schmid, 2002a, 2002b), but until now have received only scant attention from policy makers. Instead, a new law has recently entered in force to facilitate the saving up of working time accounts with tax incentives, but this law is very modest and entails budgetary measures with reduced leave facilities.[28]

Social partners, employers, and works councils can also play an important role in policies aimed at reducing the risks relating to temporary career breaks, part-time work, fixed-term contracts and other flexible working relations. Working time plans could be developed in larger undertakings. Social partners can also further stimulate the development of possibilities for paid and long-term leave. Further measures are required by the legislator, as well as the social partners, in order to enable women and men, more so than has been the case up until now, to share their time between employment and care activities. Recognising the importance of care and increasing possibilities to adjust working time to the changing needs during workers'

---

[27] See www.emancipatieweb.nl/dagindeling_nieuw#537.
[28] *Wet aanpassing fiscale behandeling VUT/prepensioen en introductie levensloopregeling,* Stb 2005, 115 and Stb 2005, 178 (Act amending fiscal treatment of early retirement/prepension and introduction of life course arrangement), in force since 1 January 2005.

life cycles provide useful starting points. But measures to alleviate the financial and career risks involved in a reduction of working time should also form an integral part of a policy for encouraging more differentiation of working time during one's lifetime.

15

Engendering Flexibility in a World of Precarious Work

ROSEMARY OWENS*

INTRODUCTION

THE FEMINISATION OF work through the extraordinary growth in precarious work in the new global economy raises issues of concern for all workers in industrialised market economies (Standing, 1999b). There are also matters of particular significance to women workers arising from this phenomenon. Certainly that is the case in Australia (Preston and Burgess, 2003), where, although women's labour market participation rates have increased dramatically over the previous two decades, they remain comparatively low when compared with other industrialised market economies (OECD, 2004a, 2005).

In Australia, women have long predominated in all forms of non-standard or atypical work, as precarious work is more usually described there (Stewart, 1992; Owens, 1993; Brooks, 1994; Creighton, 1995; O'Donnell, 2004; cf Owens, 2002). The conflict between work and family life is usually proffered as the explanation for women's over-representation in non-standard forms of work, and while this may go some small way to explaining the phenomenon, it is also clear that there is no necessary or natural causal connection between the two. In Australia, it is not only women with young children who work part time, for instance; rather, working part time has become the defining cultural indicator of women's work (Australian Bureau of Statistics (ABS), 2002). In every age group at least one third of the women who do participate in the labour market work part time, so that Australia is only a little behind the Netherlands in the percentage of women who are employed on a part-time basis (OECD,

* I would like to thank all the participants at the IISL workshop, and especially Judy Fudge, for their comments on the earlier version of this chapter. I would also like to express my thanks to the two reviewers for additional comments.

2004a, 2005).[1] Part-time work in Australia usually takes a precarious form—as casual, agency, seasonal, or home-based work—to which few legal rights attach (Owens, 2002; Pocock *et al*, 2004; Hunter, chapter 12 in this volume). There is further overlap between these precarious forms of work: thus, for instance, by 2002 one third of all women employees in Australia worked as casuals, many of them employed through agencies, or working seasonally, or from home, and the majority of them part time (ABS, 2002; Preston and Burgess, 2003).

The proliferation of precarious forms of work has occurred in the context of the 'deregulation' of Australia's labour market and changes to its century-old system of conciliation and arbitration (Mitchell and Rimmer, 1990; Mitchell, 1998). Although, as Rosemary Hunter (chapter 12 in this volume) points out, much of the growth of precarious work occurred prior to the major legislative reforms of the mid-1990s, the radical changes introduced by the Workplace Relations Act 1996 (Cth) did emphasise the nexus between precarious work and flexibility. This chapter examines the implications of these reforms for women in the labour market, focusing on the claims that flexibility enables workers to accommodate the demands of work and care. It finds them greatly overstated; for women, flexible work is invariably precarious work. But rather than accept this relationship as necessary or inevitable the last section of the chapter evaluates three strategies for engendering flexibility. First, anti-discrimination case-law is analysed. The increased use of anti-discrimination law in recent years demonstrates the precarious hold that many women have on secure employment when they also bear care responsibilities. Anti-discrimination law also emphasises the importance of equality in making explicit the relation between paid or productive and unpaid or reproductive work. Second, the strategy of promoting conversion from casual to on-going employment is examined, for it seeks to address in a direct way the insecurity of the largest group of precarious workers in Australia, casual employees. Finally, the case for the extension of flexible family-friendly standards is explored. The emphasis here is on investigating whether the unique jurisdiction of the Australian Industrial Relations Commission (AIRC) exercising superintendence over workplace standards in awards might be more conducive to the attainment of all three goals of equality, security, and flexibility.

---

[1] Statistical comparisons can be somewhat unreliable because the base methods of calculation may differ between countries. Nonetheless, the figures in relation to part-time work in the Netherlands and Australia stand out from those of other market industrialised economies. In addition, counting precarious workers in Australia is a particularly complex task given various and mismatching meanings at the conversational, statistical, and legal levels (see O'Donnell, 2004).

CREATING FLEXIBILITY AT WORK

Over the past two decades, flexibility in the organisation and management of the workplace has been perceived in industrialised market economies as necessary for successful integration into the new global economy. Australia has proved no exception. Its embrace of flexibility has occurred through an intricate double movement involving the proliferation of non-standard or atypical forms of work and the transformation of the regulatory system governing the workplace.[2]

The concept of the standard worker as a 'harvester man', a male breadwinner with a wife and dependent children, who works 'full time' and for a 'lifetime' was an integral assumption of the legal norms regulating the Australian workplace until the 1970s (Hunter, 1988). The modern reincarnation of this normative worker is one who is 'unencumbered' (Williams, 2000b; Berns, 2002; Chapman, 2005). The description of a worker as 'standard' is linked to the range of benefits and protections offered by the legal norms operating in the workplace: the 'standard' serves as the 'regulatory pivot' around which the law both constructs and protects its normative worker (O'Donnell, 2004, n 2).

The proliferation of non-standard workers in Australia is at once indicative of attempts to evade legal protections and of changing protective standards, many of which have diminished or been transformed from substantive to procedural rights. In the context of the drive for workplace flexibility, the examination of precarious work is thus connected to questions about the nature of the standard worker *and* the legal standards governing the workplace in the new economy. In the flexible workplace of the new economy it becomes imperative to question whether there is any role for legal standards in the form of rules establishing fixed substantive rights; whether such substantive rights should only be minimum standards; whether all legal standards, be they minimum or other, necessarily entrench a concept of a normative worker and encourage the precariousness of those who deviate from it; whether legal standards, even where they establish substantive rights, ought to be flexible; or whether procedural mechanisms are the only relevant standards relevant to those labouring in the new economy (cf Collins, 2001).

Although there were originally multiple categories of worker recognised in Australian labour law (Brooks, 1988; Howe and Mitchell, 1999), by the middle of the twentieth century these were largely consolidated into two

---

[2] There is a wide range of regulation (including taxation and welfare law) influencing the construction of the labour market and women's position in the new economy—for a fuller discussion of these issues, see Barnes and Preston, 2002, and see more generally Arup, 1995, Gahan and Mitchell, 1995, Mitchell, 1995, Arup, 2001, Johnstone and Mitchell, 2004, and Mitchell, 2005.

groups: employees or independent contractors. The incorporation of this binary division of workers into the structure of the law of work ensured that it was separate and distinct from the law of commercial arrangements (see also Fudge, chapter 9 in this volume). Labour and industrial relations law gave protection to employees, while other independent workers were considered to accept the risks of participation in the marketplace. Yet in operation this bifurcation of workers was never absolutely comprehensive: it never demarcated two separate, distinct and homogenous types (see also Fredman, chapter 8, and Fudge, chapter 9 in this volume). Some worked at the periphery of labour law: for instance, outworkers in the informal economy, many of whom were women and whose assumed status of independence was never matched by the reality of their working lives (Hunter, 1992; Owens, 1995a). Others, like casuals, were acknowledged as employees but excluded from much of labour law's protection and carried the risks of working in the marketplace despite being employees.

With the advent of the new economy, business began to explore with a stronger sense of purpose the possibilities for a greater utilisation of the existing forms of non-standard work relationships. The dramatic growth of casual employment was facilitated from the outset by existing classifications in industrial awards and the 'deregulatory' moves initiated in the 1980s and early 1990s to open up the Australian labour market to the new economy (Owens, 1993; Hunter, chapter 12 in this volume). In addition, business also began to investigate more seriously ways of structuring work relations that would minimise the costs and risks of its own operations in the marketplace, including dispensing with the costs of protecting workers, while simultaneously maintaining many of the aspects of the standard employment relationship it found useful, such as managerial control over workers.

Tripartite work arrangements through agencies provided one practical solution. The first major case, the *Troubleshooters' Case*, involved such arrangements in the building industry, where typically many male workers straddled the divide between employee and independent contractor by working through family-based partnerships.[3] Following the law's imprimatur of legitimacy in this case (that is, its judgment that such arrangements were *sui generis* and did not fit within the legal definition of the employment relation), agency work flourished in a wide range of industries (see Stewart, 2002; Hunter, chapter 12 in this volume). Confidence quickly grew amongst business and its lawyers that any work relation could be constructed, through the strokes of a pen, to avoid the reach of labour law's protection: form could dominate substance (Stewart, 2002). Gradually it became clear

---

[3] *Building Workers' Industrial Union of Australia v Odco Pty Ltd (t/a Troubleshooters)* (1991), 29 FCR 104 (*Troubleshooters' case*). For comment, see Fenwick, 1992.

that such confidence was not entirely well placed. Even where the contractual arrangements used by the parties were identical to those employed in the *Troubleshooters' case*, the legal classification of the work relationship was not always the same, indicating the importance of the policy dimensions of the law (see also Fudge, chapter 9 in this volume). A low-paid, unskilled woman working casually as a seasonal tomato picker was not someone who was considered, for the purposes of workers' compensation legislation, to be working in business on her own account and responsible for the risk of injury incurred at work.[4] Nor could cleaners be 'transformed' from employees to independent contractors by business requiring that they transfer to an employment agency simply to avoid paying them their award entitlements and to evade the statutory requirements governing unfair dismissals.[5] Nonetheless, even though agency workers are now often recognised as employees, difficult questions exist as to the identity of their employer (Stewart, 2002), and invariably their employment is precarious or casual in nature with no guarantee of on-going work. In practice, these tripartite agency arrangements have continued to serve the purposes of business well.

While the increasing adoption of non-standard forms of work reflected the desire of business to avoid the constraints of compliance with the protective regime of labour law, simultaneously policy makers set about introducing more flexibility into the regulatory system. The next major step in the reform process came with the enactment of the Workplace Relations Act 1996 (Cth).[6]

An important part of the 1996 reforms involved eliminating some of the pre-existing regulatory constraints on the employment of certain classes of non-standard workers. Hitherto, part-time work had been quite restricted, in contrast to casual employment. The Workplace Relations Act appeared to encourage more on-going part-time employment with access to pro-rata rights, by declaring that industrial awards could no longer be used either to impose limits upon the numbers or proportions of workers in different classifications, or to place restrictions upon the maximum number of hours part-time workers could work.[7]

The model clauses developed by the AIRC in the *Award Simplification Decision* to implement this legislative change ensured that three classes of

---

[4] In *Country Metropolitan Agency Contracting Services Pty Ltd v Slater* (2003), 124 IR 293 (*Slater*).

[5] *Damevski v Giudice* (2003), 133 FCR 438 (*Damevski*).

[6] See also the Industrial Relations Act 1988 (Cth) and the Industrial Relations Reform Act 1993 (Cth). In 2005, a further wave of reform was introduced by the Liberal Coalition government. In Australia both the Commonwealth and the states regulate work relations. This chapter focuses predominantly on Commonwealth or federal arrangements.

[7] Workplace Relations Act 1996 (Cth), s 89A(4)–(5).

employment—full-time, regular part-time, and casual—were provided for in most industrial awards.[8] Limitations on the maximum periods of engagement of part-time employees and related overtime arrangements, which had been common prior to the decision, were also removed. Regular part-time employees were now defined in awards as anyone who 'works less than full-time hours of thirty-eight per week', and they were to receive all the rights and conditions of full-time employees on a pro-rata basis. There remained, however, a requirement that part-time employees were to be offered a minimum of three hours' work for any one period of engagement. The AIRC, pointing to its statutory duty also to ensure fairness to employees, rejected the employers' request for a two-hour minimum based on productivity issues.

However, at the same time the AIRC also adopted a definition of a casual employee that was proposed by employers: a casual worker was, for the purposes of industrial awards, 'one who is engaged and paid as such'. This definition handed to business complete control in determining whether a worker would be taken on in a casual or on-going capacity. In addition, because casual employees could waive their right to be paid at the termination of each engagement and instead be paid weekly or fortnightly, the decision eliminated a number of costs and inefficiencies (for example, in the administration of the payroll) that would otherwise be incurred when employing casuals. Thus, although the restrictions on part-time employment were removed, there was no legal incentive to offer on-going employment even to those engaged for lengthy periods. Nor did the requirement to pay a premium to those who were employed as casuals for their lack of security (a practice known as 'casual loading') create a strong economic disincentive against the employment of casuals (Pocock *et al*, 2004). The 1996 reforms thus did not inhibit the trend for precarious (especially casual) employment to outgrow more secure forms of work (Pocock *et al*, 2004).

At first blush, the Workplace Relations Act also appeared to ensure that some precarious workers who had often previously been assumed to fall outside the protection of the system, such as outworkers,[9] would be brought within it. The Act made it clear that the pay and conditions of those outworkers, defined as those who 'for the purposes of the business of the employer, [perform] work at a private residential premises or at other premises that are not business or commercial premises of the employer,'[10] could be regulated by industrial awards. However, there was a rider.

---

[8] *Award Simplification Decision* (1997), 75 IR 272.

[9] This assumption was evident in *R v Commonwealth Industrial Court & Ors; ex parte Cocks & Ors* (1968), 43 ALJR 32. Cf *Re Application to Vary The Clothing Trades Award 1982* (1987), 19 IR 416.

[10] Workplace Relations Act 1996 (Cth), s 89A(9).

Outworkers were to be protected in this way 'only to the extent necessary to ensure that their *overall* pay and conditions of employment are fair and reasonable in comparison with the pay and conditions specified in a relevant award or awards for employees who perform the same kind of work at an employer's business or commercial premises.'[11] There was thus a degree of regulatory flexibility rather than a requirement to match identically the protections afforded to standard workers. However, the legislation simultaneously established an incentive to get rid of the standard employee, who worked in the factory or office and who was a necessary comparator for home-based workers to access workplace rights (cf Fredman, 1997a; Vosko, chapter 3 in this volume). By effectively guaranteeing that any industry operating entirely beyond the factory, office, or other premise of the employer would be free from the regulation of industrial awards, the 1996 legislation could be seen as specifically encouraging this form of work.

However, despite the prospects for more flexibility through an increase in home-based telework and other forms of work in the knowledge economy, and the promotion of home-based work as a flexible alternative for workers with family responsibilities, during the 1990s there was a reluctance to provide home-based work for employees (Pittard, 2003). Where provision is made for home-based work in awards (or statutory agreements) it has invariably been on condition that it is entirely at the discretion of the employer; it is not a matter of right for the employee and it is not a substitute for dependent care (Pittard, 2003). Since the 1996 reforms over one third of home-based workers in Australia are classified as 'own account' workers (ABS, 2001), ostensibly putting them beyond regulatory reach, although many may well be dependent rather that independent contractors (cf Fudge, chapter 9 in this volume). In old-economy industries, such as clothing and textiles, outwork continues to operate, but the complex contractual arrangements that characterise it continue to pose enormous obstacles to the effective protection of these workers' most basic rights (Burgess and Strachan, 2002; cf The State of Victoria, 2000; Nossar *et al*, 2004).

Even more significant than the changes expressly concerning precarious forms of non-standard work, the 1996 reforms drastically reduced the system of workplace standards. Australia has never had a strong set of *universal* statutory norms governing work relations and protecting employees. This is primarily a consequence of its constitutional arrangements, which restrict Commonwealth legislation to certain enumerated topics, none of which comprehensively cover work-related matters.[12] At the national level such

---

[11] *Ibid*, s 89A(2)(t) (emphasis added).
[12] See the Commonwealth of Australia Constitution Act 1900 (63 & 64 Vic, Ch 12), ss 51, 52.

universal work-related standards as have existed in the past have usually depended upon the 'external affairs' power, which supports the legislative implementation of international conventions.[13] To the extent that the norms contained in international instruments, such as those of the International Labour Organization (ILO), allow for the exclusion of non-standard workers from workplace rights (Vosko, chapter 3 in this volume), Australian regulation has tended to follow suit. Hence many non-standard workers, and in particular casuals and seasonal workers, were excluded from the federal statutory right to unpaid parental leave[14] and the statutory protection offered against unfair dismissal.[15]

However, prior to 1996, awards that were established under the conciliation and arbitration system operating in Australia for most of the twentieth century contained numerous detailed provisions that regulated work on an industry-wide basis. The 1996 reforms mandated a significant contraction in the range of workplace issues that could be regulated through Commonwealth industrial awards. Henceforth they were to be restricted to 20 'allowable' matters, covering such things as classification of workers; working hours; rates of pay; leave entitlements; redundancy pay and notice of termination; type of employment; and superannuation and jury service.[16] Under the 1996 reforms awards were also to be 'simplified', the language serving to emphasise the idea that regulation was intrusive, complicated, and confusing. The 1996 reforms also further deregulated the labour market by transforming awards into a safety net of *minimum* entitlements underpinning statutory agreements.[17]

Although there had been a greater emphasis on enterprise-based agreements from the late 1980s, after 1996 they became the central mechanism for regulating work in Australia. Bargaining was viewed as a necessary means to increase productivity (Wooden, 2000), and any significant increase above the safety-net level in pay, conditions, or protections for workers had to be achieved through agreements. In providing for two forms of statutory agreement, collective (that could, but need not, involve trade unions) and individual 'Australian Workplace Agreements',[18] the Workplace Relations

---

[13] See *Victoria v The Commonwealth (the Industrial Relations Act Case)* (1996), 187 CLR 416.

[14] Workplace Relations Act 1996 (Cth), Part VIA, Div 5 and schs 12 and 14, implementing ILO Convention Concerning Equal Opportunities and Equal Treatment for Men and Women Workers: Workers with Family Responsibilities   (No 156) (1981); Recommendation Concerning Equal Opportunities and Equal Treatment for Men and Women Workers: Workers with Family Responsibilities (No 165).

[15] Workplace Relations Act 1996 (Cth), Part VIA, Div 1, subdivision D. See especially s 170CBA and sch 10, implementing ILO Convention Concerning Termination of Employment at the Initiative of the Employer (No 158) (1982).

[16] Workplace Relations Act 1996 (Cth), s 89A(2).

[17] *Ibid*, Part VI. See especially s 88B.

[18] *Ibid*, Parts VIB and VID.

Act made the individualisation of work relations and the exclusion of trade unions a structural goal of the regulatory system (McCallum, 1997; Deery and Mitchell, 1999). General standards or rules were derided as an outdated 'one size fits all model' (Reith, 1999).

Despite its designation as a safety net, the award system was rendered permeable. The 'no disadvantage' test, which under the 1996 reforms mediated the relation of awards and agreements, did so only in a flexible way that did not protect the basic terms and conditions of employment contained in awards (Merlo, 2000; Mitchell *et al*, 2004). In addition, after the *Award Simplification Decision*, awards no longer necessarily imposed the same industry-wide standards on all parties. Where matters could be dealt with at the workplace level, the award could represent a 'framework' document through the application of 'facilitative provisions'. Awards were prohibited from prescribing work practices that would hinder efficiency or productivity, although this was tempered by a continuing requirement of fairness to the employee. The idea of the 'inflexible' standard regulating in a uniform way employers and employees was gradually disappearing. Contracting within the standards was identified as the way ahead.

The new regulatory system introduced in 1996 thus reduced significantly the prospect of comprehensive and strong protection by fixed standards for all workers, but especially non-standard workers because they more often work in industries with little trade union coverage or in small enterprises where collective agreements are less likely. Precarious workers, and women, are much more likely to have their pay and conditions determined only by awards (Baird and Burgess, 2003; Whitehouse and Frino, 2003).

THE FLEXIBILITY AGENDA

The resistance to rule-based standards in Australia reflects the neoliberal agenda shaping the new global economy. In every industrialised economy there has been pressure to 'deregulate' labour markets. This drive has gained momentum through invoking a concept of all regulation, but especially statutory law, as an external authority imposed from above. Law becomes an interloper, a stranger to its pre-existing subjects, imposing upon them an alien logic in contrast to contractualism, the natural law of market relations. 'Public' is thus pitted against the 'private' in a false separation, which misses the background rules that structure the fields, including domestic relations and the market, within which work relations are played out (Klare, 2002: 14).

In this neoliberal discourse, flexibility of the labour market continues to be presented as necessary for successful participation in the new economy. It promises to deliver more efficient and, therefore, more profitable outcomes for business, and claims these benefits flow through to civil society in the form of increased wealth. Flexibility is also asserted to be good for workers, enabling them to have control over their working lives in a way that respects their other life choices (Reith, 1999).

However, increasingly, these claims are challenged as workers find their promises unfulfilled. Precarious or non-standard work is supposed to enable workers to develop or maintain their skills and provide a pathway to greater and more secure integration into the labour market. But this aspirational gloss on the worth of non-standard employment has not proved accurate. The value of non-standard employment in the new economy inevitably has to be qualified because it depends on a complex set of variables, including macro- and micro-economic indications of the prospects for growth of particular industries within the national economy as it intersects with the global economy. In Australia, the most common type of non-standard work, casual work, is more an alternative to unemployment than a chosen form of work (Parliamentary Library (Australia), 2004), and all the evidence suggests that it is more likely that those with non-standard jobs will lapse back into dependency on the social welfare system than move on to more secure jobs (Gregory, 2004). Likewise, the claim that flexible employment assists workers to maintain and enhance their skills is hollow when most non-standard jobs are low skilled and rarely offer additional training (see, for example, Whittard, 2003).

An enduring criticism of non-standard work is the lack of workplace rights attaching to it; flexibility has been achieved through forms of work that do not enjoy even the most basic benefits of annual leave and sick leave (Owens, 2002; Pocock *et al*, 2004). As non-standard employment becomes more common, there is also growing recognition of the double set of problems associated with it as a form of low-paid work: that is, the jobs are low paid because they are considered to be low skilled, and, since the hours usually available in such jobs are seldom equivalent to full-time hours, the pay is low (Watson, 2004).

For women, the implications of the deregulated labour market are even starker. Australian industry has long been one of the most highly sex-segregated in the world, and it remains so (OECD, 1980; Mumford, 1989; Preston and Burgess, 2003; Preston and Whitehouse, 2003). Most of the work available in industry sectors where women predominate is low skilled and non-standard and it does not form a bridge to gaining less precarious 'decent work'. For most women, non-standard work is their only work option, the only alternative to total financial dependency on either a spouse or the welfare system.

Everywhere flexibility has had a bad name among those with a special concern about the impact on women of the regulatory changes accompanying the emergence of the new economy (Dickens, 1992; Fredman, 2004b). In Australia, most of the early criticisms of flexibility as it impacted on women centred on resisting the emphasis in the 'new industrial relations'

(Hunt and Provis, 1995) on bargaining replacing the centralised system of fixing wages and conditions (Bennett, 1995). Women, who work predominantly in service industries in non-standard jobs, were predicted to gain less than men from bargaining. Australia's centralised system had in the past proved better for women in terms of pay (and conditions) when compared with regulatory systems based on collective bargaining which operated in other industrialised countries (McColgan, 1997). Now the introduction of the bargaining system in Australia has indeed borne out the early fears that women's position would deteriorate (Burgess and Strachan, 1998, 2000; Whitehouse and Frino, 2003). Indeed, a historical study of the wage disparity between men and women in Australia shows that it is the shape of the regulatory system and not any gendered resistance by women to investing in their human capital that influences their lower earnings (Gregory, 1999). Women have become trapped mostly in poor-quality, non-standard work with access to a safety net that can best be described as a 'ceiling' not 'floor of rights' (Conaghan, 2000).

While it is often claimed that flexibility operates in a way that assists workers to balance work and care responsibilities (Commonwealth of Australia, 2002), the benefits have largely been for business (Charlesworth, 1996; Berns, 2002; Pocock, 2003). Workplace flexibility has exacerbated the very work and family conflict it is supposed to resolve, by contributing, for example, to the development of a long-hours culture (Pocock, 2003). Flexibility has taken a particularly gendered form. Men, in contrast to women, do not generally avail themselves of 'family-friendly' flexibility provisions, such as those enabling workers to take unpaid breaks from the workplace or to reduce their hours of work (Commonwealth of Australia, 2002; Bittman et al, 2004;). Fearing that breaks will damage their careers, the norm of the worker as the breadwinning 'harvester man' remains in Australia quite central to masculine identity (Bittman et al, 2004). Where flexible provisions are available, it is women who use them, absenting themselves from the labour market and effectively adopting non-standard work (Owens, 2005). Thus, to say that social trends in Australia reveal 'the pervasive abandonment of the traditional cultural norm that viewed a man's role primarily as "breadwinner" and a woman's as "homemaker"'(ABS, 2000: 8) is only half-true. Women may now participate in the labour market in unprecedented numbers, but it is overwhelmingly in non-standard work because they still carry primary responsibility for work in the home. Non-standard work has become a pragmatic solution enabling women to balance the two sides of their working lives. A 'new gender contract' (Fudge, 2005)—of one-and-a-half workers: a full-time male worker and a part-time female worker—appears also to be in place in Australia.

However, in evaluating flexibility from the perspective of women, there are certain paradoxes evident. Women are more likely than men to work in some form of non-standard work and often it is because at present this is the only way to gain the flexibility they need to accommodate the double demands of work and family. Many women feel, and indeed are, trapped in non-standard work because it is constructed as socially, economically, and culturally appropriate for them. However, at the same time, the flexibility offered either by non-standard work or by other flexible standards allowing partial exit from the workplace does not always suit their needs. Women have a wide range of care responsibilities, not all of which are provided for in the presently existing workplace flexible standards. Furthermore, what flexibility exists is often quite restricted or one-dimensional: it is not the kind of flexibility that is responsive to ever-changing demands and needs as they occur over a lifetime. There are a wide range of other problems: the lack of certainty of work hours for many casual workers, for example, does not allow them to organise child care or to deal with the requirements of other societal institutions such as schools. However, it is not rigidity in working hours, days, or weeks that women want. There are also many women, especially those in more highly skilled or senior positions, who find that their work is either absolutely inflexible or demands the flexibility of complete availability. Flexibility issues thus intersect with the gendered dimensions of both the vertical and horizontal segregation of the labour market.

TRANSFORMING PRECARIOUS WORK

Rather than simply amounting to a 'neoliberal shibboleth', perhaps flexibility could be a 'progressive rallying cry' (Klare, 2002: 6). Such transformation would require, as Karl Klare (2002) also observes, supportive changes or developments in the broad range of policy areas impacting upon and constructing work and workers. However, an evaluation of the most productive ways of effecting positive change in the law of work can contribute to making this a reality.

While acknowledging that men and women's 'choices' in relation to work are constrained by the legal and social environment that they inhabit, it is obvious that many (especially women) do feel that flexible work conditions are desirable. The difficult question is therefore identifying the best strategy or strategies to deal with the seemingly infinite diversity of workers and their needs. How is it possible to respond to women's and men's needs while recognising that they do not form a homogenous group? Can the legal system provide for flexibility in a way that suits women's present needs and encourages men to take up more responsibility for home or care work? Is it possible to develop flexibility in a transformative way: that is, in a way that does not entrench a divide between standard and non-standard work onto which a gender divide is superimposed? Or put another way, can flexibility be implemented in a way that provides equality and security at work for all? Can flexibility be engendered?

The second part of this chapter will explore these questions by evaluating three of the most significant strategies being played out in Australia for dealing with the intersection of precarious work, family responsibilities, and flexible work practices.

FLEXIBILITY WITH EQUALITY

Recent anti-discrimination cases in Australia provide clear evidence that women seek flexibility as a means of maintaining a secure hold on their place in the labour market while taking responsibility for family and care work. In a number of these cases women have made successful claims that the denial of flexibility in their work arrangements infringes their right to equality in the workplace. Among these cases are instances where the employer required a woman to maintain a full-time work schedule in the early years of her child's life or refused to consider her request for part-time work;[19] where the employer insisted that a woman attend at the workplace during certain fixed hours and declared that if she wished to have a short break to take her child from school to after-school care in the afternoon she must give up her full-time employment and move to part-time employment;[20] where the employer adhered to outdated ideas, refusing to countenance any other alternative than a woman giving up her senior position in exchange for a more lowly one if she was to work part time for a period after adopting a child;[21] and where, assuming that all workers will be devoted to their employment without interruption and 100 per cent of the time, managers engaged in a campaign of harassment when a woman announced her intention to take maternity leave,[22] and when a single mother exercised her legal entitlements to take leave to care for her ill child.[23]

But there is little certainty to be gained from this jurisdiction. In a significant recent case, a woman was not successful in her pursuit of flexible work arrangements through anti-discrimination law. Ms Schou, a highly skilled Hansard reporter, sought flexible-work arrangements to enable her to continue working full time while caring for her sick child. The medical advice was that the child would grow out of the illness, and so she sought an accommodation in her working conditions in the interim. At first she requested part-time work, but when this was refused by her employer she

---

[19] *Escobar v Rainbow Printing Pty Ltd (No 2)* (2002), EOC 93-229 (*Escobar*); and *Mayer v ANTSO* (2003), EOC 93-385 (*Mayer*).

[20] *Song v Ainsworth Game Technology Pty Ltd* (2002), EOC 93-194 (*Song*).

[21] *Bogle v Metropolitan Health Service Board* (2000), EOC 93-069 (*Bogle*).

[22] *Thomson v Orica Australia Pty Ltd* (2002), EOC 93-227 (*Thomson*).

[23] *Evans v National Crime Authority* (2003), EOC 93-298; aff'd *Commonwealth of Australia v Evans* (2004), EOC 93-335 (*Evans*).

abandoned the idea and instead sought to work from home on some days using modem technology to link her to the workplace. Although this could have been organised at relatively modest cost and her manager initially agreed, her employer failed to provide the modem and Ms Schou was forced to resign. Twice the Tribunal hearing her case ruled that she had been indirectly discriminated against on the ground of her status as parent and carer and found in her favour,[24] but each time the decision was successfully appealed on a point of law to the Supreme Court.[25]

The failure of the *Schou* litigation highlights a number of problems with relying on the anti-discrimination jurisdiction to deliver to women the kinds of flexible working conditions they need. In *Schou* 2004 the judges' determination of the 'reasonableness' of the requirement that she always work from her employer's offices was made with particular deference to the perspective of the employer. Once the requirement to attend at the workplace was shown to be 'appropriate and adapted' to the employer's purposes, the court required that Ms Schou demonstrate that the alternative arrangement of working via the modem was 'as efficacious', in order to establish the unreasonableness of the condition that she attend at work.[26] Despite the contrary findings of fact by the Tribunal on two occasions, the Appeal Court held by majority that it was 'plain beyond argument' that the attendance requirement was reasonable and that 'on any view' the modem proposal was 'less efficacious (on one or more grounds).'[27] The judges also approached the issue of the 'reasonableness' of the requirement to attend at the workplace from the point of view of the implications for the employer if *all* workers had parental responsibilities and wanted to work from home: they did not confine their reasoning to the specific context, which was that only Ms Schou needed such accommodation, and only she was seeking such accommodation. Fearing that the 'floodgates' would to be opened, the judges determined that, while the receipt of the 'privilege' or 'benefit' of being able to work from home was something that could be granted to an employee as a matter of good management practice by a compassionate employer, it was not a matter of 'right' to which Ms Schou was entitled under anti-discrimination law.

---

[24] The action was brought under the Equal Opportunity Act 1984 (Vic). *Schou v The State of Victoria* (2000), EOC 93-100, 93-101 (*Schou* 2000)—for comment, see MacDermott and Owens, 2000; and *Schou v State of Victoria Melbourne (Department of Parliamentary Debates)* (2002), EOC 93-217 (*Schou* 2002).

[25] See *State of Victoria v Schou*, [2001] 3 VR 655 (*Schou* 2001)—for comment, see Adams, 2002 and Gaze, 2002; and *State of Victoria v Schou* (2004), 8 VR 120 (*Schou* 2004)—for comment, see Knowles, 2004. See also *Kelly v TPG Internet Pty Ltd* (2003), 176 FLR 214 (*Kelly*), involving an action under the Sex Discrimination Act 1984 (Cth) which applied the Supreme Court's decision in *Schou* 2004.

[26] *Schou* 2004, at paras 39, 27 (per Phillips JA).

[27] *Ibid* at para 37. See also paras 24, 26 (per Phillips JA).

It is paradoxical that anti-discrimination law, which has frequently been condemned as an inadequate tool to deal with structural discrimination because of its individualistic focus (Thornton, 1990; Fredman, 1997a), should have been applied in this way. In separating the concept of discrimination into direct and indirect forms, the legislation distinguishes discrimination directed against an individual from that which is structural and impacts on a class. While it is accepted in Australia that a claim of indirect discrimination can be made by an individual,[28] anti-discrimination law seems peculiarly inept at considering the particular problems of individual workers in the context of structural discrimination. Thus, it has particular difficulty confronting the kind of structural issues raised when an individual worker seeks flexibility for reasons of family or care responsibilities. Seldom does an employer deny flexibility in a way that is directly discriminatory. Yet indirect discrimination does not always appear to be useful when there is only a class of one, and others who apparently belong to the same class as the complainant can and do comply with the requirements claimed to be discriminatory. These issues arise in large part because the idea of equality as 'sameness' has infected the concept of indirect discrimination (Collins, 2003a).

But workers with care responsibilities are not all the same. The infinite variety of needs and capacities of individual workers with care responsibilities makes proof of unreasonableness, integral to the successful prosecution of a claim of indirect discrimination in Australia, even more difficult than usual. The judgments in the *Schou* litigation reveal at once differing and contradictory reasons for not according the worker-flexible conditions: there is a fear that the 'floodgates' will open and all workers will demand such consideration, and at the same time a tenacious grip on the idea of the normative worker as 'unencumbered' (Berns, 2002), someone who is not discriminated against by a lack of flexibility. Given the interpretative approach to this legislation (see Gaze, 2002) there is little evidence that anti-discrimination law is capable of doing much to change workplace culture and structure.

In most anti-discrimination cases, even those where the claimant has been successful, the work relationship has often broken down irretrievably. Women who have lost their job may recover compensation for the harms suffered, but they frequently find that, with care responsibilities and inadequate public provision of child care, their chances of gaining another secure job with the flexibility they require are virtually non-existent. The impacts on women who are single parents or whose relationship with the father of the child breaks down after they lose their job are particularly severe.[29]

---

[28] See, eg, *French v Gosford City Council*, [2003] NSWADT 273 at 94–96 (*French*).
[29] See, eg, *Escobar*, above n 19, and *Evans*, above n 23.

The systemic problem of women leaving secure employment only to find that they are thereafter consigned to precarious work has also proved a problem intractable of solution in the anti-discrimination arena. The inequality that results from forced career breaks (see also Kilpatrick, chapter 7 in this volume) has been especially problematic where discriminatory practices are sanctioned by the decisions of industrial tribunals but remain immune from the reach of anti-discrimination law.[30] Even in jurisdictions where this immunity has been removed, cases can be drawn out demonstrating a continuing difficulty on the part of decision-making bodies in understanding the issues. Thus in *Amery v New South Wales*, a large number of female schoolteachers, who had resigned their on-going positions in order to care for their young children, discovered that if they wished to return to employment in a permanent position they had to accept a placement anywhere in the state. Without geographic mobility the only option available to them was casual work, which under the relevant state industrial agreement was restricted to lower classifications than they would otherwise have been eligible for if they could access a permanent position.[31] Yet an Appeal Panel overturned the finding of the Tribunal at first instance and held that these women exercised a 'subjective preference' not to travel, and that the lower pay rates and conditions that applied to them as casuals were not the result of an unreasonable requirement imposed by the employer but had a rational basis in the relevant industrial agreement.[32] A further appeal in the Supreme Court of New South Wales had to be initiated to restore the decision of the Tribunal at first instance.[33]

In most instances anti-discrimination law provides at best monetary compensation, although this will be reduced where a woman's situation is that she can only work part time because she has family or care responsibilities.[34] In only very few cases have there been orders to restructure the workplace to provide a flexible work option to a complainant.[35] And, in any event, it can be observed that where, as is often the case, a woman seeks some form of non-standard work as a flexible solution to her problems,[36] the accommodation she is wanting is also very much one to be made in her

---

[30] See, eg, Sex Discrimination Act 1984 (Cth), s 40(1a)(c).

[31] See *The State of New South Wales v Amery & Others (EOD)* (2003), 129 IR 300, successful appealed in *Amery & Ors v State of New South Wales (Director-General NSW Department of Education and Training)* (2004), EOC 93-352 (*Amery*).

[32] *Ibid*, at 50–54. On assumed geographic mobility, see also *Gardiner v Workcover Authority of New South Wales*, [2004] NSWADTAP 1 (*Gardiner*).

[33] *Amery*, above n 31. Leave to appeal this decision was then granted by the High Court (*State of New South Wales v Amery & Ors*, [2005] HCA Trans 366 (27 May 2005)), and the case is expected to be heard in 2006.

[34] *Mayer*, above n 19.

[35] See, eg, *Bogle*, above n 21, and *Song*, above n 20.

[36] *Escobar*, above n 19; *Mayer*, above n 19; *Kelly*, above n 25.

life, for it is usually she who will leave the workplace for at least part of the time. Thus, in seeking a remedy of transferring to non-standard work to accommodate care responsibilities, the worker who brings a complaint under anti-discrimination law is always constructed in the shadow of the normative standard worker. The gendered structure of work is thus entrenched in a double sense. Women are assumed to have responsibility for care work, and/or workers with care responsibilities are assumed to deviate from the standard worker.

Where the woman seeks a real transformation in workplace practice, anti-discrimination law is reluctant to intervene. Indeed, intervention is almost always dependent upon evidence that flexibility is *already* part of a workplace culture. If others at the workplace already have an entitlement to flexible work conditions, then a complainant is likely to win an equivalent concession because it is easier to demonstrate that the employer's denial of flexible work arrangements is unreasonable.[37] But there is no guarantee of success. In *Schou*, the relevant Parliamentary Officers Employment Agreement required:

> the provision of a work environment which fosters an appropriately trained, skilled and adaptable staff committed to facilitating improved work practices; the adoption of flexible and progressive work practices and reasonable changes in the way the work is organised; and the application of personnel policies and principles which are based on the principles of merit and equity.[38]

However, only the dissenting judge found that management's action was discriminatory because of the *inflexibility* of the requirement to attend at the workplace.[39] Again, another paradox is presented: a complainant must show that the refusal of flexibility is unreasonable, but success also depends on finding a comparator who does not need flexibility.

There are other problems with using anti-discrimination law as a strategy to achieve flexibility at work. A worker's inability to comply with an inflexible requirement at the workplace is often a temporary matter. Indeed, in the context of the lifetime of the worker, many of the worker's needs are transitory, lasting from hours to years. In *Schou*, the evidence was that in a few months Ms Schou would have been able to return to work full time at her employer's premises. Her situation while her child was ill was very different from when she commenced employment more than 15 years earlier, and very different again when her child had recovered his health. Thus

---

[37] See eg *Song*, above n 20; *Mayer*, above n 19. Cf *Kelly*, above n 25, where part of the reason that the complaint was rejected was because there were no other women in the employer's business working flexible part-time hours. Indeed, the only ones with flexible work in the organisation were male students in the business's call centre.

[38] *Schou* 2000, above n 24.

[39] *Schou* 2004, above n 25, at para 41 (per Callaway JA).

workers need flexibility that can enable them to respond to the changing circumstances across their working lifetime, but there is little evidence of tribunal or judicial willingness to grant remedies that are themselves flexible and vary over time.

Thus, while anti-discrimination law has provided some individuals with recompense for their employers' failure to accord them flexible work conditions, the Australian experience does not quite provide the basis for the optimism of some US feminists, who argue that anti-discrimination legislation can provide an effective strategy to produce more flexible and equal workplaces and change the conception of the normative worker (Chamallas, 1999; Williams, 1999, 2000a, 2000b). In Australia, while there have been some individual successes to date, anti-discrimination law has either replicated women's participation in non-standard work while maintaining the image of the standard worker as one without care responsibilities or refused to acknowledge the discriminatory impact of inflexible work practices. Providing little certainty of outcome, it is unlikely to offer any real path to achieving greater *structural* change in the workplace. The industrial system recognised as establishing the standards that structure work in the marketplace could be expected to offer a better prospect for dealing with structural problems posed by flexibility and non-standard work.

FLEXIBILITY WITH SECURITY

A different concern of many women (and men too) is that the only flexible work available to them has inferior workplace rights. Casual work is the most common example of this in Australia. The precariousness of casual work is manifest at a number of levels: there is usually a lack of certainty and control for the worker in the number and pattern of hours worked; and this is attended by lack of certainty in income from week to week. Where the work is low skilled there is the ever-present threat of other willing replacement workers, and the general insecurity in the relationship between employer and employee induces a tolerance of behaviour such as harassment and bullying, and workers' unwillingness to complain about their exclusion from formal workplace rights (Pocock *et al*, 2004; Thornton, 2004).

A common perception is that the problem with casual work is one of abuse: that is, workers are treated as casuals, not only when their work is short term and intermittent, but when they are in reality long-term employees. A relatively new industrial strategy used in Australia to deal with the problem of the long-term casual is to provide a legal right for these workers to request a transfer to an on-going position. This right to request a transfer has already been incorporated in some industrial awards and some enterprise agreements.[40] The strategy is also endorsed by some think tanks (Pocock *et al*, 2004) and is encouraged as part of a policy of 'flexibility with fairness' adopted by the Australian Labor Party (Latham and Emerson, 2004). However, the move to introduce conversion provisions more widely into awards has met resistance, although an attempt at the federal level to prohibit by statute their inclusion in the award safety net was defeated.[41]

The political contest over the incorporation of conversion clauses in the safety net is of particular significance because casual workers are amongst the most vulnerable workers and are less likely to be covered by enterprise agreements. The contest is also a gendered one, for there are double the numbers of female compared with male workers who are covered only by awards (ABS, 2002).

In so far as the conversion strategy provides for movement between categories of workers it represents a positive development. And for many workers a transfer to on-going work would eliminate many of the unwanted aspects of precariousness, especially as it would in many cases be accompanied by more certainty as to the number and pattern of hours to be worked and hence the weekly pay, as well as providing entitlements to paid sick leave and annual leave. Moreover, the process for conversion provides workers with control: a duty to inform the worker of the right to convert is placed on the employer, but thereafter the decision as to whether to make an application for conversion to on-going employment is with the worker. Conversion is nowhere suggested as compulsory, an important strategic element in deflecting criticisms both from business that it diminishes choice and from casual workers who may be reluctant to relinquish their pay loading.

However, while touted as a method for eliminating precarious work altogether and giving better access to safety-net standards, there are a number of significant problems with this conversion strategy. While on-going work would provide certainties seldom available to casuals and thus enable the worker to make, for instance, child-care arrangements, it may also come with a set of undesired rigidities. Conversion to on-going work could also expose the worker to other different uncertainties, as elements of precariousness and flexibility have infiltrated even so-called standard work in the new economy, (Junor, 1998; Stone, chapter 11 in this volume; Hunter, chapter 12 in this volume).

While the idea of allowing a transition between forms of work may be desirable for a number of reasons, the conversion strategy allows movement

---

[40] See *Re Metal, Engineering and Associated Industries Award* (2001), 110 IR 247. An example in the education sector is the conversion provision for general staff in the Enterprise Certified Agreement, The University of Adelaide, Cl 16.11–16.16 (see also Owens, 2002).

[41] Workplace Relations Amendment (Award Simplification) Bill 2003 (Cth). However, this prohibition has now became law with the enactment of the Workplace Relations Amendment (Work Choices) Act 2005 (Cth), S116(1) (b).

once only and in only one direction. The strategy thus builds upon and assumes a norm of standard work. Eligibility to use the conversion process is determined by the length of time working for, and the expectation of on-going employment with, a particular employer. The conversion strategy thus seeks to assimilate the casual to the standard, the norm of the on-going worker, albeit a norm sometimes slightly modified as a part-time worker. This strategy is thus based on the view that there is a binary divide in the Australian workforce between casual, or non-standard, work and standard work. Furthermore, it maintains that binary divide, simply shifting the line that defines it. This immediately risks encouraging the construction of employment practices around that definitional division.[42] A far more equitable response, and therefore from the worker's perspective a more secure approach, to the problem of casual work and its exclusion from the protection of labour law is to ensure that *every* worker is entitled on a pro-rata basis to fundamental workplace rights (Fredman, 1997a; Owens, 2002; Fredman, 2004b), using reasonable probation thresholds to protect business's legitimate interests in securing the right worker for the job. The conversion strategy can also be criticised because it attacks only some elements of precariousness and harkens back to the notion of security with a single employer rather than facilitating a more general notion of security of participation in the workplace more appropriate to the new economy (see Supiot *et al*, 2001).

Furthermore, because access to the conversion strategy is modelled on characteristics of the standard worker it is also easy to evade. Agency work provides a case in point. In some of the service sectors of the labour market where women predominate, for instance in clerical work and in health care and nursing, agency work has become the standard form of work arrangement. In seasonal work it is also becoming more common. Except in those instances where an agency worker has been placed with a client of the agency for a lengthy period and might realistically have an expectation of continuing in that position,[43] workers will be unlikely to be able to satisfy the required length of tenure and expectations of on-going employment which comprise the eligibility requirements for gaining access to the right to request conversion to on-going employment. This is not to deny that at present many agency workers may satisfy those requirements. But again, it would be relatively easy for an agency and its client businesses to restructure employment patterns to ensure that in the future the possibility of access to the conversion strategy is foreclosed to its workers.

---

[42] In other jurisdictions such behaviour has been evident with hours thresholds, and their impacts have been held to be discriminatory—see *Equal Opportunity Commission v Secretary of State for Employment*, [1994] 1 All ER 910.

[43] See, eg, *Clerks (South Australia) Award*, [2004] SAIR Comm 4.

Finally, in common with anti-discrimination legislation, the conversion strategy offers an individual solution to a structural problem. It depends upon the individual worker electing to convert and then reaching agreement with the individual employing business. Just as conversion is not mandatory for the worker, it can also be resisted by the employer where to do so is 'reasonable'. The reality of the power of managerial prerogative over the conversion process will no doubt replicate many of the problems already witnessed in the judgment of reasonableness in the anti-discrimination jurisdiction. Very few vulnerable workers are likely to press their conversion case through an arbitral process that does not guarantee success when their employer resists their request. Not surprising then, in the limited sectors where conversion rights have already been introduced they have not been greatly utilised. While choice and control of flexibility in the hands of employees may be desirable, most casual workers feel too powerless even to raise the matter let alone negotiate it to conclusion with their employers (Owens, 2002; Pocock *et al*, 2004). The lack of real individual autonomy in vulnerable women workers is compounded by the socio-cultural view, which they may internalise, that their work in the marketplace is very much secondary to their primary responsibility for reproductive work, and that their main objective is to maximise their income. The 'cashing out' of standard workplace rights through the loading that is part of the structure of casual employment in Australia is thus also likely to undermine attempts to eliminate long-term casual employment through strategies such as voluntary conversion.

FLEXIBLE STANDARDS

Even if it is preferable to ensure that all workers are covered by the same workplace standards, applied pro rata for part-time workers, there nonetheless remain questions about the nature of those standards. Some researchers argue that in enabling workers to have some power over their working lives and to balance the different aspects of their working lives satisfactorily, there is a need for policy interventions and legal reforms that do not to pit 'standards' against 'flexibility'. Rather, the challenge is to devise 'standards for flexibility'(Watson *et al*, 2003: 207).

The *Family Provisions Test Case*[44] presented one such opportunity. Business and employers agreed an increase to ten days per year of paid leave for workers (and more limited access to unpaid leave for casuals) to provide care to the family and members of their household. The remaining claims of the trade unions sought to provide in the award safety net a range of flexible

---

[44] See *Family Provisions Test Case*, 8 August 2005, PR 082005 (AIRC).

options to workers to enable them to accommodate work and family and care responsibilities. These options included extending unpaid parental leave from 12 months to 24 months, eight weeks of which may be taken by both parents concurrently; the availability of part-time work to care for a child up to the time he or she goes to school; the right to request a variation in hours of work, time of work and physical location of work; and the possibility to purchase extra leave to be taken in conjunction with annual leave or for emergency reasons. The great advantage of the claimed provisions over any existing regulation was that they sought to impose on employers a positive responsibility to respond to the needs of workers for flexibility, including a duty on employers to consider and agree to employee requests for flexibility, a duty to find alternatives that accommodate the needs of the worker where the requested measure is not possible, and a test of necessity rather than of mere reasonableness if the employer is to be excused for not responding to the requests of workers. The claimed provisions were far stricter than the approach under anti-discrimination law[45] and were less concerned with evaluating existing arrangements in the workplace and more focused on creating a workplace that would provide needed flexibility to workers. Furthermore, as regulatory standards established under the auspices of the AIRC, they could institute structural change more effectively than the individual complaint-based approach of anti-discrimination law.[46] In its arbitrated decision in the case, the AIRC provided only three new entitlements: it increased the amount of leave that could be taken simultaneously by parents of a new child from one week to eight weeks; it gave employees a right to request a second year of unpaid parental leave; and it gave a right to parents to request a return to part-time work until their child reaches school age. While the employer can only refuse the request on reasonable grounds related to the effect on the workplace or the employer's business, no formal process for dealing with a request was laid down. Nonetheless, the establishment of a right to request is an important starting point in facilitating multiple transitions enabling a true balancing of care work and paid work in the marketplace without destroying the security of a worker's attachment to the labour market.

The attainment of equality through flexible standards may, however, prove elusive. Already in Australia the possibility exists for flexible standards, known as facilitative clauses, which allow for individual variation of standards within a broad framework (sometimes requiring prior approval by collective agreement by a majority of workers at the workplace) to be

---

[45] In Australia, the test for indirect discrimination has never been as strict as 'necessity', but has always been the lesser standard of 'reasonableness'.

[46] Cf experience in the United Kingdom, which shows that even the introduction of a right for employees to request a flexible working pattern has increased employer willingness to consider such requests seriously (Palmer, 2004).

included in awards.[47] These facilitative provisions aim to allow individuals to tailor a wide range of workplace rights to suit their own needs, allowing, for instance, annual leave to be taken in single days, or a broader spans of hours within which ordinary time work hours can be worked.

Although identified as an important means of enabling workers to accommodate the otherwise conflicting demands of work and family, there is evidence that, to date, facilitative provisions have been little used especially by men (Commonwealth of Australia, 2002; Bittman *et al*, 2004). The 'right to request' provisions established by the *Family Provisions Test Case* will not necessarily mean that men will volunteer to take up the new opportunities for flexibility any more than they have in the past. Encouraging greater equality in the responsibility for family and care work is clearly a complex task. But there is some prospect that the AIRC (which is under a statutory obligation when exercising its powers in relation to the safety net[48] to take account of the public interest, the principles embodied in anti-discrimination legislation, and the principles in ILO Convention concerning Workers with Family Responsibilities (No 156)) may be able to contribute to this by also limiting the other side of flexibility, such as the long-hours culture. The decision of the AIRC to refuse to certify a collective agreement providing for '14 days on and 14 days off' for oil riggers because it would mean fathers would be too long away from their children is an example of the possibilities here, and shows that such considerations have the potential to override the protestations of business that such arrangements are conducive to greater productivity and efficiency.[49] Indeed, there is a growing worldwide recognition that the encouragement of flexible workplaces needs to go hand in hand with enabling men and boys to take greater responsibility for care work (United Nations Commission on the Status of Women, 2004). But even if the AIRC is here following rather than leading social attitudes (compare Hunter, 1988), it nonetheless adds an important element of 'public' control over what otherwise would remain a 'private' process with economic and social power unchecked. For similar reasons, too, it is important to include 'family provisions' in the award safety net because in a highly sex-segregated labour market such issues are not a high priority on the bargaining table in male-dominated enterprises (see

---

[47] See the *Family Leave Test Case* (1994), 57 IR 121 and the *Award Simplification Decision*, above n 8. For discussion, see Owens, 2005.

[48] See Workplace Relations Act 1996 (Cth), ss 90, 93, and 93A. These provisions can be seen as an example of 'fourth generation' equality duties (see Fredman, 2001).

[49] *Kellogg Brown and Root, Bass Strait (ESSO) Onshore/Offshore Facilities Certified Agreement 2000*, (7 September 2004) PR 951725 (AIRC) (Commissioner Whelan). Note this decision was successfully appealed in *Kellogg Brown and Root Pty Ltd and Ors and Esso Australia Pty Ltd* (31 January 2005) PR 955357 (AIRC) (President Justice Giudice, Vice-President Ross and Commissioner Gay).

Department of Employment and Workplace Relations and Office of the Employment Advocate, 2002, 2004; Owens, 2005). However, with the passage of the Work Choices Act 2005(Cth) only those awards that have incorporated the *Family Provisions Test Case* standards by March 2006 will be able to include them as safety net standards—in all other instances they will have to be incorporated in agreements.[50] Finally, none of this is to ignore the other major impediment to the transformative potential of flexible standards, the issue of pay equity, for as long as the economic consequences to families of men taking responsibility for family and care are more severe than when women do this work, there is little prospect of men taking a more equal share of care work.

PRECARIOUS WORK AND FLEXIBILITY: CHALLENGING LEGAL NORMS?

Of the three strategies discussed in this chapter, each offers some transformative possibilities. None of them alone can adequately address the problems of precarious work, and especially its gendered dimensions. Each has quite serious defects. None of the strategies challenges in a radical way the norms that underpin the law of work—its standard worker and its standards. Instead each, though in slightly different ways, assumes those norms. To gain flexibility anti-discrimination law requires women to prove they cannot comply with the workplace standards made for the normative worker; conversion assumes that much precarious work is in reality little different from that performed by law's normative worker; and flexible standards depend on an equal access and uptake by men and women. Each of the strategies, to varying degrees, assume workers to be an autonomous individual able to initiate actions that will change the circumstances of their working lives. Yet none appears to acknowledge explicitly the gendered contexts that shape and limit the choices those individual workers must make. While the strategy of using anti-discrimination is rejected in this chapter as unlikely to produce any real structural change in Australian workplaces, there is greater transformative potential in both strategies of conversion and flexible standards, although this chapter has suggested that some modifications are necessary to make them work. In combination, however, they offer some prospect for moving forward into a world where work might be more flexible, secure, and equal for all workers.

---

[50] Work Choices Act 2005(Cth), ss116, 116G and 117.

References

32 Hours, *Action for Full Employment*, online: <http://www.web.net/32hours> (date accessed: 22 August 2004).

Abraham, Katherine (1990) 'Restructuring the Employment Relationship: The Growth of Market Mediated Employment Relationships' in K Abraham (ed), *New Developments in the Labour Market* (Boston: MIT).

Abrams, Kathryn (1998) 'The New Jurisprudence of Sexual Harassment' *Cornell L Rev* 83 at 1169–230.

Acker, Joan (1988) 'Class, Gender, and the Relation of Distribution' *Signs* 13 at 473–97.

Adams, Edward S (2002) 'Using Evaluations to Break Down the Male Corporate Hierarchy: A Full Circle Approach' *Colorado Law Review* 73 at 117–72.

Adams, George (1995) *Canadian Labour Law*, 2nd edn (Aurora, Ontario: Canada Law Book Inc).

Adams, K Lee (2002) 'A Step Backward in Job Protection for Carers' *Australian Journal of Labour Law* 15 at 93–103.

Allan, Cameron (1998) 'Stabilising the Non-Standard Workforce: Managing Labour Utilisation in Private Hospitals' *Labour & Industry* 8(3) at 61–76.

Alston, Philip (2004) '"Core Labour Standards" and the Transformation of the International Labour Rights Regime' *European Journal of International Law* 15 at 457–521.

Alstott, Anne (2004) *No Exit: What Parents Owe Their Children and What Society Owes Parents* (New York: Oxford University Press).

Amsden, Alice (2001) *The Rise of 'the Rest': Challenges to the West from Late-Industrializing Economies* (New York: Oxford University Press).

Anctil, Hervé *et al* (2000) *Pour une politique de soutien à domicile des personnes ayant des incapacités et de soutien aux proches, Rapport du Comité pour la révision du Cadre de référence sur les services à domicile* (Quebec: Government of Quebec) ('Anctil Report').

Anderson, Bridget (2000) *Doing Dirty Work? The Global Politics of Domestic Labour* (London: Zed Books).

—— (2001) 'Just another job? Paying for Domestic Work' *Gender and Development* 9:1 at 25–33.

Anderson, Lucy (2003) 'Soundbite Legislation: the Employment Act 2002 and the New Flexible Working "Rights" for Parents' *Industrial Law Journal* 32 at 37–42.

Anghie, Antony (2002) 'Colonialism and the Birth of International Institutions: Sovereignty, Economy, and the Mandate System of the League of Nations' *New York University Journal of International Law and Politics* 34 at 513–633.

Antilla, Timo (2004) 'Why is it Difficult to Implement Daily Working Time Reduction?' Draft prepared for 9th International Symposium on Working Time, Paris, February 26–28 (draft manuscript).

Anttalainen, Marja-Liisa (1985) *Kvinnors förändrade ställning i samhället: De tude-lade arbetsmarknaderna* (Oslo: Nordisk ministerråd).

Aoyama, Yuko and Castells, Manuel (2002) 'An Empirical Assessment of the Informational Society: Employment and Occupational Structures of G-7 Countries, 1920–2000' *International Labour Review* 141 at 123–59.

Applebaum, Eileen (2001) 'Transformation of Work and Employment and New Insecurities' in P Auer and C Daniel (eds), *The Future of Work, Employment and Social Protection: The Search for New Securities in a World of Growing Uncertainties*. (Geneva: Ministry of Employment and Solidarity, France/International Labour Organization).

Arai, A Bruce (2000) 'Self-Employment as a Response to the Double Day for Women and Men in Canada' *The Canadian Review of Sociology and Anthropology* 37(2) at 125–42.

Arbeidsinspectie (2004) *Onderscheid naar arbeidsduur in cao's* (The Hague: Arbeidsinspectie).

Armstrong, Kenneth (2003) 'Tackling Social Exclusion through OMC: Reshaping the Boundaries of EU Governance' in Tanja Börzel and Rachel Cichowski (eds), *State of the Union: Law, Politics and Society* (Oxford: Oxford University Press).

Armstrong, Patricia (2001) 'The Context for Health Care Reform in Canada' in Patricia Armstrong *et al* (eds), *Exposing Privatization*. (Toronto: Garamond Press).

Armstrong, Patricia, and Armstrong, Hugh (2004) 'Thinking It Through: Women, Work and Caring in the New Millennium' in Karen R Grant *et al* (eds), *Caring For/Caring About: Women, Home Care and Unpaid Caregiving*. (Aurora, Ontario: Garamond Press).

Armstrong, Patricia and Kits, Olga (2004) 'One Hundred Years of Caregiving' in Karen R Grant *et al* (eds), *Caring For/Caring About: Women, Home Care and Unpaid Caregiving*. (Aurora, Ontario: Garamond Press).

Armstrong, Patricia and Laxer, Kate (2005) 'Precariousness in the Canadian Health Industry: Privatization, Ancillary Work and Women's Health' in Leah F Vosko (ed), *Precarious Employment: Understanding Labour Market Insecurity in Canada* (Montreal and Kingston: McGill-Queen's University Press).

Aronson, Jane (2004) '"Just Fed and Watered": Women's Experiences of the Gutting of Home Care in Ontario' in Karen R Grant *et al* (eds), *Caring For/Caring About: Women, Home Care and Unpaid Caregiving*. (Aurora, Ontario: Garamond Press).

Aronson, Jane and Neysmith, Sheila M (2001) 'Manufacturing Social Exclusion in the Home Care Market' *Canadian Public Policy* 27(2) at 151–65.

Aronsson, Gunnar (2002) 'Hälsoaspekter på tidsbegränsade anställningar' in *Hållfast arbetsrätt för ett föränderligt arbetsliv*, Government report, Ds 2002: 56 (appendix V) (Stockholm: Fritzes).

Arrow, Kenneth J (1998) 'What Has Economics to Say about Racial Discrimination?' *Journal of Economic Perspectives* 91–100.

Arthurs, Harry (1965) 'The Dependent Contractor: A Study of the Legal Problems of Countervailing Power' *University of Toronto Law Journal* 16 at 89–117.

—— (1996) 'Labour Law without the State' *University of Toronto Law Journal* 46 at 1–45.

—— (2002) 'Private Ordering and Workers' Rights in a Global Economy: Corporate Codes of Conduct in a Regime of Labour Market Regulation' in

Joanne Conaghan, Richard Michael Fischl, and Karl Klare (eds) *Labour Law in an Era of Globalization* (Oxford: Oxford University Press).

Arup, Chris (1995) 'Labour Market Regulation as a Focus for a Labour Law Discipline' in Richard Mitchell (ed) *Redefining Labour Law: New Perspectives on the Future of Teaching and Research* (Melbourne: Centre for Employment and Labour Relations Law, University of Melbourne).

—— (2001) 'Labour Law as Regulation – Promises and Pitfalls' *Australian Journal of Labour Law* 14 at 229–36.

Association des Aides Familiales du Québec (2002) 'Mémoire présenté au Ministre d'État aux Ressources humaines et au Travail sur le document', in *Revoir les normes du travail du Québec, un défi collectif* (Montréal: Association des Aides Familiales du Québec).

Association des Éducatrices et Éducateurs en Milieu Familial du Québec Inc 2003 *Mémoire de l'Association des éducatrices et éducateurs en milieu familial du Québec Inc (AÉMFQ) sur le projet de loi no 8 intitulé Loi modifiant la Loi sur les centres de la petite enfance et autres services de garde à l'enfance*, online: <www.aemfq.com/PDF%20et%20autres/Memoire_projet_loi_8.pdf> (date accessed: 15 August 2004).

Association féminine d'éducation et d'action sociale (AFÉAS) (Denyse Côté, Éric Gagnon, Claude Gilbert, Nancy Guberman, Francine Saillant, Nicole Thivierge, Marielle Tremblay) (1998) *Who Will Be Responsible for Providing Care? The Impact of the Shift to Ambulatory Care and of Social Economy Policies on Quebec Women* (Ottawa: Status of Women Canada).

Atkinson, John (1984) *Flexibility, Uncertainty and Manpower Management* (Brighton: Institute of Manpower Studies).

—— (1987) 'Flexibility or Fragmentation: the UK Labour Market in the Eighties' *Labour and Society* 12 at 87.

Australian Bureau of Statistics (ABS) (1988a) *Weekly Earnings of Employees (Distribution) Australia*, Cat No 6310.0 (Canberra: ABS).

—— (1988b) *Part-time, Casual and Temporary Employment, New South Wales*, Cat No 6247.1 (Canberra: ABS).

—— (2000) *Australian Social Trends. Population – Population Characteristics: 20th century: beginning and end* (Canberra: Yearbook, ABS).

—— (2002) *Australia Social Trends Work – Paid Work* (Canberra: Yearbook, ABS).

—— (2003) *Employee Earnings and Hours Survey, May 2002*, Cat No 6306 (Canberra: ABS).

—— (2004a) *Labour Force Status of Aboriginal and Torres Strait Islander Peoples* (Canberra: Yearbook Australia).

—— (2004b) *Employee Earnings, Benefits and Trade Union Membership*, Cat No 6310.0 (Canberra: ABS).

Ayres, Ian and Braithwaite, John (1992) *Responsive Regulation: Transcending the Deregulation Debate* (Oxford: Oxford University Press).

Baines, Susan and Gelder, Ulrike (2003) 'What is family friendly about the workplace in the home? The case of self-employed parents and their children' *New Technology, Work and Employment* 16 at 223–34.

Baird, Marion and Burgess, John (2003) 'Employment Entitlements: Development Access, Flexibility and Protection' *Australian Bulletin of Labour* 29 at 1–13.

Bakan, Abigail and Stasiulis, Daiva (1997) 'Foreign Domestic Worker Policy in Canada and the Social Boundaries of Modern Citizenship' in Abigail Bakan and Daiva Stasiulis, *Not One of the Family* (Toronto: University of Toronto Press).

Bankert, Ellen, Lee, Mary Dean, and Lange, Candace (2001) *SAS Institute: A Case on the Role of Senior Business Leaders in Driving Work/Life Cultural Change* (Philadelphia: The Wharton Work/Life Integration Project).

Banks, Olive (1981) *Faces of Feminism: A Study of Feminism as a Social Movement* (London: Martin Robertson).

Barenberg, Mark (1994) 'Democracy and Domination in the Law of Workplace Cooperation: From Bureaucratic to Flexible Production' *Columbia Law Review* 94 at 753–983.

Barnard, Catherine (1999) 'European "Social" Policy' in Paul Craig and Grainne de Burca (eds), *The Evolution of EU Law* (Oxford: Oxford University Press).

—— (2000) *EC Employment Law*, 2nd edn (Oxford: Oxford University Press).

Barnard, Catherine and Deakin, Simon (2002) 'Corporate Governance, European Governance, and Social Rights' in Bob Hepple (ed), *Social and Labour Rights in a Global Context* (Cambridge, UK: Cambridge University Press) at 122–50.

Barnard, Catherine, Deakin, Simon, and Hobbs, Richard (2003) 'Opting Out of the 48-Hour Week Employer Necessity or Individual Choice? An Empirical Study of the Operation of Article 18(1)(b) of the Working Time Directive in the UK' *Industrial Law Journal* 32(4) at 223–53.

Barnes, Angela and Preston, Alison (2002) 'Women, Work and Welfare: Globalisation, Labour Market Reform and the Rhetoric of Choice' *Australian Feminist Law Journal* 17 at 17–32.

Barnett, Rosalind C and Rivers, Caryl (1998) *She Works, He Works: How Two-Income Families are Happy, Healthy and Thriving* (Cambridge, MA: Harvard University Press).

Basok, Tanya (2002) *Tortillas and Tomatoes: Transmigrant Mexican Harvesters in Canada* (Montreal & Kingston: McGill-Queen's Press).

Båvner, Per (2001) *Half Full or Half Empty—Part-Time Work and Well-being Among Swedish Women* (Stockholm: Institutet för social forskning/Swedish Institute for Social Research).

Beck, Ulrich (2000) *The Brave New World of Work* (Cambridge, UK: Polity Press).

Beek, AMLJ, van Doorne-Huiskens, A and Veldman, A (2002) *Wet aanpassing arbeidsduur* (The Hague: Ministerie van SZW).

Befort, Stephen F (2003) 'Revisiting the Black Hole of Workplace Regulation: A Historical and Comparative Perspective of Contingent Work' *Berkeley Journal of Employment and Labour Law* 24 at 153–78.

Behrendt, Larissa (2003) *Achieving Social Justice: Indigenous Rights and Australia's Future* (Annandale, NSW: Federation Press).

Bell, Linda (1998) 'Differences in Work Hours and Hours Preferences By Race in the US' *Review of Social Economy* 56 at 481–500.

Bellman, Dale and Golden, Lonnie (2002) 'Which Workers are Non-Standard and Contingent and Does it Pay?' in Isik Urla Zeytinoglu (ed), *Flexible Work Arrangements: Conceptualizations and International Experiences* (The Hague: Kluwer Law International).

Bendel, Michael (1982) 'The Dependent Contractor: An Unnecessary and Flawed Development in Canadian Labour Law' *University of Toronto Law Journal* 32 at 374–411.

Beneria, Lourdes (1999) 'The Enduring Debate over Unpaid Labour' *International Labour Review* 138 at 237–309.

Benjamin, Paul (2002) 'Who Needs Labour Law? Defining the Scope of Labour Protection' in Joanne Conaghan, Richard Michael Fischl, and Karl Klare (eds), *Labour Law in an Era of Globalization* (Oxford: Oxford University Press).

Bennett, Laura (1995) 'Women and Enterprise Bargaining: The Legal and Institutional Framework' in Margaret Thornton, *Public and Private: Feminist Legal Debates* (Melbourne: Oxford University Press).

Berg, Peter, Appelbaum, Eileen, Bailey, Tom and Kalleberg, L. Arne (2004) 'Contesting Time. International Comparisons of Employee Control over Working Time' *Industrial and Labor Relations Review* 57 at 331–79.

Bergmann, Barbara (1986) *The Economic Emergence of Women* (New York: Basic Books).

—— (1996) *Saving Our Children From Poverty* (New York: Russell Sage Foundation).

Bergmann, Barbara and Heidi Hartmann (1995) 'A Welfare Reform Based on Help for Working Parents' *Feminist Economics*, January at 85–89.

Bernhardt, Annette and Marcotte, Dave E (2000) 'Is "Standard Employment" Still What It Used to Be?' in Françoise Carre, Marianne A Ferber, Lonnie Golden, and Stephen A Herzenberg (eds), *Nonstandard Work: The Nature and Challenges of Changing Employment Arrangements.* (Champaign, IL: Industrial Relations Research Association).

Berns, Sandra (2002) *Women Going Backwards: Law and Change in a Family-unfriendly Society* (Aldershot: Ashgate).

Bernstein, Stéphanie (2005) 'Precarious Employment in Quebec: Adapting Minimum Employment Standards Legislation to Serve Workers' in Leah F Vosko (ed), *Precarious Employment: Understanding Labour Market Insecurity in Canada*, (Montreal and Kingston: McGill-Queen's University Press).

Bernstein, Stéphanie, Lippel, Katherine, and Lamarche, Lucie (2001) *Women and Homework: The Canadian Legislative Framework* (Ottawa: Status of Women Canada).

Beveridge, William (1942) *Social insurance and allied services*, Cmnd 6404 (London, HMSO).

Bilous, Alexandre (2000) '35-Hour Working Week Law Adopted' *European Industrial Relations Observatory On-Line.* (Dublin: European Foundation for the Improvement of Living and Working Conditions), online: <www.eiro.euro-found.ie/>.

Bittman Michael and Pixley, Jocelyn (1997) *The Double Life of the Family: Myth, Hope and Experience* (St Leonards, NSW: Allen and Unwin).

Bittman, Michael, Hoffman, Sonia, and Thompson, Denise (2004) *Men's Uptake of Family Friendly Employment Provisions*, Canberra: Department of Family and Community Services, Social Policy Research Centre Paper No 22, online: <www.facs.gov.au/internet/facsinternet.nsf/aboutfacs/respubs/research-policyrespaperseries_twentytwo.htm> (date accessed: 6 December 2004).

Blackett, Adelle (1998) *Making Domestic Work Visible: The Case for Specific Regulation* (Geneva: International Labour Office).

—— (2001) 'Global Governance, Legal Pluralism and the Decentred State: A Labor Law Critique of Codes of Conduct' *Indiana Journal of Global Legal Studies* 8 at 401–47.

Blacklock, Cathy (2000) *Women and Trade in Canada: An Overview of Key Issues* (Ottawa: Status of Women Canada).

Blair, Tony (1998) 'Foreword' in Department of Trade and Industry (DTI), *Fairness at Work*, Paper presented to Parliament by the President of the Board of Trade, Cm 3968 (London: DTI).

—— (2002) *The Courage of our Convictions* (London: Fabian Society).

Blanchflower, David G. and Slaughter, Matthew (1998) 'The Causes and Consequences of Changing Earnings Inequality: W(h)ither the Debate?' in Frank Ackerman, Neva Goodwin, Laurie Dougherty, and Kevin Gallagher (eds) *The Changing Nature of Work*. (Washington, DC: Island Press).

Blau, Francine D (1986) 'Occupational Segregation and Labor Market Discrimination' in Barbara F Reskin (ed), *Sex Segregation in the Workplace* (Washington, DC: National Academy Press).

Blau, Francine D, Ferber, Marianne, and Winkler, Anne E. (1998) *The Economics of Women, Men and Work*, 3rd edn (Englewood Cliffs, NJ: Prentice-Hall).

Bloch-London, Catherine (2004) 'Assessment of the 35 Hour Week in France: From Goals to Results' in Patrick Fridenson and Benedicte Reynaud (eds), *France and the Age of Work, 1814–2004*, (Paris: Odile Jacob). Translated excerpt from chapter co-authored with Philippe Askenazy and Muriel Roger from book in French, online: <www.cnam.fr/griot/ComSITT/CBL.htm> (date accessed: 26 August 2004).

Boden, Richard (1999) 'Flexible Working Hours, Family Responsibilities, and Female Self-Employment' *American Journal of Economics and Sociology* 58 at 71–83.

Boris, Eileen and Prügl, Elizabeth (1996) *Homeworkers in Global Perspective: Invisible No More* (London: Routledge).

Borland, Jeff, Gregory, Bob, and Sheehan, Peter (2001) 'Inequality and economic change' in Jeff Borland, Bob Gregory, and Peter Sheehan *Inequality and Economic Change in Australia* (Melbourne, Centre for Strategic Economic Studies, Victoria University).

Bosch, Gerhard (1999) 'Working Time: Tendencies and Emerging Issues' *International Labour Review* 138 at 131–49.

—— (2000) 'Working time reductions, employment consequences and lessons from Europe: defusing a quasi-religious controversy' in Lonnie Golden and Deborah M Figart (eds), *Working Time: International trends, theory and policy perspectives* (London: Routledge), at 177–95.

Boyd, Susan B (1997) 'Challenging the Public/Private Divide: An Overview' in Susan B Boyd (ed), *Challenging the Public/Private Divide* (Toronto: University of Toronto Press).

Boydston, Jeanne 1990) *Home and Work: Housework, Wages, and the Ideology of Labor in the Early Republic* (New York/Oxford: Oxford University Press).

Boyer, Robert and Drache, Daniel (1996) 'Introduction' in Robert Boyer and Daniel Drache (eds) *States Against Markets: The Limits of Globalization* (London: Routledge).

Bradley, Harriet (1989) *Men's work, women's work—A sociological history of the sexual division of labour in employment* (Cambridge: Polity Press, in association with Basil Blackwell).

Bradshaw, John, Finch, Naomi, Kemp, Peter, Mayhew, Emise, and Williams, Julie (2003) *Gender and Poverty in Britain* (London: Equal Opportunities Commission).

Brodie, Stewart, Stanworth, John, and Wotuba, Thomas (2002) 'Direct Sales Franchises in the UK: A Self-Employment Grey Area' *International Small Business Journal* 20(1) at 53–76.

Brodsky, Gwen and Day, Shelagh (1996) 'The Duty to Accommodate: Who will Benefit?' *Canadian Bar Review* 75 at 433–73.

Brooks, Adrian (1988) 'Myth and Muddle – An Examination of Contracts for the Performance of Work' *University of New South Wales Law Journal* 11 at 48–101.

—— (1994) 'Approaches to the Regulation of Atypical Working Arrangements or Labour Law and Science Fiction' in Ron McCallum, Greg McCarry, and Paul Ronfeldt (eds), *Employment Security* (Sydney: Federation Press).

Brosnan, Peter and Thornthwaite, Louise (1998) '"The TV work is not so bad": The Experience of a Group of Homeworkers' *Labour & Industry* 8(3) at 97–113.

Brosnan, Peter and Walsh, Pat (1998) 'Employment Security in Australia and New Zealand' *Labour & Industry* 8(3) at 23–41.

Brown, William, Deakin, Simon, and Ryan, Paul (1997) 'The Effects of British Industrial Relations Legislation 1979–1997' *National Institute Economic Review* 161 at 69-83.

Bruegel, Irene (1998) 'The restructuring of the family wage system, wage relations and gender' in Linda Clarke, Peter de Gijsel, and Jorn Janssen (eds), *The Dynamics of Wage Relations in the New Europe* (London: Kluwer), at 214–28.

Bruegel, Irene and Diane Perrons (1998) 'Deregulation and Women's Employment: The Diverse Experience of Women in Britain' *Feminist Economics* 4 at 103–25.

Bryson Alex, and White, Michael (1996) *From Unemployment to Self-Employment* (London: Policy Studies Institute).

Buechtemann, Christopher and Quack, Sigrid (1989) 'Bridges or Traps: Non-Standard Employment in the Federal Republic of Germany' in Gerry Rodgers and Janine Rodgers (eds), *Precarious Jobs in Labour Market Regulation: The Growth of Atypical Employment in Western Europe* (Geneva: ILO).

—— (1990) 'How Precarious is "Non-standard" Employment? Evidence for West Germany' *Cambridge Journal of Economics* 14 at 315–29.

Bulow, Jeremy I and Summers, Lawrence H (1986) 'A Theory of Dual Labor Markets with Application to Industrial Policy, Discrimination, and Keynesian Unemployment' *Journal of Labour Economics* 4 at 376–414.

Burchell, Brendan and Rubery, Jill (1992) 'Categorizing Self-Employment: Some Evidence from the Social Change and Economic Life Initiative in the UK' in Patricia Leighton and Alan Felstead (eds), *The New Entrepreneurs: Self-employment and Small Business in Europe* (London: Kegan Paul Ltd).

Burchell, Brendan, Deakin, Simon, and Honey, Shelia (1999) *The Employment Status of Individuals in Non-Standard Employment*. Report prepared for the Department of Trade and Industry, England.

Burgess, John and Campbell, Iain (1998) 'The Nature and Dimensions of Precarious Employment in Australia' *Labour & Industry* 8(3) at 5–21.

Burgess, John and Strachan, Glenda (1998) 'Equal Employment Opportunity, Employment Restructuring and Enterprise Bargaining: Complementary or Contradictory?' *Journal of Interdisciplinary Gender Studies* 3 at 23–37.

—— (2000) 'The Incompatibility of Decentralised Bargaining and Equal Opportunity in Australia' *British Journal of Industrial Relations* 38 at 361–80.

—— (2002) 'The Home as the Workplace: Developments in Homeworking in Australia' in Gregor Murray, Collette Bernier, Denis Harrison, and Terry H Wagner (eds) *Rethinking Institutions for Work and Employment* (Quebec: University of Laval).

Burri, Susanne (2000) *Tijd delen. Deeltijd, gelijkheid en gender in Europees- en nationaalrechtelijk perspectief* (Deventer: Kluwer).*

—— (2001) 'Part-time Work in the Netherlands. Towards Policies on Differentiation of Working Time During One's Lifetime?' *EuroAS* 11 at 208–17.

—— (2004) 'Aanpassing van de arbeidsduur: evaluatie en rechtspraak' *Sociaal Maandblad Arbeid 2004* at 502–12.

—— (2005) 'Working Time Adjustment Policies in the Netherlands' in A Hegewisch (ed), *Working Time for Working Families: Europe and the United States. Contributions to a Program of the Washington Office of the Friedrich Ebert Foundation in Cooperation with the Work Life Program at American University Washington College of Law and the Hans Böckler Foundation* (Washington, DC: Friedrich Ebert Stiftung).

Burri, Susanne, Opitz, Heike, and Veldman, Albertine (2003) 'Work Family Policies on Working Time put into Practice. A Comparison of Dutch and German Case Law on Working Time Adjustment' *The International Journal of Comparative Labour Law and Industrial Relations* 19 at 321–46.

Cahn, Naomi R (2001) ,The Coin of the Realm: Poverty and the Commodification of Gendered Labor' *Journal of Gender, Race and Justice* 5 at 1–30.

Callus, Ron and Lansbury, Russell D (eds) (2002) *Working Futures: The Changing Nature of Work and Employment Relations in Australia* (Sydney: The Federation Press).

Campbell, Iain (1996) 'Casual Employment, Labour Regulation and Australian Trade Unions' *Journal of Industrial Relations* 38 at 571–99.

—— (1997) 'Working-Time: Comparing Australia and Germany'. in Paul James, Walter F Veit, and Steve Wright (eds), *Work of the Future: Global Perspectives* (St Leonards, NSW: Allen and Unwin).

—— (2000) 'The Spreading Net: Age and Gender in the Process of Casualisation in Australia' *Journal of Australian Political Economy* 45 at 68–99.

Campbell, Iain and Burgess, John (2001) 'A New Estimate of Casual Employment' *Australian Bulletin of Labour* 27(2) at 85–108.

Canada Employment Insurance Commission (2004) 'Employment Insurance 2003 Monitoring and Assessment Report', submitted to the Minister of Human Resources and Skills Development Canada (Ottawa: Government of Canada).

Canada, House of Commons (2001) Standing Committee on Human Resources Development and the Status of Persons with Disabilities, Third Report: *Employment Insurance.*

Cancedda, Alessandra (2001) *Employment in Household Services* (Dublin: European Foundation for the Improvement of Living and Working Conditions).

Caracciolo di Torella, Eugenia (2001) 'The "Family-Friendly" Workplace: The EC Position' *International Journal of Comparative Labour Law and Industrial Relations* 17 at 325–44.

Carter, Donald, England, Geoff, Etherington, Brian, and Trudeau. Gilles (2002) *Labour Law in Canada* (The Hague: Kluwer Law International).

Caruso, Bruno (2002) 'Immigration Policies in Southern Europe: More State, Less Market?' in Joanne Conaghan, Richard Michael Fischl, and Karl Klare (eds), *Labour Law in an Era of Globalization: Transformative Practices and Possibilities* (Oxford: Oxford University Press).

Castells, Manuel (1996) *The Rise of the Network Society* (Oxford: Blackwells).

—— (2000) *The Rise of the Network Society, vol I, The Information Age: Economy Society and Culture*, 2nd edn (Oxford: Blackwells).

Center for Religion, Ethics, and Social Policy at Cornell University *Take Back Your Time Day*, online: <www.timeday.org> (date accessed: 22 August 2004).

Chamallas, Martha (1999) 'Mothers and Disparate Treatment: The Ghost of *Martin Marietta*' *Villanova Law Review* 44 at 337–54.

Chantier de l'Économie Sociale (2000) *Mémoire du Chantier de l'économie sociale à la Commission sur l'organisation des services de santé et des services sociaux* (Montreal: Chantier de l'Économie Sociale).

Chapman, Anna (2005) 'Work/Family, Australian Labour Law and the Normative Worker' in Joanne Conaghan and Kerry Rittich (eds), *Labour Law, Work and Family: Critical and Comparative Perspectives* (Oxford: Oxford University Press).

Charlesworth, Sara (1996) *Stretching Flexibility: Enterprise Bargaining, Women Workers and Changes to Working Hours* (Australia: Human Rights and Equal Opportunity Commission).

Citizenship and Immigration Canada (2004) *Foreign Worker Manual—FW I* (Ottawa: Government of Canada).

Clarkson, Stephen (2002) *Uncle Sam and Us: Globalization, Neoconservatism, and the Canadian State* (Toronto: Toronto University Press).

Collins, Hugh (1990) 'Independent Contractors and the Challenge of Vertical Disintegration to Employment Protection Laws' *Oxford Journal of Legal Studies* 10 at 331–80.

—— (2000) 'Employment Rights of Casual Workers' *Industrial Law Journal* 29 at 73–78.

—— (2001) 'Regulating the Employment Relation for Competitiveness' *Industrial Law Journal* 30 at 17–47.

—— (2002) 'Is There a Third Way in Labour Law?' in Joanne Conaghan, Richard Michael Fischl and Karl Klare (eds), *Labour Law in an Era of Globalization* (Oxford: Oxford University Press) at 449–70.

—— (2003a) 'Discrimination, Equality and Social Inclusion' *Modern Law Review* 66 at 16–43.

—— (2003b) *Employment Law* (Oxford: Oxford University Press).

—— (2005) 'The Right to Flexibility' in Joanne Conaghan and Kerry Rittich (eds), *Labour Law, Work and Family: Critical and Comparative Perspectives* (Oxford: Oxford University Press).

Coltrane, Scott (1996) *Family Man: Fatherhood, Housework, and Gender Equity* (New York, NY: Oxford University Press).

Comeau, Yvan (2003) 'La diversité du rapport salarial dans le troisième secteur' *Service Social* 50 at 199–230.

Commission of the European Communities (CEC) (1997a) *Employment in Europe 1997*, (Luxembourg: Office for Official Publications of the European Communities).

—— (1997b) *Green Paper: Partnership for a New Organisation of Work* (Luxembourg: Office for Official Publications of the European Communities).

—— (1999) *Joint Employment Report 1999* (Luxembourg: Office for Official Publications of the European Communities).

—— (2000) *Towards a Community Framework Strategy on Gender Equality (2001–2005)* (Luxembourg: Office for Official Publications of the European Communities).

—— (2001a) *Employment and Social Policies: A Framework for Investing in Quality* (Luxembourg: Office for Official Publications of the European Communities).

—— (2001b) *Employment in Europe 2001: Recent Trends and Prospects* (Luxembourg: Office for Official Publications of the European Communities).

—— (2001c) *Draft Joint Social Inclusion Report* (Luxembourg: Office for Official Publications of the European Communities).

—— (2001d) Communication from the Commission to the Council, the European Parliament, and the Economic and Social Committee, *Promoting Core Labour Standards and Improving Social Governance in the Context of Globalisation* (Luxembourg: Office for Official Publications of the European Communities).

—— (2002a) *Joint Employment Report 2001* (Luxembourg: Office for Official Publications of the European Communities).

—— (2002b) *Employment in Europe 2002: Recent Trends and Prospects* (Luxembourg: Office for Official Publications of the European Communities).

—— (2003a) *Employment in Europe 2003: Recent Trends and Prospects* (Luxembourg: Office for Official Publications of the European Communities).

—— (2003b) Communication, *Improving Quality in Work: A Review of Recent Progress* (Luxembourg: Office for Official Publications of the European Communities).

—— (2003c) Communication from the Commission, *The Future of the European Employment Strategy (EES): A Strategy for Full Employment and Better Jobs for All*, COM (2003) 6 final (Luxembourg: Office for Official Publications of the European Communities).

—— (2004a) *Joint Employment Report 2003/4*, COM (2004) 24 final, Brussels, 9 January (Luxembourg: Office for Official Publications of the European Communities).

—— (2004b) Report from the Commission to the Council, the European Parliament, the European Economic and Social Committee and the Committee of the Regions *Report on Equality between Men and Women* COM (2004) 115 final, Brussels, 19 February (Luxembourg: Office for Official Publications of the European Communities)

Commission of the European Communities and Council (2004) *Joint report by the Commission and the Council on social inclusion: The Joint Inclusion Report 2003* (Luxembourg: Office for Official Publications of the European Communities).

Commission on Labor Cooperation (2003) *The Rights of Nonstandard Workers: A North American Guide* (Washington, DC: Secretariat of the Commission for Labor Cooperation).

Commission des normes du travail (CNT) et Ministère du Travail (2002) *Évaluation des impacts économiques des modifications proposées à la Loi sur les normes du travail* (Quebec: CNT and Ministère du Travail).

Commission of Social Justice (1994) *Social Justice: Strategies for Renewal* (London: Vintage).

Committee on Women's Employment and Related Social Issues (1986) (Barbara F Reskin and Heidi I Hartmann (eds)) *Women's Work, Men's Work: Sex Segregation on the Job* (Washington, DC: National Academy Press).

Commonwealth of Australia (2002) *OECD Review of Family friendly Policies: The Reconciliation of Work and Family Australia's Background Report*, prepared by the Department of Family and Community Services and Department of Employment and Workplace Relations, with assistance from the Work and Family Life Consortium, online: <www.oecd.org> (date accessed: 1 September 2004).

Conaghan, Joanne (1986) 'The Invisibility of Women in Labour Law' *International Journal of the Sociology of Law* 14 at 377–92.

—— (1999) 'Feminism and Labour Law: Contesting the Terrain' in Anne Morris and Therese O'Donnell (eds), *Feminist Perspectives on Employment Law* (London: Cavendish Publishing).

—— (2000) 'The Family-Friendly Workplace in Labour Law Discourse: Some Reflections on *London Underground v Edwards*' in Hugh Collins, Paul Davies, and Roger Rideout, *Legal Regulation of the Employment Relation* (London: Kluwer Law International).

—— (2002) 'Women, Work and Family: A British Revolution?' in Joanne Conaghan, Richard Michael Fischl, and Karl Klare (eds), *Labour Law in an Era of Globalization: Transformative Practices and Possibilities* (London: Oxford University Press), 54–73.

—— (2003) 'Labour Law and "New Economy" Discourse' *Australian Journal of Labour Law* 16 at 9–27.

Conaghan, Joanne and Chudleigh, Louise (1987) 'Women in Confinement: Can Labour Law Deliver the Goods?' *Journal of Law and Society* 14 at 133–48.

Conaghan, Joanne and Rittich, Kerry (eds) (2005) *Labour Law, Work and Family: Critical and Comparative Perspectives* (Oxford: Oxford University Press).

Connell, Robert William (1987) *Gender and Power* (Cambridge: Polity Press).

Conseil du Statut de la Femme (CSF) (1990) *Mémoire présenté à la Commission des affaires sociales sur l'avant-projet de loi modifiant la Loi sur les normes du travail: Avis adopté par les membres du Conseil du statut de la femme à l'assemblée des 17 et 18 janvier 1990* (Québec: CSF).

—— (2002a) *Avis du Conseil du statut de la femme: Mémoire sur le document de consultation 'Revoir les normes du travail: un défi collectif'* (Quebec: CSF).

—— (2002b) *Avis: Mémoire sur le projet de loi no 143, Loi modifiant la Loi sur les normes du travail et d'autres dispositions législatives* (Quebec: CSF).

Cooke-Reynolds, Melissa and Zukewich, Nancy (2004) 'The Feminization of Work' in *Canadian Social Trends* (Ottawa: Statistics Canada—Catalogue No 11-008), 24–29.

Cooney, Sean (1999) 'Testing Times for the ILO: Institutional Reform for the New International Political Economy' *Comparative Labour and Policy Journal* 20 at 365–400.

Costa, Dora L (2000) 'Hours of Work and the Fair Labor Standards Act: A Study of Retail and Wholesale Trade 1938–1950' *Industrial and Labor Relations Review* 53 at 648–64.

Cousins, Christine (1999) 'Changing Regulatory Frameworks and Non-Standard Employment: A Comparison of Germany, Spain, Sweden and the UK' in Alan Felstead and Nick Jewson. (eds), *Global Trends in Flexible Labour* (Basingstoke, England: Macmillan Business).

Coussins, Jean (1979) *The Shift-work Scandal* (London: National Council of Civil Liberties).

Cox, Rachel (2005) *Making Family Child Care Work: Strategies for Improving the Working Conditions of Family Childcare Providers* (Ottawa, Status of Women Canada).

Crain, Marion (1999) 'Where have all the Cowboys Gone? Marriage and Breadwinning in Post-industrial Society' *Ohio State Law Journal* 60 at 1877–963.

Cranford, Cynthia, Fudge, Judy, Tucker, Eric, and Vosko, Leah (2005) *Self-Employed Workers Organize: Law, Policy and Unions* (Montreal and Kingston: McGill-Queen's University Press).

Crawley, Miles (2000) 'Labour Hire and the Employment Relationship' *Australian Journal of Labour Law* 13 at 291–96.

Creighton, Breen (1995) 'Employment Security and "Atypical" Work in Australia'. *Comparative Labour Law Journal* 16 at 285–316.

Creighton, Breen and Stewart, Andrew (2000) *Labour Law: An Introduction*, 3rd edn (Sydney: Federation Press).

Cully, Mark (2002) 'The Cleaner, the Waiter and the Computer Operator: Job Change 1986–2001' *Australian Bulletin of Labour* 28 at 141–62.

Curry, Chris (2003) *The Under-Pensioned: Women* (London: Pensions Policy Institute).

Dale, Angela (1986) 'Social Class and The Self-Employed' *Sociology* 20 at 430–34.

Dale, Angela (1991) 'Self-Employment and entrepreneurship: notes on two problematic concepts' in R Burrows (ed), *Deciphering Self-Employment* (London and New York: Routledge).

Darity, William A and Mason, Patrick L (1998) 'Evidence of Discrimination in Employment: Codes of Colour, Codes of Gender' *Journal of Economic Perspectives* 12 at 63–90.

Davies, Paul and Freedland, Mark (1983) *Kahn Freund's Labour and the Law* (London: Stevens & Sons).

—— (1984) *Labour Law: Text, Cases and Materials*, 2nd edn (London: Weidenfeld and Nicolson).

—— (2001) 'Employees, Workers, and the Autonomy of Labour Law' in Dieter Simon and Manfred Weiss (eds), *Zur Autonomie des Individuums* (Baden-Baden: Nomos Verlagsgellschaft), at 31–46.

Davidov, Guy (2002) 'The Three Axes of Employment Relationships: A Characterization of Workers in Need of Protection' *University of Toronto Law Journal* 52 at 356–418.

De Geus, AJ (2004a) Letter from the Minister of Social Affairs and Employment De Geus (2 April 2004) to the Second Chamber of Parliament, AV/WTZ/ 2000/24015.

—— (2004b) Letter from the Minister of Social Affairs and Employment De Geus (8 April 2004) to the Second Chamber of Parliament, AV/IR/2004/21163.

De Groot, Raphaëlle and Ouellet, Elizabeth (2001) *Plus que parfaits: Les aides familiales à Montréal 1850–2000* (Montreal: Éditions du Remue-Ménage).

De Soto, Hernando (2000) *The Mystery of Capital: Why Capitalism Triumphs in the West and Fails Everywhere Else* (New York: Basic Books).

Deakin, Simon (1998) 'The Evolution of the Contract of Employment, 1900–1950' in N Whiteside and R Salais (eds), *Governance, Industry and Labour Markets in Britain and France* (London: Routledge).

—— (2001) 'The Contract of Employment: A Study in Legal Evolution' *Historical Studies in Industrial Relations* 11 at 1–36.

—— (2002) 'The Many Futures of the Contract of Employment' in Joanne Conaghan, Richard Michael Fischl, and Karl Klare (eds), *Labour Law in an Era of Globalization: Transformative Practices and Possibilities* (Oxford: Oxford University Press).

Deakin, Simon and Browne, Jude (2003) 'Social Rights and Market Order: Adapting the Capability Approach' in Tamarra K Hervey and Jeff Kenner (eds), *Economic and Social Rights under the EU Charter of Fundamental Rights* (Oxford: Hart Publishing), at 27–44.

Deakin, Simon and Morris, Gillian (1998) *Labour Law*, 2nd edn (London: Butterworths).

—— (2001) *Labour Law*, 3rd edn (London: Butterworths).

Deakin, Simon and Wilkinson, Frank (2000) 'Labour Law and Economic Theory: A Reappraisal' in Hugh Collins, Paul Davies, and Roger Rideout (eds), *Legal Regulation of the Employment Relation* (London: Kluwer Law International), at 29–62.

Deery, Stephen and Mitchell, Richard (eds) (1999) *Employment Relations: Individualisation and Union Exclusion—An International Study* (Sydney, NSW: The Federation Press).

Delage, Benoit (2002) *Results from the survey of self-employment in Canada* (Hull, Québec: Human Resources Development Canada, online: <dsp-psd.communi- cation.gc.ca/Collection?RH64-12-2001E.pdf> (date accessed: 16 September 2004).

Department of Employment and Workplace Relations and Office of the Employment Advocate (DEWR & OEA) (2002) *Agreement Making in Australia under the Workplace Relations Act 2000–2001* (Canberra: Commonwealth of Australia).

—— (2004) *Agreement Making in Australia under the Workplace Relations Act 2002–2003* (Canberra: Commonwealth of Australia).

Deutsch, Francine (1999) *Halving it all: How equally shared parenting works* (Cambridge, MA: Harvard University Press).

Dickens, Linda (1992) *Whose flexibility?: Discrimination and Equality Issues in Atypical Work* (London: The Institute of Employment Rights).

—— (2004) 'Problems of Fit: Changing Employment and Labour Regulation' *British Journal of Industrial Relations* 42(4) at 595–616.

Dif, M'hamed (1998) 'Flexibilité du travail et ses implications pour l'emploi: réflexions sur les modèles émergents' *Économies et Sociétés* 20: 3 at 231–46.

Dobrzynski, Judith H (1996) 'Somber News for Women on Corporate Ladder' *New York Times*, 6 November, p D1.

Dombois, Rainer, Hornberger, Erhard, and Winter, Jens (2003) 'Transnational Labor Regulation and the NAFTA—A Problem of Institutional Design? The Case of the North American Agreement on Labor Cooperation between the USA, Mexico and Canada' *Comparative Labour Law and Industrial Relations* 19 at 421–40.

Donahue, John and Heckman, James (1991) 'Continuous vs Episodic Change: The Impact of Civil Rights Policy on the Economic Status of Blacks' *Journal of Economic Literature* 29 at 1603–72.

Dowling, Craig and Howe, John (2002) 'Fried Chicken, Unfair Dismissal and Job Creation: One of These Things is Not Like the Other' *Australian Journal of Labour Law* 15 at 1–7.

Drago, Robert *et al* (2001) Final Report to the Alfred P Sloan Foundation for the Faculty and Families Project, Work–Family Working Paper 01–02, Pennsylvania State University.

Dunlop, John Thomas *et al* (1994) *The Dunlop Commission on the Future of Worker-Management Relations* (Washington, DC: United States Department of Commerce and Department of Labor).

Eardley, Tony and Corden, Anne (1996) *Low Income Self-Employment* (Aldershot: Avebury).

Egger, Phillippe (2002) 'Towards a policy framework for decent work' *International Labour Review* 141 at 161–74.

Eisenbrey, Ross (2003) 'The Naked Truth About Comp Time: Current Proposal is like Emperor's New Clothes: There's Nothing There for Workers' *EPI Issue Brief*, 31 March, p 1.

Elder, Sara and Schmidt, Dorothea (2004) *Global EmploymentTrends for Women, 2004* (Geneva: Employment Trends Unit, Employment Strategy Development, International Labour Organization).

Elias, Peter (2000) 'Status in Employment: A world survey of practices and problems' *Bulletin of Labour Statistics* 1 at XI–XIX.

Elson, Diane (1999) 'Labour Markets as Gendered Institutions: Equality, Efficiency and Empowerment Issues' *World Development* 27 at 611–27.

Elvin-Nowak, Ylva (1999. *Accompanied by guilt—Modern motherhood the Swedish way* (Edsbruk: Stockholm University).

Engblom, Samuel (2001) 'Equal Treatment of Employees and Self-employed Workers' *International Journal of Comparative Labour Law and Industrial Relations* 17 at 211–31.

Engels, Frederick (1972) *The Origin of the Family, Private Property and the State* (London: Lawrence and Wishart) (original edition, 1884).

—— (1977) *The Condition of the Working Class in England* (London: Progress Publications) (original edition, 1845).

England, Geoffrey, Wood, Roderick, and Christie, Innis (2005) *Employment Law in Canada*, 4th edn (Toronto: Butterworths).

Equal Opportunities Commission (EOC) (1979) *Health and Safety Legislation: Should we Distinguish between Men and Women?* (Manchester: EOC).

—— (2003) *Facts about Men and Women in Great Britain* (Manchester: EOC).

—— (2004) *Facts about Men and Women in Britain* (Manchester: EOC).

Ertman, Martha M (1998) 'Commercializing Marriage: A Proposal for Valuing Women's Work through Premarital Security Agreements' *Texas Law Review* 77 at 17–110.

Esping-Andersen, Gosta (1999) *Social Foundations of Post-industrial Economies* (Oxford: Oxford University Press).

Estlund, Cynthia (2004) 'Reconstituting Employee Representation in an Era of Self-Regulation' (draft manuscript).

European Commission (1998) *Transformation of Labour and Future of Labour Law in Europe* (Luxembourg: Office for Official Publications of the European Communities).

—— (2003a) *Economically Dependent/quasi subordinate (para subordinate) employment* (Luxembourg: Office for Official Publications of the European Communities).

—— (2003b) *Employment in Europe 2003* (Luxembourg: Office for Official Publications of the European Communities).

—— (2004) *Employment in Europe 2004. Recent Trends and Prospects* (Luxembourg: Office for Official Publications of the European Communities).

European Foundation for the Improvement of Living and Working Conditions (2002) *Temporary Agency Work in the European Union* (Luxembourg: Office for Official Publications of the European Communities).

European Study of Precarious Employment (ESOPE) (2002) 'Defining and Assessing Precarious Employment in Europe: A Review of Main Studies and Surveys. A Tentative Approach to Precarious Employment in France' in Jean-Claude Barbier, Angélina Brygoo and Frédéric Viguier, *Precarious Employment in Europe: A Comparative Study of Labour Market related Risks in Flexible Economies* (Paris: Centre d'études de l'emploi).

—— (2003) (Jean-Claude Barbier, Angélina Brygoo, Frédéric Viguier, and Françoise Tarquis (eds)) *Normative and regulatory frameworks influencing the flexibility, security, quality and precariousness of jobs in France, Germany, Italy, Spain and the United Kingdom* (Paris: Centre d'études de l'emploi).

—— (2004) (Miguel Laparra, Jean-Claude Barbier, Isabelle Darmon, Nicola Düll, Carlos Frade, Luigi Frey, Robert Lindley, and Kurt Vogler-Ludwig (eds)) *Managing labour market related risks in Europe: Policy implications* (Paris: Centre d'études de l'emploi).

Eurostat (Statistical Office of the European Communities in Luxembourg) (1999) *News Release 78/99*, 10 August (Luxembourg: Eurostat).

—— (2002a) *Eurostat News Release No 60/2002* (Luxembourg: Eurostat).

—— (2002b) *News Release No 86/2002*, 'Temporary work in the EU', 19 July (Luxembourg: Eurostat).

—— (2004a) *News Release 72/2004*, 2 June (Luxembourg: Eurostat).

—— (2004b) *News Release 97/2004*, 3 August (Luxembourg: Eurostat).

Fagan, Collette and Warren, Tracey (2001) *Gender, Employment and Working Time Preferences in Europe* (Dublin: European Foundation for the Improvement of Living and Working Conditions).

Fajertag, Giuseppe (1999) 'New Paths in Working-Time Policies in Europe: The Difficult Challenge of Reconciling Employers' and Employees' Need for Flexibility' *Labour & Industry* 9 at 145–60.

Felstead, Alan (1991) 'The Social Organization of the Franchise: A case of controlled self-employment' *Work, Employment and Society* 5(1) at 37–57.

Felstead, Alan and Jewson, Nick (1999) 'Flexible Labour and Non-Standard Employment: An Agenda of Issues' in Alan Felstead and Nick Jewson (eds), *Global Trends in Flexible Labour*. (Basingstoke, England: MacMillan Business).

Felstead, Alan and Leighton, Patricia (1992) 'Issues, Themes and Reflections on the "Enterprise Culture"' in Patricia Leighton, and Alan Felstead (eds), *The New Entrepreneurs: Self-employment and Small Business in Europe* (London: Kegan Paul Ltd).

Fenwick, Colin (1992) 'Shooting for Trouble? Contract Labour in the Victorian Building Industry' *Australian Journal of Labour Law* 5 at 237–61.

Figart, Deborah M and Mutari, Ellen (1998) 'Degendering Work Time in Comparative Perspective: Alternative Policy Frameworks' *Review of Social Economy* 56 at 460–80.

—— (2000) 'Work Time Regimes in Europe: Can Flexibility and Gender Equity Coexist?' *Journal of Economic Issues* 34 at 847–71.

Fineman, Martha Albertson (1995) *The Neutered Mother, the Sexual Family and Other Twentieth Century Tragedies* (New York: Routledge).

Flanagan, Robert J (2003) 'Labor Standards and International Competitive Advantage' in Robert J Flanagan and William B Gould IV (eds), *International Labor Standards* (Stanford, CA: Stanford Law and Politics).

Florin, Christina and Nilsson, Bengt (2002) *"Något som liknar en oblodig revolution"—jämställdhetens politisering under 1960- och 1970-talen* (Umeå: Umeå Universitet).

Folbre, Nancy (2001) 'Accounting for Care in the United States' in Mary Daly (ed), *Care Work: The Quest for Security* (Geneva: International Labour Office), at 175–191.

Frader, Laura L and Rose, Sonya O (1996) 'Introduction: Gender and the Reconstruction of European Working-Class History' in Laura L Frader and Sonya O Rose (eds), *Gender and Class in Modern Europe* (Ithaca: Cornell University Press).

Franco, Ana and Winquist, Karin (2002) 'Women and men reconciling work and family life' *Statistics in focus* Theme, 3-9/2002 (Luxembourg: Eurostat).

Frangeur, Renée (1998) *Yrkeskvinna eller makens tjänarinna? Striden om yrkesrätten för gifta kvinnor i mellankrigstidens Sverige* (Lund: Arkiv).

Fraser, Nancy (1993) 'After the Family Wage: Gender Equity and the Welfare State' *Political Theory* 22(4) at 591–618.

—— (1997) *Justice Interruptus: Critical Reflections on the "Postsocialist" Condition* (New York: Routledge).

Fraser, Nancy and Gordon, Linda (1994) 'A Genealogy of Dependency: Tracing a Keyword for the US Welfare State' *Signs* 19(2) at 309–34.

Fredman, Sandra (1997a) *Women and the Law* (Oxford: Clarendon Press).

—— (1997b) 'Labour Law in Flux: The Changing Composition of the Workforce' *Industrial Law Journal* 26 at 337–52.

—— (2001) 'Equality: A New Generation?' *Industrial Law Journal* 30 at 145–68.

—— (2004a) 'The Ideology of New Labour Law' in Catherine Barnard, Simon Deakin, and Gillian S Morris (eds), *Essays in Honour of Bob Hepple* (Oxford: Hart Publishing), at 9–41.

—— (2004b) 'Women at Work: The Broken Promise of Flexicurity' *Industrial Law Journal* 33 at 299–319.

Freedland, Mark (1999) UK National Study, *ILO Meeting of Experts on Workers in Situations Needing Protection* (Geneva: International Labour Office).

—— (2003) *The Personal Employment Contract* (Oxford: Oxford University Press).

Freeman, Richard (1998) 'War of the Models: Which Labour Market Institutions for the 21st Century?' *Labour Economics* 5 at 1–24.

Frenette, Marc (2002) 'Do the Falling Earnings of Immigrants Apply to Self-Employed Immigrants', Analytic Studies Branch, Research Paper Series, No 195 (Ottawa: Statistics Canada).

Fudge, Judy (1997a) *Precarious Work and Families* (Toronto: Centre for Research on Work and Society, York University).

—— (1997b) 'Little Victories, Big Defeats: The Rise and Fall of Collective Bargaining Rights for Domestic Workers' Rights in Ontario', in Abigail B Bakan and Daiva Stasiulis (eds), *Not One of the Family: Foreign Domestic Workers in Canada* (Toronto: University of Toronto Press).

—— (1999) 'Legal Forms and Social Norms: Class, Gender and the Legal Regulation of Women's Work from 1870 to 1920' in Elizabeth Comack (ed), *Locating Law: Race/Class/Gender Connection* (Halifax: Fernwood).

—— (2000a) 'Consumers to the Rescue? Corporate Campaigns Against Labour Abuse' in Susan B Boyd, Dorothy Chunn, and Bob Menzies (eds), *Abusing Power* (Halifax: Fernwood).

—— (2000b) 'The Paradoxes of Pay Equity: Reflections on the Law and The Market in *Bell Canada* and the *Public Service Alliance of Canada*' *Canadian Journal of Women and the Law* 12 at 313–44.

—— (2001) 'Flexibility and Feminization: The New Ontario Employment Standards Act' *Journal of Law and Social Policy* 16 at 1–22.

—— (2002) 'From Segregation to Privatization: Equality, the Law, and Women Public Servants, 1980-2001' in Judy Fudge and Brenda Cossman *Privatization, Law and the Challenge to Feminism* (Toronto: University of Toronto Press).

—— (2003) 'Legal Protection for Self-Employed Workers' *Just Labour* 3 at 36–44.

—— (2005) 'A New Gender Contract? Work–Life Balance and Working Time Flexibility' in Joanne Conaghan and Kerry Rittich (eds), *(Re)Producing Work: Labour Law, Work and Family* (Oxford: Oxford University Press.

Fudge, Judy and Cossman, Brenda (2002) 'Privatization, Law and the Challenge to Feminism' in Judy Fudge and Brenda Cossman (eds) *Privatization, Law and the Challenge to Feminism* (Toronto: University of Toronto Press).

Fudge, Judy and Vosko, Leah (2001a) 'Gender, Segmentation and the Standard Employment Relationship in Canadian Labour Law and Policy' *Economic and Industrial Democracy* 22 at 271–310.

—— (2001b) 'By Whose Standards? Re-regulating the Canadian Labour Market' *Economic and Industrial Democracy* 22 at 327–56.

—— (2003) 'Gendered Paradoxes and the Rise of Contingent Work: Towards a Transformative Feminist Political Economy of the Labour Market' in Wallace Clement and Leah F Vosko (eds), *Changing Canada: Political Economy as Transformation* (Montreal and Kingston: McGill-Queen's University Press).

Fudge, Judy, Tucker, Eric, and Vosko, Leah (2002) *The Legal Concept of Employment: Marginalizing Workers* (Ottawa: Law Commission of Canada).

—— (2003a) 'Employee or Independent Contractor? Charting the Legal Significance of the Distinction in Canada' *Canada Labour and Employment Law Journal* 10(2) at 193–230.

—— (2003b) 'Changing Boundaries in Employment: Developing a New Platform for Labour Law' *Canada Labour and Employment Law Journal* 10(3) at 361–99.

Gahan, Peter and Mitchell, Richard (1995) 'The Limits of Labour Law and the Necessity of Interdisciplinary Analysis' in Richard Mitchell (ed), *Redefining Labour Law: New Perspectives on the Future of Teaching and Research* (Melbourne: Centre for Employment and Labour Relations Law, University of Melbourne).

Galabuzi, Grace-Edward (2001) *Canada's Creeping Economic Apartheid* (Toronto: CSJ Foundation for Research and Education).

Gallie, Duncan and Paugam, Serge (2003) *Social Precarity and Social Integration: Report for the European Commission Based on Eurobarometer 56.1* (Luxembourg: EC).

Gash, Vanessa (2003) 'Moving Up, Moving Out: The Transitions of Atypical Workers to the Standard Employment Contract' in *Les données longitudinales dans l'analyse du marché du travail, 10emes Journées d'étude Céreq* (Paris: Centre National de la Recherche Scientifique).

Gaze, Beth (2002) 'Context and Interpretation in Anti-Discrimination Legislation' *Melbourne University Law Review* 26 at 325–54.

George, B Glenn (2001) 'If You're Not Part of the Solution, You're Part of the Problem: Employer Liability for Sexual Harassment' *Yale Journal of Law & Feminism* 13 at 133–74.

Gershuny, Jonathan and Robinson, John P (1998) 'Historical Changes in the Household Division of Labor' in Frank Ackerman, Neva R Goodwin, Laurie Dougherty, and Kevin Gallagher (eds), *The Changing Nature of Work* (Washington, DC: Island Press).

Gill, Stephen (1995) 'Globalization, Market Civilization, and Disciplinary Neoliberalism' *Millennium: Journal of International Studies* 24 at 399–423.

Gilmour, Joan M (2002) 'Creeping Privatization in Health Care: Implications for Women as the State Redraws Its Role' in Brenda Cossman and Judy Fudge (eds), *Privatization, Law and the Challenge to Feminism* (Toronto: University of Toronto Press).

Glass, Jennifer (2004) 'Blessing or Curse? Work–Family Policies and Mother's Wage Growth Over Time' *Work and Occupations* 31 at 367–94.

Godard, John (2003) 'Labour Unions and Workplace Rights' *Canadian Public Policy* XXIX at 449–68.

Golden, Lonnie (1998) 'Working Time and the Impact of Policy Institutions: Reforming the Overtime Hours Law and Regulation' *Review of Social Economy* 56 at 522–41.

—— (2000) 'Better timing?: Work schedule flexibility among US workers and policy directions' in Lonnie Golden and Deborah M Figart (eds), *Working Time: International trends, theory and policy perspectives* (London: Routledge), at 212–32.

Goldin, Claudia D (1990) *Understanding the Gender Gap: An Economic History of American Women* (New York: Oxford University Press).

Gordon, Robert W (1984) 'Critical Legal Histories' *Stanford Law Review* 36 at 57–125.

Gould IV, William B (2003) 'Labor Law for a Global Economy: The Uneasy Case for International Labor Standards' in Robert J Flanagan and William B Gould IV *International Labor Standards* (Stanford, CA: Stanford Law and Politics).

Government of Canada, 'National Occupational Classification 2001 (NOC 2001)', online: <www23.hrdc-drhc.gc.ca/2001/generic/welcome.shtml> (date accessed: 1 June 2004).

Granovetter, Mark S (1974) *Getting a Job: A Study of Contracts and Careers* (Cambridge, MA: Harvard University Press).

Gregory. Bob (1999) 'Labour Market Institutions and the Gender Pay Ratio' *The Australian Economic Review* 32 at 273–78.

—— (2004) 'Where to now?: Welfare and labour market regulation in Australia' *Australian Bulletin of Labour* 30 at 33–45.

Gregory, Bob, Klug, Eva, and Martin, Yew May (1999) 'Labour Market Deregulation, Relative Wages and the Social Security System' in Sue Richardson (ed), *Reshaping the Labour Market: Regulation, Efficiency and Equality in Australia* (Cambridge, UK: Cambridge University Press).

Grinspun, Ricardo and Kreklewich, Robert (1994) 'Consolidating Neoliberal Reforms:"Free Trade" as a Conditioning Framework' *Studies in Political Economy* 43 at 33–62.

Grodin, Joseph R (1996) 'Arbitration of Employment Discrimination Claims: Doctrine and Policy in the Wake of Gilmer' *Hofstra Lab & Emp LJ* 14 at 1–55.

Grootscholte, M, Bouwmeester, JA, and de Klaver, P (2000) *Evaluatie Wet op het ouderschapsverlof. Onderzoek onder rechthebbenden en werkgevers. Eindrapport* (The Hague: Ministerie van SZW).

Gryst, Roma (2000) *Contracting Employment: A Case Study of How the Use of Agency Workers in the SA Power Industry is Reshaping Employment* (Sydney, Australian Centre for Industrial Relations Research and Training Working Paper No 59).

Guay, Danielle, Corbeil, Christine, and Descarries, Francine (2003) *Coup de main à domicile: Monographie d'une entreprise d'économie sociale en aide domestique (Cahiers du LAREPPS No 03-11)* (Montreal: Laboratoire de recherche sur les pratiques et les politiques sociales, Université du Québec à Montréal).

Guberman, Nancy (2002) *L'analyse différenciée selon les sexes et les politiques québécoises pour les personnes âgées en perte d'autonomie. Lien social et politiques – RIAC 47 (Spring)*, 155–169.

—— (2004) 'Designing Home and Community Care for the Future: Who Needs to Care?' in Karen R Grant *et al* (eds), *Caring For/Caring About: Women, Home Care and Unpaid Caregiving* (Aurora, Ontario: Garamond Press).

Gurstein, Penny (2001) *Wired to the World, Chained to the Home: Telework in Daily Life* (Vancouver: University of British Columbia Press).

Håkansson, Kristina (2001). *Språngbräda eller segmentering? En longitudinell studie av tidsbegränsat anställda* (Uppsala: Institute for Labour Market Policy Evaluation (IFAU)).

Hakim, Catherine (1987) 'Trends in the Flexible Workforce' *Employment Gazette* 95 at 549–60.

Hamermesh, Daniel J and Trejo, Stephen J (2000) 'The Demand for Hours of Labor: Direct Evidence From California' *The Review of Economics and Statistics* 82 at 38–47.

Handelstjänstemannaförbundet HTF (The Salaried Employees' Union) (2003) *Tid i balans—en arbetstidsundersökning med fokus på jämvikt* (Stockholm: Handelstjänstemannaförbundet HTF).

Hankivsky, Olena and Morrow, Marina, with Patricia Armstrong, Lindsey Galvin and Holly Grinvalds (2004) *Trade Agreements, Home Care and Women's Health* (Ottawa: Status of Women Canada).

Harkness, Susan (2002) *Low Pay, Times of Work and Gender* (Manchester: EOC).

Harley, Bill and Whitehouse, Gillian (2001) 'Women in Part-Time Work: A Comparative Study of Australia and the United Kingdom' *Labour & Industry* 12(2) at 33–59.

Hartmann, Heidi (1976) 'Capitalism, Patriarchy, and Job Segregation by Sex' *Signs: Journal of Women in Culture and Society* 1 at 137–69.

Hepple, Bob (1997) 'New Approaches to International Labour Regulation' *Industrial Law Journal* 26 at 353–66.

—— (1999) 'A Race to the Top? International Investment Guidelines and Corporate Codes of Conduct' *Comparative Labor Law & Policy Journal* 20 at 347–63.

—— (2002) 'Enforcement: The Law and Politics of Cooperation and Compliance' in Bob Hepple (ed), *Social and Labour Rights in a Global Context: International and Comparative Perspectives* (Cambridge: Cambridge University Press).

Hewitt, P (1993) 'Flexible Working: Asset or Cost' *Journal of Policy Studies* 14 at 18.

Hirshmann, Nancy (1999) 'Difference as an Occasion for Rights: A Feminist Rethinking of Rights, Liberalism and Difference' in Susan Hekman (ed), *Feminism, Identity, and Difference* (London: Frank Cass), at 27–55.

Hochschild, Arlie (1997) *The Time Bind: When Work Becomes Home and Home Becomes Work* (New York: H Holt and Company/Metropolitan Books).

Hollis, Patricia (1979) *Women in Public: The Women's Movement 1850–1900* (London: George Allen & Unwin).

Holmlund, Bertil, and Storrie, Donald (2002) 'Temporary Work in Turbulent Times' *The Economic Journal* 112 at 245–69.

Howe, John and Mitchell, Richard (1999) 'The Evolution of the Contract of Employment in Australia: A Discussion' *Australian Journal of Labour Law* 12 at 113–30.

Hughes, Karen (1999) *Gender and Self-Employment in Canada: Assessing Trends and Policy Implications*, Changing Employment Relationships Series, Canadian Policy Research Networks (CPRN) Study No W04 (Ottawa: CPRN).

—— (2003a) 'How are Women Faring in the Entrepreneurial Economy?' (Ottawa: Breakfast on the Hill Seminar Series, sponsored by Canadian Federation for the Humanities and Social Services).

—— (2003b) 'Pushed or Pulled? Women's Entry into Self-Employment and Small Business Ownership' *Gender, Work and Organization* 10 at 433–54.

—— (2004) 'Rethinking Policy for the "New Economy": The Case of Self-Employed Women' *Saskatchewan Law Review* 67(2) at 571–90.

Human Rights Watch (2000) 'Unfair Advantage: Worker's Freedom of Association in the United States under International Human Rights Standards', online: <www.hrw.org/reports/2000/uslabor/> (date accessed: 20 September 2004).

Humphries, Jane (1981) 'Protective Legislation, the Capitalist State and Working-Class Men: The Case of the 1842 Mines Regulation Act' *Feminist Review* 7 at 1–33.

Hundley, Greg (2000) 'Male/female earnings differences in self-employment: The effects of marriage, children, and the household division of labour' *Industrial and Labor Relations Review* 54 at 95–114.

Hunnicutt, Benjamin Kline (1996) *Kellogg's Six-Hour Day* (Philadelphia: Temple University Press).

—— (1998) *Work Without End: Abandoning Shorter Hours for the Right to Work* (Philadelphia: Temple University Press).

Hunt, Ian and Provis, Chris (eds) (1995) *The New Industrial Relations in Australia* (Sydney, NSW: The Federation Press).

Hunt, Jennifer (1999) 'Has Work Sharing Worked in Germany?' *Quarterly Journal of Economics* February at 117–48.

Hunter, Rosemary (1988) 'Women Workers in Australian Federal Industrial Relations Law: From *Harvestor* to Comparable Worth' *Australian Journal of Labour Law* 1 at 147–71.

—— (1992) 'The Regulation of Independent Contractors: A Feminist Perspective' *Corporate & Business Law Journal* 5 at 165–88.

—— (1995) 'Women workers and the liberal state: Legal regulation of the workplace, 1880s–1980s', in Diane Elizabeth Kirby (ed), *Sex, Power and Justice: Historical Perspectives in Law in Australia* (Melbourne: Oxford).

—— (2000) *The Beauty Therapist, the Mechanic, the Geoscientist, and the Librarian: Addressing Undervaluation of Women's Work* (Sydney: ATN WEXDEV).

—— (2002) 'The Mirage of Justice: Women and the Shrinking State' *Australian Feminist Law Journal* 16 at 53–74.

Hunter, Laurie, McGregor, Alan, MacInnes, John and Sproull, Alan (1993) 'The "Flexible Firm": Strategy and Segmentation' *British Journal of Industrial Relations* 31 at 383–407.

Hutchins, Leigh and Harrison, Amy (1926). *A History of Factory Legislation* (London: P.S. Kings and Son) (original edition, 1903).

Hutton, Will (2002) *The World We're In* (London: Abacus).

Hyde, Alan (2000) *Classification of US Working People and Its Impact on Workers' Protection* (Geneva: ILO).

—— (2003) *Working in Silicon Valley: Economic and Legal Analysis of a High-Velocity Labor Market* (Armonk, NY: ME Sharpe).

International Labour Organization (ILO) (1988) *Asian Sub-Regional Tripartite Seminar on the Protection of Homeworkers: Proceedings of PIACT [International Programme for the Improvement of Working Conditions and Environment]* (Manila: International Labour Office).

—— (1990a) *Documents of the Meeting of Experts on the Social Protection of Homeworkers* (Geneva: International Labour Office).

—— (1990b) *Resolution Concerning the Promotion of Self-Employment*, International Labour Conference, 77th Session, Provisional Report 34 (Geneva: International Labour Office).

—— (1990c) *Report VII: The Promotion of Self-employment*, International Labour Conference, 77th Session (Geneva: International Labour Office).

—— (1993a) *Report V (1): Part-time work* (Geneva: International Labour Office).

—— (1993b) *Report V (2): Part-time work* (Geneva: International Labour Office).

—— (1995) *Report V (2): Homework* (Geneva: International Labour Office).

—— (1997a) *Report VI (2): Contract Labour*, International Labour Conference, 85th Session (Geneva, International Labour Office).

—— (1998a) *Report V (2B): Contract Labour*, International Labour Conference, 86th Session. (Geneva: International Labour Office).

—— (1998b). *Report V (2B) Addendum*, Committee on Contract Labour, International Labour Conference, 86th Session (Geneva: International Labour Office).

—— (1998c) *Report of the Committee on Contract Labour* Provisional Record, International Labour Conference, 86th Session (Geneva: International Labour Office).

—— (1999) *Decent Work: Report of the Director General* (Geneva: International Labour Office).

—— (2000a) *Meeting of Experts in Workers in Situations Needing Protection (The Employment Relationship: Scope)* Basic Technical Document (Geneva: International Labour Office).

—— (2000b) *Report of the discussion of the Meeting of Experts in Workers in Situations Needing Protection* (Geneva: International Labour Office).

—— (2001) Second Item on the Agenda, 280th Session, Governing Body (Geneva: International Labour Office).

—— (2002) *Decent Work and the Informal Economy*, International Labour Conference, 90th session (Geneva: International Labour Office).

—— (2003a) *Report V: The scope of the employment relationship* (Geneva: International Labour Office).

—— (2003b) *Report of the Committee on the Employment Relationship*, Provisional Record, 91st Session of the International Labour Conference (Geneva: International Labour Office).

—— (2003c) *Time for Equality at Work*. Report of the Director-General, Global Report under the Follow-up to the ILO Declaration on Fundamental Principles and Rights at Work, 91st Session of the International Labour Conference (Geneva: International Labour Office).

—— (2004a) *A Fair Globalization: Creating Opportunities for All*, Final Report, World Commission on the Social Dimensions of Globalization, online: <www.ilo.org/public/english/wcsdg/index.htm> (date accessed: 20 September 2004).

—— (2004b) *Global Employment Trends for Women* (Geneva: International Labour Office).

—— (2004c) Second Item on the Agenda, 'Date, Place, and Agenda of the 95th Session (2006) of the International Labour Conference', 289th Session, Governing Body (Geneva: International Labour Office).

—— (2004d) *Social Dialogue: Both a means and an end*, online: <www.ilo.org/public/english/dialogue/ifpdial/sd/index.htm> (date accessed: 20 September 2004).

—— (2004e) *World Commission says globalization can and must change, calls for urgent rethink of global governance*, 24 February, ILO/04/07, online: <www.ilo.org/public/english/bureau/inf/pr/2004/7.htm> (date accessed: 19 September 2004).

—— (2005) *The Employment Relationship*, Report V(1), International Labour Conference, 95th Session, Geneva.

ILO Committee on Freedom of Association (2004) *334th Report of the Committee on Freedom of Association*, GB 290/5 (Part 1), 290th Session (Geneva: ILO).

International Monetary Fund (IMF) (1999a) *World Economic Outlook: International Financial Contagion*, online: <www.imf.org/external/pubs/ft/weo/1999/01/index.htm> (date accessed: 20 September 2004).

—— (1999b) *A Role for Labour Standards in the New International Economy?*, online: <www.imf.org/external/np/tr/1999/tr990929.htm> (date accessed: 20 September 2004).

—— (2003) *World Economic Outlook: Growth and institutions*, online: <www.imf.org/external/pubs/ft/weo/2003/01/index.htm> (date accessed: 19 September 2004).

—— (2004) *World Economic Outlook: Advancing Structural Reforms* (Washington, DC: IMF).

Isuma – Canadian Journal of Policy Research (2002) 3(1), Editorial at 1–2.

Jackson, Andrew (2002) *Is Work Working for People of Colour?*, Research Paper No 18 (Ottawa: Canadian Labour of Congress).

Jacobs, Jerry A (1989) *Revolving Doors: Sex Segregation and Women's Careers* (Stanford, CA: Stanford University Press).

Jacobs, Jerry A and Gerson, Kathleen (1998a) 'Who Are the Overworked Americans?' *Review of Social Economy* 56 at 442–59.

—— (1998b) 'Toward a Family-Friendly, Gender Equitable Workweek' *University of Pennsylvania Journal of Labor and Employment Law* 1 at 457–72.

—— (2004) *The Time Divide: Work, Family, and Gender Inequality* (Cambridge, MA: Harvard University Press).

Jeffery, Mark (1998) 'Not Really Going to Work? Of the Directive on Part-Time Work, "Atypical Work" and Attempts to Regulate It' *Industrial Law Journal* 27(3) at 193–213.

Johnstone, Richard and Mitchell, Richard (2004) 'Regulating Labour Law' in Christine Parker, Nicola Lacey *et al* (eds), *Regulating Law* (Oxford: Oxford University Press).

Jolls, Christine (2000) 'Accommodation Mandates' *Stanford Law Review* 53 at 223–305.

Jonsson, Inger (2003) 'Deltidsarbete och deltidsarbetslöshet inom svensk detaljhandel—utvecklingslinjer och tidigare insatser, Working Paper from the HELA-project' *Working Life Report 21* (Stockholm: National Institute for Working Life).

Julén, Jenny (2001) 'A Blessing or a Ban? About the Discrimination of Pregnant Job-Seekers', in Ann Numhauser-Henning (ed), *Legal Perspectives on Equal Treatment and Non-Discrimination* (The Hague: Kluwer Law International).

Junor, Anne (1998) 'Permanent Part-Time Work: New Family-Friendly Standard or High Intensity Cheap Skills?' *Labour and Industry* 8(3) at 77–95.

Kalleberg, Arne L, Rasell, Edith, Hudson, Ken, Webster, David, Reskin, Barbara F, Cassirer, Naomi and Appelbaum Eileen (1997) *Nonstandard Work, Substandard Jobs: Flexible Work Arrangements in the US* (Washington: Economic Policy Institute).

Kalleberg, Arne L, Rasell, Edith, Cassirer, Naomi, Reskin, Barbara F, Hudson, Ken, Webster, David, Appelbaum, Eileen, and Spalter-Roth. Roberta M (1998) 'Nonstandard Work, Substandard Jobs: Flexible Work Arrangements in the United States' in Frank Ackerman, Neva R Goodwin, Laurie Dougherty, and Kevin Gallagher (eds), *The Changing Nature of Work* (Washington, DC: Island Press).

Kamenka, Eugene (1983) *The Portable Karl Marx* (Harmondsworth: Penguin).

Kamerman, Sheila, Neuman, Michelle, Waldfoge, Jane, and Brooks-Gunn. Jeanne (2003) *Social Policies, Family Types and Child Outcomes in Selected OECD Countries*, OECD Social, Employment and Migration Working Papers No 6 (Paris: Employment, Labour and Social Affairs Committee, OECD).

Kamhi, Nadja and Leung, Danny (2005) *Recent Developments in Self-Employment in Canada*, Working Paper 2005-8. (Ottawa: Bank of Canada).

Kanter, Rosabeth Moss (1977) *Men and Women of the Corporation* (New York: Basic Books).

Kelly, Erin L (2003) 'Discrimination Against Caregivers?: Gendered Family Responsibilities, Employer Practices, and Work Rewards', in *Rights and Realities: Legal and Social Scientific Approaches to Employment Discrimination* (New York: Kluwer Academic Press).

Kessler-Harris, Alice (2001) *In Pursuit of Equity: Women, Men, and the Quest for Economic Citizenship in 20th-Century America* (New York: Oxford University Press).

Kilpatrick, Claire (2003) 'Has New Labour Reconfigured Employment Legislation?' *Industrial Law Journal* 32 at 135–63.

Kilpatrick, Claire and Freedland, Mark (2004) 'How is EU Governance Transformative? Part-time Work in the UK' in Silvana Sciarra, Paul Davies, and Mark Freedland (eds) *Employment Policy and the Regulation of Part-time Work in the EU: A Comparative Analysis* (Cambridge: Cambridge University Press).

Klare, Karl (2000). 'Countervailing Workers' Power as Regulative Strategy', in Hugh Collins, Paul Davies, and Roger Rideout (eds), *Legal Regulation of the Employment Relation* (London: Kluwer Law International).

—— (2002) 'The Horizons of Transformative Labour and Employment Law' in Joanne Conaghan, Richard Michael Fischl, and Karl Klare (eds), *Labour Law in an Era of Globalization: Transformative Practices and Possibilities* (Oxford: Oxford University Press), at 3–29.

Knijn, Trudie and Kremer, Monique (1997) 'Gender and the Caring Dimension of Welfare States: Toward Inclusive Citizenship' *Social Politics* (Fall) at 328–61.

Knowles, Fiona (2004) 'Misdirection for Indirect Discrimination' *Australian Journal of Labour Law* 17 at 185–96.

Langbein, John H and Wolk. Bruce A (2000) *Pension and Employee Benefit Law*, 3rd edn (New York: Foundation Press).

Langevin, Louise and Belleau, Marie-Claire (2001) *Trafficking in Women in Canada: A Critical Analysis of the Legal Framework Governing Immigrant*

Live-In Caregivers and Mail-Order Brides (Ottawa: Status of Women Canada).

Langille, Brian (1996) 'General Reflections on the Relationship of Trade and Labor (Or: Fair Trade is Free Trade's Destiny)' in Jagdish N Bhagwati and Robert E Hudec (eds), *Fair Trade and Harmonization: Prerequisites for Free Trade—Legal Analysis, vol 2,* (Cambridge, MA: MIT Press).

—— (1997) 'Eight Ways to Think About Labour Standards' *Journal of World Trade Law* 31 at 27–53.

—— (2002) 'Labour Policy in Canada—New Platform, New Paradigm' *Canadian Public Policy* 28 at 133–42.

Langille, Brian and Guy Davidov (1999) 'Beyond Employees and Independent Contractors: A View From Canada' *Comparative Labour Law and Policy Journal* 21(1) at 6–45.

Laslett, Barbara and Johanna Brenner (1989) 'Gender and Social Reproduction: Historical Perspective' *Annual Review of Sociology* 15 at 381–404.

Latham, Mark and Emerson, Craig (2004) *Flexibility with Fairness for Australia's Workforce*, Australian Labour Party, Policy Document, 6 August 2004, online: <www.alp.org.au/policy/index.php> (accessed: 2 October 2004).

Laville, Jean-Louis and Nyssens, Marthe (eds) (2001) *Les services sociaux entre associations, marché et État. L'aide aux personnes âgées* (Paris: Éditions La Découverte).

Lawler, Edward E III. (1994) 'From Job-based to Competency-based Organizations' *Journal of Organizational Behaviour* 15 at 3–15.

Lee, Eddie (1997) 'Is Full Employment Still Desirable and Feasible?' *Economic and Industrial Democracy* 18(1) at 35–53.

Lehndorff, Steffen (2004) 'Working Time in Germany: The Effectiveness of and Crisis in Regulation by Collective Agreement', Paper prepared for International Symposium on Working Time Conference, Paris, 26–28 February.

Leijnse, Frans, Goudswaard, Kees, and Plantenga, Janneke (2002) *Anders denken over sociale zekerheid. Levenslopen, risico en verantwoordelijkheid* (The Hague: Ministerie van SZW).

Lester, Gillian (1998) 'Careers and Contingency' *Stanford Law Review* 51 at 73–145.

—— (2005) 'In Defense of Paid Family Leave' *Harvard Journal of Law and Gender* 28 at 1–85.

Lewis, Jane (2001) 'The Decline of the Male Breadwinner Model: Implications for Work and Care' *Social Politics* (Summer) at 152–69.

Linder, Marc (1992) *Farewell to the Self-Employed: Deconstructing a Socioeconomic and Legal Solipsism* (New York: Greenwood Press).

Lippel, Katherine (2005) 'Precarious Employment and Occupational Health and Safety Regulation in Quebec' in Leah F Vosko (ed), *Precarious Employment: Understanding Labour Market Insecurity in Canada* (Montreal and Kingston: McGill-Queen's University Press).

Lobel, Orly (2004) 'The Renew Deal: The Fall of Regulation and the Rise of Governance in Contemporary Legal Thought' (draft manuscript).

Loutfi, Martha (1991) 'Self-Employment Patterns and Policy Issues in Europe' *International Labour Review* 130(1) at 1–19.

Low Pay Commission (2003) *Building on Success: Fourth Report of the Law Pay Commission* (London: The Stationery Office).

Lowe, Graham and Schellenberg, Grant (2001) *What's a Good Job?.The Importance of Employment Relationships*, Changing Employment Relationships Series, Canadian Policy Research Networks (CPRN) Study No W05 (Ottawa: CPRN).

MacDermott, Therese and Owens, Rosemary (2000) 'Equality and Flexibility for Workers with Family Responsibilities: A Troubled Union?' *Australian Journal of Labour Law* 13 at 278–90.

Macklin, Audrey (1992) 'Foreign Domestic Worker: Surrogate Housewife or Mail Order Servant?' *McGill Law Journal* 37(3) at 681–760.

—— (2002) 'Public Entrance/Private Member' in Brenda Cossman and Judy Fudge (eds), *Privatization, Law and the Challenge to Feminism* (Toronto: University of Toronto Press).

MacPherson, Elizabeth (1999) 'Collective Bargaining for Independent Contractors: Is the Status of the Artist Act a Model for other Industrial Sectors?' *Canadian Labour and Employment Law Journal* 7 at 355–89.

Mahoney, Rhona (1995) *Kidding Ourselves: Breadwinning, Babies, and Bargaining Power* (New York: Basic Books).

Malamud, Deborah C (1998) 'Engineering the Middle Classes: Class Line-Drawing in New Deal Hours Legislation' *Michigan Law Review* 96 at 2212–321.

Mantz, Beth M (2001) 'J & J Discrimination Suit may be One of Largest Ever' *Dow Jones News Wires*, 16 November, p 40.

Marin, Enrique (2005). 'The Employment Relationship: The Issue at the International Level', Paper presented to 'The Scope of Labour Law – Re-drawing the Boundaries of Protection', Conference organised by the Rockefeller Centre and Institute for Labour Studies, Bellagio, May.

Markus, Maria (1987) 'Women, Success and Civil Society: Submission to, or Subversion of, the Achievement Principle' in Seyla Benhabib and Drucilla Cornell (eds), *Feminism as Critique* (Padstow: Polity Press).

Marsh, Catherine (1991) *Hours of Work of Women and Men in Britain* (Manchester: EOC).

Marshall, Katherine (1999) 'Employment after Childbirth' *Perspectives on Labour and Income 11(3)*, Ottawa: Statistics Canada Catalogue No. 75-001-XPE.

Marx, Karl (1983) *Capital, vol 1* (London: Lawrence & Wishart Ltd) (reproducing the text of the 1887 edition edited by Frederick Engels).

McBride, Steven (2001) *Paradigm Shift: Globalization and the Canadian State* (Halifax: Fernwood).

McCallum, Ronald C (1997) 'Australian Workplace Agreements–An Analysis' *Australian Journal of Labour Law* 10 at 50–61.

McColgan, Aileen (1997) *Just Wages for Women* (Oxford: Clarendon Press).

—— (2000a) 'Family-Friendly Frolics? The Maternity and Parental Leave Regulations 1999' *Industrial Law Journal* 29 at 125–44.

—— (2000b) 'Missing the Point? The Part-Time Workers (Prevention of Less Favourable Treatment) Regulations 2000' *Industrial Law Journal* 29 at 260–67.

—— (2000c) 'Regulating pay discrimination' in Hugh Collins, Paul Davies and Roger Rideout (eds), *Legal Regulation of the Employment Relation* (London: Kluwer Law International), at 203–23.

—— (2003) 'The Fixed-Term Employees (Prevention of Less Favourable Treatment) Regulations 2002: Fiddling while Rome Burns?' *Industrial Law Journal* 32 at 194–99.

McDowell, Linda (1991) 'Life Without Father and Ford: The New Gender Order of Post-Fordism' *Transactions of the Institute of British Geographers* 16 at 100–19.

McGinley, Ann C (2000). '!Viva La Evolucion!: Recognizing Unconscious Motive in Title VII' *Cornell Journal of Law & Public Policy* 9 at 415–92.

McGlynn, Clare (2001) 'Reclaiming a Feminist Vision: The Reconciliation of Work and Family Life in European Union Law and Policy' *Columbia Journal of European Law* 7 at 241–72.

McKnight, Abigail, Elias, Peter, and Wilson, Rob (1998) *Low Pay and the National Insurance System* (London: EOC).

Meager, Nigel (1991) *Self-Employment in the UK* (Brighton, Sussex: University of Sussex Institute of Manpower Studies).

Merlo, Otto (2000) 'Flexibility and Stretching Rights: The No-Disadvantage Test in Enterprise Bargaining' *Australian Journal of Labour Law* 13 at 207–35.

Milkman, Ruth (1997) *Farewell to the Factory: Auto Workers in the Late Twentieth Century*. (Berkeley, CA: University of California Press).

Ministère du Développement Économique et Régional (2002) *Portrait des entreprises en aide domestique* (Quebec: Government of Quebec).

Ministère de l'Emploi, de la Solidarité Sociale et de la Famille (MESSF) (2003) *Scénarios de développement et de financement pour assurer la pérennité, l'accessibilité et la qualité des services de garde: Consultation 2003* (Quebec: Government of Quebec).

Ministère de la Santé et des Services Sociaux (MSSS) (1999) *La complémentarité du secteur privé dans la poursuite des objectifs fondamentaux du système public de santé au Québec. Rapport du Groupe de travail* (Quebec: Government of Quebec) ('Arpin Report').

—— (2003) *Chez soi, le premier choix: La politique de soutien à domicile* (Quebec, MSSS).

—— (2004) 'Vous recevez de l'aide ... Les services d'aide à domicile et le chèque emploi-service', online: <ftp.msss.gouv.qc.ca/publications/acrobat/f/documentation/2004/04-513-05.pdf> (date accessed: 15 August 2004).

Ministère du Travail (2004) 'Dossiers pratiques: chèque emploi-service', Ministère du Travail, France, online: <www.travail.gouv.fr/infos_pratiques/ch_emploi-service.html (date accessed: 15 August 2004).

Ministerie van SZW (2004) *Wet aanpassing arbeidsduur. Jurisprudentieonderzoek 3e meting* (Den Haag: Ministerie van SZW).

Minow, Martha (1990) *Making All the Difference: Inclusion, Exclusion, and American Law* (Ithaca: Cornell University Press).

Miras, Rolf, Smith, Roger, and Karoliff, Vladimir (1994) 'Canada's Underground Economy Revisited: Update and Critique' *Canadian Public Policy* 20(3) at 235–52.

Mirchandani, Kiran (1999) 'Feminist Insight on Gendered Work; New Directions in Research on Women and Entrepreneurship' *Gender, Work and Organization* 6(4) at 224–35.

Mitchell, Richard (ed) (1995) *Redefining Labour Law: New Perspectives on the Future of Teaching and Research* (Melbourne: Centre for Employment and Labour Relations Law, University of Melbourne).

—— (1998) 'Juridification and Labour Law: A Legal Response to the Flexibility Debate in Australia' *International Journal of Comparative Labour Law and Industrial Relations* 14 at 113–35.

—— (2005) 'Labour Law and Labour Market Regulation: Beyond the Employment Relationship',. Paper presented at conference 'Labour Law, Equity and Eficiency: Structuring and Regulating the Labour Market for the 21st Century', 8–9 July (Melbourne: Centre for Employment and Labour Relations Law, University of Melbourne).

Mitchell, Richard and Rimmer, Malcolm (1990) 'Labour Law, De-Regulation, and Flexibility in Australian Industrial Relations' *Comparative Labour Law Journal* 12 at 1–34.

Mitchell Richard, Campbell, Rebecca, Barnes, Andrew, Bicknell, Emma, Creighton, Kate, Fetter Joel, and Korman, Samantha (2004) *Protecting the Worker's Interest in Enterprise Bargaining: The 'No-Disadvantage' Test in the Australian Federal Jurisdiction, Final Report* (Melbourne, Victoria: Workplace Innovation Unit, Industrial Relations Victoria).

Morris, Marika (2004) 'What Research Reveals About Gender, Home Care and Caregiving: Overview and the Case for Gender Analysis' in Karen R Grant *et al* (eds)*Caring For/Caring About: Women, Home Care and Unpaid Caregiving* (Aurora, Ontario: Garamond Press).

Morris, Marika, Robinson, Jane, and Simpson, Janet (1999) *The Changing Nature of Home Care and its Impact on Women's Vulnerability to Poverty* (Ottawa: Status of Women Canada).

Muckenberger, Ulrich (1989) 'Non-Standard Forms of Work and the Role of Changes in Labour and Social Security Legislation' *International Journal of the Sociology of Law* 17 at 381–402.

MuConsult (2003) *Onderzoek ten behoeve van evaluatie Waa en Woa. Eindrapport* (Amersfoort: MuConsult).*

Mumford, Karen (1989) *Women Working: Economics and Reality* (Sydney: Allen and Unwin).

Mumford, Karen and Parera, Antonia (2003) 'The Labour Force Participation of Married Mothers: A Tale of International Catch-Up' *Australian Journal of Labour and Economics* 6 at 619–30.

Mundlak, Guy (2005) 'Re-commodifying Time: Working Hours of Live-in Domestic Workers' in Joanne Conaghan and Kerry Rittich (eds), *Labour Law, Work and Family: Critical and Comparative Perspectives* (Oxford: Oxford University Press).

Murray, Jill (1999a) 'Normalising Temporary Work: The Proposed Directive on Fixed-Term Work' *Industrial Law Journal* 28 at 269–75.

—— (1999b) 'Social Justice for Women? The ILO's Convention on Part-Time Work' *International Journal of Comparative Labour Law and Industrial Relations* 15(1) at 3–20.

—— (2001a) 'The International Regulation of Maternity: Still Waiting for the Reconciliation of Work and Family Life' *International Journal of Comparative Labour Law and Industrial Relations* 17(1) at 25–46.

—— (2001b) *Transnational Labour Regulation the ILO and EC Compared* (The Hague: Kluwer Law International).

Mutari, Ellen and Figart, Deborah (2000) 'The social implications of European work time policies: promoting gender equity?' in Lonnie Golden and Deborah Figart (eds) *Working Time: International trends, theory and policy perspectives* (London: Routledge), at 232–51.

—— (2001) 'Finland Experiments with a Six-Hour Work Day a Family Friendly Policy?' *Dollar & Sense*, 1 September, p 32.

National Assembly, Permanent Commission on the Economy and Labour, CET-67: 21-7, 6 December 2002, 36th Legislature, 2nd Session.

Nelander, Sven and Goding, Ingela (2003) *Anställningsformer och arbetstider 2003* (Stockholm: LO Löne-och välfärdsenheten).

Neumark, David and Reed, Deborah (2002) 'Employment Relationships in the New Economy', NBER Working Paper No w8910 (Cambridge, MA: National Bureau of Economic Research).

New South Wales Industrial Relations Commission (1998) *Pay Equity Inquiry: Report to the Minister, vol 1* (Sydney: NSWIRC).

Nierop, Cees (2003) *Flexible Work-Arrangements and the Quality of Life* (Amsterdam: AIAS (Amsterdam Institute for Advanced Labour Studies)).

Nossar, Igor, Johnstone, Richard, and Quinlan, Michael (2004) 'Regulating Supply Chains to Address the Occupational Health and Safety Problems associated with Precarious Employment: the Case of Home-Based Clothing Workers in Australia' *Australian Journal of Labour Law* 17 at 137–60.

Numhauser-Henning, Ann (2004) 'Balancing values to build a legitimate society' in *Work in the Global Economy. Papers and proceedings of an international symposium. Tokyo, 1–3 December 2003* (France, International Institute for Labour Studies).

O'Brien, Margaret and Shemilt, Ian (2003) *Working Fathers: Earning and Caring* (London. EOC).

O'Donnell, Anthony (2004) '"Non-Standard" Workers in Australia: Courts and Controversies' *Australian Journal of Labour Law* 17 at 1–28.

O'Reilly, Jacqueline, Cebrián, Immaculada, and Lallement, Michel (2000) *Working-Time Changes. Social Integration Through Transitional Labour Markets* (Berlin: Wissenschaftszentrum Berlin Für Sozialforschung).

Oakley, Ann (1976) *Housewife* (Harmondsworth: Penguin Books).

OECD (1980) *Women and Employment: Policies for equal opportunities* (Paris: OECD).

—— (1994a) *Employment Outlook* (Paris: OECD).

—— (1994b) 'Part I: Labour Market Trends and Underlying Forces of Change' and 'Part II: The Adjustment Potential of the Labour Market' in *The OECD Jobs Study—Evidence and Explanations* (Paris: OECD).

—— (1996) *Employment and Labour Standards: A Study of Core Workers' Rights and International Trade* (Paris: OECD).

—— (1999) *Public Subsidies for Home Care for the Frail Elderly and Their Impact on Women Care-Givers* (DEELSA/ELSA (99)12 (Paris: OECD (Employment, Labour and Social Affairs Committee)).

—— (2000) *Employment Outlook* (Paris: OECD).

—— (2001) *Employment Outlook* (Paris: OECD).

—— (2002a) *Babies and Bosses, Vol 1: Australia, Denmark and Netherlands* (Paris: OECD).

—— (2002b) *Employment Outlook* (Paris: OECD).

—— (2003a) *Babies and Bosses, Vol 2: Austria, Ireland and Japan* (Paris: OECD).

—— (2003b) Meeting of the Employment, Labour, and Social Affairs Committee at Ministerial Level, *Trade Union Advisory Committee Statement*, DELSA/ELSA/MIN 4, 23 September.

—— (2004a) 'Women in Employment' by Paul Swain in *Putting More Women to Work: A Colloquium on Employment, Child Care and Taxes* (Paris: OECD). Available at www.oecd.org (accessed: 19 May 2004).

—— (2004b) *Employment Outlook* (Paris: OECD).

—— (2005) *Statistical Profile of Australia – 2005* (Paris: OECD). Available at www.oecd.org (accessed: 19 June 2005).

Office of the Equal Opportunities Ombudsman (1999). *JämO:s Rapport om föräldraskap*.

Olsen, Francis E (1983) 'The Family and the Market: A Study of Ideology and Legal Reform. *Harvard Law Review* 96 at 1497–578.

Oppenheim Mason, Karen (1984) 'Commentary: Strober's Theory of Occupational Sex Segregation' in Barbara F Reskin (ed), *Sex Segregation in the Workplace* (Washington, DC: National Academy Press).

Owens, Rosemary J (1993) 'Women, "Atypical" Work Relationships and the Law' *Melbourne University Law Review* 19 at 399–430.

—— (1995a) 'The Peripheral Worker: Women and the Legal Regulation of Outwork' in Margaret Thornton (ed), *Public and Private: Feminist Legal Debates* (Melbourne: Oxford University Press).

—— (1995b) 'The Traditional Labour Law Framework: A Critical Evaluation' in Richard Mitchell (ed), *Redefining Labour Law: New Perspectives on the Future of Teaching and Research* (Melbourne: Centre for Employment and Labour Relations Law, University of Melbourne).

—— (2001) 'The Long-term or Permanent Casual—An Oxymoron or "a well enough understood Australianism" in the Law' *Australian Bulletin of Labour* 27 at 118–36.

—— (2002) 'Decent Work for the Contingent Workforce in the New Economy' *Australian Journal of Labour Law* 15 at 209–34.

—— (2005) 'Taking Leave: Work and Family in Australian Law and Policy' in Joanne Conaghan and Kerry Rittich (eds), *Labour Law, Work and Family: Critical and Comparative Perspectives* (Oxford: Oxford University Press).

Pal, Leslie A and Maxwell, Judith (2004) *Assessing the Public Interest in the 21st Century: A Framework*, Paper prepared for the External Advisory Committee on Smart Regulation (Ottawa: Canadian Policy Research Networks).

Palmer, Tom (2004) *Results of the First Flexible Working Employee Survey* (London, UK: Employment Relations Occasional Papers, Department of Trade and Industry).

Parliamentary Library (Australia) (2004) *Casual Employment: Trends and Characteristics. Research Note* (Canberra, Australia), online: <www.aph.gov.au/library/pubs/rn/Index.htm> (date accessed: 2 December 2004).

Pateman, Carole (1988) 'The Patriarchal Welfare State' in Amy Gutmann (ed), *Democracy and the Welfare State* (Princeton, NJ: Princeton University Press).

Paterson, Emma (1874) 'The Position of Women and How to Improve it', reproduced in Patricia Hollis (ed) (1979), *Women in Public: the Women's Movement 1850–1900* (London: George Allen & Unwin).

Paterson, Wendy A (2003)'Desire for Social Justice: Equal Pay, the International Labour Organization, and Australian Government Policy, 1919–1975' in *Schools of Humanities and Liberal Arts, Faculty of Education and Arts* (Newcastle: University of Newcastle).

Peck, Jamie. A and Theodore, Nicholas (2002) 'Temped Out? Industry Rhetoric, Labor Regulation and Economic Restructuring in the Temporary Staffing Business' *Economic and Industrial Democracy* 23(2) at 143–75.

Pedersini, Roberto (2002) '"Economically dependent workers", Employment law and industrial relations', online: European Industrial Relations Observatory <www.eiro.eurofound.eu.int/2002/05/study/index.html> (date accessed: 25 May 2004).

Pélisse, Jérôme (2004a) 'Time, Legal Consciousness, and Power: The Case of France's 35-Hour Workweek Laws', Paper prepared for Annual Meeting of the Law and Society Association.

—— (2004b) 'From Negotiation to Implementation: A Study of the Reduction of Working Time in France (1998–2000)' *Time and Society* 13 at 221–24.

Perulli, Adalberto *Economically Dependent /Quasi-Subordinate (Para-Subordinate) Employment: Legal, Social and Economic Aspects* (Brussels: European Commission).

Philipps, Lisa (2002) 'Tax Law and Social Reproduction: The Gender of Fiscal Policy in and Age of Privatization' in Brenda Cossman and Judy Fudge (eds), *Privatization, Law and the Challenge to Feminism* (Toronto: University of Toronto Press).

Picchio, Antonella (1992) *Social Reproduction: The Political Economy of the Labour Market* (Cambridge: Cambridge University Press).

—— (1998) 'Wages as a Reflection of Socially Embedded Production and Reproduction Processes' in Linda Clarke, Peter de Gijsel, and Jorn Janssen (eds) *The Dynamics of Wage Relations in the New Europe* (London: Kluwer), 195–214.

Picciotto, Sol (2003) 'Rights, Responsibilities and Regulation of International Business' *Columbia Journal of Transnational Law* 42 at 123–51.

Picot, Garnett and Heisz, Andrew (2000) *The Performance of the 1990s Canadian Labour Markets* (Ottawa: Statistics Canada).

Piore, Michael (2002) 'The reconfiguration of work and employment relations in the United States at the turn of the 21st century' in Peter Auer and Bernard Glazer (eds), *The Future of Work, Employment and Social Protection: The dynamics of change and the protection of workers* (Geneva: Ministry of Social Affairs, Labour and Solidarity, France/International Institute for Studies).

Pittard, Marilyn (1997) 'Collective Employment Relationships: Reforms to Arbitrated Awards and Certified Agreements' *Australian Journal of Labour Law* 10 at 62–88.

—— (2003) 'The Dispersing and Transformed Workplace: Labour Law and the Effect of Electronic Work' *Australian Journal of Labour Law* 16 at 69–93.

Pittard, Marilyn and Naughton, Richard (2003) *Australian Labour Law: Cases and Materials*, 4th edn (Sydney: Butterworths).

Pocock, Barbara (1998) 'All Change, Still Gendered: The Australian Labour Market in the 1990s' *Journal of Industrial Relations* 40 at 580–604.

—— (2003) *The Work/Life Collision* (Sydney: Federation Press).

Pocock, Barbara, Buchanan, John, and Campbell, Iain (2004) *Securing Quality Employment: Policy Options for Casual and Part-time Workers* (Australia: Chifley Research Centre), online: <www.chifley.org.au> (date accessed: 2 December 2004).

Posner, Richard (1989) 'An Economic Analysis of Sex Discrimination Law' *University of Chicago Law Review* 56 at 1311–35.

Preston, Alison C (2001a) *The Structure and Determinants of Wage Relativities: Evidence from Australia* (Aldershot: Ashgate Publishing Ltd).

—— (2001b) 'The Changing Australian Labour Market: Developments During the 1990s' *Australian Bulletin of Labour* 27(3) at 153–76.

Preston, Alison and Burgess, John (2003) 'Women's Work in Australia: Trends, Issues and Prospects' *Australian Journal of Labour and Economics* 6 at 497–518.

Preston, Alison C and Whitehouse, Gillian (2003) *Gender Differences in Occupation of Employment within Australia. Perth* (Australia: Curtin University of Technology, Women's Economic Policy Analysis Unit, Mimeo).

Prime Minister's Task Force on Women Entrepreneurs (2003) 'Report and Recommendation' Ottawa: House of Commons, online: <www.liberal.parl.gc.ca/entrepreneur/documents/031029_final_report_en.pd> (date accessed: 25 May 2004).

Probert, Belinda (1995) *Part-time Work and Managerial Strategy: Flexibility in the New Industrial Relations Framework* (Canberra: AGPS).

—— (1997) 'Gender and Choice: The Structure of Opportunity' in Paul Warren James, Walter F Veit, and Steve Wright (eds), *Work of the Future: Global Perspectives* (Sydney: Allen & Unwin).

Prügl, Elizabeth B (1996) 'Biases in Labor Law: A Critique from the Standpoint of Home based Workers' in *Homeworkers in Global Perspective: Invisible No More* (New York, Routledge) at 203–81.

—— (1999) *The Global Construction of Gender: Home-based Work in the Political Economy of the Twentieth Century* (New York: Columbia University Press).

Purcell, Kate (2000) 'Changing Boundaries in Employment and Organisations in Kate Purcell (ed) *Changing Boundaries in Employment* (Bristol: Bristol University Press) at 1–30.

Quebec, National Assembly (Permanent Commission on the Economy and Labour). 2002. 36th Leg, No CET-67 at 21–7, 6 December.

Quinlan, Michael (2001) 'Negotiating Flexibility: The Role of the Social Partners and the State' (Book Review) *Labour & Industry* 11(3) at 128–31.

Rainbird, Helen (1991) 'The Self-Employed: Small Entrepreneurs or Disguised Wage Labourers?' in Anna Pollert (ed), *Farewell to Flexibilit* (Oxford: Blackwell).

Ramirez-Machado, José Maria (2003) *Domestic Work, Conditions of Work and Employment: A Legal Perspective* in Conditions of Work and Employment Series No 7 (Geneva: International Labour Office).

Regini, Marino (2003) 'Work and Labour in Global Economies: The Case of Western Europe' *Socio-Economic Review* 1 at 165–84.

Reith, The Honourable Peter, MP (1999) 'Delivering on Work and Family: The Workplace Relations Act' *Australian Bulletin of Labour* 25(3) at 221–28.

Resnik, Judith (2004) 'The Rights of Remedies: Collective Accountings for and Insuring Against the Harms of Sexual Harassment' in Catherine MacKinnon and Riva Siegal (eds), *Directions in Sexual Harassment Law* (New Haven, CT: Yale University Press), at 247–72.

Rifkin, Jeremy (1995) *The End of Work and the Decline of the Global Labour Force and the Dawn of the Post Market Era* (New York: Putnam).

Rittich, Kerry (2002a) 'Feminization and Contingency: Regulating the Stakes of Work for Women' in Joanne Conaghan, Richard Michael Fischl, and Karl Klare (eds) *Labour Law in an Era of Globalization: Transformative Practices and Possibilities* (Oxford: Oxford University Press), at 117–36.

—— (2002b) *Recharacterizing Restructuring: Law, Distribution and Gender in Market Reform* (The Hague: Kluwer International).

—— (2003a) 'Core Labour Rights and Labour Market Flexibility: Two Paths Entwined? Permanent Court of Arbitration/Peace Palace Papers' in *Labor Law Beyond Borders: ADR and the Internationalization of Labor Dispute Resolution* (London: Kluwer Law International).

—— (2003b) 'Engendering Development/Marketing Equality' *Albany Law Review* 67 at 575–92.

Rochette, Maude (2003) *Le travail atypique des parents et la garde des enfants: Description du phénomène et recension des expériences étrangères de garde à horaires non usuels* (Quebec: Ministère de l'Emploi, de la Solidarité Sociale et de la Famille (MESSF)).

Rodgers, Gerry and Janine Rodgers (eds) (1989) *Precarious Jobs in Labour Market Regulation: The Growth of Atypical Employment in Western Europe* (Belgium: International Institute for Labour Studies).

Rodrik, Dani (1997) *Has Globalization Gone Too Far?* (Washington, DC: Institute for International Economics).

—— (1998) 'Consequences of Trade for Labor Markets and the Employment Relationship' in Frank Ackerman, Neva R Goodwin, Laurie Dougherty, and Kevin Gallagher (eds), *The Changing Nature of Work* (Washington, DC: Island Press).

Rodrik, Dani, Subramanian, Arvind, and Trebbi, Francesco (2002) 'Institutions Rule: The Primacy of Institutions over Geography and Integration in Economic Development', NBER Working Paper 9305 (Cambridge, MA: National Bureau of Economic Research).

Romero, Mary (1999) 'Immigration, the Servant Problem, and the Legacy of the Domestic Labor Debate: "Where Can You Find Good Help These Days!"' *University of Miami Law Review* 53 at 1045–64.

Rooney, Jennifer *et al* (2003) *Self-Employment for Women: Policy Options that Promote equality and Equal Opportunities* (Ottawa: Status of Women Canada).

Roos, Patricia A and Resnick, Barbara F (1984) 'Insitutional Factors Contributing to Sex Segregation in the Workplace' in *Sex Segregation in the Workplace: Trends, Explanations, Remedies* (Washington, DC: National Academy Press).

Rubery, Jill (1998) *Women in the Labour Market: A Gender Equality Perspective* (Paris: OECD Directorate for Education, Employment, Labour and Social Affairs).

—— (2002) 'Gender mainstreaming and gender equality in the EU: The impact of the EU employment strategy' *Industrial Relations Journal* 33(5) at 500–22.

—— (2003) *Gender mainstreaming and the open method of coordination: is the open method too open for gender equality policy?* (Manchester: European Work and Employment Research Centre, University of Manchester).

Rubery, Jill and Grimshaw, Damain (2003) *The Organization of Employment: An International Perspective* (Houndsmill, Basingstoke: Palgrave MacMillan).

Rubery, Jill, Smith, Mark, and Fagan, Colette (1998) 'National Working-Time Regimes and Equal Opportunities' *Feminist Economics* 4 at 71–101.

—— (1999) *Women's Employment in Europe: Trends and Prospects* (London: Routledge).

Rubery, Jill, Smith, Mark, Figueiredo, Hugo, Fagan, Colette, and Grimshaw, Damian (2004) *Gender Mainstreaming and the European Employment Strategy and Social Inclusion Process* (Manchester: Manchester School of Management, University of Manchester (European Work and Employment Research Centre, EWERC)).

Safer, Morley (2003) 'The Royal Treatment', *60 Minutes* (transcript), 20 April.

Salazar Parrenas, Rhacel (2001) *Servants of Globalization: Women, Migration and Domestic Work* (Stanford: Stanford University Press).

Saltzman, Amy (1997) 'When Less Is More' *US News & World Report*, 27 October, p 78.

Sankaran, Kamala (2002) 'The ILO, Women and Work: Evolving Labor Standards to Advance Women's Status in the Informal Economy' *The Georgetown Journal of Gender and the Law* III at 851–69.

Sassen, Saskia (1991) *The Global City* (Princeton, NJ: Princeton University Press).

—— (2002) 'Global Cities and Survival Circuits' in Barbara Ehrenreich and Arlie Hochschild (eds), *Global Woman: Nannies, Maids and Sex Workers in the New Economy* (New York: Metropolitan), at 254–74.

Saunders, Ron (2003) *Defining Vulnerability in the Labour Market*, Research Paper W/21 Work Network (Ottawa: CPRN).

Schellenberg, Grant and Clark, Christopher (1996) *Temporary Employment in Canada: Profiles, Patterns and Policy Considerations* (Ottawa: Canadian Council on Social Development).

Schmid, Günther (2002a) 'Transitional Labour Markets and the European Social Model: Towards a New Employment Compact' in Günther Schmid and Bernard Gazier (eds), *The Dynamics of Full Employment. Social Integration Through Transitional Labour Markets* (Cheltenham, UK, and Northampton; MA, USA: Edward Elgar).

—— (2002b) 'Employment Insurance for Managing Critical Transitions During the Life Cycle' in Peter Auer and Bernard Gazier (eds), *The Future of Work, Employment and Social Protection* (Geneva: International Institute for Labour Studies).

Schneiderman, David (2000) 'Investment Rules and the New Constitutionalism' *Law and Social Inquiry* 25 at 757–89.

Schor, Juliet B (1991) *The Overworked American* (New York: Basic Books).

—— (1994) 'The Piper Lecture: Working in Contemporary Context: Amending the Fair Labor Standards Act' *Chicago-Kent Law Review* 70 at 157.

Schultz, Vicki (1990) 'Telling Stories About Women and Work: Judicial Interpretations of Sex Segregation in the Workplace in Title VII Cases: Raising the Lack of Interest Argument' *Harvard Law Review* 103 at 1750–843.

—— (1998) 'Reconceptualizing Sexual Harassment' *Yale Law Journal* 107 at 1683–805.

—— (2000) 'Life's Work' *Columbia Law Review* 100 at 1881–964.

Schwartz, David S (1989) 'When is Sex Because of Sex? The Causation Problem in Sexual Harassment Law' *U Penn L Rev* 150 at 1697–794.

—— (1997) 'Enforcing Small Print to Protect Big Business: Employee and Consumer Rights Claims in an Age of Compelled Arbitration' *Wis L Rev* 33 at 33–132.

Schwartz, Felice (1989) 'Management Women and the New Facts of Life' *Harvard Business Review* 67 at 65–76.

Sciarra, Silvana (2004) 'New Discourses in Labour Law: Part-time Work and the Paradigm of Flexibility' in Silvana Sciarra, Paul Davies, and Mark Freedland (eds), *Employment Policy and the Regulation of Part-time Work in The European Union: A Comparative Analysis* (Cambridge, UK: Cambridge University Press).

Sciarra, Silvana, Davies, Paul, and Freedland, Mark (2004) *Employment Policy and the Regulation of Part-time Work in the European Union: A Comparative Analysis* (Cambridge, UK: Cambridge University Press).

Scott, Joan (1988) 'Deconstructing Equality Versus Difference: Or the Uses of Poststructuralist Theory for Feminism' *Feminist Studies* 14(1) at 33–50.

Seccombe, Wally (1992) *A Millennium of Family Change* (London: Verso).

Sen, Amartya (1999) *Development as Freedom* (New York: Anchor Books).

—— (2000) 'Work and Rights' *International Labour Review* 139 at 119–28.

SER (2001) 'Commissie Sociaal-Economisch Deskundigen' *Levensloopbanen: gevolgen voor veranderende arbeidspatronen* (The Hague: SER).

Shank, Susan (1986) 'Preferred Hours of Work and Corresponding Earnings' *Monthly Labor Review*, November at 40–44.

Shihata, Ibrahim (1991) 'The World Bank and Human Rights' in *The World Bank in a Changing World, vol 1* (Dordrecht: Martinus Nijhoff), at 97–134.

—— (1997) *Complementary Reform: Essay on Legal, Judical and Other Institutional Reforms Supported by the World Bank* (The Hague: Kluwer).

—— (2000) 'Issues of "Governance" in Borrowing Members – The Extent of their Relevance under the Bank's Articles of Agreement' in *The World Bank Legal Papers* (The Hague: Martinus Nijhoff), at 245–82.

Siegel, Reva (1994) 'Home As Work: The First Woman's Rights Claims Concerning Wives' Household Labor, 1850–1880' *Yale Law Journal* 103 at 1073–217.

Silbaugh, Katharine (1996) 'Turning Labor Into Love: Housework and the Law' *Northwestern University Law Review* 91(1) at 1–86.

—— (1998) 'Marriage Contracts and the Family Economy' *Northwestern University Law Review* 93 at 65–143.

Simpson, Bob (2004) 'The National Minimum Wage Five Years On: Reflections on Some General Issues' *Industrial Law Journal* 33 at 22–41.

Skocpol, Theda (2000) *The Missing Middle: Working Families and the Future of American Social Policy* (New York: WW Norton).

Smith, Belinda (2002) 'Time Norms in the Workplace: their Exclusionary Effect and Potential for Change' *Columbia Journal of Gender and Law* 11 at 271–360.

Smith, Peggie (1999) 'Regulating Paid Household Work: Class, Gender, Race, and Agendas of Reform' *American University Law Review* 48 at 851–925.

Smith, PR (2000) 'Organizing the Unorganizable: Private Paid Household Workers and Approaches to Employee Representation' *North Carolina Law Review* 79 at 45–110.

Smith, Meg and Ewer, Peter (1999) *Choice and Coercion: Women's Experiences of Casual Work* (Sydney: Evatt Foundation).

Sociaal Cultureel Planbureau (SCP) and Centraal Bureau voor de Statistiek (CBS) (2002) *Emancipatiemonitor* (The Hague: SCP and CBS).*

—— (2004) *Emancipatiemonitor 2004* (The Hague: SCP and CBS).*

Standing, Guy (1989) 'Global Feminisation through Flexible Labour' *World Development* 17 at 1077–95.

—— (1999a) 'Global Feminisation Through Flexible Labor: A Theme Revisited' *World Development* 27 at 583–602.

—— (1999b) *Global Labour Flexibility: Seeking Distributive Justice* (Basingstoke: Macmillan Press Ltd).

—— (2000) 'Brave New Words? A Critique of Stiglitz's World Bank Rethink' *Development and Change* 31 at 737–63.

—— (2001) 'Care Work: Overcoming Insecurity and Neglect' in Mary Daly (ed) *Care Work: The Quest for Security* (Geneva: International Labour Office).

—— (2002) *Beyond the New Parternalism: Basic Security as Equality* (London, UK: Verso).

Stanworth Celia, and Stanworth, John (1997) 'Managing an Externalized Workforce: Freelance Labour' *Industrial Relations Journal* 28 at 43–55.

State of Victoria (2000) *Independent Report of the Victorian Industrial Relations Taskforce, Part I: Report and Recommendations* (Melbourne, Victoria: Department of State and Regional Development, Industrial Relations Division).

Statistics Canada (2000) *Survey of Labour and Income Dynamics* (Public Use Micro Data, Special Run).

Statistics Sweden (2004) *Labour Force Surveys 2003* (Orebro, Sweden: Statistics Sweden Publication Services).

Stewart, Andrew (1992) '"Atypical" Employment and the Failure of Labour Law' *Australian Bulletin of Labour* 18 at 217.

—— (2002) 'Redefining Employment? Meeting the Challenge of Contract and Agency Labour' *Australian Journal of Labour Law* 15 at 235–76.

Stiglitz, Joseph E (2002) *Globalization and its Discontents* (New York: Norton).

Stone, Katherine (1995) 'Labor and the Global Economy: Four Approaches to Transnational Labor Regulation' *Michigan Journal of International Law* 16 at 987–1028.

—— (1996) 'Mandatory Arbitration of Individual Employment Rights: The Yellow Dog Contract of the 1990s' *Denver Law Review* 73 at 1017–50.

—— (1998) 'The Prospects for Transnational Labor Regulation: Reconciling Globalization and Labor Rights in the EU and NAFTA' in Ton Wilthagen (ed), *Advancing Theory in Labour and Industrial Relations in a Global Context: Proceedings of a Colloquium, Amsterdam 18–19 April* (Amsterdam: Royal Netherlands Academy of Arts and Sciences).

—— (1999) 'Rustic Justice: Community and Coercion Under the Federal Arbitration Act' *North Carolina Law Review* 77 at 931–1036.

—— (2001) 'The New Psychological Contract: Implications of the Changing Workplace for Labour and Employment Law' *University of California, Los Angeles Law Review* 48 at 519–661.

—— (2003) 'The New Face of Employment Discrimination' in David Sherwyn and Michael Yelnosky (eds), *NYU Selected Essays on Labor and Employment Law* 1 (New York: Kluwer).

—— (2004) *From Widgets to Digits: Employment Regulation for the Changing Workplace* (Cambridge: Cambridge University Press).

Storrie, Donald (2002) *Temporary agency work in the European Union* (Dublin: European Foundation for the Protection of Living and Working Conditions).

Stråth, Bo (2001) 'After Full Employment and the Breakdown of Conventions of Social Responsibility' in Bo Stråth (ed), *After Full Employment: European Discourses on Work and Flexibility* (Brussels: PIE-Peter Lang).

Sturm, Susan (1998) 'Race, Gender and the Law of the Twenty-First Century Workplace' *University of Pennsylvania Journal of Labour and Employment Law* 1 at 639–789.

—— (2001) 'Second Generation Employment Discrimination: A Structural Approach' *Columbia Law Review* 101 at 458–568.

Summers, Lawrence (1989) 'Some Simple Economics of Mandated Benefits' *American Economics Review* 79(2) at 177.

Supiot, Alain (2002) 'Introductory Remarks: Between market and regulation: new social regulations for life long security' in Peter Auer and Bernard Gazier (eds), *The Future of Work, Employment and Social Protection* (Geneva: Ministry of Social Affairs, Labour and Solidarity at France: International Institute for Labour Studies).

Supiot, Alain *et al* (2001) *Beyond Employment: Changes in Work and the Future of Labour Law in Europe* (London: Oxford University Press).

Taub, Nadine and Schneider, Elizabeth M (1982) 'Perspectives on Women's Subordination and the Role of the Law' in David Kairys (ed), *The Politics of Law: A Progressive Critique* (New York, Pantheon).

Taylor, Robert (2002) *Britain's World of Work: Myths and Realities* (Swindon. ESRC).

Thompson, EP (1991) 'Time, Work-Discipline and Industrial Capitalism' in *Customs in Common* (Harmondsworth: Penguin), at 352–403 (original publication (1967) *Past and Present* 38).

Thompson, Mark (1994) *Rights and Responsibilities in a Changing Workplace, A Review of Employment Standards in British Columbia* (Victoria: BC Ministry of Skills, Training and Labour).

Thornton, Margaret (1990) *The Liberal Promise: Anti-Discrimination Legislation in Australia* (Melbourne: Oxford University Press).

—— (ed) 1995 *Public and Private: Feminist Legal Debates* (Melbourne: Oxford University Press).

—— (2004) 'Corrosive Leadership (or Bullying by Another Name): A Corollary of the Corporatised Academy' *Australian Journal of Labour Law* 17 at 161–84.

Thurow, Lester C (1975) *Generating Inequality: Mechanisms of Distribution in the US Economy* (New York: Basic Books).

Tijdens, Kea (2002) *Employees' Preferences for More or Fewer Working Hours: The Effect of Usual, Contractual and Standard Working Time, Family Phase and Household Characteristics, and Job Satisfaction* (Amsterdam: AIAS (Amsterdam Institute for Advances Labour Studies)).

Tilly, Chris (1996) *Half a Job: Bad and Good Part-time Jobs in a Changing Labor Market* (Philadelphia: Temple University Press).

Tilly, Chris and Tilly, Charles (1998) *Work Under Capitalism* (Boulder, Co: Westview Press).

Tobler, Christa (1999) 'Part-time-Work in the Context of Indirect Discrimination' in Y Kravaritou (ed), *The Regulation of Working Time in the European Union: Gender Approach* (Brussels: PIE-Peter Lang).

Tornes, Kristin (1994) 'The Timing of Women's Commodification—How Part-time Solutions Became Part-time Traps' in Thomas Boje and Sven Olsson Hort (eds), *Scandinavia in a New Europe* (Kristiansand: Scandinavian University Press).

Townson, Monica (2002) *Women in Non-Standard Jobs: The Public Policy Challenge* (Ottawa: Status of Women Canada).

Trades Union Congress (TUC) (2002) *About Time. A New Agenda for Shaping Working Hours* (London: TUC).

—— (2003) *The Use and Abuse of the 'Opt-Out' in the UK* (London: TUC).

Traversa, Enrico (2003) 'Protection of Part-time Workers in the Case law of the Court of Justice of the European Communities' *The International Journal of Comparative Labour Law and Industrial Relations* 19 at 219–41.

Travis, Michelle (2003) 'Equality in the Virtual Workplace' *Berkeley Journal of Employment & Labor Law* 24 at 283–376.

Trejo, Stephen J (1991) 'The Effects of Overtime Pay Regulation on Worker Compensation' *The American Economic Review* 81 at 719–40.

—— (2001) 'Does the Statutory Overtime Premium Discourage Long Workweeks?' IZA Discussion Paper No 373, October 2001 (Bonn, Germany: Institute of the Study of Labor).

Trubek, David M and Mosher, James S (2003) 'New Governance, Employment Policy and the European Social Model' in *Governing Work and Welfare in a New Economy: European and American Experiments* (Oxford: Oxford University Press), at 33–58.

Trudeau, Gilles (1998) 'Temporary Employees Hired Through A Personnel Agency: Who Is The Real Employer?' *Canadian Labour and Employment Law Journal* 5 at 359–75.

Trumbull, Gunnar (2001) 'France's 35 Hour Work Week: Flexibility Through Regulation' in *US France Analysis* (Washington, DC: The Brookings Institution).

Tulgan, Bruce (2001) *Winning the Talent Wars* (New York, NY: WW Norton and Co Inc).

United Nations (UN) (1995) *Report of the World Conference for Social Development*, UN Docs A/CONF166.9, 19 April, online: <http://daccessdds.un.org/doc/UNDOC/GEN/N95/116/51/PDF/N9511651.pdf?OpenElement>

—— (1999) *World Survey on the Role of Women in Development*, online: <www.un.org/womenwatch/daw/followup/a54227.pdf> (date accessed: 20 September 2004).

—— (2005) *Gender Equality: Striving for Justice in an Unequal World*, Policy Report on Gender and Development: 10 Years after Beijing (France: United Nations Research Institute for Social Development).

UN Commission on the Status of Women (2004) *The Role of Men and Boys in Achieving Gender Equality: Agreed Conclusions*, 48th Session, 1–12 March.

UN Department of Economic and Social Affairs (1995) *Copenhagen Declaration on Social Development*, World Summit for Social Development, online: <www.un.org/esa/socdev/wssd/agreements/index.html> (date accessed: 20 September 2004).

United Nations Development Programme (UNDP) (1995) *Human Development Report 1995* (New York, NY: Oxford University Press).

—— (1999) *Human Development Report 1999* (New York, NY: Oxford University Press).

UNDP Commission on the Private Sector and Development (2004) *Unleashing Entrepreneurship: Making Business Work for the Poor* (New York, NY: UNDP).

Underhill, Elsa and Fernando, Hubert (1998) 'Deregulating Precarious Employment in Victoria: Trends in Employee Complaints' *Labour & Industry* 8(3) at 43–60.

Ungerson, Claire (1997) 'Social Politics and the Commodification of Care' *Social Politics* (Fall) at 362–81.

Vaillancourt, Yves and Jetté, Christian (1999) 'L'aide à domicile au Québec: relecture de l'histoire et pistes d'action' in *Cahier du LAREPPS No 99-01* (Montreal: Université du Québec à Montréal).

Van Cruchten, Jo and Kuijpers, Rob (2003) *Webmagazine*, 7 April (The Hague: Centraal Bureau voor de Statistiek (CBS)).

Van der Toren, JP, Evers, GHM, and Commissaris, EJ (2002) *Flexibiliteit en zekerheid. Effecten en doeltreffendheid van de Wet flexibiliteit en zekerheid* (The Hague: Ministerie van Sociale Zaken en Werkgelegenheid).

Van Luijn, Heleen and Keuzenkamp, Saskia (2004) *Werkt verlof? Het gebruik van regelingen voor verlof en aanpassing van de arbeidsduur* (The Hague: SCP).*

Visser, Jelle (2002) 'The first part-time economy in the world: a model to be followed?' *Journal of European Social Policy* 12 at 23–42.

Vosko, Leah F (1997) 'Legitimizing the Triangular Employment Relationship: Emerging International Labour Standards from a Comparative Perspective' *Comparative Labor Law and Policy Journal* (Fall) at 43–77.

—— (2000) *Temporary Work: The Gendered Rise of a Precarious Employment Relationship* (Toronto: University of Toronto Press).

—— (2002) '"Decent Work": The Shifting Role of the ILO and the Struggle for Global Social Justice' *Global Social Policy* 2 (April) at 19–46.

—— (2004a) *Confronting the Norm: Gender and the International Regulation of Precarious Work* (Ottawa, Law Commission of Canada).

—— (2004b) 'Standard Setting at the ILO: The Case of Precarious Employment' in J Kirkton and MJ Trebilcock (eds) *Hard Choices, Soft Law: Combining Trade, Environment, and Social Cohesion in Global Governance* (New York: Ashgate), at 139–57.

Vosko, Leah F and Nancy.Zukewich (2005) 'Precarious by Choice: Gender and Self-Employment' in Leah Vosko (ed), *Precarious Employment: Understanding*

Labour Market Insecurity in Canada (Montreal and Kingston: McGill-Queen's University Press), at 67–89.

Vosko, Leah F, Zukewich, Nancy, and Cranford, Cynthia (2003) 'Precarious Jobs: A New Typology of Employment' *Perspectives on Labour and Income. Statistics Canada—Catalogue No 75-001-XIE 4* at 16–24.

Walby, Sylvia (1986) *Patriarchy at Work* (London: Polity Press).

—— (1990) *Theorizing Patriarchy* (Oxford: Basil Blackwell).

Waring, Marilyn (1988) *Counting For Nothing: A New Feminist Economics* (San Fransciso: Harper and Row).

—— (1996) *Three Masquerades: Essays on Equality, Work and Human Rights* (Toronto: University of Toronto).

Watson, Ian (2004) 'Wages of part-time workers in Australia: An initial appraisal using HILDA', Paper for the Centre for Applied Social Research Workshop on *The Quality of Part-time Work*, 19 July 2004 (Melbourne: RMIT).

Watson, Ian, Buchanan, John, Campbell, Iain, and Briggs, Chris (2003) *Fragmented Futures: New Challenges in Working Life* (Sydney, NSW: The Federation Press).

Webb, Beatrice (1896) *Women and the Factory Acts*, Fabian Tract No 67 (London: Fabian Society).

Webster, Juliet (2001) *Reconciling Adaptability and Equal Opportunities in European Workplaces*, Report for DG-Employment of the European Commission, online: <europa.eu.int/comm/employment_social/equ_opp/index_en.htm> (date accessed: 19 September 2004).

Wech, Jack F Jr, Tichy, Noel, and Charan, Ram (1989) 'Speed, Simplicity, Self-Confidence: An Interview with Jack Welch' *Harvard Business Review* at 112–29.

Wedderburn, KW (1965). *The Worker and the Law*, 1st edn (Harmondsworth: Penguin).

Wedderburn, Lord (1986) *The Worker and the Law*, 3rd edn (Harmondsworth: Penguin).

Weller, Sally, Cussen, Jane, and Webber, Michael (1999) 'Casual Employment and Employer Strategy' *Labour & Industry* 10(1) at 15–33.

White, Linda A (2001) 'Child Care, Women's Labour Market Participation and Labour Market Policy Effectiveness in Canada' *Canadian Public Policy* 27(4) at 386–405.

White, Lucie E (2001) 'Closing the Care Gap That Welfare Reform Left Behind' *The Annals of the American Academy* 577 at 131–43.

White, Stuart (2001) 'The Ambiguities of the Third Way' in Stuart White (ed), *New Labour: The Progressive Future?* (New York: Palgrave).

Whitehouse, Gillian (2001) 'Recent Trends in Pay Equity: Beyond the Aggregate Statistics' *Journal of Industrial Relations* 43 at 66–78.

Whitehouse, Gillian and Frino, Betty (2003) 'Women, Wages and Industrial Agreements' *Australian Journal of Labour and Economics* 6 at 579–96.

Whittard, Jenny (2003) 'Training and Career Experiences of Women Part-time Workers in a Finance Sector Organisation: Persistent Remnant of the "Reserve Army"?' *Australian Journal of Labour and Economics* 6 at 537–57.

Wikman, Anders (2002) 'Temporära kontrakt och inlåsningseffekter' in *Hållfast arbetsrätt för ett föränderligt arbetsliv*, Government report, Ds 2002:56 (appendix III) (Stockholm: Fritzes).

Williams, Joan (1999) 'Market Work and Family Work in the 21st Century' *Villanova Law Review* 44 at 305–36.

—— (2000a) 'Exploring the Economic Meanings of Gender' *American University Law Review* 49 at 987–1020.

—— (2000b) *Unbending Gender: Why Family and Work Conflict and What to Do About It* (New York, NY: Oxford University Press).

—— (2001) 'From Difference to Dominance to Domesticity: Care as Work, Gender as Tradition' *Chicago-Kent Law Review* 76 at 1441–93.

Williams, Joan and Segal, Nancy (2003) 'Beyond the Maternal Wall: Relief for Family Caregivers Who are Discriminated Against on the Job' *Harvard Women's Law Journal* 26 at 77–162.

Williams, Lucy (2002) 'Beyond Labour Law's Parochialism: A Re-envisioning of the Discourse of Redistribution' in Joanne Conaghan, Richard Michael Fischl, and Karl Klare (eds), *Labour Law in an Era of Globalization: Transformative Practices and Possibilities* (Oxford: Oxford University Press).

Wilthagen, Ton (1998) *Flexicurity: A New Paradigm for Labour Market Policy Reform?*, Working Paper FS I 98-202 (Berlin: Wissenschaftszentrum Berlin für Sozialforschung (Social Science Research Centre Berlin)).

Wolfensohn, James D (1999) *A Proposal for a Comprehensive Development Framework (A Discussion Draft)* (Washington, DC: World Bank).

Wooden, Mark (2000) *The Transformation of Australian Industrial Relations* (Sydney, NSW: The Federation Press).

World Bank (1989) *Sub-Saharan Africa – from Crisis to Sustainable Growth: A Long-Term Perspective Study* (Washington, DC: World Bank).

—— (1995) *World Development Report 1995: Workers in an Integrating World* (Oxford; New York: Oxford University Press).

—— (1998) 'Core Labour Standards and the World Bank', Background Document for ICFTU/ITS/World Bank Meetings on Core Labour Standards, 20 January.

—— (2000) *World Development Report 2000/2001: Attacking Poverty* (Oxford; New York: Oxford University Press).

—— (2001) *Engendering Development: Through Gender Equality in Rights, Resources and Voice* (Washington, DC: World Bank).

—— (2002) *Integrating Gender into the World Bank's Work: A Strategy for Action* (Washington, DC: World Bank)

—— (2003) *Policy Research Report. 2003: Land Policies for Growth and Poverty Reduction* (New York: Oxford University Press).

—— (2004) *Doing Business in 2004: Understanding Regulation* (Washington, DC: World Bank).

—— (2005) *World Development Report 2006: Equity and Development* (Washington, DC and New York: World Bank and Oxford University Press).

World Commission on the Social Dimension of Globalization (2004) *A Fair Globalization: Creating Opportunity for All* (Geneva: ILO).

Wright, Erik Olin and Dwyer, Rachel E (2003) 'The Patterns of Job Expansions in the USA: A Comparison of the 1960s and 1990s' *Socio-Economic Review* 1(3) at 289–325.

Yamada, David C (2000) 'The Phenomenon of "Workplace Bullying" and the Need for Status-Blind Hostile Work Environment Protection' *Georgetown Law Journal* 88 at 475–536.

Young, Donna E (2001) 'Working Across Borders: Global Restructuring and Women's Work' *Utah Law Review* 1 at 1–73.

Young, Iris Marion (2000) 'Disability and the Definition of Work' in Leslie Pickering Francis and Anita Silvers (eds), *Americans with Disabilities: Exploring Implications of the Law for Individuals and Institutions* (New York: Routledge).

—— (2003) 'Autonomy, Welfare Reform and Meaningful Work' in Eva Feder Kittay and Ellen Feder (eds), *The Subject of Care: Feminist Perspectives on Dependency* (Lanham, MD: Rowman and Littlefield).

Zatz, Noah (2004) 'Beyond Employment: Work Requirements, Caretaking, and Liberal Justice' [unpublished manuscript].

Zeytinoglu, Isik Urla (ed) (2002) *Flexible Work Arrangements: Conceptualizations and International Experiences* (The Hague: Kluwer Law International).

Zeytinoglu, Isik Urla and Muteshi, Jacinta Khasiala (2000) 'Gender, Race and Class Dimensions of Nonstandard Work' *Relations Industrielles* 55(1) at 133–67.

Zeytinoglu, Isik Urla and Weber, Caroline (2002) 'Heterogeneity in the Periphery: An Analysis of Non-Standard Employment Contracts' in Isik Urla Zeytinoglu (ed), *Flexible Work Arrangements: Conceptualizations and International Experiences* (The Hague: Kluwer Law International).

* *with a summary in English*

Index

Lightning Source UK Ltd.
Milton Keynes UK
09 November 2010

162575UK00001B/5/P